Negotiating India's Past

Essays in Memory of Partha Sarathi Gupta

edited by

Biswamoy Pati
Bhairabi Prasad Sahu
T.K. Venkatasubramanian

Negotiating India's Past

Essays in Memory of Partha Sarathi Gupta

edited by

Biswamoy Pati
Bhairabi Prasad Sahu
T.K. Venkatasubramanian

Tulika Books

Published by **Tulika Books**
35A/1 (third floor), Shahpur Jat, New Delhi 110 049, India

First published in India 2003

ISBN: 81-85229-81-3 (Hb)

Designed by Ram Rahman, typeset in Minion at Tulika Print Communication Services, New Delhi, and printed at Chaman Enterprises, 1603 Pataudi House, Daryaganj, Delhi 110 006

Contents

Preface

The idea behind this collection of essays goes back to the condolence meeting organized at the Delhi School of Economics shortly after Professor Partha Sarathi Gupta passed away. Many of Professor Gupta's contemporaries, including Professor Amartya Sen, spoke on that occasion. Some of us who attended the meeting came up with the idea of a volume in memory of Professor Gupta, and discussed it amongst ourselves before we dispersed that evening. The response to our proposal, which was overwhelming, has been a vital factor in sustaining the project and led to the successful completion of this book.

The essays collected in this volume weave together, issues and concerns of different scholars from the world of Indian history. The themes examined reflect a common desire to understand historical processes over time and from the perspective of different regions, without losing sight of the broader historical context. Through this attempt, the book perhaps demonstrates not only the fascinating possibilities of India's historical scholarship but also the fact that it has indeed come of age.

The essays that focus on early Indian history delineate the change of orientation in this field. This is borne out by the ground that has been covered: the history of archaeology in colonial India, political processes and the structure of the polity, social history, gender, the relevance of both text and context and the environment—all these are taken up for scrutiny. The engagement with interpretation of evidence extends from archaeological data to regional chronicles, and from inscriptional evidence to archival sources.

The essays that examine different aspects of 'medieval' India are based on a wide variety of sources. They question several of the assumptions of historians and historiography centred around subversive cults and nomadic peoples, and examine crucial aspects related to the monetary system and the dynamics of early trading contacts with the English. They also bring to light the hidden tensions and diversities of this period.

The essays dealing with 'modern' India discuss the complex interactions associated with the 'colonial encounter' and the negotiations they entailed. While the focus is on the subaltern classes, the process of colonization, through which the feudal order was transformed and integrated to it, provides the backdrop to most of these essays. Drawing upon a variety of sources, they critique the existing historiography and chart out new ways of looking at the colonial past, taking into account the mechanism and working of internal contradictions within Indian society.

The fifteen contributions included in this collection are organized under three sections. The first section focuses on aspects of ideology, legitimacy and the state; the second examines issues in economic history; and the third takes up aspects of society.

We would like to thank all the contributors for their unstinting cooperation, as also Tulika Books, especially Indira and Purnima, and Rajen, for the effort that has gone into the publication of this book.

BISWAMOY PATI
BHAIRABI PRASAD SAHU
T.K. VENKATASUBRAMANIAN

Partha Sarathi Gupta (1934–1999)

Biswamoy Pati
Bhairabi Prasad Sahu
T.K. Venkatasubramanian

This collection of essays is in memory of Professor Partha Sarathi Gupta, whose teaching career, spanning thirty-eight years, began at Burdwan University (1961) and the Delhi School of Economics (1961–62). Subsequently, he moved to the Department of History, Delhi University (1962), where he taught till his retirement in 1999. Partha Sarathi Gupta graduated from Presidency College, Calcutta, and was awarded the Ishan Scholarship for scoring the highest marks among Arts students. Among his class-fellows were Professors Sukhamoy Chakravarty, Benoy Bhushan Chaudhuri, Barun De and Amartya Sen. Professor Gupta did his Master's and D.Phil. at Oxford University. He held a Smuts Visiting Fellowship at Cambridge (1980–81) and a Fellowship at the Centre for Contemporary Studies, New Delhi (1986–89), and was elected a Fellow of the Royal Historical Society. He was Sectional President of the Indian History Congress for the 'Countries other than India' section in 1976, and General President of the Indian History Congress in 1998. He passed away suddenly on 10 August 1999, a few days after his retirement.

Professor Gupta's intellectual development was rooted in the diversities that he was exposed to and the research that he pursued all through his career. It may be relevant to mention here that he was secretary of the Oxford University Socialist Club and, later, a member of the Labour Party of Britain. It was perhaps no coincidence that, given his interest in the history of labour, Partha Sarathi Gupta's doctoral work investigated the trade union movement of railway workers in Britain, in the late nineteenth and early twentieth centuries. His first major publication, *Imperialism and the British Labour Movement, 1914–1964*,[1] was based on a vast range of sources. Regarded as one of the standard works on imperial history, it was a comprehensive account of the policies of the Labour Party and of labour groups towards various sections of the British empire. It explored how social reforms were won as concessions through struggles waged by the British working class. By that time, E.P. Thompson had already studied the 'making' of the English working class,[2] and Lenin's argument about a 'labour aristocracy' in the age of imperialism, which sought to improve its living standards through reforms, was well known. Professor Gupta's work, extending and complementing vital aspects suggested by Lenin and Thompson, provided an understanding of the complex dynamics that underlined the social history of the working class and labour movement in Britain.

Dr Gupta's research interests also extended to Indian history. A major project with which he was associated, as Editor, was the Indian Council for Historical Research's *Towards Freedom* series. He put together a massive collection, in three volumes, of documents about the movement for freedom during two critical years of the Second War.[3] These cover a wide-ranging array of subjects: the aftermath of the 'Quit India' movement, the 1943 famine, the Mahatma's charisma, the Communist Party of India, the Forward Bloc and the Radical Democratic Party, peasants' and workers' movements, the Indian National Army, the Hindu Mahasabha, the Akali Dal and the Dravida Kazhagam, business groups, the cultural movement, developments in the princely states, censorship, the colonial army, and the courts of law.

Many of us who were in touch with him during the course of this project remember his detailed questions and the hours of discussions he had with a vast range of people, to elicit connections and clarifications. His painstaking efforts led to the collection of a wealth of material from governmental as well as non-governmental agencies, which will encourage research and provide scholars an entry-point to primary sources. They reveal the passionate involvement and dedication of a historian with a zeal for exactitude, which Professor Gupta regarded as sacrosanct.

His other scholarly contributions—'British Labour and the Indian Left, 1919–1939',[4] 'Imperial Strategy and the Transfer of Power, 1939–1951',[5] 'Radio and the Raj',[6] 'Music and Political Consciousness'[7] and 'Identity Formation and Nation-States: Some Reflections'[8]—reflect his diverse interests and concerns. The project that he did not live to see completed was a volume titled *The British Raj and Its Indian Armed Forces 1857–1939*, which was published after he left us; it includes a contribution by him on the debate on the Indianization of the army.[9]

Professor Gupta's recollections of his early days, in the period when India gained independence, have influenced many of us and been incorporated into our research work. He once narrated a conversation he had about the implications of independence with Ramachandra Barik, a domestic servant (originally from coastal Orissa). Partha Sarathi was then thirteen years old, and lived in East Bengal with his parents. Barik had wanted to know if independence would enable him to write off his loans and recover his mortgaged land from the village *sahukar*. And, despite receiving an answer in the affirmative, Barik had remained silent, perhaps because he was not entirely convinced by his young master's assurance.

Professor Gupta interacted with generations of students and guided research both formally and informally.[10] Many of his students are established historians in their own right today. Some of us who have got together for this volume have fond memories of being taught and inspired by him. His first M.A. (Previous) lecture used to be followed by taking the students to Delhi University's Central Library and teaching them how to locate books. After this, reading lists would be handed out and details given about where to find the books. Everyone familiar with him will remember not only his erudite scholarship but also his great interest in and singleminded devotion to building up the History section—especially, European History—of the Delhi University Library. Many of the non-Indian historical journals available in this library today are a direct legacy of the hard work put in by Professor Gupta.

His idea of organizing students' seminars was indeed a new experiment in the 1970s. He actively reinforced the significance of economic history, which had almost lapsed as an optional subject in the M.A. Final course. He initiated the first major revision of the undergraduate and postgraduate courses, in a democratic process involving all college and university faculty. 'The Rise of the Modern West'—a vital course taught at the undergraduate level today—was his brainchild. He initiated the preparation of good textbooks in Hindi, as cooperative enterprises by the teaching faculty. He was enthusiastically committed to the expansion and development of the History Department of Delhi University. In many ways, thus, Professor Partha Sarathi Gupta was 'an institution within an institution'.

Notes and References

[1] Published by Macmillan Press, London and Basingstoke, 1975; reprinted by Sage Publications, Delhi, 2002.

[2] E.P. Thompson, *The Making of the English Working Class*, Penguin Books, Harmondsworth, 1968 (first published in 1963).

[3] Partha Sarathi Gupta, ed., *Towards Freedom: Documents on the Movement for Independence in India 1943–1944*, Parts I–III, Oxford University Press, Delhi, 1997; together, the three volumes comprise 3,517 pages.

[4] In B.R. Nanda, ed., *Socialism in India*, Vikas Publishers, Delhi, 1972. For details related to Professor Gupta's academic publications, see Partha Sarathi Gupta, *Power, Politics and the People: Studies in British Imperialism and Indian Nationalism*, Permanent Black, Delhi, 2002.

[5] In Amit Kumar Gupta, ed., *Myth and Reality: The Struggle for Freedom in India, 1945–47*, Manohar Publishers, Delhi, 1987.

[6] This was presented as the S.G. Deuskar Lecture on Indian History and Society, at the Centre for Studies in Social Sciences, Calcutta, in 1993, and subsequently published by K.P. Bagchi and Sons, Calcutta, 1995.

[7] 'Music and Political Consciousness: A Critical Study of D.L. Roy and Nazrul Islam', Occasional Papers, 2nd series, XV, Nehru Memorial Museum and Library, Delhi.

[8] This was the Presidential Address to the Patiala session of the Indian History Congress, 1998; see *Proceedings of the Indian History Congress*, 1999.

[9] This was co-edited with Anirudh Deshpande and published by Oxford University Press, Delhi, 2002.

[10] Besides supervising a number of M.Phil. dissertations, Professor Gupta guided the research of half a dozen Ph.D. scholars on subjects related to European history and colonial Indian history.

Ideology, Legitimacy and the State

The Discovery of the Indus Civilization

Early Intuitions and Unknown Reports, 1826–1920

Nayanjot Lahiri

Most students of the Indian past are aware that the discovery of 'the civilization of the Indus valley'—now more commonly described as either the Indus or the Harappan civilization—was announced by Sir John Marshall in 1924, although fragments of that archaeological puzzle had begun to fall in place from 1921 onwards. Less well known is the 'prehistory' of that discovery: clues about an unknown, yet distinctive culture that had long been available from what would later become famous Indus sites, as also the ideas and intuitions of travellers, government officials and professional archaeologists about them. This essay is about that story. Because they were relegated to the shelves of a voluminous archive, the details of this little known saga have till now remained hidden and only rarely appear in the vast published literature on the subject. Theoretically, of course, they have always been available, but hardly anyone had previously thought of exhuming them from the file-room of the Archaeological Survey of India.

Professor Partha Sarathi Gupta, in whose memory this volume has been published, through his own writing and in the course of his legendary lectures, displayed a mastery of archival material that many of us greatly admired. This essay has been written in the hope that Professor Gupta would have approved of a story pertaining to the construction of India's ancient past based on an exploration of the archival sources of British India.

Pathbreaking discoveries are often portrayed as culminating events or outcomes of long evolutionary processes. In truth, they appear in this form more in reminiscences than in reality. The discovery trail leading to the Indus civilization illustrates this rather well. If one were to describe the process within the contours of an evolutionary unfolding, a reassuringly smooth sketch made up of a progressive sequence of discoveries, excavations and ideas about them would be produced. In unravelling the threads in the story of how this third-millennium BC culture was unearthed, we are, however, confronted with a much more untidy tale.

It is a tale of ancient mounds scattered across a large area, stretching from the Punjab to Rajasthan, waiting for the right explorers to turn up. When the first explorers came, they certainly appreciated what they saw. They even stumbled upon distinctive objects, juxtaposed in ways that were unique. The challenge posed by such archaeological 'aberrations', evidence at odds with what was then known about India's material past, was not, however, taken up by them. It was not taken up even by other more discerning archaeologists and scholars who visited and excavated these mounds in the decades that followed. What today appear as momentous clues were, before the 1920s, either interpreted in a way that would 'prove' the testimony of ancient texts, or simply assimilated within what was then regarded as an appropriate historical framework. There were several flashes of extraordinary insight but, for one reason or another, these were not followed through.

Harappa and Nineteenth-Century Investigators

Harappa is the first known site of the Indus civilization and it became a famous city site much before its significance was seriously understood. Nineteenth-century travellers believed that an old historic city lay buried in the mounds of the village of that name, then in the Montgomery area of Punjab and now in Pakistan's Sahiwal district. In 1826, almost a century before John Marshall's dramatic announcement in the *Illustrated London News* of the discovery of long-forgotten cities in the Indus valley, a British army deserter, deeply interested in things antiquarian, came there. This was James Lewis, better known as Charles Masson, and he left the earliest available modern account of that site. He seems to have been impressed by the large circular mound and the long-deserted 'ruinous brick castle' with its high walls and towers, as also its traditions which affirmed 'the existence of a city, so considerable that it extended to Chicha Watni, thirteen cosses distant'.[1] Masson also mentioned other stories that were circulating around the archaeological remains of Harappa. It used to be believed, for instance, that the circular perforated stones which had emerged from the remains were the bangles of a local '*faqir* of renown'. 'Tradition also affirmed', according to Masson, that Harappa had been 'destroyed by the lust and crimes' of its sovereign.[2]

Lieutenant Alexander Burnes, who visited it a few years later in the summer of 1831, like Masson, recognized the extensive brick ruins of Harappa as the remains of an ancient city. He too was impressed by its size: 'The remains are extensive, and the place, which had been built of brick, is about three miles in circumference.'[3] Burnes visited Amri in the province of Sind as well, which would later became a reputed type site of the Indus culture. There too Burnes noted 'a mound of earth, some 40 feet high, which the traditions of the country point out as the halting-place of a king, who ordered the dung of his cavalry to be gathered together, and hence the mound Amree!'[4]

Burnes and Masson were remarkable individuals in their own way but cannot be described as archaeologists. Charles Masson is best remembered as an 'itinerant antiquarian' who searched the sites of Persia and Afghanistan for coins and *objets d'art*. Although he claimed to be an American from Kentucky, he was not an American at all and seems to have tried to change his identity after he deserted the Company's forces. Masson passed through Harappa on his way to Sind and Baluchistan and eventually he reached Afghanistan, where he is known to have settled in 1833. From that time onwards, for a number of years, he received a retainership from the East India Company for collecting ancient artefacts, and shortly thereafter came to be paid a regular annual stipend as the Company's accredited intelligence agent in Kabul. Such intelligence information was crucial to the frontier drama of dangerous adventure and diplomacy, popularly known as the 'Great Game', that was fast unfolding in the early part of the nineteenth century.[5] Basically a struggle for political ascendancy between Russia and Great Britain, 'played' across the mountainous tracts and passes of High Asia, it started before the time of Masson, in 1810 to be exact, and ended with Frances Younghusband, nearly a century later.

Alexander Burnes, like Masson, could also be described as a 'player' in the 'Great Game'. One of the most promising officers of the Company's army and fluent in Persian, Arabic and Hindi, he is well known for his clandestine survey of the Indus river. He sailed from Kutch to Sind and then up the Indus till Lahore, under the pretence of escorting a gift of English dray horses from the British sovereign William IV to Raja Ranjit Singh of Punjab. It was in the course of that navigation that he visited Harappa, after disembarking at Tolumba and travelling some miles inland. In 1832 Burnes was to come to the Punjab again, this time on a more risky adventure. He was on his way to Kabul and Central Asia in order to acquire political information about the countries bordering the Oxus. It was in Kabul that he died, in 1841, at the hands of a violent mob. By then many Afghans blamed Burnes for the diplomatic manoeuvres that had resulted in the British advance into Kabul in 1838. This was a hugely unpopular move, especially because it coincided with the installation of a puppet, Shah Shujah, as the ruler of the realm.

The first archaeologist to visit Harappa was Alexander Cunningham. One of the pioneers of Indian archaeology, Cunningham (1814–1893) came to India as a military engineer, rose to the rank of a general and, subsequently, served as the first Director of the Archaeological Survey of India from 1861 till 1885, with a gap between 1866 and 1870 when the Survey was suspended. His command over India's historical geography was unparalleled and some of the most famous places mentioned in ancient literature, including Taxila, Kausambi and Sankisa, were first identified on the ground by him. His documentation and disfiguring of the major Buddhist *stupa* complexes in central India are equally famous. Lepel Griffin, Agent to the Governor General in central India, was certainly referring to Cunningham when he said that 'the chief injury and the one most difficult to repair to the Sanchi Tope is that caused by the vandalism of the archaeologists themselves, whose path through India may be traced by the monuments irreparably injured by their hands'.[6]

As for Harappa, Cunningham first visited it in 1853, and over the next couple of decades he returned twice, excavating it only in 1872–73. Describing it as the most extensive of ancient sites along the banks of the Ravi river, his account is the earliest archaeological report of excavations there. The account is interesting for other reasons as well.[7] For one thing, it tells us about the ways in which the ancient mounds were used and viewed. Punjab's railway contractors regarded the seemingly limitless brick remains that formed the mounds as a convenient source for ballast. Apparently, a hundred miles of the Lahore–Multan railway was constructed from the bricks of Harappa. Among the local people, myths circulated about Harappa's ruins and antiquities. We learn from Cunningham that a Hindu temple was believed to lie buried in what is now described as Mound AB, just as perforated stones which had been recovered from the mounds and are presently recognized as a specific class of chalcolithic ring stones, were regarded by inhabitants as the thumb rings of a renowned *faqir*. The 'rings of the *faqir*' had been earlier noticed by Masson but Cunningham's report mentions his 'identity'. This was a *Naogaza* named Nur Shah, and they were kept at his tomb.

On the archaeological side, the alignment of the mounds and their location in relation to the old bed of the Ravi river are graphically illustrated in Cunningham's site plan. Most important, he provides visual details of objects that would later become 'type fossils' or archetypal objects of the civilization—an inscribed, rectangular stone seal and flint implements. Less than a decade later, in the field season of 1883–84, and this is little known, his assistant H.B.W. Garrick also dug at Harappa and found bracelets, rings, a spinning weight, 'catapelt balls' and 10 to 12 pounds of charred wheat.[8]

The nineteenth century, thus, did see Harappa 'discovered', in the sense that it came to be recognized as an 'archaeological site' where an ancient city lay buried. What is striking about these early reports are the hints that their authors understood that they had encountered archaeological features which were unlike what was usually seen at Indian sites. By 1872 Cunningham was a veteran archaeologist with field experience of over thirty years in scores of places across a swathe of territory that stretched from Kashmir to Bihar. Cunningham was also an enthusiastic collector of Buddhist sculptures very commonly found at sites in Punjab and the northwest, and, interestingly enough, his contract as the Director General of the Survey allowed him a share in the antiquities that he discovered! Yet, neither Cunningham nor his assistant Garrick seems to have reaped the usual harvest of riches at Harappa that excavations at other places had yielded. Instead, they found a few unique features. Among other things, Cunningham recognized that the engraved seal of Harappa was in a script he had not seen anywhere in India. Similarly, Garrick was struck by the singular absence of sculpture at Harappa, so commonly found at other subcontinental sites.

Why did these pioneer explorers fail to understand the significance of such clues? Perhaps the most important reason was that Cunningham and Garrick belonged to an age when discourses about the Indian past were formed around a predominantly literary grid. Within a referential context made up of Hindu and Buddhist religious literature, classical accounts and itineraries of Chinese pilgrims, it must have been difficult to imagine that there were monumental sites that existed beyond textual boundaries and topographies. And so, in spite of its unique features, Harappa's antiquity came to be perceived within this framework. Charles Masson believed that 'every condition of Arrian's Sangala was here fulfilled', while for Alexander Cunningham this was *Po-fa-to-lo,* the city visited by Huien Tsang in the seventh century BC. A few years later, though, he extended the antiquity of the site to the sixth century BC, when he described the characters on the Harappan seal as 'archaic Indian letters of as early an age as Buddha himself'.[9]

Visualizing Unknown Vistas: From Nal to Harappa

The seal which had so impressed Cunningham, along with a couple of others from Harappa, ultimately reached the British Museum in London[10] where, in late 1901, the young John Marshall, preparing for his departure for India, saw them for the first time.[11]

The twenty-five-year-old Marshall had just been appointed Director General of Archaeology in India, and was spending some days examining antiquities of Indian origin in the British Museum.[12] This was necessary because Marshall, a Cambridge-trained archaeologist whose fieldwork had been in Greece, southern Turkey and Crete, had no background or training in Indian studies.[13] When he was chosen for this post, he had been actively exploring the possibility of a professorship in Greek at Sydney University. The reasons why a man without any 'India' connections was recruited for the top job were many, but mainly connected with George Nathaniel Curzon's appointment as Viceroy of India (1899–1905) and the revival in 1901 of the post that Marshall was to occupy. Archaeology and the restoration of India's architectural heritage were a high priority for Curzon. Apart from his own deep interest in monuments, this vision was shaped by the social context in England and by the need to make imperial governance appear more 'enlightened'. Historic buildings that had been pillaged or converted into dingy governmental spaces were encountered by the Viceroy across much of India, and proved to be an embarrassing reminder of 'a century of British vandalism and crime' (these are Curzon's own words). So, their restoration came to be perceived as an urgent, necessary step in promoting a more cultured image of colonial rule.

Appropriately, the Viceroy used his influential position with George Hamilton, Secretary of State for India, to lobby for more money and posts for the Archaeological Survey. Within a few months of his arrival in India, Curzon got him to approve an increase in the annual budget for archaeology; this was followed by his obtaining sanction, in May 1901, to revive the post of Director General of the Archaeological Survey, which had been abolished by the government in 1889. The search for an appropriate candidate was left by the India Office to Sir Edward Maunde Thompson, Director of the British Museum in London. However, Curzon made it reasonably clear that he was not looking for a scholar in Oriental studies but for a 'comparatively young man who has distinguished himself as a scholar at one of the English Universities and who has since devoted himself to archaeological work in Greece or Egypt or Asia Minor, and who has the capacity and energy and power of work'.[14] Clearly, the young John Marshall, with his flawless Cambridge classical archaeology training, was tailormade for the post.

Coming back to Harappa, we do not know what Marshall's immediate impressions about the seals in the British Museum were, although he remembered, decades later, that they had interested him.[15] Yet it is reasonably clear that they did not inspire him sufficiently, because he did not visit Harappa during his early years in India. During those years, the young Director General was almost exclusively concerned with overseeing a large-scale programme of architectural conservation and restoration which had been visualized and was closely watched over by Curzon.[16] Moreover, at that point of time, field exploration and excavation were hardly a priority of the Archaeological Department that Marshall headed. That a sum of Rs 5,000 was spent on excavations during his first year in India, a mere 5 per cent of the archaeological budget, reflects this.

Discharging Curzon's ambitious programme of conservation took up most of Marshall's time. Extensive tours had to be made across the country, sometimes in the company of the Viceroy, during which he followed up Curzon's written notes and instructions or advised local authorities on such matters. In his first year alone over eight months were spent in such surveys. Conservation work also required a constant interaction with all kinds of people in whose custody the monuments were, ranging from military authorities to religious organizations. Further, Marshall himself kept in direct touch with firms handling restoration schemes. In the case of Mughal buildings at Delhi and Agra, the work was executed through the firm of 'Nuthoo Ram and Sons' of

Agra, with whom Marshall regularly corresponded and haggled about estimates for marble inlay, the number of workers being employed by them, their pace of work and so on. Conservation work was also underway at the medieval monuments of Lahore, which Marshall visited on a number of occasions. Harappa is fairly close to that city. Marshall did not visit it, however, during his sojourns to Lahore.

Although monument conservation was his main preoccupation, even in those busy years John Marshall did make some time for field excavations. Interestingly enough, from the wealth of research possibilities open to him, he began by traversing familiar ground—historically documented sites—instead of Harappa, with its intriguing seals. Charsada in the North West Frontier Province was his first choice, which he excavated in 1903 with J.Ph. Vogel, then in charge of the Frontier Circle of the Survey. Charsada is ancient Pushkalavati and is situated in an area that is alive with classical antecedents, a world that Marshall, fresh from fieldwork in Greece, was familiar with.[17] Till then, most of the archaeological work that had been undertaken there was in the nature of desultory idol-digging. Marshall hoped to show that, instead of seeing sites as a source of sculpture, excavations could be used for understanding their evolution and history; accordingly, four mounds were opened up, including the fortified acropolis of Bala Hissar. Additionally, ancient cities fascinated Marshall and in his early years he seems to have considered exploring both Kausambi in the Allahabad region and Ujjain in Malwa. Eventually, though, it was the historic, fortified urban landscape of Rajagriha in Bihar that he excavated in 1905, because he considered it to be the most promising buried site that he had seen till then in India.[18]

More relevant, from the perspective of this essay, is his instinctive perception that there was an archaeological canvas waiting to be found that preceded the birth of Indian cities, a space which was to remain largely blank until the Indus cities were discovered. So, it may be worthwhile to try and explore the way in which Marshall, at that stage, conceived of this problem, and how he tried to follow up a few archaeological leads in the Ganga–Yamuna *doab*, Baluchistan and Bahrain.

In 1903 Marshall deputed one of his assistants, Pandit Hirananda Sastri, to explore the Ganga–Yamuna *doab* and survey sites that had yielded copper hoard objects. During the course of that tour, Hirananda visited Rajpur, Parasu, Bithur and Pariar, and at the latter place he noticed that they were being treated as objects of worship and considered as relics of a fight 'between Rama's hosts and sons!'[19] Today, however, copper hoard objects in the *doab* are recognized to be of Harappan, Late Harappan and related vintage, since some such objects have been found in Harappan contexts at sites like Lothal in Gujarat and Mitathal in Haryana. What is most interesting is that Hirananda had been asked to visit copper hoard sites because Marshall was trying to collect information about a 'Bronze age' which, he believed, could be correlated with the Early Vedic age.[20] The beginning of the Early Vedic period, around that time, was generally dated to *c.* 2000 BC, and this means that Marshall was seriously considering the possibility of an archaeological culture of comparable antiquity in India.

In the same year that Hirananda Sastri explored copper hoard sites, Marshall made his first tentative steps towards visualizing a much earlier historical beginning for Baluchistan as well. And the man responsible for this was an Indian Civil Service officer, Hughes Buller. Compiler of several volumes of the *Baluchistan District Gazetteer*, Buller, few are aware, thought of himself as a kind of amateur archaeologist, collecting all kinds of artefacts and archaeological information in the course of his official duties. In order to ascertain the nature and chronology of his finds, he corresponded with several people all over the country. One of them was Marshall. By 1903 a lively correspondence had developed between them, and in October that year Buller wrote to Marshall about 59 bowls which his assistant in the Jhalawan country, Mirza Sher Muhammad, had brought from a mound called Sohr Damb at Nal.[21]

When photographs of the Nal pottery reached Marshall, he immediately declared it to be the most interesting and finest pottery yet procured in India. He also thought that it bore analogies with Mediterranean forms of 800 BC. Marshall's preoccupation with Mediterranean analogies is understandable in the light of his training. After having taken a first in the Classics Tripos at Cambridge, in 1900 he had spent the winter months at Athens and on Crete, comparing the Mycenaean remains from Crete with those of the mainland.[22] He had also been associated with the excavations conducted at Praisos and Kato Zakro in eastern Crete under the auspices of the Cretan Exploration Fund. So, in 1903, with the Mediterranean experience still fresh in his memory, he urgently asked Buller for more information:

> Could you find anything at all in the way of implements or other things which would give a possible clue. The trenches from which they come must be of supreme interest. Will you ask your agent to procure every single specimen he can on this pottery? I am quite willing to pay anything upto 25 a piece. . . . Is the country, where the mound is situated, such that we could dig there ourselves? The sight of this pottery has made me intensely keen. I cannot be rash enough to commit writing my own yet vague ideas about it, but I believe if other objects could be discovered we may show that *we have got back to a date as yet unrepresented in the region by any antiquities.* (Emphasis added)[23]

A few months later he felt confident enough to state that

> they are closely allied to a type found in Cyprus, Phoenicia, etc. about the eighth century BC, which show a decadent Mycenaean technique and design combined with more purely Asiatic influences. . . . I want very much to have some more excavations done in the mound at Nal. I believe that we shall probably get most important results from it, perhaps some of the most important that have ever been obtained in this country.[24]

These are very interesting observations and although Marshall himself did not excavate at Nal, his intuition that the date of the ceramics from there could push back the existing chronology of Baluchistan was correct. As we realize today, Nal is part of the cultural horizon that is integrally associated with the evolutionary sequence that culminates in the Indus civilization. Indeed, when its antiquity came to be finally understood, Nal turned out to be much older than Marshall had imagined.[25]

It was with a view to following up the 'definite traces of Phoenician influence in Baluchistan' and unearthing fresh links in the chain of connections between it and the Mediterranean that, in 1904, Marshall also seriously contemplated excavations at Bahrain. J.G. Lorrimer of the Foreign Office had aroused his curiosity about a huge necropolis there which had yielded objects that had been identified by a British Museum man as being of Phoenician workmanship. Marshall's communications reveal his excitement about undertaking work there, and by January 1905 the practical arrangements were underway. At the last moment, however, the Viceroy's veto preempted the expedition. Curzon believed that India's Director General of Archaeology, 'paid out of Indian revenues, and surrounded by a field of work, which we are simultaneously assuring the Secretary of State will occupy his undivided energies for many years to come', had no business to be going outside of India.[26]

Today, we know a great deal about Bahrain and its connections with the third-millennium BC 'Bronze age' world. But we will never know whether a field expedition to Bahrain may have hastened Marshall's understanding of the traces of a civilization of comparable antiquity in India.

In any case, like Bahrain, the copper hoard sites of Gangetic India or the Baluchi terrain, where Nal stood, were also not seriously followed up during Marshall's early years in India. In fact, neither was Harappa. Harappa, however, must have remained with him because a few years later, three Archaeological Survey men—Pandit Hirananda Sastri, Maulvi Zafar Hasan and Harold Hargreaves—visited and produced reports on it. These were all prepared within the course of five years, between 1909 and 1914.

What can possibly explain the timing of this interest? It appears that in 1906, when Marshall's department came to be put on a permanent footing and he proceeded on furlough to England, one of the subjects that he proposed to investigate was the pottery from Baluchistan, which appeared to him to be closely related to certain wares of the eastern Mediterranean.[27] He even carried with him a dozen paintings of the Nal ceramics[28] and spent time in the British Museum looking (unsuccessfully) for analogies. In the British Museum, he also re-examined the Harappa seals. Whether that re-examination led to any special revelations, is not known. The only thing we are certain about is that, after returning to India, Marshall set in motion a process for purchasing the mounds of Harappa.

By February 1908 specific information about the modalities of purchase were known, when the Deputy Commissioner, Montgomery, wrote to say that these could be purchased from the owners for Rs 4,706. They were, however, not purchased. Nor was Harappa excavated at that point in time. In 1909, Hirananda Sastri was sent there, probably to archaeologically whet Harappa before the mounds were purchased. Sastri had by then moved on to become an assistant to J.Ph. Vogel. The latter was now the Archaeological Surveyor of Hindu and Buddhist Monuments of the Northern Circle, and it was in his territory that Harappa was located. Only few details about Sastri's report, apparently not a very optimistic one, are known from secondary sources. Significant, for instance, is the fact that he mentioned that bricks of the size of 12"x 6"x 3" were found at Harappa. Bricks of this kind, that is, in the ratio of 1:2:4, today recognized as typical of the Indus cities, were practically unknown from subcontinental archaeological sites with ancient antecedents. The original report of Sastri, however, remains elusive.

On the other hand, a copy of the note of Maulvi Zafar Hasan penned in 1912 is available, and is of intrinsic interest in the trail that leads to the discovery of the Indus civilization. It seems to have been entirely forgotten, though, even by fellow archaeologists who were his contemporaries.[29] Zafar Hasan had joined the Archaeological Department three years earlier, when he was awarded an Arabic and Persian scholarship after having graduated from the Mohammadan College at Aligarh. Initially the young man was attached to the office of the Director General, and it is likely that he was sent to Harappa by Marshall himself.

The note briefly describes the mounds, the small village of Harappa, and considers the possibility that the ancient town was destroyed by fire since apparently burnt timber, bricks and grain were found within a mound there. Several objects were purchased, which included beads, terracottas, coins and, most importantly, two seals. What adds to the importance of Zafar Hasan's report is that a month after it was submitted to Marshall, the latter wrote that he thought that Harappa was likely to open quite a new chapter in Indian history. Marshall made this statement in a letter to Miles Irving, an ICS officer stationed at Montgomery, also mentioning that he was seriously contemplating excavation there.[30] This correspondence between Marshall and Irving was filed by his office under the subject heading, 'Proposed Excavations at Harappa in the Montgomery District, Punjab'. Irving drew Marshall's attention to the ruins of another ancient city on the banks of the Ravi, four miles from Harappa, called Rajanpur. This was marked by a mound similar to Harappa and yielded large-sized bricks. He, of course, could not say if it was

> as old as Harappa—it may be an offshoot from it, founded on the bank of the river when it changed its course in which case, of course,

> it must be much more recent. But it is also possible that the river once flowed between them and that it is of the same age.[31]

So, once again, the process for undertaking an archaeological dig at Harappa was revived. In 1914, Harold Hargreaves visited Harappa with the purpose of surveying the proposed land that was to be acquired for the excavation. Originally headmaster of the Government High School at Amritsar in Punjab, unlike other Archaeological Survey officers, Hargreaves was neither trained as an architect nor as an Oriental scholar, but was simply a man who was deeply interested in monuments and archaeological remains. His formal association with the Survey began in 1911 when he was asked to officiate in the Frontier Circle during the absence and deputation in England of Marc Aurel Stein, one of the most famous explorers of Asia, who also happened to be an officer in the Archaeological Survey.[32] Hargreaves performed his duties with great zeal and acumen when acting as Superintendent of the Frontier, especially those related to the cataloguing of antiquities at the Lahore Museum and listing the monuments of the province. For these reasons, when J.Ph. Vogel resigned from the Archaeological Department, instead of going through the tedium of recruiting and training a scholar from England, Marshall had no hesitation in recommending that he be permanently inducted. In 1914, in fact, Hargreaves had just been appointed as Superintendent of Hindu and Buddhist Monuments in the Northern Circle, and it was in that capacity that Marshall requested him to go to Harappa. After his proposed inspection he was expected to undertake excavations in the following year, or so Marshall believed.

Hargreaves visited Harappa in October 1914 and submitted an inspection note the following month, along with photographs. These are probably the earliest available photographs of the mounds of Harappa and of the artefacts that were turning up from there. There is also a photograph of two seals from there which had been procured by his assistant, J.R. Gupte.[33] Hargreaves considered Harappa to have been a large and important city. His estimate of its size, though, was much less than that of Cunningham—around 94 acres. The countless bricks and the extensive remains of pottery also suggested to him that it had been occupied for a very long time. But what is surprising is that the very features that are recognizable today as pointers towards the great antiquity of Harappa—the absence of coins, the small size of the bricks—seemed to Hargreaves as suggesting that the site was not particularly old: 'the seemingly total absence of coins at the present day, the comparatively small size of the bricks and the admission by Cunningham that no coins of the Indo–Greeks have been found at Harappa, all seem to indicate a fairly late date for its foundation.'

The main purpose for which Hargreaves had been sent to Harappa was to assess the desirability of acquiring the mounds there for an archaeological dig. From that perspective, the continued exploitation of bricks which had particularly denuded areas E and D did not augur well for any future excavation:

> the whole surface is pitted with these excavations which look like newly opened graves. . . . Quite apart from the millions of bricks removed for the railway before Cunningham's visit, by means of a temporary line laid to the mounds, the continuous removal of walls by the villages must have destroyed so much archaeological evidence that beyond odd stretches of walling here and there it seems very improbable that anything in the way of a plan of buildings could be recovered by systematic excavation of the two principal mounds.[34]

There was, however, one mound which appeared to be relatively undisturbed, where Hargreaves recommended a trial excavation. His other specific recommendations were:

> In view, therefore, of the great devastation wrought by contractors and villagers and the fact that sites of known antiquity such as Kausambi, Kanauj, Sankisa, etc., await regular exploration, I cannot recommend the purchase of the mounds for Rs 4,706 which is the sum stated in letter No. 60 of 20th February 1908 from the Deputy Commissioner, Montgomery to the Commissioner, Lahore Division, and we cannot 'protect' the mounds without purchase. I note in the letter under reference that 'the owners are not willing to accept land elsewhere in exchange' but as a new canal runs within two miles of Harappa I fancy the owners of the mounds would now consider themselves very fortunate to get land in exchange. If the owners will not agree to anything less than purchase I would suggest that an endeavour be made to arrange with them for the temporary occupation by the Archaeological Survey, for say two years, of the uncultivated and seemingly undisturbed mound referred to above so

> that at least trial excavations should be carried out there and some idea formed as to the desirability, or otherwise, of acquiring the whole site. I find that labour in this district is very scarce and consequently expensive and the Deputy Commissioner informs me that neither diggers nor carriers can be procured for less than *8 annas* per day and when the new canal is opened and waste land brought under cultivation the price of labour in the district is likely for some years to be even more expensive.[35]

Unlike Hargreaves, Marshall was not particularly concerned about the extensive brick-robbing at Harappa. This is because he then considered it unlikely that the brick buildings on or near the surface belonged to the same epoch as the inscribed seals! And it was

> the interesting seals with pictographic signs which are what we want to follow up. The latter, probably, were in a lower stratum, and, in that case, it would not matter how many of the superimposed brick buildings had been removed. Indeed, the more that have gone the better, as it would facilitate our digging.[36]

Evidently, while Marshall was convinced about the unique character of the Harappa seals and that the site would open up unknown historical vistas, he did not at that stage imagine they could be associated with extensive brick structures.

Instead of immediately acquiring any part of the mounds, it was suggested to the civil authorities at Montgomery that Hargreaves should carry out a trial excavation at Harappa in the winter of 1915–16, and then the Archaeological Department would decide whether the land ought to be purchased.[37] The excavation, however, did not take place and this is somewhat puzzling, although there is a probable explanation. Following the outbreak of the First World War in 1914, there was considerable displacement of personnel within the portals of government departments. From the Archaeological Department Gordon Sanderson, who was Superintendent of Muhammadan Monuments in the Northern Circle, joined the Indian army in February 1915, and within a few months, died in active service. Following his untimely death, Hargreaves had to temporarily hold charge of Sanderson's office (from May 1915 till January 1916).[38] By the end of 1916 Hargreaves had also opted for military duty and, in his place, Daya Ram Sahni, then Superintendent of Archaeology, Kashmir State, was appointed.[39] Sahni's association with the Archaeological Survey went back to 1903, when he was selected for the first Sanskrit scholarship in the department. Since then he had assisted Marshall in about half a dozen excavations, and had also studied and deciphered scores of inscriptions pertaining to all periods of Indian history, including Persian ones. His work in the Lucknow and Sarnath Museums was especially thorough, and involved classifying, arranging and labelling the large collections of antiquities preserved there. Eventually, in 1931, Sahni would become Director General of the Survey, the first Indian to occupy the top job in archaeology during British times.

Sahni inspected Harappa for the first time in 1917. He had obviously seen the note by Hargreaves, and the latter's suggestion to begin excavations on Mound F strongly appealed to him. He submitted a proposal for its acquisition as also a portion of Mound AB, where an old wall of considerable thickness below the Naogaza tomb raised hopes of the existence of some important brick monument.[40] Rs 2,771 was paid as compensation for the two mounds. The other mounds were not acquired but were brought under the operation of the Ancient Monuments Act in order to stop unauthorized diggings for building material.

Kalibangan, Bahawalpur and Sind, 1918–20

Daya Ram Sahni's dig at Harappa commenced only in 1921, and formed the starting point for the process by which fragments of the Indus archaeological puzzle were pieced together. That excavation is beyond the scope of this essay, since here we are only looking at the disconnected segments themselves, not the process by which they were pieced together to form an idea about the phenomenon called the Indus civilization. So, for the moment, let us stay with 1917 since in that year, in adjacent Rajasthan, mounds which are now recognized to be of Indus antiquity were being explored. The mounds were the Kalibangan *theris*, the site of a provincial Harappan city, and the explorer, an Italian called Luigi Pio Tessitori.

An accomplished linguist who specialized in west Indian vernaculars as also Jaina texts, Tessitori was the translator into Italian of the *Upadeshamala*, *Dhruvavairagyashataka* and *Indriyaparajayashataka*.[41] He began his work on the 'Bardic and Historical Survey of Rajputana' in 1914 under the aegis of the Asiatic Society of Bengal, after having earned a doctorate on the subject of Tulsidas's

Ramayana. From 1916, his work on Rajputana came to be financed by grants from the Education Department of the imperial government and from the archaeological grant of the Archaeological Department. In return for the latter's support, Tessitori toured Bikaner extensively in search of antiquarian remains and by May 1918, submitted a 228-page manuscript on his work to Marshall. The latter was so impressed that he proposed to publish it as a separate volume, once the monument lists for Bikaner were completed. Tessitori, however, died of double pneumonia on 22 November 1919;[42] the report (which had been returned to him) remained incomplete, unpublished and is now untraceable. Among the only contemporary published references to it is Marshall's summary, which noted that along with temples and forts, Tessitori explored and collected antiquities from a number of *theris* or ancient mounds in the Ghaggar–Hakra tract, including Rang Mahal, Bhadrakali, Pir Sultan, Munda, Dotheri and *'Kali Banga'*.[43]

There are virtually no details in the published literature about what Tessitori had observed and collected at Kalibangan. However, he did send extracts from his 'Touring Report for 1917–18' to D.B. Spooner in August 1917, when the latter was officiating in Marshall's place while he was away at Kashmir. Tessitori was then grappling with the question of finding equivalences for the cinerary vases that he had found at Kalibangan, and wrote to Spooner asking for books that would help him to understand their nature and age. Spooner promised to do so but asked for photographs that would help him to select the right literature. Since Tessitori had no photographs of 'Kali Banga', he enclosed an extract from his tour report.[44] This mentions the presence of two mounds there, one of them relatively large, and the fact that, as at Harappa, the site had served as a source of railway ballast:

> The two *theris* are found about ¾ of a mile south-west of the village, and they are close to one another, being separated only by a small depression running across. One of the two is very large, but very irregular in shape. Much material was asportated [*sic*] from the spot in 1900 when the section of the Jodhpur–Bikaner Railway connecting Suratgadh with Hanumangadh was being constructed, the materials being utilized as ballast on the line. Mr Warren of the Jodhpur–Bikaner Railway, who superintended the work, has told me that when he had the *theris* dug in search of ballast, he unearthed in several places rectangular chambers of about 5 x 6 feet, closed by

walls of large bricks and having no entrance. He also found a considerable quantity of balls of burnt clay and of fragments of pottery, but no traces of moulded bricks, nor of any implements, so far as he could recollect. He did not go very deep, however, and abandoned the spot when he saw that the materials obtained were no longer paying the cost of excavating.

The traces of Mr Warren's excavations are still evident all over the two mounds. In places one sees regular square holes, and these probably mark the spots where the chambers mentioned by Mr Warren were found. In one place, on the slope of the smaller mound, a deep trench has been cut, about three yards deep. It is evident that hardly one spot was left unexplored and wherever bricks were found within easy reach, they were ruthlessly asportated [*sic*].[45]

Tessitori noted that the burnt clay balls which Warren had taken away from Kalibangan in large quantities were still abundantly found all over the mounds, along with 'flat lumps' or what we recognize as terracotta cakes—objects commonly found at Harappan sites. Pottery, brick bats, earthen rings and human bone fragments were reported as well. Moreover, a pot burial, of the type that was later excavated by the Archaeological Survey of India in the 1960s, was unearthed:

In one place on the top of the larger mound, from the side of a ditch which had probably been excavated by the railway ballast-hunters, there was emerging what seemed to be the mouth of a very large vase. I had the earth dug all around and found that it really was a large earthen pot, which had been broken on one side, as well as around the orifice, but was still intact in the main body and the inside. It was round in shape except for some oblongness in the lower part, which made the lower half of the vessel roughly resemble the pointed half of an egg. The height, measured internally, was about 2'4', and the maximum diameter 2'1'. The mouth, which must have been very wide, had a rim curving to the outside. The thickness of the clay was ½ inch. I found no traces of any cover, but the vessel probably had one and it was destroyed. The pot was buried in a perpendicular position, and the orifice was about 1 foot under the surface of the ground.

The vessel was filled with earth forming a very compact mass with fragments of pottery. It took about three hours to dig the inside and here is a list of what I found: (a) An oblong earthen vase almost

> intact but for some abrasions round the mouth and the pedestal. The height was 5½′, and the diameter 3¼′ at the mouth, 3¾′ in the middle, and only 1¼′ in the pedestal. The thickness of the clay was only ⅛′. The vase contained fragments of burnt bones and ashes besides a few pieces of clay. (b) Fragments of five or six other vases, whereof two or three of about the same size as the above, one very large with a mouth about 6½′ in diameter, and one a dimunitive size with a mouth of only 1¼′ in diameter. Some of the vases were externally decorated with lines in black or white paint. (c) Three fragments of covers of the diameter of about 7½″, 4½″ and 1½″ respectively. The form was that of a round plate or dish, raised in the middle, with a protruberance for lifting it. (d) Two earthen rings 1″ in diameter, and fragments of at least another eight rings or bangles from 1″ to 2″ in diameter. The thickness of the clay varied from ½″ in the rings of smaller dimensions, to ¼″ in the rings of larger dimensions. Some were decorated with transversal lines in black paint. (e) Three round lumps of baked clay, and fragments of two or three others, and also fragments of one or two triangular tiles. (f) Fragments of human bones, and traces of ashes, and small fragments of coal.
>
> The find leaves no doubt that the mound was a burying ground, where relics of cremated bodies were reserved.[46]

Later, photographs of Kalibangan and its excavated objects were taken. We know this because they have been catalogued in Volume 8 (1917–19) of the Rajputana albums in the photographic library of the Archaeological Survey's head office. One cannot be quite certain about when these were taken, although it is likely that it was during the lifetime of Tessitori. The photographs show excavations of the site, including that of a brick well and artefacts ranging from Harappan pottery and related stone beads to bone and ivory objects. While a number of objects were found, as is evident from the tour report and the photographs, there is no mention of either coins or sculpture; in other words, of any antiquities that can be recognized as belonging to the historical period. Marshall must have read this account, seen the photographs of the site and its antiquities, and one wonders if the distinctive character of the excavated artefacts or the similarity in the descriptions of Harappa and Kalibangan struck him.

Some years before Tessitori's report on Kalibangan, in the

same desert stretch towards the west, other mounds had been brought to Marshall's notice. These are described in an account of the tour of Malik Muhammad Din along the old bed of the Hakra river in the Bahawalpur state.[47] Not much is known about Malik Muhammad or in what capacity he explored this area. What is certain, however, is that he was interested in old sites and objects, and had been collecting coins from the Bahawalpur mounds since 1903. However, in 1916, when he began actively corresponding with the Archaeological Survey, Malik Muhammad was not in the vicinity of Bahawalpur but was the manager of the Mandal estates in Karnal.

Possibly, Malik Muhammad's most significant archaeological tour in the Cholistan stretch of Bahawalpur was in the cold season of 1909–10, when he travelled from the area opposite Ahmadpur down to the extreme southwest corner of Bahawalpur state with half a dozen desert men who knew every inch of that part of the country. His companions not only pointed out scores of ruined mounds but also recounted traditions connected with them, including one that identified a spot 10 miles east of Manjgarh fort with the place where the rapacious invader Sultan Mahmud of Ghazni had encamped on his return from Somnath! He sent a report about them, along with the coins that several of the mounds had yielded, to the Archaeological Survey in 1913, in the hope that they would be identified and published. The coins were mainly medieval, although a few belonged to the Scytho–Parthians and Kushanas, but since none of them were of a rare type, it was not thought worthwhile to compile a special report on them.[48]

From the perspective of the present essay, this unpublished report is of interest.[49] Malik Muhammad describes some mounds there which were surveyed in the 1970s by the premier archaeological explorer of Bahawalpur, Mohammad Rafique Mughal, and found to yield chalcolithic pottery. For instance, there are two mounds in Malik Muhammad's report called 'Ratta Dahr' and 'Ratta Tibba' (also Chitta Tibba and Ratta Theh), situated about a mile apart. These were substantial structural archaeological sites:

> the height of each mound is more than a hundred feet above the ground level of the desert around. Tradition asserts that these were two flourishing towns long before the Islamic period, and were inhabited by the *Sohdas* or *Sodhas* (probably the *Sogdii* of the Greek historians). . . . The *chitta* and *ratta* mounds are very extensive and

large cyclopean bricks have been unearthed from them from time to time by the people in the neighbourhood.[50]

These two mounds, in all probability, are two of the three mentioned as Nos 353, 354 and 355, or Ratta-I, Ratta-II and Ratta-III, in Mughal's site list, and his survey of them yielded Hakra wares and Mature Harappan material.[51]

The Bahawalpur mounds and Malik Muhammad's report must have stayed in Marshall's mind, because, in 1924, following the announcement of the discovery of the Indus civilization in the *Illustrated London News*, he did consider the possibility of buried Indus cities in Bahawalpur and in Rajasthan. However, no particular site or mound in Bahawalpur was mentioned by him, nor is there anything to suggest that, in the context of Rajasthan, Marshall specifically remembered Kalibangan or understood the relevance of Tessitori's work there for Indus studies.

Theoretically speaking, Kalibangan could also have provided a flash of insight, especially in its relationship with the Indus area, to Rakhal Das Banerji. As a scholar Banerji was a man of uncanny historical intuition, and many of his writings on Indian history, especially those pertaining to Bengal, are full of masterly insights. His association with the celebrated Indus city of Mohenjodaro, however, is what he is popularly remembered for; more will be said about that later. Banerji began his career as an assistant in the Indian Museum at Calcutta and subsequently joined the Archaeological Survey.

Coming back to the possible insights that, hypothetically speaking, Banerji may have had in 1920, the details of his visit to the Bikaner Museum as Superintendent of the Western Circle suggest that he went specifically for the purpose of examining the Tessitori collection of antiquities there. This means that he must have seen the Kalibangan material.[52] Furthermore, Banerji examined some of the mounds that Tessitori had excavated along both banks of that part of the Ghaggar/Hakra river bed which lay in the Bikaner state. These were the mounds at Bhatner, Hanumangarh and Suratgarh, and, significantly, he found that 'they resembled to a very great extent the stupa mounds of Sind. These mounds are strewn over with potsherds and broken bricks but there was no evidence of stone work in any of them.'[53] Banerji's observation about a general resemblance between Sind's *stupa* sites—and he must have certainly had Mohenjodaro in mind, a site which he had visited in December 1919—and the Bikaner mounds undoubtedly suggests that he perceived a general similarity in the archaeological remains of the two areas. At the same time, there is nothing in Banerji's writings that can be taken to imply that he was specifically reminded of the Kalibangan antiquities when he excavated at Mohenjodaro.

In the same year that Tessitori wrote his account of Kalibangan, an Indian Civil Service officer, H.E.L. Carter, was exploring what he called the 'Stone age' of Sind, by which he meant sites where flint implements were found.[54] Carter was then Municipal Commissioner at Hyderabad (Sind), and many of his letters to Marshall on his finds are very diffuse and disjointed. However, what is important is the information in them that pointed to unknown cultural elements in Sind. For instance, one of the sites that he mentioned in his correspondence with Marshall is Tharro. Described by him as a 'walled Stone age city', it is a site that we recognize today as a Harappan one. Here, Carter found beautiful flints on the very ground which was covered with potsherds: 'It is a fine red pottery painted in patterns with the common reddish-brown colour. I kept a few pieces, one because of a very peculiar pattern which I thought at the time to be a variant of the swastika.'[55] Carter believed that most of his finds should be classified as palaeolithic. However, in terms of what was known about archaeological sites in northwest India, the presence of flints along with painted pottery could hardly have been regarded as palaeolithic assemblages by Marshall. Incidentally, the same juxtaposition of artefacts—flints along with pottery—had been described by Cunningham at Harappa. But at this point in time, there is no hint that John Marshall was struck by this extraordinary coincidence. Later, as we shall see, he acknowledged the importance of Carter's work and came to believe that the presence of long flint blades was one of the best indicators of an Indus site.

Finally, a word about Mohenjodaro. This monumental city site was actually visited by an archaeologist, Devadatta Ramkrishna Bhandarkar, in 1911–12. Son of R.G. Bhandarkar, former Vice-Chancellor of Bombay University, he was the first Indian to be appointed as an officer in the Survey; he became Assistant Archaeological Surveyor in 1904. His formal association with the Survey, though, ended in 1917, when he was handpicked by Sir Ashutosh Mookherji, Vice-Chancellor of Calcutta University, for the

Chair of Carmichael Professor of Ancient Indian History and Culture.

In 1911 Bhandarkar was in charge of the Western Circle of the Survey and thus Mohenjodaro was very much within his range of responsibilities. Bhandarkar came to the site hoping to find an impressive Buddhist *stupa*, of the type that is commonly found in other parts of Sind. As it happened, he failed to recognize the *stupa* at Mohenjodaro and quickly concluded that it was unlikely that there would be such a structure there. The ruins, he believed, were probably just two hundred years old, because the bricks were of 'modern type', with not even a single carved moulded brick.[56] Bhandarkar was wrong on both counts. There is a solid brick *stupa* at Mohenjodaro, erected on the summit of the highest mound, as also a settlement which goes back several millennia. Mohenjodaro was again visited in 1919, this time by Rakhal Das Banerji, who instantly recognized the *stupa* there but little else.[57] However, he did note that the site failed to yield human images or coins. The significance of this negative evidence was not realized by Banerji then. Mohenjodaro would have to wait another decade before this discerning explorer could truly appreciate her antiquity.

Conclusion

Such then was the state of exploration and understanding prior to 1920. Looking back, what one recognizes is the growing presence in the northwest of artefacts and cultures then unrepresented in the archaeological narrative of India's past: a new kind of pottery from Nal in Baluchistan; unique seals from Harappa in Punjab; a combination of painted pottery and flints as observed at Harappa scattered on the surface of Tharro in Sind; an absence of coins as also of images from structural mounds like Kalibangan in Rajasthan and Mohenjodaro in Sind. There must be many other such clues.

Yet, simultaneously, one also senses a curious reticence about following up these clues. Specific clues came from Nal as early as 1903 and from Tharro in 1918; two sites, Mohenjodaro and Kalibangan, whose cultural resemblance, with the benefit of hindsight, could have been discovered by 1920; Harappa, which since the nineteenth century had intrigued a number of archaeologists; an awareness as early as 1912 in at least one of them, John Marshall, that Harappa was likely to open up unknown vistas of the Indian past, and yet, the lack of single-mindedness to follow up his exceptional intuition.

Home Department and Foreign Department files were consulted at the National Archives of India (New Delhi), Revenue and Statistics Department files at the India Office Library (London), and Archaeological Survey of India files at the Archaeological Survey of India (New Delhi).

Notes and References

1 C. Masson, *Narrative of Various Journeys in Balochistan, Afghanistan and the Punjab*, Vol. 1, London, 1842, pp. 452–53; also see G. Possehl, *Indus Age: The Beginnings*, New Delhi, 1999, pp. 44–49.

2 Masson, *Narrative of Various Journeys.*

3 A. Burnes, *Travels into Bokhara together with a Narrative of a Voyage on the Indus*, Vol. III, Karachi, London, New York, first edition 1834, reprint 1973, pp. 137–38.

4 Ibid., pp. 58–59.

5 For an immensely readable account of the 'Great Game', read P. Hopkirk, *The Great Game on Secret Service in High Asia*, Oxford, 1990.

6 Proceedings of the Home Department (PHD hereafter)–A (Archaeology and Conservation), October 1882, Nos 6–11, Lepel Griffin's letter, dated 5 August 1882, to the Foreign Department of the Government of India.

7 Burnes, *Travels into Bokhara*, pp. 48–51.

8 PHD–A (Archaeology and Conservation), October 1884, Nos 21–24.

9 See J.F. Fleet, 'Seals from Harappa', *Journal of the Royal Asiatic Society of Great Britain and Ireland*, 1912, pp. 699–701.

10 Three seals seem to have reached the British Museum. One was presented by Major General Clark (this had figured in Cunningham's 1875 report), another by J. Harvey of the Indian Educational Service and the third by Mr Dames, who also published a note on the seals in volume 15 of *Indian Antiquary* (1886). The seal presented by Mr Dames had not been found by him but was dug up by T.A. O'Connor, District Superintendent of Police. For details, see Fleet, 'Seals from Harappa'.

11 See D.K. Chakrabarti, *A History of Indian Archaeology from the Beginning to 1947*, New Delhi, 1988, p. 156. There, he cites a statement of Pandit Madho Sarup Vats that clearly suggests this: 'Even before coming to India, as far back as 1901, and again in 1906, when he went home to England, Sir John had interested himself in the British Museum seals from Harappa.'

12 Revenue and Statistics Department (R&S hereafter), No. 326 of 1901, letter from John Marshall to Arthur Godley, dated 11 October 1901.

13 For details about Marshall's education and appointment as Director General of the Archaeological Survey of India, see N. Lahiri , 'John Marshall's appointment as Director General of the Archaeological Survey of India: A Survey of the Papers Pertaining to his Selection', *South Asian Studies 13*, 1997, pp. 127–40.

14 Ibid., p. 135.

15 Chakrabarti, *History of Indian Archaeology*, p. 156.

16 Curzon's conservation agenda with Marshall serving as his right-hand man is discussed in N. Lahiri, 'Coming to Grips with the Indian Past: John

Marshall's Early Years as Lord Curzon's Director General of Archaeology in India—Part I', *South Asian Studies 14*,1998, pp. 1–23.

[17] Archaeological Survey of India (ASI hereafter), No. 86, May 1902, Vogel's letter to Marshall, dated 15 March 1903.

[18] ASI, No. 175, November 1904, Marshall's letter to Burgess, dated 20 December 1904.

[19] ASI, No. 206, June 1903, Hirananda Sastri's letter to Marshall, dated 11 January 1904.

[20] ASI, No. 55, September 1903, Marshall's letter to Secretary, Revenue & Agriculture Department, dated 21 March 1903.

[21] ASI, No. 104, July 1903, Hughes Buller's letter to Marshall, dated 12 October 1903.

[22] Marshall's Cretan career has been closely documented by D.W. Gill in 'Collecting for Cambridge: John Hubert Marshall on Crete', manuscript copy.

[23] ASI, No. 104, July 1903, Marshall's letter to Hughes Buller, dated October 1903.

[24] Ibid., Marshall's letter to Hughes Buller, dated 30 July 1904.

[25] ASI, No. 119, September 1904, 'Notes'.

[26] Proceedings of the Foreign Department–B (External), Nos 173–81 of March 1905, Curzon's note, dated 30 December 1904, in 'Foreign Department Notes'.

[27] PHD–A (Archaeology & Epigraphy), June 1906, Nos 13–35, Marshall's letter to Secretary, Home Department, dated 2 April 1906. He wrote: 'The second subject which I propose to investigate concerns certain antiquities which were acquired last year from Baluchistan and which appear to be closely related to certain Cypro–Phoenician wares of the eastern Mediterranean. The problem is one which merits investigation not only for the sake of elucidating this particular chapter in the prehistoric civilization of Baluchistan, but also by reasons of its bearing on the early civilization of the Persian Gulf and particularly of the island of Bahrein.'

[28] ASI, No. 71, May 1905. See 'Notes'.

[29] ASI, No. 350, Serial Nos 1–20, 1915, Zafar Hasan's report, dated 5 September 1912. Marshall's writings on the Indus civilization contain no mention of either Zafar Hasan's visit to Harappa or his note.

[30] ASI, No. 371, Serial Nos 1–2, December 1912, Marshall's letter to Miles Irving, dated 15 November 1912.

[31] Ibid., Irving's letter to Marshall, dated 22 October 1912.

[32] ASI, No. 169, Serial Nos 1–9, June 1911, see note of J.Ph. Vogel, dated 28 April 1911.

[33] ASI, No. 400, Serial No. 1, 1914, H.A. Hargreaves's 'Inspection Note on Harappa, Montgomery District, Punjab'. The note suggests that the Superintendent was accompanied by J.R. Gupte, who Marshall had recommended to Hargreaves as a replacement for Pandit Hirananda. Earlier Gupte was a sub-registrar at Nasik and, during that time, had published papers on epigraphy and numismatics.

34 Ibid.
35 Ibid.
36 ASI, No. 400, Serial No. 1, 1914, Marshall's note, dated 19 November 1914.
37 Ibid.
38 *Annual Report of the Archaeological Survey of India* (*ARASI* hereafter), 1915–16, Part I, p. 28.
39 *ARASI*, 1916–17, p. 26.
40 ASI, No. 548, 1920, manuscript note by Daya Ram Sahni entitled 'Excavations at Harappa'.
41 ASI, No. 476, Part I, 1919. See obituary notice by G.K. Nariman entitled 'The Late Dr Tessitori', *Bombay Chronicle*, 11 January 1920.
42 ASI, No. 476, Part I, 1919.
43 *ARASI*, 1918–19, p. 23.
44 ASI, No. 300, 1918. See Tessitori's 'Extract from my Touring Report for 1917–18', dated 19 August 1917.
45 Ibid.
46 Ibid.
47 Marshall was only informed of this in 1915. See ASI, No. 283, Serial Nos 1–3, 1915. The account is titled 'A List of the Ruined Mounds in Bahawalpur State from which ancient coins were discovered between 1903 and 1909'.
48 ASI, No. 283, Serial Nos 1–3, 1915, Director General of Archaeology's letter to Malik Muhammad Din, dated 17 August 1916.
49 ASI, No. 283, Serial Nos 1–3, 1915, undated report entitled ' A List of the Ruined Mounds in Bahawalpur State from which ancient coins were discovered between 1908 and 1909'.
50 Malik Muhammad, 'A List of Ruined Mounds in Bahawalpur'.
51 M.R. Mughal, 'Recent Archaeological Research in the Cholistan Desert', in G. Possehl (ed.), *Harappan Civilization: A Contemporary Perspective*, New Delhi, 1982, pp. 87–90.
52 ASI, No. [not stated on the file], 1921, Banerji's letter to the First Assistant to the Agent to the Governor General at Rajputana, dated 10 May 1920.
53 R.D. Banerji, Bikaner State, *Progress Report of the Archaeological Survey of India, Western Circle, for the year ending 31 March 1921*, p. 113.
54 ASI, No. 425, 1918, letter of Carter to the Director General of Archaeology, dated 13 December 1917.
55 Ibid., see Carter's letter to Marshall, dated 18 March 1918. The quoted excerpt is from Carter's letter to Marshall dated 18 May 1918.
56 D.R. Bhandarkar, Mohenjodaro, *Progress Report of the Archaeological Survey of India, Western Circle, for the year ending 31 March 1912*, pp. 4–5.
57 R.D. Banerji, Mohenjodaro, *Progress Report of the Archaeological Survey of India, Western Circle, for the year ending 31 March 1920*, 121, pp. 79–80. Banerji probably visited Mohenjodaro in the middle of December since his diary (see Appendix A in the *Progress Report*) mentions 15 December as the date on which he was at Dokri. That is the railway station closest to Mohenjodaro.

The Early State in Orissa

From the Perspective of Changing Forms of Patronage and Legitimation

Bhairabi Prasad Sahu

Power is a broader and more comprehensive concept than authority, which is a form of power but not the only one. Authority is legitimate power and as such, is associated with assured, regular obedience of subjects. While the distinction between power and authority is an important one, people seeking to sustain and consolidate their power always look for ways to legitimize it. All forms of power, including domination, concentrate on a variety of justifications.[1] Ruling elites find it difficult to justify their power by *de facto* possession of it, and therefore try to find a moral and/or ethical basis for it. Validation of power was necessary not only in communities passing from the pre-state stage to the stage of state society but also in established complex societies. Legitimation helps in addressing the concerns and compulsions emanating from within local society, as well as in conforming to and becoming a part of the pan-Indian tradition. Legitimation of temporal power and the making of dominant ideology are issues more complex than have generally been assumed. Legitimation, instead of being perceived in simple reductionist terms, is increasingly located as an arena of continuous engagement involving contestation and negotiation, and as being constantly restructured and redefined.[2]

Patronage, with its inherent capacity to confer status and influence the domain of popular perceptions, has always been an important factor in socio-political processes, including the legitimation of royal authority. Rulers derived their legitimation through patronage of brahmanas, local deities and religious centres, among others. Studies on patronage and legitimation in early India range from analysis of the brahmana–kshatriya relationship and grant of land and resources to monastic establishments, through the study of puranic genealogies and the imageries of kingship in inscriptional evidence, to temple-building activities, including the formation of cultic centres.[3] In ancient societies, as so often today, patronage was usually not disinterested. The objective implicit in the act, more often than not, was the creation of inequitous social bonds and interactive networks of asymmetrical relationships, and, consequently, further strengthening of the prevalent authority structure.[4] The patron, the recipient and the objects of exchange were the interacting elements in the act. The dynamics of the relationship between the constituent elements were rooted in the particular society, for, ultimately, conceptions of status, power and authority were culturally patterned. Patronage included not only impressive monuments but also more modest efforts and services, for what really mattered was the perception that such activities created at the popular level and the image that they helped to project.[5] Community patronage, as distinguished from that of the power elite, implied, among other things, popular acquiescence in the social advancement of individuals and/or groups. Patronage, thus, viewed in a broader perspective, bound people in complex relationships of domination and subordination, and in doing so, institutionalized unequal relations in society. Patronage being a significant component of the dominant ideology and, therefore, of the strategies of domination, its changing forms, it is hoped, will reflect the trajectory of socio-political transformation in early Orissa.

Studies on early Orissa are usually limited to the construction of political and dynastic history. It is presumed that administered bureaucratic states were the normal prevailing condition from the time of the Mahameghavahanas, the first local dynasty. The state is also perceived as something that was natural and given. Such assumptions, deriving perhaps from the imperialist and nationalist discourses on empire, contributed to the image of the all-powerful, omnipresent state in early India, divorced from its material foundations and having little to do with popular opinion.[6] In an effort to re-evaluate some of these questions, this essay explores the complex links between patronage and legitimation in the particular regional context, its immense variety, changing forms and the social categories involved in the act. It focuses on the relationships between art, religion, state and society on the basis of archaeological, sculptural and epigraphic sources. The period covered is roughly between the first century BC and *c.* AD 600. The lower limit of this time-span is defined by the Hathigumpha inscription and the group of rock-cut caves at Udayagiri and Khandagiri.

The terminal date perhaps warrants some explanation. By the seventh century, the manifest socio-political profile in many areas, especially in the littoral region, indicated an early stage of the transition to the early medieval period. It then constituted a turning point in the history of the region.

II

Udayagiri and Khandagiri provide the earliest evidence of systematically organized rock-cut monuments in the region. The Dhauli elephant sculpted just above the set of Ashokan edicts is perhaps the only piece of incontrovertible evidence of an earlier art form, dating to the middle of the third century BC. The elephant gives the impression of emerging out of the woods, for only the first half has been sculpted. Historians hold diametrically opposite views on the remnant of a lion figure and the bell capital, now placed in the Orissa State Museum, and the *linga* identified as a part of a pillar, in the Bhaskareswara temple at Bhubaneswar.[7] Though these sculptural relics need not have been part of an Ashokan pillar or even contemporary to each other, at the present stage of research it is difficult to be precise about their antiquity and authorship.

The series of caves at Udayagiri and Khandagiri dedicated to Jaina monks are situated not far away from Sisupalgarh, identified with Kalinganagara, the ancient capital of Kharavela. The inscriptions in some of them indicate that these were excavated between the first century BC and first century AD, under the patronage of the Mahameghavahanas. Kharavela, the most illustrious of them, is known to us by his lengthy Hathigumpha inscription. Despite the fact that the data are not voluminous, the donors may be divided into two broad categories. The first includes those belonging to the ruling class, for example, Kharavela himself, his chief queen, King Kudepasiri (probably a successor of Kharavela), Prince Vadukha,[8] the town judge (*nagara akhadamsa*) Bhutti, and Nakiya, the wife of the *mahamada*,[9] while the second category comprises humble individual donors, most probably lay devotees and monks.[10] In the latter category donations by (*padamulika*) Kusuma, a servant or menial, and the monks of Dohada are noteworthy. The donation by Jaina monks is unambiguously stated, unlike the indirect, hesitant references to similar donations at Mathura. In addition, it indicates that, like the Buddhist monks in the Deccan and central India, the Jaina monks too possibly did not renounce all their worldly possessions and could have used these for worthy purposes.[11] Each cave (*lena*) was usually a gift by a separate individual and the donations may have been more substantial as compared to those at Sanchi.[12] The possible explanation for this lies in the elite nature of most donations. The paucity of donative records at Udayagiri–Khandagiri may be accounted for by the fact that Kharavela seems to have provided the funds for construction of most of the caves.[13]

The evidence also provides insights into the socio-political dimensions of art in early Orissa. The fact that the donors considered it necessary to record their gifts, so that they could be read, suggests that they were seeking advertisement for their acts and, flowing from it, recognition and status, apart from religious merit. The donative record of the chief queen also mentions her pedigree, connecting her to another ruling family. She is said to be the daughter of King Lalaka, the grandson or great-grandson of Hastisahasa/Hastisimha.[14] It is tempting to invoke parallels with Nayanika's marriage to the Satavahana king Satkarni in the Deccan, with all its political implications. However, in doing so at this stage, there is the danger of reading more than what is provided in this short inscription.[15] Another aspect of these inscriptions is that they record three donations by women: one by a queen, the second by the wife of a state functionary, and the third by a menial(?) woman.[16] On their own these may not suggest anything significant. However, they acquire meaning in the light of the rich sculptural representation of women in a variety of contexts, both in the private and public domains.[17] The social visibility of women may imply the absence of an entrenched, brahmanical society premised on *varna*/caste ideology and gender hierarchy.[18]

For purposes of piety the recording and display of the donor's name is not necessary, and less so is a lengthy public statement encapsulating the career and achievements of the donor, as in the case of the Hathigumpha inscription. Apparently, the purpose of the Hathigumpha inscription was not merely to record the donation to the Jaina recluses. The image or self-image of Kharavela was also aimed to be projected through it. A carefully constructed image of royalty runs through the length of the record, especially in the first two and last two lines, revealing various elements that were invoked in its making. The elements include the picture of a successful warrior, a hero, a conqueror/*chakravartin*,[19] a liberal donor, a benevolent and responsive administrator, a patron of the arts and religions, etc.

In the narrative reliefs on the façade of the caves, particularly those on the lower storey of Ranigumpha, the representations bear witness to an emphasis on royal actions. In the sculptural arrangement, one finds a corroborative and repetitive image of kingship. This is an early, perhaps the earliest, instance of historical and political allegory in contemporary art. The use of metaphors in lithic art and the spatial spread of such art forms are usually associated with the Gupta period and beyond. The sculptural elements range from war to entertainment on the elaborate façade to carefully selected narrative stories, and are focused on themes relating to the career and conquests of Kharavela.[20] The sculptures celebrate the political success of the *chakravartin* king symbolized in the installation of the Kalinga Jina after its recovery from Magadha following the defeat of its ruler, who, perhaps, is shown bowing at the feet of Kharavela in one of the scenes.[21] The remarkable correspondence between the visual imagery of the sculptures and the content and spirit of the epigraph is striking, and only the naive would believe that it was accidental, not designed. Their propaganda and, deriving from it, their legitimation value, cannot be underestimated. These symbols of substance at the Udayagiri–Khandagiri complex vividly convey the self-image(s) of kingship, and are possibly visible markers of the political structure of early Kalinga. Monuments are indicators of, as well as mediums for, the control over produce and labour. Their capacity for generating respect and awe, and conferring esteem needs no emphasis. They are thus acts of political wisdom and not merely related to personal religious faith. While the simplicity of the architectural plan conforms to the Jaina ethics and ethos, the sculptural arrangement in general has much that is mundane. Not everything is religious, or Jaina in this case. Scenes of combat, dance, music, songs, festivities, rejoicing, etc.,[22] although they might militate against the self-denying, austere, supposedly Jaina ambience of the site, are still very much there. Kharavela's faith in Jainism notwithstanding, he relentlessly engaged in political aggrandizement, war and booty—indicating perhaps the pragmatism associated with the political compulsions of a ruler.

Kharavela, in spite of his personal faith in Jainism, was liberal to all sects. This catholicity is evidenced by the expression *sava-*

pasamdapujako sava-devayatana-samkarakarako (the worshipper of all religious orders, the repairer of shrines of all gods) in line seventeen of the Hathigumpha inscription. Royal generosity was widespread and there is a mention of donations to brahmanas as well.[23] Again, this non-sectarian attitude of the ruler is corroborated by sculptural art. Naga figures are found on the door arches at Anantagumpha. Tree worship has been depicted in one of the tympana on the façade of Anantagumpha and at Jaya-Vijayagumpha in the space between the arches.[24] Interestingly, the six *yaksha* images and three large images of Nagaraja reported from sites in the vicinity of Bhubaneswar are broadly dated around the time of the Mahameghavahanas.[25] Miniature *yakshas* occur at the Ranigumpha and Ganeshagumpha in Udayagiri, and the Anantagumpha at Khandagiri.[26] All this evidence, together, point towards religious pluralism, characterized by harmonious coexistence of popular cults and beliefs. Kharavela may be seen to have been responding to the religious and cultural aspirations of a diverse ethno-cultural setting, quite like the Kushanas in north India. Compulsions of royal power made it necessary for the king not to be perceived as being partisan and/or sectarian.[27] The broad-based religious patronage, thus, was not entirely disinterested.

The reconstructional beautification of Kalinganagara, the capital, the arrangements for the restoration of the aqueduct, the entertainment of the people with music, dance and festivities, the building of the victory palace, and the remission of taxes and cesses,[28] perhaps, were largely acts of benevolence, for they led to the creation of a special kind of a bond between the ruler and his subjects because of their potential to provide better conditions for agriculture, employment opportunities and such other benefits.[29] Such acts were neither entirely personal acts of charity nor impersonal conduct, as are commodity relations, especially when these were prominently listed as achievements, as part of a lengthy public statement, by the king. Moreover, the poverty and misery of the masses, it is said, is the breeding ground for aristocratic patronage.[30] The relationship between deprivation and patronage focuses on an important dimension of temporal power and authority.

The evidence suggests that the Udayagiri–Khandagiri complex and the associated projects were products as much of power and politics as of piety. The images of kingship and of forms of patronage as gleaned from the inscriptional and sculptural data may be better understood in the context of the power structure and the nature of the polity.

The earliest manifestation of some form of institutionalized state in ancient Kalinga under Kharavela seems to have derived largely from the Mauryan interaction with the region, as were the contemporaneous, similar developments in the Deccan.[31] The details of the processes leading to this are exasperatingly elusive in the archaeological record.[32] The two sets of Ashokan inscriptions at Dhauli and Jaugada suggest that the Mahanadi delta and Rishikulya valley were scenes of activity during the Mauryan period. Ashokan Kalinga roughly extended from the Cuttack–Puri area to the modern Ganjam–Srikakulam districts. Though apparently a digression, it is imperative to mention that the term Kalinga had varying connotations at different points of history, and probably covered the area up to Godavari–Krishna along the Andhra coast in the early historical period.[33] Coming back to the Mauryan context, it is difficult to be precise about the administrative details and its consequences, on the basis of the available evidence. We may infer that there was a great deal of socio-political flux after the end of the Nanda–Mauryan experience and the region's interaction with the metropolitan centre. Maximum opportunities for the growth of chieftainships would have arisen at the centres of Mauryan interaction in the wake of such a momentous development. The hitherto coopted periphery or 'locality' elites, with their power and status enhanced within their own societies because of the said interaction, could acquire a more meaningful and visible political profile.

Sisupalgarh, identified with Tosali, one of the administrative centres in Ashokan Kalinga near Dhauli, has produced evidence for continuous occupation between the earlier part of the third century BC and *c.* AD 300.[34] It is situated on the outskirts of Bhubaneswar on the way to Dhauli. Jaugada, identified with Samapa, the other contemporary political centre in the region, has yielded similar data.[35] It may not be entirely coincidental that the Mahameghavahanas—Kharavela being the third in the family—rose to power around Bhubaneswar and the Mahanadi delta. At the risk of repetition one may reiterate that Kharavela's chief queen came from a ruling lineage with three to four generations of history. The expression *Kalinga purvaraja nivesitam* (founded by the earlier rulers of Kalinga), in line eleven of the Hathigumpha inscription, implies the existence of ruling chiefs in Kalinga prior to the Mahameghavahanas. Inscriptional evidence, thus, indicates the continued presence of 'locality' chiefs in the post-Mauryan period.

Notwithstanding the adoption of exalted titles such as *chakradharo, chakravarti, Kalingadhipati* and *maharaja* by the Mahameghavahanas,[36] the power structure over which they presided seems to have been in an early stage of evolution. It is doubtful if they were able to provide for an 'administered' polity. There is very little evidence for a state exercising control over a precisely delimited territory with the help of a bureaucratic command structure, where the contours of power relations and the jurisdiction of the officials are defined. The *mahamada* and *nagara akhadamsa* are two high state functionaries mentioned in the donative records discussed above. The interpretation of the words *kamma, chulakamma* and *padamulika* is far from satisfactory, and one is not sure whether the first two constitute personal names or administrative designations.[37] Even if we concede, for the moment, the latter possibility, our understanding of the administrative structure is by no means enhanced. Certainly, it was not a state with a bureaucratic structure, characterized by officials with distinct and specific jurisdiction. The possibility of individuals holding multiple responsibilities cannot be ignored. Taxes and cesses are mentioned in the context of their remission. Surprisingly, neither Kharavela nor his successors seem to have issued any dynastic coins. More so because Kharavela refers to colossal state expenditure on his construction projects, among other things.[38] One may consider the possibility of some of the available punch-marked coins being used as the medium of exchange. However, most of the coins from Sisupalgarh, including the silver punch-marked coin, date from *c.* AD 100 onwards. Besides, coins with their motifs and symbols are also signs and statements of royal sovereignty, and their absence cannot be wholly unrelated to the compulsions and nature of the socio-political system. A comparison with the contemporary Deccan makes the paucity of metallic money in Kalinga more conspicuous.[39] The rudimentary administrative mechanism and such other associated problems[40] were sought to be compensated, perhaps, by the forging of ties through various forms of cultural transactions in a post-tribal state, as it were.

Kharavela's unusual inscription was an important, and possibly effective, medium of communication. Indubitably, it was a discourse in power and conveys the notion of authority. It eulogizes war, valour and victory, and highlights the prospects of booty and tribute.

However, nowhere does the image of a compelling, assertive or even persuasive ruler emerge, either from the language or tone of discourse. To make a more general point about the importance of such evidence for understanding the nature of contemporary political structures, it may be useful to briefly reflect on the Ashokan inscriptions, for instance. Even a cursory reading of the Ashokan inscriptions reveals that the mode of discourse in such mediums of communication is important and is likely to provide significant insights into the nature of power and authority. The paternalistic attitude and image of a father figure that the Ashokan inscriptions exude, while simultaneously conveying the king's striking self-confidence and notion of authority, are noteworthy.[41] The point of inference is that the state under Kharavela, with an independent socio-political organization, a vaguely defined territory and centre of government, and an ideology based on the concept of reciprocity, apparently, was an early state. The military successes of Kharavela in general, and his victories over such categories as the Bhojakas, Rathikas and the people of Pithunda in particular, seem to have been overstated.[42] The military campaigns appear to have been plundering raids, because there is nothing to suggest a consolidation of gains from these conquests. Moreover, such localities/communities were themselves in a stage of transition to the early historical phase.[43] These raids, however, had the potentiality of generating the necessary resources for the extensive patronage at home, which could sustain the ruling elite's strategies of domination and, consequently, help the consolidation of authority.

In spite of the fact that there is a reference to *paurajanapada* and evidence for royal indulgence, the vagueness that surrounds the ordinary people is striking. The community and the common man/woman are elusive. Given the limitations of the data, one can see depictions of society in the art of Udayagiri and Khandagiri and in artefacts from sites like Sisupalgarh. But, as for the larger issue relating to the nature of society itself, the available evidence is not unequivocal. The adaptation of terms such as *chakravartin*, *agamahisi*, *nagara*, *rajarsi* and *Bharatavarsha*, terms with perhaps northern moorings, is instructive. References to northern political centres in the Hatigumpha record also indicate the ongoing cultural interactions. The existence of brahmana households may be inferred from line nine of the said epigraph. It mentions them as recipients of royal munificence, among others. Nevertheless, vedic sacrifices and patronage of brahmanas were not yet integral to the legitimation process. Kharavela significantly claimed to be a descendant of Rajarsi Vasu. Brahmanas and brahmanical ideology, structures and institutions were still not intrinsic to the making of strategies of domination. Society, though largely casteless, was not necessarily classless. Material prosperity, growing technical skill, trade and cultural contacts are demonstrable in the archaeological record.[44] However, there is little on the organizational aspects of manufacture and trade. A casual comparison with the data from the Deccan concerning the varieties of guilds, their activities, and intra-regional and inter-regional exchange networks, shows up the poverty of information in the Orissan context. In addition, the non-issuance of coins by the Mahameghavahanas, among other things, perhaps reveals the state of the market economy and the level of the society. It has generally been recognized that early historical trade was conducted by guilds, cutting across political formations.[45] However, in Orissa during the said period, we do not come across terms denoting traders, commercial centres or guilds. Kalinga, because of its geographical location, perhaps acted as a bridge in the eastern coastal trade; but that is far from saying that mercantile activities were in the making in the region.[46] Kosambi's thesis on the socio-economic role of the cave-monasteries on trade routes[47] is enticing but, given the nature and limitations of the data, it is difficult to ascribe a very active role to the group of caves at Udayagiri–Khandagiri, not far away from Sisupalgarh, in the trade network along the east coast.

Material remains, coins, pottery, ornaments, etc., are more numerous in the second–third century AD layers at Sisupalgarh.[48] The earliest evidence of rouletted ware from the site is dated to the latter half of the first century AD, and the glass bangles and clay bullae belong to the second century. The gold coin of Dharmadamadara, a Murunda ruler supposedly, and the clay seal of *amatya* Prasannaka belong to the third century.[49] This brief survey does not focus on factual details, important though these may be, but on the overall pattern that emerges from the material remains.[50] Interestingly, defences were in good condition till the mid-first century AD and thereafter were neglected, coinciding perhaps with the decline of the Mahameghavahanas. Under Kharavela, therefore, Sisupalgarh appears to have been more of a political centre than anything else. The cultural sequence and data obtained at Jaugada, to the south, in Ganjam district, broadly conform to the Sisupalgarh evidence.

What emerges from this amorphous evidence is a society in a stage of transition to the historical period where the contours of development were not fully established and, hence, providing conflicting signals. It seems to have been a loosely organized, primarily agrarian society, in which the basic distinction was between the ruling elite and the ruled. Beyond this the differences appear to have been considerably blurred and not hierarchically structured, as in later societies.

III

The process leading to the emergence of ruling elites at the level of 'localities'[51] did not end with Kharavela and his immediate successors. Continued manifestation of the process in the early Christian centuries is discernible in the dispersed data from various pockets of the region. They demonstrate uneven and perhaps dissimilar patterns of growth in the region, while simultaneously revealing the inherent complexities. The expansion of the Mahameghavahanas into the Godavari–Guntur area of modern Andhra Pradesh in the mid-second century AD[52] manifests a continuation of the process of locality formation. Whether this was an offshoot of one of Kharavela's campaigns or a consequence of fission, that is, segmentation of the ruling family, or both, is not clear. The two relevant inscriptions, the Guntupalli inscriptions[53] and the Velpuru inscription,[54] record the donation of two *mandapas*, one each by the scribe of Mahameghavahana Sri Sada and the lady attendant (Deva, the lamp-bearer) of Aira Maharaja Manasada. Though it is difficult to determine the exact relationship between the Mahameghavahanas and this Aira Maharaja, it is significant that *Aira* as a family name also occurs in the record of the Mahameghavahanas of Kalinga, and the title *maharaja* was used by them as well. The grants were made in favour of, what appear to be, autochthonous deities. Donations to deities and the association of the donors in some capacity or the other with the state, attract attention. Commoners, for example, peasants, artisans and traders, continue to be absent from the scene. The accrued political profile of the said locality, implicit in the inscriptions, may have to be viewed in the context of a further stage in the transition to the historical period. Similarly, the Bhadrak stone inscription of the time of Gana, dated to the second half of the third century AD, recording the donation of a certain measure of land or grains in favour of a shrine or religious establishment,[55] has important socio-political implications. It has a bearing on the question of the evolution of ownership rights in land and/or control over produce. In addition, the tentative political visibility of the locality suggests that its internal transformation, leading to the emergence of the historical phase, was far from complete.[56] The process there, in all likelihood, came into its own during the late fifth or sixth century.[57]

The subsequent emergence of the Bhanjas in the Keonjhar area, and Maharaja Tustikara around Asurgarh, in Kalahandi district, will have to be viewed in terms of the continuation of the same trend. However, these localities, far as they are from the coast, help us to appreciate the phased evolution and development of the variegated areas in the region. The patronage extended to the local, autochthonous deity Stambeshwari by Maharaja Tustikara, referred to in his Terasinga Plates,[58] perhaps finds archaeological corroboration in the excavated circular brick structure at Asurgarh. The site yields some very inconclusive, yet significantly suggestive, information on the developments leading to this stage in the fifth century. Fine black polished ware, a broken piece of chunar sandstone with Mauryan polish, red glazed Kushana-type pottery, unfinished or broken pieces of stone ornaments and a mould for the preparation of ornaments,[59] among other finds, reflect the earlier history of the site. The fragmentary evidence from Manmunda, located close to the confluence of the Mahanadi and the Tel in Phulbani district, and Ganiapalli, near the confluence of the Ang and Magar rivers in the district of Sambalpur, relate to the early Christian centuries.[60] They suggest the formative beginnings of these areas. In western and southwestern Orissa, the formation of 'localities' and the transition to the historical period seem to have been generally later than similar developments in the coastal districts.

The Asanapat inscription of Maharaja Satrubhanja of the Naga family records the construction of a shrine (*Deva-yatana*) by the king,[61] while the inscription on the stone image of Shiva from the same site in Keonjhar district describes events during Satrubhanja's rule.[62] At Sitabinji in the same district, there is a tempera showing a royal procession. The name of the king is mentioned as Rajaraja Sri Disabhanja. In its vicinity are a *chaturmukha lingam* and boulders, some of which are inscribed with the names of Shaiva ascetics. The associated finds include a female figurine, a ruined brick structure, bronze ear ornaments, pottery and Puri–Kushana coins. Khiching, in the neighbouring Mayurbhanj district, has yielded a stone seal with the letters reading *ragaraja* (*rajaraja*),[63] implying the presence of some ruling chief. There is a visible pattern in the apparently scattered data which conforms to the emerging ubiquitous trend. They focus on the linkages between temporal power and the sacred domain, the networks of patronage and legitimation that rulers with a name ending in 'bhanja' sponsored and participated in at the locality level, during the fourth to sixth centuries.

Patronage centred around locality deities and their shrines or establishments may be understood in the context of the need to create larger community identities by transcending kinship considerations. Autochthonous chiefs without the support of a kshatriya status for legitimacy extended patronage to locality deities. The politics of patronage would legitimize power and help the emergence of a stratum of ruling elites. Consequently, it would accentuate differentiation within communities and lead to the formation of complex relationships of domination and subordination.

On the basis of the spatial distribution of punch-marked coins, covering both western and coastal Orissa, and the discovery of the coin mould from Sisupalgarh, the presence of an organized currency system in the post-Kharavela period may be suggested. The chronology of these coins is, however, debatable. While most of the coins have been conventionally dated from the middle of the first millennium BC onwards, the date of the Sisupalgarh find is around AD 100 and the Asurgarh collection of fifty coins came from the uppermost layer assigned to the fifth century.[64] It is not unlikely, therefore, that these coins were in circulation up to the fourth–fifth centuries AD. Hoards of Puri–Kushana coins (local Kushana imitations), usually in association with some Kushana coins, have been reported from different parts of northern and coastal Orissa. The abundance of these coins, among other things, suggests that it was the regional currency during the second–fourth/fifth centuries.[65] The find-spots of these coins point to the possibility of a trade route from the Singbhum area to coastal Orissa and Andhra through the northern districts of Keonjhar and Mayurbhanj. The Mahanadi valley could have been used as a communication route between the littoral and the flood plains of western Orissa. The concentration of both punch-marked and Puri–Kushana coins in the coastal districts is perhaps indicative of their growing social complexity. Familiar beliefs about ancient Orissa's transoceanic trade networks may be disturbed but the actual evidence for trade with Southeast Asia is little,[66] and the data for Roman contacts are limited to the rouletted ware and clay bullae from Sisupalgarh and the few Roman coins from Bamanghati in Mayurbhanj.[67] With the available information it is difficult to be precise about the organization, nature and impact of early historical trade in the region.[68]

The details of the processes and stages in the emergence of 'localities' and the transition to the early historical period are not clear. It is, however, obvious that historico-cultural stages were uneven over the region.[69] While some localities, particularly those in the coastal tract, acquired early visibility, others inland were still characterized by ill-defined, at times even exasperatingly hazy, contours of development. However, the early socio-political manifestations even in the relatively difficult terrains of northern and western Orissa suggest that both the movement of men, ideas and goods, and human interactions, including perhaps exchange networks, cut across geographical categories such as heartland, periphery and frontier.[70]

IV

Land grants to brahmanas and the growth of temples, the two ostensible markers of patronage since the Gupta period, can be appreciated in the context of the formation of sub-regional agrarian bases and the need to legitimize the emerging political structure and society.[71] Royalty patronized brahmanas, subscribed to the brahmanical ideology and dispersed their resources as donations to brahmanical institutions, due to their own compulsions. Such patronage ensured the extension and consolidation of authority.[72] Ruling lineages used the mystique of vedic rituals, shastric ideas and puranic symbolism to strengthen their authority. The relationship between the king and the brahmana was crucial to the processes of state formation and socio-economic transformation. In Orissa, these processes began to operate simultaneously from the fourth and fifth centuries onwards. The formation of agrarian bases at the locality and sub-regional levels was an ongoing process and it introduced a comparable socio-political structure throughout.

The spread and entrenchment of vedic, shastric and puranic discourses can be gleaned from the early epigraphic records and sculptures of Orissa. The Mathara, early eastern Ganga and Sailodbhava inscriptions bear testimony to these developments. These records refer to the Vedas, Vedangas, vedic sacrifices, Puranas, puranic deities and stories.[73] Kings begin to be compared with heroes of the epics, such as Arjuna and Hanumana.[74] Moreover, statements suggesting the destruction of the impurities or stains of the Kali age in the early eastern Ganga and Sailodbhava records, among others, are suggestive of cultural and ideological transformation.[75] The references to the Kali age in puranic literature have been interpreted to symbolize a systemic crisis in northern India.[76] However, in the context of Orissa, Kali may be perceived differently. Repeated references to the removal of the stains of the Kali age are usually juxtaposed with the virtue and purity of the king, which helped him to accomplish the act. A contextualized analysis of the notion of virtue/purity of the ruler shows that it meant the patronage of vedic sacrifices, *varnasrama dharma* and the shastric–puranic value system.[77] Kali, thus, was a metaphor for a society not conforming to the normative, ideal brahmanical prescriptions. It symbolized the negation of *dharma* and, flowing from it, the king, representing order, had to be distanced from it. The notion of the Kali, while distinctly highlighting kingly virtues by contrast, unmistakably suggests the formation of monarchical states with reference to the dominant ideology.[78]

The early temples of Bhubaneswar, such as Satrughneswara, Lakshmaneswara, Parasurameswara and Suvarnajaleswara, depict scenes from the epics and the Puranas. Themes relating to the marriage of Shiva and Parvati, Shiva curbing the pride of Ravana, Shiva begging food of his consort, the discussion between Rama and Sugriva, Rama killing the golden deer, Bali's death at the hands of Rama, the fight between Shiva as Kirata and Arjuna, etc., constitute the subject matter of the narrative panels in these temples. These sculptures indicate the familiarity of the artists with stories from the epics and Puranas, and constitute significant evidence of the process of internalizing cultural forms. The Shaiva *acharyas* who were associated with this earliest group of temples may be seen as contributors to the propagation of these new ideas and institutions. Brahmanas and temples were thus the agencies for disseminating these ideas. The spread of such ideas would achieve socio-cultural integration over wider areas, and across communities. Consequently, the associated symbols would be used to exercise domination[79] in a hierarchically structured society in-the-making.

Accompanying this process of sub-regional state formation

and the power elite configuration, involving patronage for one and validation for the other, was a process of social change. The community, which had so far been elusive in our records and was therefore presumably in the background, was now becoming visible. The occurrence of terms such as *kutumbin, grihasvami, grihadhyaksha, praja, mahattara* and *mahamahattara*[80] (in the land-grant charters of the various ruling lineages during the fifth–seventh centuries) in a general context of agrarian expansion[81] suggests the emergence of a stratified peasantry. The upwardly mobile among them would look for channels of status advancement. The foundations of the early phase of temple-building activities in the region were laid around *c.* AD 600. The royal records convey evidence of donations to temples for repairs, offerings, services and maintenance, but quite strikingly, not one of the early donative charters alludes to their construction by royalty.[82] The beginnings of the temple movement, then, may be credited to the long architectural tradition in the region and to community patronage. Individual or group patronage would emanate from the desire to acquire upward mobility in the asymmetrically structured society in-the-making and to gain acceptance for the assumed status. Besides, common people too, perhaps, looked to men of substance for the performance of services that were important for the everyday life of the community. Patronage of religious establishments, thus, provided a major channel for status enhancement to those who wanted to move up within the hierarchical, apparently static, caste society.

The interacting elements in the act of patronage changed through time. However, the nexus that was created between power, religious institutions and the people continued throughout. The structure of legitimation reflects both the cultural basis of power and its cultural domain. The shift in patronage from rock-cut monuments and public entertainment programmes to shastric–puranic ideology and temples, through local folk deities/cults, exhibits early forms of socio-cultural transformation. The autochthonous deities had strong local roots. The spatial spread of these deities and/or cults provided the emerging local/trans-local ruling lineages an assured dimension of territoriality as their principal patrons. The varying forms of legitimation in early Orissa provide insights into the intra-regional variations. These distinctions extended to the domain of art as well. The artists of Kalinga and the *shilpis* of the lower Mahanadi valley did not follow identical traditions in the early phase of temple-building activities.[83] Though the pace and stage of socio-political developments across sub-regions were not uniform, they existed not in immutable isolation but in a state of interaction and transformation. The transfer of land as gift (*dana*) introduced complex agrarian relations and, flowing from it, greater differentiation within society. However, the patronage extended to brahmanas and temples may be understood in the context of the contemporary society which was beginning to experience simultaneous processes of change—agrarian expansion, state formation, evolution of caste society and cultic integration.[84] Both contributed towards the growth and subsequent consolidation of a hierarchically structured, complex socio-political order.

An earlier version of this essay, under the title 'Power and the Politics of Patronage: Political and Social Processes in Early Orissa', was presented at the National Seminar on 'From Cultural History to the History of Culture', organized by the Department of History, Hyderabad University, Hyderabad, in October 1996. I am grateful to Professor B.D. Chattopadhyaya for his comments on an earlier draft of this paper.

Notes and References

1 The ingenuity of the people of antiquity in devising mechanisms to sustain the socio-political order need not be underestimated. For a recent discussion, see the relevant essays in Anton Powell (ed.), *Classical Sparta: Techniques behind her Success*, London, 1989; also M.I. Finley, *Politics in the Ancient World*, Cambridge University Press, Cambridge, 1984 (reprint).

2 See, for example, B.D. Chattopadhyaya, 'Political Processes and the Structure of Polity in Early Medieval India: Problems of Perspective', Presidential Address, Ancient India section, *Proceedings of the Indian History Congress*, Burdwan session, 1983, pp. 25–63; Hermann Kulke, *Kings and Cults: State Formation and Legitimation in India and Southeast Asia*, Manohar Publishers, Delhi, 1993; 'The Early and the Imperial Kingdom: A Processual Model of Integrative State Formation in Early Medieval India', in Kulke (ed.), *The State in India 1000–1700*, Oxford University Press, Delhi, 1997, pp. 233–62; and Kesavan Veluthat, 'Religious Symbols in Political Legitimation: The Case of Early Medieval South India', *Social Scientist*, Nos 236–37, 1993, pp. 23–33.

3 Ibid. Also see Sibesh Bhattacharya, 'Political Authority and Brahmana-Kshatriya Relationship in Early India: An Aspect of the Power Elite Configuration', *Indian Historical Review*, Vol. X, Nos 1–2, pp. 1–20; Romila Thapar, 'Genealogy as a Source of Social History', in *Ancient Indian Social History: Some Interpretations*, Orient Longman, Delhi, 1987 (reprint), pp. 326–60; and B.S. Miller (ed.), *The Powers of Art: Patronage in Indian Culture*, Oxford University Press, Delhi, 1992, sections I and II.

4 For a good general discussion on the problem of authority and patronage

in the ancient world, see Finley, *Politics in the Ancient World*, Chapter 2, pp. 24–49.

5 For the socio-political dimensions of patronage, see Romila Thapar, *Cultural Transaction and Early India: Tradition and Patronage*, Oxford University Press, Delhi, 1987, especially pp. 26–28. Also, the Introduction by Barbara S. Miller and Richard Eaton, in Miller (ed.), *The Powers of Art*, particularly pp. 1–4.

6 For a recent statement of this kind, see A.K. Mohanty, *State and Government in Ancient Orissa*, Vidyapuri, Cuttack, 1993.

7 See R.L. Mitra, *Antiquities of Orissa*, Vol. 2, *Indian Studies: Past and Present*, Calcutta, 1880, p. 98; K.P. Jayaswal, 'Evidence of an Ashokan Pillar at Bhubaneswar in Orissa', *Indian Antiquary*, Vol. 58, 1929, pp. 218–19; N.K. Basu, 'Some Ancient Remains from Bhubaneswar', *The Journal of Bihar–Orissa Research Society*, Vol. 15, 1929, p. 261; K.C. Panigrahi, *Archaeological Remains at Bhubaneswar*, Kitab Mahal, Calcutta, 1961, pp. 184–87; N.K. Sahu, *History of Orissa*, Vol. I, Utkal University, Cuttack, 1964, pp. 273–77; and Debala Mitra, 'A Note on the Bhaskareswara Linga', *Journal of the Asiatic Society*, Vol. 1, No. 1, 1959.

8 The upper storey of cave 9, known as Svargapuri, at Udayagiri, was dedicated by the queen. Two of the cells on the ground floor of the same cave, popularly known as Manchapuri, were gifts by Maharaja Kudepasri and Kumara Vadukha. See R.D. Banerji, 'Inscriptions in the Udayagiri and Khandagiri Caves', *Epigraphia Indica*, Vol. XIII, 1915–16, Nos I, II and III, pp. 159–61; also H. Luders, 'A List of Brahmi Inscriptions from the Earliest Times to about AD 400', *Epigraphia Indica*, Vol. X, Appendix, 1912, Nos 1346, 1347 and 1348.

9 Banerji, 'Inscriptions in the Udayagiri and Khandagiri Caves', Nos VII and VIII, pp. 163–64; Luders, 'List of Brahmi Inscriptions', Nos 1351 and 1352.

10 Luders, 'List of Brahmi Inscriptions', Nos 1344, 1349, 1350, 1353; also see Banerji, 'Inscriptions in the Udayagiri and Khandagiri Caves', Nos IV, V, VI and IX–XIII, pp. 162–65. It is necessary to mention that in inscriptions IX, XII and XIII, the donors have not been properly identified owing to the poor state of the said records.

11 For such evidence in the Deccan and central India, see Vidya Dehejia, 'The Collective and Popular Basis of Early Buddhist Patronage: Sacred Monuments, 100 BC–AD 250', in Miller (ed.), *The Powers of Art*, p. 37.

12 The exceptions are the donation by the monks and the one by Kamma and Harakshina. Banerji, 'Inscriptions in the Udayagiri and Khandagiri Caves', Nos V and XI.

13 The Hathigumpha inscription points in this direction. K.P. Jayaswal and R.D. Banerji, 'Kharavela's Hatigumpha Inscriptions', *Epigraphia Indica*, Vol. XX, line 15, p. 89.

14 Some differences are noted in the readings of Luders and Banerji. See *Epigraphia Indica*, Vol. X, No. 1346, p. 161, and *Epigraphia Indica*, Vol. XIII, p. 160.

15 Matrimonial alliances, even later, continued to help the consolidation of

power and status elevation of the newly rising ruling families. For an example, see Devangana Desai, 'The Patronage of the Lakshmana Temple at Khajuraho', in Miller (ed.), *The Powers of Art,* p. 79.

[16] Luders, 'List of Brahmi Inscriptions', Nos 1344, 1346, 1352.

[17] For details, one may see N.K. Sahu, *Kharavela,* Orissa State Museum, Bhubaneswar, 1984, pp. 109, 111, 117–20, 197; also see R.P. Mahapatra, 'Position of Women as Depicted in the Early Sculptures of Udayagiri and Khandagiri Caves', *Orissa Historical Research Journal,* Vols XXIV–XXVI, 1980, pp. 61–64.

[18] The hierarchical caste system and subordination of women are inextricably inter-related because the purity of caste is contingent upon the purity of women.

[19] While Kharavela uses the epithet *Chakradhara* (holder of the wheel of sovereignty) for himself, his chief queen refers to him as *Chakravartin. Epigraphia Indica,* Vol. XX, line 17, p. 80; and Luders, 'List of Brahmi Inscriptions', No. 1346.

[20] Some of the photographs and sketches are available in N.K. Sahu, *Kharavela,* pp. 63, 65, and 68; and Debala Mitra, *Udayagiri and Khandagiri,* Archaeological Survey of India, New Delhi, 1975, plates IIIA, VB, VIB, etc.

[21] For plates and sketches, see Mitra, ibid., plates IIIB and VIIIB; N.K. Sahu, *Kharavela,* pp. 70, 82, 241.

[22] N.K. Sahu deals with them at length. See ibid., Chapters VI and VII, especially the sketches on pp. 156, 158–59, 210.

[23] Jayaswal and Banerji, 'Kharavela's Hatigumpha Inscriptions', line 9.

[24] In both instances the tree is within railings, under umbrellas, being worshipped with offerings of flowers. Photographs and sketches of the same are available in N.K. Sahu, *Kharavela,* pp. 146 and 217; and Mitra, *Udayagiri and Khandagiri,* plate XIVB.

[25] See B.P. Sahu, 'Ancient Orissan Cultural Relations', *Indica,* Vol. 21, No. 1, 1984, p. 6.

[26] Ibid.

[27] Various dynasties in ancient India addressed the problem by ensuring that members of the royal family, especially women, patronized sects other than those encouraged by the ruler himself. See A.K. Narain, 'Religious Policy and Toleration in Ancient India with Particular Reference to the Gupta Age', in B.L. Smith (ed.), *Essays on Gupta Culture,* Motilal Banarsidass, Delhi, 1983, pp. 17–51.

[28] Lines 3 and 5–7 in the Hathigumpha inscription mention these activities. See Jayaswal and Banerji, 'Kharavela's Hatigumpha Inscriptions'.

[29] It is recorded in the inscription that such works were paid for and that they were not products of involuntary labour. See lines 4, 6–7, 10 and 16, referring to state expenditure.

[30] Finley, *Politics in the Ancient World,* p. 47.

[31] The implications of the Mauryan interaction with the Deccan are both convincingly and lucidly presented in S. Seneviratne, 'Kalinga and Andhra: The Process of Secondary State Formation in Early India', *The Indian Historical*

Review, Vol. VII, Nos 1–2, pp. 54–69; and B.D. Chattopadhyaya, 'Transition to the Early Historical Phase in the Deccan: A Note', in B.M. Pande and B.D. Chattopadhyaya (eds), *Archaeology and History*, Vol. II, Agam Kala Prakashan, Delhi, 1988, pp. 727–32.

[32] B.P. Sahu, 'Ancient Orissa: The Dynamics of Internal Transformation of the Tribal Society', in K.M. Shrimali (ed.), *Essays in Art, Religion and Society*, Munshiram Manoharlal, Delhi, 1987, pp. 170–71.

[33] The territories of many ruling lineages associated with Kalinga encompassed areas of both modern Andhra and Orissa. For a historical explanation, see N.K. Bose, *Culture and Society in India*, Asia Publishing House, Bombay, 1977 (reprint), pp. 25–26. For a recent statement and the most comprehensive treatment of the idea of Kalinga, see Martin Brandtner, 'Representations of Kalinga: The Changing Image and Geography of a Historical Region', in H. Kulke and B. Schnepel (eds), *Jagannath Revisited: Studying Society, Religion and the State in Orissa*, Manohar Publishers, Delhi, 2001, pp. 179–210.

[34] B.B. Lal, 'Sisupalgarh 1948: An Early Historical Fort in Eastern India', *Ancient India*, Vol. V, 1949.

[35] *Indian Archaeology—A Review*, 1956–57, pp. 30–31.

[36] See Hathigumpha inscription, lines 1 and 17, *Epigraphia Indica*, Vol. XX, pp. 79–80; Luders, 'List of Brahmi Inscriptions', Nos 1346 and 1347.

[37] N.K. Sahu interprets these terms as official designations. He suggests that 'Kamma' stands for *Karma Sachiva* and 'Chula Kamma' was his junior in the Department of Works. Sahu, *Kharavela*, p. 91.

[38] See B.P. Sahu, 'Ancient Orissan Cultural Relations', *Indica*, Vol. 21, No. 1, 1984, p. 6.

[39] See R.S. Sharma, 'Urbanism in Early Historic India', in Indu Banga (ed.), *The City in Indian History*, Manohar Publishers, Delhi, 1991, pp. 13–14.

[40] A good discussion of the administrative organizations of the earliest states and their socio-political implications is provided in Shereen Ratnagar, *Enquiries into the Political Organization of Harappan Society*, Ravish Publishers, Pune, 1990, pp. 162–64.

[41] The Ashokan inscriptions portray not only the king's sense of indebtedness to the people and his activities for their welfare, but also define a lot of marginal groups and reveal the king's/state's desire to regulate them, besides contrasting his achievements with the ephemeral activities of earlier rulers and constantly focusing on him.

[42] The exaggeration and unduly favourable picture presented in the record is obvious from statements such as his army marching through Bharatavarsha for conquest. Line 10 in Hathigumpha.

[43] For the Rathikas and Bhojakas, see Chattopadhyaya, 'Transition to the Early Historical Phase in the Deccan'.

[44] B.P. Sahu, 'Ancient Orissan Cultural Relations'; 'Ancient Orissa: The Dynamics of Internal Transformation of the Tribal Society', p. 172.

[45] For a survey of early historical trade and a good discussion of eastern coastal and trans-oceanic trade, see H.P. Ray, 'Early Historical Trade: An

Overview', *The Indian Economic and Social History Review*, Vol. XXVI, No. 4, 1989, pp. 437–57; and 'Early Trade in the Bay of Bengal', *The Indian Historical Review*, Vol. XIV, 1990, pp. 79–89.

[46] For a critical appraisal of the situation in Orissa, see B.P. Sahu, 'Situating Early Historical Trade in Orissa', in K.M. Shrimali (ed.), *Indian Archaeology since Independence*, Association for Study of History and Archaeology, Delhi, 1996, pp. 95–109.

[47] D.D. Kosambi, 'Dhenukakata', in A.J. Syed (ed.), *D.D. Kosambi on History and Society: Problems of Interpretation*, Department of History, University of Bombay, Bombay, 1985, especially pp. 198–201.

[48] See B.B. Lal, 'Sisupalgarh 1948', *Ancient India*, Vol. V, 1949.

[49] A.S. Altekar, 'A Note on the Kushana Gold Coin', *Ancient India*, Vol. V, 1949, pp. 100–01, and 'A Unique Kushano-Roman Gold Coin of King Dharmadamadara', *The Journal of the Numismatic Society of India*, Vol. 12, 1950, pp. 1–4; S.C. De, 'A Peep in the Dark Period', *Orissa Historical Research Journal*, Vol. III, No. 2, 1954, p. 106.

[50] For details, see B.P. Sahu, 'Situating Early Historical Trade'.

[51] Chattopadhyaya explains the term by invoking the *janapada* parallel from northern India. See Chattopadhyaya, 'Transition to the Early Historical Phase in the Deccan'.

[52] D.C. Sircar, 'Two Inscriptions from Guntur District', *Epigraphia Indica*, Vol. XXXII, 1957–58, pp. 83; also see note 2.

[53] N.K. Sahu, *Kharavela*, pp. 368–72.

[54] Ibid., pp. 373–76; Sircar, 'Two Inscriptions', pp. 82–87.

[55] D.C. Sircar, 'Bhadrak Inscription of the Time of Gana, of Regnal Year 8', *Epigraphia Indica*, Vol. XXIX, 1951–52, pp. 169–72; S.N. Ghosal, 'The Bhadrak Stone Inscription of the Time of Gana', *Journal of the Asiatic Society*, XXII, Nos 1–2, pp. 36–38.

[56] The image of goddess Bhadrakali at Bhadrak is as old as the third century AD. The Bhadrakali temple inscription suggests that the deity was originally known as Parnnadevati. See A.N. Parida, 'The Sculptural Art and the Early Temples of Orissa', *Utkal Historical Research Journal*, Vol. 1, 1990, p. 98 and note 13.

[57] The inscription of Gopachandra, the Gandibedha copper coins and subsequent inscriptions from the district of Balasore point in that direction. See Rajaguru, *Inscriptions of Orissa*, Vol. I, Pt II, Orissa State Museum, Berhampur, 1958, inscription Nos 22, 25, 26, 28 and 29; for the coins, see ibid., p. 57.

[58] Ibid., pp. 81–85.

[59] S.C. Behera (ed.), *Interim Excavation Reports*, Sambalpur University, 1982, pp. 5–6.

[60] Ibid., pp. 9–22.

[61] *Indian Archaeology—A Review*, 1974–75, pp. 55.

[62] See A. Das, 'Asanapat', *Orissa Historical Research Journal*, Vol. XIII, No. 2, 1965, pp. 1–8; S. Tripathy, 'A Note on the Asanapat Stone Inscription', *Journal of Orissan History*, Vol. I, No. 2, July 1980. In all fairness, it should

be mentioned that one is not sure if the two Satrubhanjas were one and the same person.

63 P. Acharya, *Studies in Orissan History, Archaeology and Archives*, Cuttack Students Store, Cuttack, 1969, p. 374.

64 Behera (ed.), *Interim Excavation Reports*, p. 3.

65 For the early coins, see S. Tripathy, *Early and Medieval Coins and Currency System in Orissa*, Punthi Pustak, Calcutta, 1986.

66 See Ray, 'Early Trade in the Bay of Bengal', p. 82.

67 Cited in Acharya, *Studies in Orissan History*, p. 573.

68 For an assessment, see B.P. Sahu, 'Situating Early Historical Trade'.

69 For an analysis of a similar yet clearer situation in the Deccan, see Aloka Parasher, 'Social Structure and Economy of Settlements in the Central Deccan (200 BC–AD 200)', *Social Science Probings*, Vol. 5, Nos 1–4, 1992, particularly pp. 6–19.

70 For an analysis of such categories, see Shereen Ratnagar, 'A Bronze Age Frontier: Problems of Interpretation', paper presented at the symposium on 'Frontiers in Indian History', Indian History Congress, Warangal session, 1992, pp. 6–8, 14.

71 For a discussion, see B.D. Chattopadhyaya, 'Historiography, History and Religious Centres: Early Medieval North India, *circa* AD 700–1200', in Vishakha N. Desai *et al.* (eds), *Gods, Guardians and Love: North Indian Temple Sculptures (700–1200)*, New York and Ahmedabad, 1993, pp. 37–43.

72 H. Kulke, 'Fragmentation and Segmentation versus Integration: Reflections on the Concept of Indian Feudalism and Segmentary State in Indian History', *Studies in History*, Vol. IV, No. 2, 1982, pp. 247–48; B.P. Sahu, 'Aspects of Rural Economy in Early Medieval Orissa', *Social Scientist*, Nos 236–37, January–February 1993, pp. 56–57.

73 K.N. Mahapatra, 'Puranic Stories in the Early Records and Sculptures of Orissa', *Orissa Historical Research Journal*, Vol. X, pp. 59–74; Debala Mitra, *Bhubaneswar*, Archaeological Survey of India, New Delhi, 1978 (fourth edition), pp. 29–34; and R.P. Mohapatra, 'Krishna Themes in Orissan Sculptures', *Orissa Historical Research Journal*, Vol. XXXI, Nos 2–4, 1985, pp. 77–79.

74 For example, see the Banapur Plates of Madhyamaraja and Midnapur Plate of Somadatta in S.N. Rajaguru, *Inscriptions of Orissa*, Vol. I, Pt II, lines 45 and 48, pp. 194 and 198, and lines 3–9, pp. 140–41.

75 For Kali references see, for example, Puri Plates of Madhavavarman, ibid., line 15, p. 179, and Paralakhemedi Plates of Indravarman, ibid., Vol. II, 1960, lines 2–3, p. 35.

76 See R.S. Sharma, 'The Kali Age: A Period of Social Crisis', in S.N. Mukherjee (ed.), *India: History and Thought*, Subarnarekha, Calcutta, 1982, pp. 186–203; and B.N.S. Yadava, 'The Accounts of the Kali Age and the Social Transition from Antiquity to the Middle Ages', *Indian Historical Review*, Vol. V, Nos 1–2, 1979, pp. 31–63.

77 For the performance of the *Aswamedha* and *Vajpeya* sacrifices, expressions

of reverence to brahmanas and the projection of rulers as *parama-brahmana*, see for example, *Inscriptions of Orissa*, Vol. I, Pt 2, p. 220, lines 39–40; pp. 141–42, lines 3–9; p. 55, line 6.

[78] For details of the argument, see B.P. Sahu, 'Conception of the Kali Age in Early India: A Regional Perspective', *Trends in Social Science Research*, Vol. 4, No. 1, 1997, pp. 27–36.

[79] For a good discussion, see Kesavan Veluthat, 'Religious Symbols in Political Legitimation: The Case of Early Medieval South India', *Social Scientist*, Nos 236–237, January–February 1993, pp. 23–33.

[80] B.P. Sahu, 'Ancient Orissa: The Dynamics of Internal Transformation', pp. 176–77, also see fns 72 and 74. *Mahattaras* and *Mahamahattaras* are addressed in the records of the Early Gangas, Mudgalas and Dattas.

[81] B.P. Sahu, 'Aspects of Rural Economy', pp. 48–68.

[82] Not before around the ninth century do we have definite evidence for such constructions by royalty. See Vidya Dehejia, *Early Stone Temples of Orissa*, Vikas Publishing House, Delhi, 1979, pp. 173–74, 183.

[83] D.R. Das, 'Saiva Images on Orissan Temple Walls (from the seventh to the ninth century AD)', *Journal of Ancient Indian History*, Vol. XII, 1978–79, p. 107.

[84] For a comprehensive discussion, see B.D. Chattopadhyaya, *The Making of Early Medieval India*, Oxford University Press, Delhi, 1994, particularly the Introduction. Also see the Introduction in B.P. Sahu (ed.), *Land System and Rural Society in Early India*, Manohar Publishers, Delhi, 1997.

The Making of a *Mandala*

Fuzzy Frontiers of Kalhana's Kashmir

Kumkum Roy

I first met Partho-da nearly twenty years ago: I was a nervous aspirant for a job and he, amongst others, was on the interview board. I was aware of his reputation as one of the most erudite and meticulous teacher–scholars in the country, but what impressed me most during that meeting, and remains as an abiding memory, was his gentle, yet focused interventions, ensuring that I could be at ease in spite of my ignorance. Our areas of specialization and research interests were vastly different, but the felicity with which he transcended these boundaries permitted us to discover common spaces. It is one of these that I propose to explore here.

As President of the Indian History Congress in 1998, Partho-da drew attention to the question of identity formation and nation-states, and with his characteristic wide-ranging scholarship, drew on both European and Indian histories to open up the theme in its complexity. While the precolonial phase in South Asia was somewhat marginal to his central concern, he was nonetheless interested in tracing antecedents. Some of these can be understood in terms of the emergence of regions and regional polities in the subcontinent, a process that has been the subject of both theoretical formulations and empirical investigations over the last two or three decades.

It is in this context that we can, I hope fruitfully, return to one of our acknowledged classics, Kalhana's *Rajatarangini,* composed in twelfth-century Kashmir, but purporting to trace its history from the inception of the physical world as we know it, literally from the beginning of the present *kalpa.*[1] Elsewhere,[2] I have suggested that Kalhana's text can be understood in terms of the rich diversity of intellectual and cultural traditions that marked early medieval Kashmir. It can also be contextualized in terms of the identities that seem to have been of immediate importance to the author: as son of the great minister of Kashmir, Chanpaka,[3] and as a poet.[4]

In terms of structure and content, the eight *tarangas* (literally, waves or sections) of the text can be grouped into three broad strata. The first includes the first three *tarangas*. These are relatively short but deal with what is projected as an immense span of history, from the inception of the world to a relatively more precise point in time, *c*. seventh century AD. This is a time-frame within which literal truth is somewhat irrelevant: what seems to be central is the creation of a mythical past, a space within which an ideal socio-political order could be projected. Kalhana envisages this in terms of the relatively smooth succession of both named and unnamed kings, and the establishment and maintenance of both *varna* and gender hierarchies.

The second stratum includes *tarangas* four to six, and deals with the recent past. Here, Kalhana's account of socio-political relations becomes both more vivid and complicated. We also encounter deviations from the norm that are recounted with obvious disapproval. These trends are far more commonplace in the last two *tarangas*, which constitute the third stratum, where Kalhana grimly enumerates sordid details of more or less contemporary events, far removed from the idyllic stereotypes of his normative world.

Embedded within this threefold stratification and related to it, is Kalhana's understanding of Kashmir. This can be viewed at two connected levels: one, in terms of the uniqueness of the realm, which the author establishes with painstaking care at the very outset of his work; and two, defining relations between the realm on the one hand and the world outside on the other. The second project was more complicated, evident in variations in the narrative within the three strata. What I will attempt to do is to trace some of these variations and, if possible, examine their implications.

I

In the very first *taranga*, Kalhana traces the origin of Kashmir from a mythical lake, the Satisaras or the lake of Sati, consort of Shiva.[5] The creation of land from water is linked to a conflict between divine and demonic forces: the puranic trinity of Brahma, Vishnu and Shiva on the one hand, and a demon named Jalodbhava (literally, he who emerges from the water) on the other. This is attributed to the instigation of Prajapati Kashyapa (after whom the realm is named), and leads to the emergence of the *mandala* of Kashmir.[6]

While this myth connects the emergence of the realm to major brahmanical/brahmanized deities, both male and female, other origin myths cited by Kalhana are less closely bound to the great tradition. These relate to the Nagas or serpent deities, especially Nila, their supreme lord,[7] the protector of the realm, endowed with fluid signs of royalty; the Vitasta or Jhelum, which serves as his *danda* or staff; and the Nilakunda, identified with Verinag[8] as his parasol. Besides, the mountains themselves are viewed as a rampart to protect the Nagas from Garuda,[9] an allusion to one of the enduring themes of puranic mythology, the battle between the serpents and the mythical bird, also associated with Vishnu, in which the latter is invariably victorious. The persistence of 'naga'/'nag' endings for place names associated with lakes and springs even at present, points to the resilience of regional traditions.

The tension between locating Kashmir in terms of a wider puranic cosmogony and geography and more specific local beliefs is perhaps best exemplified in Kalhana's treatment of the Vitasta. On the one hand, as we have just seen, he associates it with the Nagas. But on the other, he equates it with Gauri, a manifestation of the goddess associated with Shiva.[10] While such associations may not have been invented by the author, his juxtaposition of them was integral to his definition of the region.

In effect, Kalhana locates Kashmir at the intersection of both unique and more broad-based notions of sacred space. The former understanding is reinforced by mentioning specific shrines and sacred spots. These include Papasudana, the site of a Shaiva shrine;[11] a shrine to the goddess of twilight, Sandhya;[12] a volcano (literally, a self-originating fire);[13] and the shrines of Nandikshetra and Sharada, most of which are also mentioned in the *Nilamata Purana*.[14] More generally, Kalhana resorts to a popular expression and informs his audience that not even a tiny speck of land, enough to hold a sesamum grain, can be found without a *tirtha* to either Shiva or Vishnu in their manifold forms in the realm.[15]

Kalhana moves from the sacred to the mundane with remarkable ease. We are told that Kashmir can be conquered through merit (*punya*) rather than with weapons *(shastra)*. It is also endowed with hot baths, safe rivers, mild sunshine, learning, saffron, cold water and grapes. Given such diverse attributes, not surprisingly, it rivals heaven.[16] What is more, Kalhana reinforces the notion of the centrality of the *mandala* by locating it at the epicentre of a series of concentric circles. The outermost realm is the earth with its wealth of jewels, within which the north, the direction of the lord of wealth, is worthy of praise; within this the father of Gauri, that is, the Himalayas, is particularly distinguished; and finally, within the mountains, the *mandala* of Kashmir.[17] The very first king Kalhana mentions, Gonanda, is represented as exercising benign control over this realm, with the northern direction typified by Mount Kailasha, the abode of Shiva, and the Ganga (or Vitasta) paying homage to him.[18]

As is obvious, Kalhana attempts to locate Kashmir within a contextualized space. This is also evident in his notion of time, with his account ostensibly beginning with the end of the *Dvapara Yuga*, the age associated with the *Mahabharata* war. This is thought to coincide with a less exalted phase in human existence, marked in particular by a general decline in ethics.[19] Nevertheless, given that we are fated to belong to this dreary age, Kalhana attempts to enable his audience to come to terms with it.

If Kalhana represents Kashmir as constituting the apex of the universe, it is not surprising that at least occasionally rulers of Kashmir are portrayed as exercising universal sway. This is true of Gonanda as well as Jalauka, for instance.[20] Such claims, more often than not, are couched in comfortingly vague terms. At the same time, there are other references suggestive of more specific interventions, attributed to the rulers of Kashmir in the world beyond this realm.

We can attempt to classify the way such contacts are described. One area that figures, expectedly, in the text is the Ganga valley, recognized by Kalhana as the heartland of political activity, as well as of ideal social and cultural norms. In spite of such associations, or perhaps because of them, there is a certain ambivalence in Kalhana's treatment of contacts between Kashmir and the recognized core of brahmanical traditions. On the one hand, he suggests that these links can be traced back to a respectable antiquity. This is evident in his attempt to weave in the history of Kashmir with the traditions of the *Mahabharata*. Gonanda, we are told, went to fight the Yadavas at Mathura at the instance of Jarasandha, and died fighting.[21] Yet another ruler, represented as a contemporary of the Kurus and Pandavas, was apparently not able to participate in the battle at Kurukshetra, as he was a minor.[22] It is obvious that such stories cannot be evaluated in terms of their literal accuracy or otherwise. What seems likely is that they were a part of constructed traditions that attempted to claim a space for Kashmir within dominant supra-regional narratives. At the same time, it is interesting that the easy and logical expedient of claiming that the rulers of Kashmir were allies of the victorious Pandavas and their associates, the Yadavas, is not adopted. In fact, connections with the Ganga valley were conceived of in terms of hostility towards the Yadavas[23] and an alliance with Jarasandha, whose association with Magadha and a *rakshasa* foster-mother were rather dubious from the perspective of both brahmanical and kshatriya traditions. Both the allies and the opponents attributed to the early rulers of Kashmir may be an indication that relations between Kashmir and the polities of the Ganga valley were not necessarily harmonious. As in the case of myths of origin of the land, this would also suggest that forging connections between regional and wider traditions was not a seamless or mechanical process.

To an extent, this is reinforced by Kalhana's references to Kanyakubja or Kanauj, which was the most important political centre in the Ganga valley in the early medieval period. In the first *taranga*, Kanyakubja figures amongst the conquests attributed to Jalauka, identified as the son of Ashoka.[24] Once again, the reference is literally ahistorical, as Kanauj was not an important centre in Mauryan times.[25] What is perhaps more interesting is the author's suggestion that this conquest enabled Jalauka to set up the *varna* order in his own realm. In other words, claims to political domination are juxtaposed somewhat uneasily with an acceptance of the social norms of those allegedly conquered. Elsewhere,[26] I have suggested that the *varna* order was contested, if not irrelevant, in the context of early medieval Kashmir. As such, claiming that it had been adopted from Kanauj may have been part of a process of asserting its legitimacy. This may have been part of a strategy that was of immediate relevance to Kalhana, who was working within a tradition that may be broadly defined as sanskritic and brahmanical.

The first three *tarangas* also include descriptions of expeditions to the south. The first of these is attributed to Mihirakula,[27] the fierce ruler who resembled the god of death. He is credited with having marched up to Simhala or Sri Lanka, in order to avenge a supposed insult.[28] After reaching the southern ocean he apparently uprooted the king, replaced him with one of his choice and returned after defeating the rulers of Chola, Karnata and Lata, that is, the Cholas of the Tamil region, the rulers of the southwest coast and of Gujarat.[29]

The second expedition is characterized by conquest of a different kind, associated as it is with Meghavahana, recognized by Kalhana as being a Buddhist ruler who spread the message of *ahimsa*. He is so successful that the water god Varuna agrees to help him cross the ocean, while Vibhishana, the contemporary ruler of Lanka, pays homage to him, and even the *rakshasas*, as well as all living creatures, adopt non-violence.[30]

As is evident, both accounts are marked by elements drawn from legends and folklore. What is perhaps more striking is that there is none of the ambivalence that characterizes accounts of encounters with rulers of the Ganga valley: in the case of the remote south, such encounters are invariably represented in terms of the unquestioned victory of the rulers of Kashmir, whether in terms of military might or moral authority. It is obvious that distance, apart from lending enchantment to the view, provided the author with space for constructing ideal political relations. Such constructs would probably have appeared less plausible had they been located within realms that were more easily accessible and relatively well known.

Interestingly enough, central India figures as an intermediate zone. This is evident in the narrative about Vikramaditya of Ujjayini.[31] Here, it is Vikramaditya who is portrayed as taking the initiative in intervening in the internal affairs of Kashmir, by appointing the poet Matriagupta as its ruler. This is contested by Pravarasena, the other claimant to the throne, but the resolution is non-violent as Vikramaditya dies rather conveniently, just as Pravarasena decides to march against him. Pravarasena compensates for this anti-climactic end by marching to the eastern and western seas and installing Vikramaditya's son on his ancestral throne.[32]

The other context in which regions outside Kashmir figure is in terms of providing wives for rulers. These include Pragjyotisha, identified with present-day Assam,[33] and the Chola realm.[34] As is common knowledge, claims to women are often symbolic of claims to superior status amongst men. Once again, the question is not whether specific women from distant lands were actually brought to Kashmir: suggesting such possibilities created the notion of an ideal situation where the ruler could not only claim to exercise a rather vague control over the earth, invariably envisaged as feminine, but also over other, more specific realms.

What is striking about these first three *taranga*s is the virtual absence of references to peoples and places in the immediate vicinity of Kashmir. As we will see, such references proliferate in the second and third strata of the text. What seems evident is that in Kalhana's ideal world, Kashmir was located at the centre of the universe. Besides, interactions with the world beyond were ideally dominated by the rulers of Kashmir. Closer home, where actual and more frequent contact was likely, the projection of an ideal became less easy, and the relations are represented as being more untidy.

II

At first sight, the spatial contours Kalhana draws in the second stratum of the text may appear somewhat paradoxical. On the one hand, we have, especially in connection with rulers such as Lalitaditya and Jayapida in the fourth *taranga*, narratives of exploits in distant lands. On the other hand, the immediate spatial context of the realm acquires greater visibility. This apparent paradox can perhaps be resolved if we keep in mind the chronological shift: from the fourth *taranga* onwards we move closer to real time; yet, the three to four hundred years that separated Kalhana from his story perhaps allowed for a certain amount of romanticization.

Lalitaditya is explicitly described as a *sarvabhauma* ruler (literally, in control over the entire land), this being contrasted with the position of his contemporaries, who are simply regional lords (*pradeshikeshvara*).[35] As in the case of Jalauka but with possibly greater historical veracity, Kalhana represents Lalitaditya as conquering Kanauj, making the backs of men bend in terror.[36] We also have mention of the contemporary ruler Yashovarman, who is portrayed as paying tribute to him.[37]

Jayapida, likewise, is credited with an expedition through the Ganga valley. This is characterized by a pilgrimage to Prayaga, where he registers his presence by offering a *dakshina* of horses, numbering 99,999, as a challenge to other donors who could remove his name only if they exceeded his generosity.[38] Besides, he is supposed to have carried away the *simhasana* or lion throne from the king of Kanauj.[39] At another level, Jayapida is associated with reinstating the study of the *Mahabhashya*, Patanjali's commentary on Panini's Sanskrit grammar, and his patronage of learning (presumably sanskritic) creates a vacuum in other lands.[40] One can read Kalhana's account of the later ruler Yashaskara as being complementary. Amongst other things, he is supposed to have established a *matha* or monastery for the benefit of students from *aryadesha*.[41] Once again, we can see that the attitude towards the Ganga valley is fraught with ambivalence. It is viewed as a region endowed with unique ritual and political significance, which needs to be appropriated by the aspiring rulers of Kashmir.

At another level, Lalitaditya is credited with leading expeditions to all three seas, reaching in the east up to Gauda and Kalinga, marching to the south up to the realm of Karnata and the banks of the Kaveri, besides travelling along the west coast through the seven Konkans before returning to central India.[42]

Once again, in the case of Jayapida, we have a variation on this theme. He acquires, amongst other things, five *rakshasas* from Lanka, with the compliance of Vibhishana (who seems to have ruled over the island for a veritable eternity).[43] He also embarks on a *digjaya* (literally, a conquest of the directions) that takes him to the eastern ocean. The vast army that is launched from the Himalayas to the sea is thought to resemble the Bhagirathi or the Ganga. Here, he sets up a city to commemorate his exploits, and enters and escapes from the castle of one Bhimasena, a ruler of the eastern direction.[44] He also has an encounter with Aramudi, the ruler of Nepala.[45] More generally, he is credited with reaching to the four oceans, which serve as mirrors for the personified feminine royal fortune, Jayashri.[46]

As in the case of rulers in the first stratum, some of Lalitaditya's exploits are represented in terms of the submission of women. This is evident in the story of Ratta, the ruler of Karnata, who resembles Durga but nonetheless bows down so that her face is reflected on the toenails of Lalitaditya.[47] He is also credited with a march to the kingdom of women (*strirajya*) beyond Pragjyotisha, where the queen trembles with both fear and sexual excitement.[48] Jayapida, likewise, ventures into *strirajya* and is credited for his conquest of the senses.[49]

At the same time, the theme of acquiring wives is worked out somewhat differently in Jayapida's case. He is represented as going on a long voyage through the subcontinent, travelling incognito in order to establish his reputation as a hero. Once again, the narration is replete with folkloristic elements. The hero ultimately reaches Paundravardhana (part of Bengal), where he is discovered when he kills a lion, and the ruler offers his daughter, Kalyanadevi, to Jayapida. In return, the latter is supposed to have conquered five Gauda princes and made them subordinate to his father-in-law.[50]

Perhaps more interesting is another variation on the theme that surfaces in these *tarangas*, involving acquiring wives from neighbouring principalities. These include Sugandha, who is given as a wife to Shankaravarman by the ruler of the northern region, and Didda, daughter of the ruler of Lohara,[51] who is given in marriage to Kshemagupta.[52] Both these women are credited with an active and independent role in the politics of the realm, which Kalhana records in spite of his obvious disapproval.[53]

Where Kalhana's narrative of Lalitaditya's campaigns literally breaks new ground is in his treatment of the Uttarapatha, or the north. On the one hand, this is represented as a mythical realm with no paths, untouched by the sun, peopled by the shadowy Uttarakurus who are duly terrorized.[54] On the other hand, we have references to named peoples. These include the Kambojas who are deprived of their horses, the Tuhkharas who flee, the Bhauttas who are pale with anxiety and the Darads who are subdued. Further, the Turuskas, or Turks, are made to shave half their head and hold their arms behind their backs as a mark of servitude.[55] Most of these peoples have been identified and localized by Stein, who suggests that the Kambojas lived in eastern Afghanistan, the Tuhkharas in the Amu Darya (Oxus) valley, the Bhauttas, possibly of Tibetan origin, in Ladakh, and the Darads or Dards to the north of Kashmir, in the regions of Gilgit and Chitral.[56] Lalitaditya seems to find mention in contemporary Chinese chronicles as well, which refer to Mu to pi (derived from Muktapida, his *viruda*) who sent an embassy to the Chinese ruler requesting help against the Tibetans.[57] What is striking is that descriptions of the northern campaigns are marked by a degree of specificity and detail that is absent in the other cases.

To an extent, this is also reinforced by references to named *mandalas* in the region, including Jalandhara and Lohara. The first is obviously the region of present-day Jullundhur, possibly extending along the Beas valley into Kangra in Himachal Pradesh, while the second has been identified with the Loharin valley, which marks one of the easiest entry points from west Punjab into Kashmir.[58] Lalitaditya is supposed to have established his dependants (*anujivin*) in both these regions.[59] What is interesting is that here, in the immediate vicinity of Kashmir, there is no question of representing the relationship between neighbours in terms of a grand conquest. What we have instead is a more modest assertion of control through intermediaries.

Such references become far more plentiful in the fifth and sixth *tarangas*. Here, we find a reworking of the notion of the *digjaya*, as for instance in the case of Shankaravarman.[60] In his case this means, effectively, war against immediate neighbours, the ruler of Darvabhisara, identified with the lower hills between the Jhelum and the Chenab, and the Gurjaras, located in Gujarat on the Chenab as well as sundry territories on the banks of the Indus.[61] Shankaravarman is credited with capturing the ruler of Darvabhisara and defeating Alakhana, the ruler of the Gurjaras, acquiring the territory of Takka from him. While the conflicts are clearly localized in the northwest of the subcontinent, Kalhana attempts to contextualize them within his ideal framework. So, Shankaravarman, placed between the Darads and the Turushkas, is compared to *aryavarta*, situated between the Himalayas and the Vindhyas.[62] In the sixth *taranga*, we come across references to other neighbouring polities, including Rajapuri, identified with present-day Rajouri, and the Shahi realm, located in the Kabul valley.[63] References to both these polities are far more frequent in the subsequent *tarangas*.

III

Kalhana focuses on his contemporary world in the third stratum of the text. As mentioned earlier, this appears to be very different from his constructions of the mythical and recent past. To start with, relations with the world beyond the *mandala* are now represented as being of almost incidental importance. There are no references to grandiose *digjayas* or to vast armies traversing the subcontinent from shore to shore. Even in the case of Jayasimha, who is idealized by the author, we are told that the rulers of Kanyakubja were honoured by his friendship,[64] a far cry from claims to carrying away the throne. Besides, while references to the Ganga valley continue, these are, more often than not, in terms of pilgrimages to Varanasi, undertaken either by disgruntled or destitute feudatories. [65]

References to other distant regions are also incidental to the narrative. In the case of Bhikshacara, one of the claimants of the throne, we are told that he was brought up by the ruler of Malava,[66] but in his actual bid for the throne he is supposed to have recruited effective support from neighbouring principalities.

What is also interesting is the treatment of women of distant lands. In the case of Harsha, we are told that he sees a portrait of the wife of Parmandi, the ruler of Karnata, and falls in love with her. However, instead of resulting in an expedition to win her, this is resolved by his fantasizing about her.[67] This is in marked contrast to earlier versions of the same theme, which invariably ended in acquiring women.

At the same time, there are continued references to drawing on the cultural resources of other lands. Kalasha is credited with introducing dancing girls from other lands (*deshantara*),[68] while Jayasimha settles both brahmanas from the Sindhu (Indus region) and Dravida brahmanas in his realm.[69]

In other instances, the rulers of Kashmir are represented as both emulating and excelling the achievements of their contemporaries. Kalasha, once again, is supposed to be versed in the languages of all *desha*s, as well as a poet, whose fame spreads through other lands.[70] Harsha, otherwise identified as a mercenary iconoclast, acquires such a reputation as a patron of poets that the renowned poet Bilhana, who had left Kashmir, regrets having done so.[71]

Yet, by and large, it is the narration of relations with neighbouring polities that is accorded centrality. This takes a variety of forms. On the one hand, we have references to attempts to conquer these polities, a strategy that does not appear to have been particularly successful. For instance, we are told that King Ananta launched attacks on both Vallapura and Urasha,[72] with no lasting success in either case.[73] A somewhat different strategy was probably adopted by his successor Kalasha, as a result of which eight rulers came to his court, evidently to pay homage. These included those of the two states just mentioned, as well as those of Nilapura (unidentified), Champa (present-day Chamba, Himachal Pradesh), Rajapuri (Rajouri), Lohara, Kanda and Kashthavata (both possibly to the southeast of Kashmir).[74]

At another level, we have references to intervening in succession disputes. Ananta, for instance, is credited with deposing the ruler of Champa and replacing him with another, presumably more favourably inclined towards the ruler of Kashmir.[75] But this was clearly a strategy that could work both ways, and what Kalhana documents in the last two *tarangas* is primarily a tangled account of succession disputes pertaining to the throne of Kashmir in which peoples and rulers from neighbouring polities were active participants, occasionally on invitation from rival factions but also seizing the initiative whenever possible. Thus, the Darads encourage rebels against Harsha,[76] and the rulers and people of Kalinjara and Rajapuri are also drawn into the conflict.[77] Others who intervene in later disputes include the Loharas and Turushkas as well as the Khashas and the *mlecchas*,[78] and peoples from the region of the Indus.[79] What is more, Kashmir itself is divided into Madavarajya and Kramarajya, the Vitasta valley to the north and south of Srinagar respectively, with rebels drawing support from one or both halves of the realm.[80] In other words, the *mandala* and the political structures that went into its making appear to be rather fragile.

Ultimately, towards the end of the text, Kalhana makes a feeble attempt to return to his grandiose ideals. This is evident in the comparison of Jayasimha's queen consort, who is represented as the embodiment of royal fortune (*rajalakshmi*), with Sati (Shiva's consort). She is in fact portrayed as equal or even superior to the goddess, as the *tirtha*s in which she bathes lose their desire to have contact with the real Sati.[81] And finally, in the concluding verse, Kalhana compares his own enterprise with the Godavari, which enters the sea with its seven mouths.[82]

Kalhana's understanding of the *mandala* was thus multi-layered. Ideally, it constituted the centre of the universe. At another level, its most powerful rulers were credited with the ability to intervene in and shape the destinies of distant lands. At the same time, there is an implicit and occasionally explicit recognition that sanskritic and brahmanical traditions were derived from the world beyond the mountains. Thus the relationship is envisaged as a two-way process. And, at yet another level, there is a somewhat reluctant acknowledgement that the *mandala* was in effect part of a constellation of relatively small principalities whose aspiring and actual rulers constantly jostled for power and influence within their own realms as well as amongst their neighbours.

Finally, how do we evaluate Kalhana's enterprise? It is perhaps useful to remember that he conceived of his work as being explicitly meant for kings,[83] who were expected to learn from his account. To an extent, his success is evident from the fact that later rulers encouraged scholars to both continue with the narrative and translate it. Kalhana's definitions of the realm were thus both available and possibly acceptable to the ruling elite. What is interesting in this context is the coexistence and survival of apparently contradictory definitions of the sphere of influence of the *mandala* and its rulers. This can be viewed as representing yet another instance of the complex process whereby regional identities were constituted in the early medieval period. It reminds us that such identities can be only partly understood in terms of intra-regional configurations: ultimately, regions emerge and sustain themselves in terms of a wider economic, socio-political and cultural context.

Notes and References

1 *Rajatarangini*, I.25. All references to the Sanskrit text are from M.A. Stein, *Kalhana's Rajatarangini: A Chronicle of the Kings of Kashmir*, Vol. III, Motilal Banarsidass, Delhi, 1988 (first published in 1892).

2 Kumkum Roy, 'Turbulent Waves: Constructions of Gender Relations in the *Rajatarangini* of Kalhana', paper presented at a symposium, Indian History Congress, Calicut, 1999.

3 This is reiterated in the colophon marking the end of each section of the text.

4 *Rajatarangini*, I.4, etc.

5 Ibid., I.25.

6 Ibid., I.26–27. These creation myths were apparently part of regional traditions, and are found in the *Nilamata Purana* as well. For details, see M.A. Stein, *Kalhana's Rajatarangini: A Chronicle of the Kings of Kashmir*, Vol. I, Motilal Banarsidass, Delhi, 1989, p. 5 ff. (first published in 1900).

7 *Nagadhisha, Rajatarangini*, I.28.

8 Stein, *Kalhana's Rajatarangini*, Vol. I, p. 5.

9 *Rajatarangini*, I.31.

10 Ibid., I.29.

11 Ibid., I.32.

12 Ibid., I.33.

13 Ibid., I.34.

14 Stein, *Kalhana's Rajatarangini*, Vol. I, p. 7.

15 *Rajatarangini*, I.38.

16 Ibid., I.39–42.

17 Ibid., I.43.

18 Ibid., I.57.

19 Ibid., I.48, 49.

20 Ibid., I.58, 115.

21 Ibid., I.59–63.

22 Ibid., I.82.

23 See also ibid., I.68–69.

24 Ibid., I.117.

[25] Incidentally, Ashoka himself figures as the great-grandson of Shakuni, suggesting links with the *Mahabharata*, ibid., I.101.

[26] Kumkum Roy, 'Turbulent Waves'.

[27] As in the case of Ashoka, this is an instance of appropriating traditions about a powerful ruler within the framework of a regional chronicle to add weight to it. Mihirakula is otherwise known as a Huna ruler. See Stein, *Kalhana's Rajatarangini*, Vol. I, p. 43.

[28] His wife apparently wore a blouse marked with the footprints of the ruler of Simhala, *Rajatarangini*, I.294–295.

[29] Ibid. I.296–300.

[30] Ibid., III.29–81.

[31] Ibid., III.125–285.

[32] Ibid., III.325–330.

[33] For example, *Rajatarangini*, II.147–148.

[34] Ibid., III.432–434.

[35] Ibid., IV.126.

[36] Ibid., IV.133. There is a play on words, as the Sanskrit name Kanyakubja is supposed to refer to the daughters of the king who were punished by the wind god, who entered their bodies, making them hunchbacked. Lalitaditya's exploit is projected as being comparable.

[37] Ibid., IV.134,135.

[38] Ibid., IV.414–415.

[39] Ibid., IV.468.

[40] Ibid., IV.488–493.

[41] Ibid., VI.87.

[42] Ibid., IV.146–164.

[43] Ibid., IV.503–506.

[44] Ibid., IV.514–528.

[45] Ibid., IV.531.

[46] Ibid., IV.590.

[47] Ibid., IV.152–154.

[48] Ibid., IV.173–174.

[49] Ibid., IV.587.

[50] Ibid., IV.421–468.

[51] For the location of Lohara, see below.

[52] Ibid., V.157, VI.176,

[53] See Kumkum Roy, 'Turbulent Waves', for further details.

[54] Ibid., IV.163, 337, 175.

[55] Ibid., IV.165–169.

[56] Stein, *Kalhana's Rajatarangini*, Vol. I, p. 47.

[57] Ibid., p. 130.

[58] Ibid., p. 138. M.A. Stein, *Kalhana's Rajatarangini: A Chronicle of the Kings of Kashmir*, Vol. II, Motilal Banarsidass, Delhi, 1989 (first published in 1900), p. 293.

[59] *Rajatarangini*, IV.177.

[60] Ibid., V.136–216.

[61] Stein, *Kalhana's Rajatarangini*, Vol. I, pp. 203–04.
[62] *Rajatarangini*, V.152–155.
[63] Stein, *Kalhana's Rajatarangini*, Vol. II, p. 337.
[64] *Rajatarangini*, VIII.2453.
[65] Ibid., VII.1007, VIII.1626.
[66] Ibid., VIII.228.
[67] Ibid., VII.1119–1125.
[68] Ibid., VII.606.
[69] Ibid., VIII.2444.
[70] Ibid., VII.610.
[71] Ibid., VII.935–38.
[72] Identified with Ballavan, the low hills to the east of Jammu and the hills along the upper course of the Vitasta and the Indus (Stein, *Kalhana's Rajatarangini*, Vol. I, pp. 287, 215).
[73] *Rajatarangini*, VII.220–221.
[74] Stein, *Kalhana's Rajatarangini*, Vol. I. p. 315.
[75] *Rajatarangini*, VII.218.
[76] Ibid., VII.912–913.
[77] Ibid., VII.1256. Kalinjara was probably a hill territory to the south of Kashmir and not the more well known polity in central India, Stein, *Kalhana's Rajatarangini*, Vol. I, p. 356.
[78] *Rajatarangini*, VIII.884–887.
[79] Ibid., VIII.2007.
[80] Ibid., VII.1228, 1240, VIII.723, 724, etc. For the identities of the two halves, see Stein, *Kalhana's Rajatarangini*, Vol. I, p. 57.
[81] *Rajatarangini*, VIII.3383–3384.
[82] Ibid., VIII.3449.
[83] Ibid., I.21.

The Legitimacy of Order

Music as Ideology in Ancient and Medieval Tamilakam

T.K. Venkatasubramanian

Music history, when taken as a part of cultural history, invites a structural approach of some kind. Music history has always contained a certain amount of cultural history either in depicting institutions and social roles, or in determining stylistic or constitutional norms and current aesthetic ideas. Obviously, the structural method finds its natural field of application in cultural history. Hence, a history of events and a structural approach are by no means mutually exclusive. A history of events has affinity to political history. A structural approach helps to strike a balance between the depiction of historical kingdoms and the elaboration of theoretical and aesthetic systems.

The social history of music appears in various guises, ranging from the modestly empirical to the ambitiously abstract and philosophical. Social history is restricted to depicting institutions and social roles. A structural approach widens the scope by not only including institutions and social roles but also other elements that make up a musical structure. Hans Robert Jauss expressed the view that musical texts become source material because 'they have the structure of inter-subjective dialogue'. He wrote:

> the process of transmitting the impact and reception of a work of art consists in a dialogue, the past subject will be in a position to say something to the other only if this present-day subject recognizes the answer implicit in the earlier discourse as also applying to a question that he himself must pose.[1]

It could be added that the musical legacy of a distant past that has its theory of art from a notion of originality is still a legitimate object of investigation.

Patterns of government are the result of human endeavour.

Man's experience with political institutions and processes are many and varied. K.N. Sivaraja Pillai, one of the early historians of Tamilnadu observed:

> In all probability, the earliest form of Tamil rule of which we are afforded some glimpses here and there . . . was a sort of communal republic wherein each adult male member of the community had a voice in the direction of public affairs. The people seem to have existed as village communities under the direction of *kilars* or village elders. In course of time, the village communities grew in number and size and then they held together as an union or confederacy of a number of such communities presided over by *vel, ko,* or king.[2]

In the life-pattern of the king (*muventhar*) we find the system had acquired uniformity and a certain amount of unwritten sanctity. '*Venthu*' seems to have come into existence after a long process of evolution.[3] The political structure of the Sangam epoch of Tamilakam was one of incessant warfare. Political jolts and frequent overturns were internal and did not break the chain of development of evolution of the tribal leader into a social captain, exhibiting the features of a monarchical system.

Craze for power and desire for expansion of territory are the main causes of warmongering.[4] Love of war and lust for glory drove kings to war camps.[5] Disparaging talk indulged in by the adversary provoked action. Refusal to give girls in marriage on demand by kings provided one more cause for provocation (*maram*).[6] An invader announced, by the beating of the tom-tom, his advent and intention to march on the capital. The announcement declared that the invader was going to shoot forth arrows directed at cows, peace-loving brahmanas, women and invalids; those who had not brought forth sons to discharge their duties to deceased ancestors were to get under shelter.[7] Raiding of the enemy's capital followed this announcement (*Anirai Kavaruthal*). We do not hear of battle engagements at night.

Uprooting the guardian tree was one of the preliminary operations indulged in by an invader. Every ruler had his favourite guardian tree, the protection of which was his sacred duty. To allow the guardian tree to get uprooted by an enemy was a mark of humiliation and a sign of defeat or discomfiture. A number of valiant warriors kept close watch over it. If the enemy succeeded in uprooting it, it signified a victory and a notable achievement.[8]

Poets and bards played a significant role in such pre-war operations. Rulers held them in high esteem. They attached much value to the eulogistic verses of the poets. There were instances of poets (*pulavar*) and bards playing one ruler against the other in their compositions.[9] Many poets made use of their intimacy with rulers to prevent war amongst them.

Among the events connected with victory celebrations, mention is to be made of the custom of allowing the elephant to play (bathe) at will in the tank belonging to the vanquished ruler. The victor made the ornament '*kajhal*' (*veerakandi*) using the gold extracted from the diadem of the vanquished, and wore it as an ankle bracelet.[10] The custom of planting the ensign of the victor's banner in the enemy's territory was another act of celebration.[11] The spoils of victory were distributed by the victor to his allies.[12] Among the recipients of such largesse were dancers, who received chariots and horses, and minstrels, who received their share of the spoils gained by destruction of the enemy's ramparts and fort walls.[13] The heads of the minstrels (*panar*) were embellished with the gold procured from ornaments adorning the faces of the enemy's elephants. The *pulavar* hailed this activity and the *panar* sang the glory of the patrons who accomplished it. The artistic skill displayed by the *pulavar* and *panar* reflected the nature of battles and state diplomacy. Such intercourse between poetry and strategy—various phases of the same culture, between religion and technical conceptions—were reflected in the compositions. It should, however, be remembered that these were spontaneous; art was not a forced product of such circumstances. Poems of the *pulavar* sung by the *panar* vividly pictured the social realm.[14] This reciprocal interaction between the ruler and the bard anticipated historical development and foreshadowed things to come in a prophetic manner. A kind of social relation between the ruler, composer and singer (artist) was predicted.

Music as an instrument of power makes people forget the general fear of jungle life, makes them believe in the harmony of civilized life and silences their misgivings. Music is ritual power when it is a question of making people forget the fear of violence, it is representative power when it is a question of making them believe, and bureaucratic power when it is a question of silencing those who oppose it. Music thus localizes and specifies power.

The primary function of music depends on its mysterious

appositeness to a code of power in the way in which it participates in the crystallization of social organization in an order. Music creates political order because it is a minor form of sacrifice. It strengthens the belief that a society is possible if individuals are sublimated. Ideas of political institutionalization germinate. At this stage, music and dance first provoke anxiety and then provide a feeling of security. They create a problem in order to solve it. Violent energies are summoned up and directed to groups to provide non-violent support. Music becomes a necessary attribute of power. The earliest attempts during the Sangam period of Tamil history demonstrate this hypothesis of music as a nascent stimulation of political organization. Music of the Sangam epoch stimulated the accepted norms of social transformation. Confucius said: 'To speak and carry into execution what you have spoken is ceremony, to act without effort or violence is music.'[15]

The political set-up of the early Tamils was exposed to environmental challenges which set limits on the ways it tended to change. The *venthu* of the time was a result of such evolution. Economic and social changes directly affected several components of the political structure. Poets who praised themselves by composing eulogies were held in high esteem. Bards held positions of high trust. We find a definitive poet–bard relationship, like that of Avvaiyar and Athiyaman Netuman Anchi, Pari and Kapilar, Pisiranthai and Kopperum Cholan. Such poets and bards were intimate and esteemed friends of the kings and patrons. The *panar* and poets served the state in many ways.[16]

The religion of the early Tamils was animistic: divine forces were conceived of as immanent within actual habits and as potentially harmful. Divine forces (*ananku*), for the most part, were not personified as gods. It is noteworthy that early Tamil literature is wholly lacking in mythology.[17] The *ananku* clings to a woman and, as long as it is controlled, it lends auspiciousness to her life and to her husband. If not controlled duly, it may wreak havoc. This was an indirect way of emphasizing the chastity of women. If a widow was young and chaste she was so imbued with magical powers that 'her youthfulness makes her sweet life quiver even though she is alone for a few seconds in the vast graded place of her husband where the eye of the drum (*mulavu*) never sleeps'.[18]

Rituals like *velanatal* and *velanveriyatal* that are mentioned in Tamil literature presuppose belief in the existence of a spirit apart from the body, and its temporary possession of another man's or woman's body for good or for evil.[19] A soldier who fell fighting was remembered by his compatriots. The spot where he fell or lived was usually marked by a hero stone (*nadukal*), which became an object of worship. The hero stone was supposed to be inhabited by the dead warrior's spirit. The doctrine of reincarnation was accepted by the Tamils of the early centuries of the Christian era. The doctrine served as an ethical check on men's lives, and also offered endless opportunity and hope for salvation.

In all these, music served as a regulating tool of society. Since, of all the other sensual pleasures, music corrupts the soul the least, it was qualified to be such a tool.[20] In the ritual *veriyatal*, music was a locus of subversion, a transcendence of the body. Society attempted to integrate it into an official religion. As a quintessential mass activity, it functioned as a necessary factor for legitimacy. Support from *venthu* was necessary to channelize it as a system of power.[21] Music in the daily life of the ruler became necessary and inseparable.[22] Since the *panan* invariably sang 'eulogies', it was deemed as court music. The compositions were elitist and monopolistic productions. They served as vehicles of political propaganda. The consumers of such music belonged to every social class—peasants, artisans, etc. The *panan* moved from place to place offering service. They organized circulation of music (propaganda) within society.

Pallava rule made Kanchipuram the centre of religious activity of Shaivites, Vaishnavites, Buddhists and Jains. The religious activity of the Shaivites and Vaishnavites centred round local temples. Temple construction and creation of endowments were deemed as noble endeavours not only by rulers, chiefs and prominent officials, but also by a large cross-section of the subjects who reflected the spiritual awakening of the epoch. The Pallava rulers claimed divine origin, as evidenced by their later charters. The most interesting aspect of this was the human body assuming divine or even supra-divine proportions. This was a confirmed invasion of the sacred domain of the gods, and to assess the quantum of encroachment into the divine domain, the relationship between the king and the fine arts and his control over temple affairs are to be probed into.

In the many-sided activities of early townships in the Pallava kingdom, the local temple was a dynamic social institution which made a notable contribution to political, social, economic and cultural life. The retinue of servants attached to a temple was known as '*kovil parivaram*' or '*tali parivaram*'.[23] *Tevaram* singers formed part of the *parivaram*. Starting with Mahendra Varman I, classical dance, evidently already popular in the royal court, spread in popularity, to achieve wide appeal during Rajasimha's reign. Dance in a modified form was introduced in the temples.[24] Rangapataka, one of the queens of Rajasimha, was perhaps an expert Bharatanatyam dancer.[25] Some sculptural representations in the Vaikuntha Perumal temple at Kanchipuram give the impression that group dances involving men and women participants were in vogue. This group dancing was encouraged by the Pallava rulers and is known from varieties of such dancing performed at the Pallava court. Dances performed in temples were ritualistic in character and had a religious significance.

Religion, philosophy and art are the most spiritualized forms of culture. They have widely differentiated content. Referring to the rule of the Pharoahs of Egypt, Gordon Childe has remarked that their administration functioned so long and so smoothly, and was able to penetrate the forms of Egyptian culture so completely, not because their subjects were aware of the king's role but because they believed unflinchingly (even if not spontaneously) in the divinity of the ruler and were reverentially devoted to him.[26] The tradition of reciting hymns in Tamilnadu is a unique feature of its cultural and religious history. This tradition became an institution in itself by acquiring consequential links. The Pallavas evinced a vital interest in the perpetuation of this pious endeavour. The creation of temples was the result of the Pallavan rulers' urge to express themselves or give expression to their 'divine selves'.

Religious themes influenced the performing arts of dance and music. Compositions in praise of kings, chieftains and patrons formed the core of 'secular music'. A patent characteristic of unbroken tradition is devotion to established norms. When convention and validity come closer towards union, the situation obviates the need to reflect on how it happened, or which logically or chronologically preceded the other. Musical genres as eulogies are autonomous.[27] 'Voluntary music' (for example, the *tevaram* of the Nayanmars and the *prabhandams* of the Alvars) is freely conceived and executed. The epic *Silappathikaram* provides varieties of 'collective singing and dancing'.[28] In these instances, composing was an on-the-spot, voluntary effort. To appreciate such ritualistic compositions, we must allow free rein to our imagination and fill gaps of aesthetic shortfalls.

Magic, music, sacrificial ritual and identity highlight the position of the artist in a majority of civilizations. During the Pallava rule, the religious sector produced a crop of artists attached to temple service, sometimes endowed with supernatural and civilizing powers. Music was inlaid with precision into the stream of power. In contrast with attempts to reduce music to the history of music of the princes, we find in Pallavan Tamilnadu a concern for channelizing music.[29] The royal concern for music was because it was a regulator of society. Women dedicated to temple service (*devaratiyar, talicheri pendukal, rishabha taliyar* and *kuttiyar*) included Hrdai—captured and handed to temple service and *alankarikai*—selected by the king.[30] This suggests that the Pallavan rulers believed that of all sensual pleasures, there is none that corrupts the soul less.

During the Sangam days, music and dance were loci of subversion, transcendence of the body. Society made no special attempt to integrate them into the official religion. *Veriyatal*, for instance, was a quintessential mass activity. What the Pallavas attempted was to integrate music with religion by linking it with temples and forging the fine arts as tools for ensuring cultural and political unity. Temples did not condemn artists.[31] Ritualistic routines based on *agamas* helped to shape religion as an instrument of order, a prop for political power and a legitimizer of royal succession. Artists rendering temple service were domesticated by royal favours. Music created ritual order, then represented a simulacrum of order and served as a stake in the game of power. Forms, sources and roles have changed along with, and by means of, changes in the support of power. Its code and original usage underwent transformation. With the advent of Pallavan rule at Kanchipuram, a fresh code emerged as a simulacrum of the first and a foundation for novel powers.[32] The birth of a new genre of music, a renewed syntax, was witnessed—a new system throwing open the field for new exploration of the possible expressions of music.

To the Hindus, an icon is a symbol of god, a tool of the devotee to concentrate on the divine and become one with it. Prayer and worship are directed to the spiritual power which directs the universe, and is conceived by the worshipper (artist) in a particular form that has special appeal for him. The icon is a concrete symbol (*pratima*) meant to aid concentration.[33] In his work *Thirukkovaiyar*, Saint Manickavasakar introduces 'bridal mysticism' (*ṇayaka–nayaki bhava*) — intimacy between God and soul. In large measure, Shaiva Siddhantha captures the history of the Nayanmars, hymnists and *acharyas* (preceptors) of the school of Shaivism. Lives, outpourings and doctrines shaped the tenets and moulded the characteristics of Shaiva Siddhantha.[34]

Vaikanasa and *Pancharathra* are Vaishnava traditions that differ in small details, as in the description and disposition of subsidiary deities (*parivara devatas*) enshrined in temples. *Pancharathras* admit innovations unknown in the older and more conservative *Vaikanasa* tradition, such as the consecration of Andal and other female devotees who were believed to have attained the status of *nachchiyar* (Lord's consort), comparable with *nayaka–nayaki bhakti* (loved one plus lover). Apart from such minor differences, both the traditions are in agreement regarding the iconic form (image, *archa*) of Vishnu as one of the true replicas of the Lord, an *avatara* (incarnation), guaranteeing easy accessibility of the Lord to the devotee who finds his surrender (*prapatti*) made easier thereby.

In the stress of conflicts with heretical rivals, there arose within Hinduism a tendency to close its ranks and foster a religious syncretism which found room within the folds of its orthodoxy for all forms of theistic belief. This syncretism was based on the conception of the *Trimurti*, the three-fold manifestation of the same godhead. The 'emotional theism' of the Nayanmars and Alvars runs parallel to Vaishnavism and Shaivism. Musical compositions were products of the Tamil religious experience. Vijayalaya Chola rule at Tanjore is said to have ushered in the 'silver age of south Indian Shaivism and Vaishnavism'. The strategic position of Kanchipuram, one of the principal cities of the Chola empire, is highly illustrative of the mutual relations of rival religious systems which were competing for royal patronage and popular favour. In religion, the aim was not to attain equality but harmony, to evolve a system in which each person and class would find a proper place, a foothold from where the next step was to be taken.

Such changes do not define in full the structural location of kingship. To move towards such a definition, kingship has to be examined in relation to temples. By this time, the Hindu temple had attained the zenith of its influence on the social life of the country. A deliberate desire to bring the temple into intimate touch with several aspects of the life of the people was evident. The form of government was monarchy, as in the Sangam days.[35] It was not primitive chieftaincy but royalty, with numerous palaces, officials and ceremonials, and a majestic display of the concentrated resources of an extensive empire. Therefore, it is inconceivable that little groups of roving bards with their tambourines and danseuses could have strolled in a casual manner into the stately mansions of such mighty potentates, and accosted them with an hour or two of feast and song. The Chola kingdom had grown to imperial dimensions and the ruler was synonymous with *chakravartin* (emperor). Official records, however, still described him as '*Udaiyavar*'. A symptom of the consciousness of change is to be found in the magnificent lithic temple of Rajarajesvara at Thanjavur (Tanjore). The rule of the Cholas covered roughly a period of four centuries (AD 850–1250), and during this long time-span the entire Tamil region was studded with stone temples (*karralis*) of different sizes.

With the rise of the Vijayalaya Chola power there ensued a broadening of the channels of literature and a more copious flow of literary effrontery: an expression of fresh energy released by the realization of an imperial state in south India. The *prasasthis* of the Chola kings, with a few exceptions, may be classed among the best specimens of the literature of the age, marked by stately diction, easy flow of verse and animated narration of historical incidents. These *prasasthi* compositions must have been the works of court poets of a high calibre. The steady demand for their services furnished great impetus to the cultivation of a secular literature.

The custom of taking the deity in procession (*utsavamurthy*) was mentioned in an earlier context.[36] Of the literary productions of the Chola period, the *ula* is noteworthy for its highlighting of the king–deity relationship. For instance, the poet Ottakkutthar chose the *ula* as the vehicle for his encomiums on three successive monarchs who followed Chola Kulottunga I. Free from the cares and anxieties of his high station, with no troubles—domestic or foreign—to cloud his happiness, the king is conceived of as going for a stroll with his retinue around the capital city. The first part of the *ula* generally gives a more or less studied account of the achievements of the king and his ancestors. It provides a detailed description of the chief persons among his courtiers who accompany him, and their status in the administrative system of the country. This is followed by a description of the amorous looks and telltale acts of the women of the city who, at the sight of the king, become agitated and lovesick.

The medieval king was an ardent worshipper and this disposition received ample recognition at the hands of the court poets.[37] The king's largesse was seen as an inherent factor. This largesse is to be distinguished from the largesse extended by rulers of the Sangam age. Acts of devotion by the king were praised by the poets.[38] The panegyric of medieval times was totally different from the early bardic style of poetry of the Sangam epoch. The prime hero of the panegyric was the deity. The king was the second hero in so far as he served the deity. It was immaterial who patronized the poet. The poet determined the king's rank within a devotional context. The patron and the poet, both saw the deity as their ultimate refuge. The Chola court poet established a suggestive graded link between king and god. A patent change in the balance of relations between patron and poet could be noticed in post-Chola times. The king who denied honour to the poet ended up sharing his throne with him.[39]

The conception of the king as a faithful servant of god is worked out in the complex economic and social functions of the south Indian temple. Temples, big and small, preserved many aspects of music and dance. The *mandapas* of temples served as theatres. Many studies have highlighted the biographies of dancers and musicians who performed in temple theatres. There was a uniform wage structure for temple artistes, and this fact is testified by temple inscriptions. Rajaraja I, the Chola king, prescribed service regulations for artistes.[40] In the event of the death of a dancer or of an artiste migrating to other regions, the next qualified person in the family performed the dance item. If no one in the family was qualified, another qualified person was appointed to perform the dance. In the event of no one qualified being available, the *nyayattar* (supervisors) elected an eligible person to perform the dance item.[41] Dancers were regulated by the orders of the king. In one instance, the king restored a dancer and her descendants, who were mistakenly taken into the royal household, to the temple.[42] In some instances, symbols were used to indicate the affinity of a dancer to a demarcated temple.[43] There were regular male dancers (*nattavam*). They were remunerated with plots of land which came to be called '*nattavakkani*'.[44] A Brihadeeshvara temple inscription speaks of assignment of shares in temple lands and income from lands transferred to artistes like Devaratiyar, *Kottimattalam* players, Muttarai Sangu, Moriyam and Padaviyam. The maximum was paid to the first-grade *ganapadi* (singer).[45]

The conception of the king as a devoted servant of god, as suggested by the evidence, also makes us infer that servants of the deity of the temple (*atiyar*) were involved in a transactional relationship with god. The relationship of human kings with temple deities was an elegant and symbolic division of sovereignty.[46] King, artiste and god seem to have sorted out their relative positions and the human patron found a perfectly acceptable place in the devotional scheme.[47]

The music master of the renowned French dramatist Molière is believed to have said that 'without music no state could survive'.[48] Any theory should not blind us to the difference in degree between firmly and less firmly established facts. Historical facts depend on interpretation. Perhaps facts are transmitted and retransmitted. Music does not lend itself as a subject to narrative dynastic history. That means, music history cannot be reduced to a clearly defined subject. It impinges significantly on the human being, its nature being defined by three potencies, namely, religion, culture and the state. The term religion is varied and ramified in its connotations and throws forth some challenges. In spite of these contradictions it is logical to claim that the creation of music is historical through and through. Musical poetics based on genre is a substantive feature of music. Genre in the present context is taken as a fixed relation between the end that music is intended to serve and the technical means appropriate to that end.[49] This is sometimes called the 'end versus means' relation, characteristic of the functional concept of music. But we see no dichotomy between the history of institutions and the history of technique. A balance between the functions served and the techniques employed is patent.

Historical evidence from the Sangam age suggests that music originated in ritual undertakings. In course of time, music became an attribute of religious and political power. The practice of remunerating artistes indicates the entry of music into a relation of commodity exchange. All these provide a rough sketch of a society under construction, a society in which music and dance were mass-produced and consumed. Music and dance became prophetic and the social organization echoed this. Since the dawn of the Bhakti movement, music and dance have served as tools for the consolidation of society in Tamilnadu. They linked the power centre to the subjects and thus became an attribute of power in various forms. The Chola state was always fascinated by the performing arts. The economic and political dynamics of Chola society led the state to invest in art. Music and dance became objects of consumption, like everything else. Their distribution was organized through the temple. Music and dance became activities essential for knowledge and social relations; they came to be inscribed with precision into the economic hierarchy of the Chola state. The artistes became economically bound to a machine of power. The state paid the artiste for creating what it needed to affirm legitimacy. The livelihood of the artistes depended on the good-will of the ruler. When official power used the arts to make people forget their woes, they became 'ritual sacrifice' (scapegoats); when the state desired to enlist the faith of the ruled, music became an 'enactment' (representation).

The transition of the religion of the Tamils from the pre-Bhakti to the Bhakti stage is a touchstone upon which the poet–king–god relationship can be tested. The *samayachari* of a later date differed from the *panan* of the Sangam period, though both wandered through the country. The pilgrimage tours of the former were not in search of permanent patrons. They adopted a pilgrim's life and before undertaking pilgrimage tours the patrons were known. As such, they did not imitate the nomadic life of the *panan*. The composers and rulers of the Nayaka and Maratha courts of Thanjavur found the court–temple relationship quite convenient.[50] Many Bhakti saints of Tamilnadu, between the fifteenth and eighteenth centuries, belonged to the tradition of Carnatic music. They helped the shaping of the '*kruthi*', the Bhakti song genre. The output of literary and musical writings during the Nayaka and Maratha periods was phenomenal. Compositions that praised royal and non-royal patrons represented the courtly perspective. The artistes revelled in the king–god symbiosis, articulating their view of it in a smooth transition of focus from temple to court and *vice versa*. The harmonious ideal of a 'shared sovereignty' and complementary and shared functions between king and god were patently brought forth. Except in instances where the author happened to be the king himself, the standard reward for authors took the form of 'showers of gold' (*kanakabishekam*), costly gifts (land, necklaces and gold ornaments) and, sometimes, musical instruments.

In their work *Symbols of Substance*, Velcheru Narayana Rao and his co-authors project the central paradox of Nayaka kingship as a 'tension between inflated claims and the limited scale of kingship'. They write, 'Both divinity and disillusion are woven into the public role of the Nayaka king.' They emphasize:

> We are used to thinking of the temple as patterned after the royal court, its God served in the idiom of kingship; but the Nayaka political centre has reassimilated the regal structure of the sacred centre and then proclaimed the primacy of its own form of the divine—not the frozen immobile image (*archavathara*) carved out of stone, but the human avatar who moves, breathes and desires—he is in short a splendid figure cut out for grandiose display, yet shockingly vulnerable to attack by both external and internal forces including his own subordinates—he is most at home in the powerful illusion fostered, but also consciously undermined by his own panegyrics.[51]

The authors thus bring out the paradoxical elements and structural peculiarities of the Nayaka state.

Music's mode of insertion into economic (thereby political) activity was different in each network. This difference played a major role in the transition from one network to another. During the Sangam epoch music did not create wealth. The distinction between the productive and the unproductive was not relevant at that stage. The *panan* remained unproductive. Accumulation of wealth through music appeared only with the advent of temple patronage. Value was created. At the same time, religious functionalism was also kept up. This meant that value was created and accumulated outside the control of the artiste.[52] Yet the labour of the artiste was not in itself productive labour. He was outside capitalism. Still, his labour was used by the king. This situation is not without significance. The income of the artiste was independent of the quantity of labour he provided. It depended on the intensity of demand for that variety of labour. His product helped to build up the king–god hypothesis as a means of legitimizing the king's power.

Maratha Tanjore has been christened as 'the last golden age of precolonial culture'. The relation of artistes to power embeds a simulacrum—of the gift to sovereignty, to divinity. In many respects, the Maratha dynasty mediated the Nayaka cultural experience. The Maratha court culture assumed Nayaka political symbolism—the king was still identified as an *avatara* (incarnation), but he was now Rama turned into Shiva.[53] Cultural activities, however, took place in a deteriorating economic setting. Rice production in the Kaveri delta recorded a dramatic crisis between AD 1776 and 1796.[54] Available evidence shows that demography recorded little change till the 1770s. There was a sharp decline thereafter. It was only in the 1820s that the population of Thanjavur touched 1.06 million (that is, the 1779–80 level). A stagnant economy is on record.[55] The common belief is that only powerful and wealthy states can patronize and create the infrastructure necessary for a cultural efflorescence. This assumed theoretical dualism between 'material' and 'cultural' is challenged by the developments at the Maratha court at Thanjavur. Politics and poetics, money and metaphysics were, in this instance, isolated. During the rule of the Nayakas, there was an expanding agrarian economy shaped by social flux. Nayaka rule can be legitimately described as 'a time of movement, innovation and cultural growth'.

The technical mastery possessed and displayed by the musical trio of Thyagaraja, Muthuswami Dikshithar and Syamasastri was unique. Thyagaraja, the bard of Thiruvaiyaru, created a distinct legend. Stories involving gifts of gold (wealth) are told about Thyagaraja's life. When King Serfoji-II invited Thyagaraja to perform at his court, the bard was asked to compose a few songs in praise of the king in addition to his other devotional compositions. *Nidhi chala sugama*? (Is wealth happiness?), was Thyagaraja's outraged reply. The composition involved a punning contrast between the semantically related words *nidhi* (wealth) and *sannidhi* (good wealth, that is the shelter of *bhakti*). The milieu of early Tamil Bhakti tolerated a range of personal styles within the community of devotees. Thyagaraja turned away from the pluralism of early Bhakti. He epitomized sainthood in his poverty, simplicity and aversion to court-life. His point of view was in opposition to the prevailing paradigm of the relationships among poets, kings and gods. Thyagaraja's rejection of the court may be taken as a Bhakti reformulation, though we lack more such instances to quote. In the milieu of Tamilnadu thus far, court and temple related to each other through a system that worked smoothly and harmoniously in the ritual and social spheres. The ambiguities and conflicts that underlay the system are patently brought out in Thyagaraja.

In his refusal of the king's request we can see the composer refusing to stay bound to a camp whose political power was dwindling. Identical situations may be noted in the music history of the west too.

Lully, in his dedication of 'Persee' to Louis XIV of France, wrote:

> It is for Your Majesty that I undertook this work, I must dedicate it only to you Sir, it is you alone who must decide its destiny. The public sentiment, however flattering it may be for me, does not suffice to make me happy, and I never believe I have succeeded till I am assured that my work has had the good fortune of pleasing you. The subject seemed to me of such beauty that I had no difficulty developing a strong fondness for it. I could not fail to find in it powerful charms. You yourself, Sire, were kind enough to make the choice, and as soon as I laid eyes upon it, I discovered in it the image of Your Majesty. . . . I well know, Sire, that on this occasion, I should not have dared publish your praise. Not only for me is your praise too elevated a topic, it is beyond even the reach of the most sublime eloquence. However I realize that in describing the true gifts Perseus received from the Gods and the astonishing deeds he so gloriously accomplished, I am tracing the heroic qualities and prodigious actions of Your Majesty. I feel that my zeal will run away with me if I neglected to retain it.[56]

Evidently, this is a political discourse of music strongly linked to royal power.

By the close of the eighteenth century, praise was no longer sung for the lord and master. At least in France, the link between music and political power had come to an end. However, royal patronage did not disappear even after the eighteenth century. Music came into contact with a new reality. It ceased to be composed solely for the pleasure of the court. In France, the Royal Academy of Music monopolized all power in the name of the king and prohibited the diffusion of music until AD 1725. Yet, the diffusion of music could not be stopped. Philidor's *Concert Spirituel* (Spiritual Concert), followed by Gossec's *Concert des Amateurs* (Concert of Amateurs) in AD 1769, brought the music of power to the bourgeoisie of France. The privilege granted to the Royal Academy of Music had been so exclusive that no one could organize a performance for which admission would be charged. Everything changed when the monopoly was broken.

The suggestion made by the western experience, particularly in France, is that music (harmony) theorizes its usage as a simulacrum of ritual by affirming that it has a pacifying effect. In a way, harmony is a representation of the absolute relationship between well-being and order in nature.[57] It makes people believe by shaping what they hear. In the eighteenth century, reason replaced the natural order and appropriated harmony as a tool for power. It made people believe in the legitimacy of order. An ideology of harmony (music) imposed itself in hierarchical organization. This idea figures in the political economy of the period and later in the theory of general economic equilibrium.[58]

The theoretical and material dimensions of the progress of music and dance in Tamilnadu are available. Music combinatories in production became central to the search for and formation of compromises, of harmony between divergent interests. Harmonious music, the creator of a form of growth, also produced the conditions for its own change. Music was prophetic and experienced the limits of the representative mode of production. Even while accepting the view that Nayaka court music was part of the ceremonial pomp that served to further the fame of the ruler and the self-image of court society, it cannot be denied that composers were permitted to display individuality. Composers' autonomy was a historical phenomenon, though its scope and significance are open to debate. Under Maratha rule, composers were actually encouraged to display their individuality. For instance, Thanjavur court poetry cannot be pinpointed as being exclusively of 'bourgeois' or 'capitalist' origin.[59]

Characteristic slow-measured reverential movements are part of the religious rites of every creed and race for the cultivation of repose and the economization of the infinite coming through man so that it can work out the best results for him.[60] It is difficult to respond sympathetically to the prognosis that art thereby gets debased. The Maratha and post-Maratha epochs witnessed a major shift in 'serious music' that tried to communicate spiritual values. Marimuttha Pillai, born at Tillai Vidankan near Chidambaram, composed songs about Nataraja as *nayaka*. The *bhakti*-laden compositions of Marimuttha Pillai stand in favourable comparison with the *padams* of Purandaradasa. A century before the advent of Gandhiji, Gopala Krishna Bharathi (AD 1800–95) delivered a stunning blow to untouchability. Bharathi made use of non-literary Tamil (people's Tamil). Kavi Kunjara Bharathi, Vedanayakam Pillai, Utthukkadu Venkatasubbier, Thirumalaikkavi and others carried the torch forward. In AD 1799, the Maratha kingdom of Thanjavur was taken over by the British. *Durbar* patronage to the arts vanished. Some *poligars*, like those of Ettayapuram (Tirunelveli district) and the Sethupathis of Ramanathapuram, continued to patronize artists and composers. The musical impact of the west on the 'serious music of the Tamils' may be said to be non-existent. Every great intellectual tradition at any moment represented the market quotations put upon the experience of the race by generations of experts. It is true that 'serious art' never influenced the masses directly. Groups of cultivated elites, groups with political and economic power, nurtured and sustained the arts. The impact of mass culture on the elite was remote and indirect. Music is a form of social action and involves particular cultural contexts and elements of social organization.

Notes and References

[1] Hans Robert Jauss (ed.), *Racines und Erzahlung*, R. Warning, Munich, 1975, p. 348.

[2] K.N. Sivaraja Pillai, *The Chronology of the Early Tamils*, Madras, 1932.

[3] T.V. Kuppuswami, *Sangam Chieftains and Their Times*, Elicitation Committee, Thanjavur, 1984, Ch. 3, pp. 29–41.

[4] *Purananuru*, verse 8.

[5] Ibid., verse 31.

[6] Ibid., verse 78.

[7] Ibid., verse 9. *Tolkappiyam: Purattinai*, 10, commentary of Nachchinarkkiniyar.

[8] *Pathirruppatthu*, 2:2, 2:9.

[9] *Purananuru*, verses 46, 48, 90, 172.

[10] Ibid., verse 40.

[11] Ibid., '*Yelir kathava merinthukaikkondu nin pelvayuluvai parik-kumarralai*'.

[12] *Ahananuru*, verse 211. *Purananuru*, verse 6.

[13] *Sirupanarruppatai*: '*Viran ven mannar manneyin murukki nayavar panar punkan theerthapin*'. *Purananuru*, verses 22, 126; services rendered by the *panar*.

[14] *Panar* are to be distinguished from *pulavar* (poets). The male artistes were Senniyar, Vairiyar, Seriyar, Matankar and Isaikkarar: *Pinkalanikandu*, 815. The female practitioners were Patini, Virali and Patal Makalir: *Divakaram*, 32. Also, *Tolkappiyam*, commentary on *Porul Nirpa*, 91.

[15] *Book of Rites*, translated by James Lagge, Vol. II, New York University Books, New Hyde Park, New York, 1967, Ch. 25, para. 15, p. 276.

[16] See T.K. Venkatasubramanian, 'Rational and Social Foundations of Music and Dance of Early Tamils', *Proceedings of the Indian History Congress*, Patiala session, 1998, pp. 186–99.

[17] It has been said, 'music is not a myth coded in sounds instead of words'. It is a 'language without meaning'. Claude Levi-Strauss, *The Naked Man*, translated by John and Doran Weightman, Jonathan Cape, London, 1981, pp. 647–59. Such conflicting views show that it is a historical fact that the

drum and song have been carriers of linguistic meaning. The meaning of a 'musical message' is expressed in a global fashion. Also vide *The Naked Man*, Ch. II.

[18] *Purananuru*, 247. The *mulavu* (drum) is one of the symbols of power of the Venthar.

[19] *Narrinai*, 173, 258, 288.

[20] The Thebans, in order to soften the manners of their youth, authorized a law of passion. Montesquieu, *The Spirit of the Laws*, translated by Thomas Nugent, Hefner Publishing Company, New York, 1965.

[21] Charlemagne had to force cultural and political unity of his kingdom by imposing the universal practice of the 'Gregorian Chant'.

[22] The practice of *panar* waking the Venthar in the morning. Other services rendered to the state are given.

[23] C. Minakshi, *Administration and Social Life under the Pallavas*, University of Madras, Madras, 1977, Ch. XII, pp. 206–22.

[24] Ibid., p. 311.

[25] The name Rangapataka indicates this.

[26] Vera Gordon Childe, *History*, Routledge and Kegan Paul, London, 1947, p. 75.

[27] 'Autonomy' in the context means the effort of the artist in bridging an economic need. Frederick Engels uses the term 'relative autonomy' to defend Marxism against charges of Philistinism (*Letters of 1890s*). Engels concedes primacy to economic considerations only in the last resort. '*Arruppatutthuthal*', the Tamil literary convention, involves 'gifts' that are economic considerations.

[28] *Aoichchiyar Kuravai, Kunrakkuravai, Vettuva vari, Kanduka vari, Ammanai*, etc.

[29] Ananda Coomaraswamy, *The Transformation of Nature in Art*, Dover Publications, New York, 1956, pp. 62, 117, 169. Coomaraswamy argues for a close affinity between theology and aesthetics. For him, art is a symbolic representation of the invisible divine essence and hence subserves religious functions. This is sometimes described as 'Coomaraswamy's aesthetic mysticism'.

[30] In Greece, there was no state supervision of music. Sparta was an exception. In Rome, emperors ensured popularity of music.

[31] Nayanmars and Alvars praised dancers: for example, '*Panchin melladip-pavaimar*' (damsels with feet soft as cotton); '*Arulmanittatam poonmulai arambaiyar*' (full-breasted damsels engaged in divine service).

[32] Nayanmars and Alvars very often mixed dissonance with harmonious chords to stimulate the hearer and to sting him, as it were, so that he became concerned with the outcome and was all the more pleased when everything was restored to order.

[33] '*Munnam avanutaiya namam kettal talaippatal nankai talaivan tale*' (First she heard his name and gained information about His native land; immediately becoming passionately attached to Him, she abandoned her parents. Renouncing earthly conventions, losing her name and herself, she started a

life of dedicated service at His feet). Thirunavukkarasar Tevaram.

34 T.G. Aravamudhan, 'The Authors of the Holy Canon of Saivism', *The Quarterly Journal of the Mystic Society*, XXV, 1935, p. 143.

35 K.A. Nilakanta Sastri characterized it as 'byzantine' and Burton Stein characterized the state as 'segmentary'. See T.K. Venkatasubramanian, 'Chiefdom to State: Reflections on Kaveri Delta Social Formations', *Proceedings of the Indian History Congress*, 57th Session, Chennai, pp. 27–110.

36 B.G.L. Swamy, 'The Four Saivite Samayacharyas of the Tamil Country in Epigraphy', *Journal of Indian History*, Vol. L, Part I, 1972.

37 Rajaraja I, the Chola king, is described as '*Sivapada Sekharan*' (Worshipper of the feet of Shiva, or Crowned by Shiva's foot).

38 Anapaya Chola (Kulottunga II) decorated the great hall at Chidambaram (*Perambalam*) with gold. This act was praised by 'Sekkilar', author of *Periyapuranam*.

39 Episode picturing the encounter between *pulavar* Kalamegam and Thirumalairayan (king of Thirumalairayan pattinam). U.V. Swaminatha Iyer (ed.), *Ninaivu Manchari*, Vol. II, 1953, p. 60 (*Vinotara Manchari*).

40 *South Indian Inscriptions*, Vol. II, No. 66.

41 Inscription No. 66 mentions two instances. In one case, the right to play on the veena was passed on to the son-in-law of the deceased person (ibid., Vol. I.10). In another instance, the right was conferred upon the brother of the deceased (ibid., Vol. I.10).

42 *Annual Reports on Epigraphy*, 1924, No. 361. The royal household had numerous servants of various descriptions, including bodyguards of sorts. Palace servants were organized into *velams* and were settled in different quarters. They were often war captives and yet were generously paid. K.A. Nilakanta Sastri, *The Cholas*, University of Madras, Madras, 1975, p. 450.

43 *Annual Reports on Epigraphy*, 1921, No. 230, Part II, para 19. The temple dancers of Banapuram during the reign of Kulottunga I were marked with a '*sulam*' (Shiva's trident), indicating that they belonged to a Shiva temple.

44 *South Indian Inscriptions*, Vol. XXIII, No. 306. *Annual Reports on Epigraphy*, 1924, No. 361.

45 *South Indian Inscriptions*, Vol. II, No. 66.

46 Arjun Appadurai, *Worship and Conflict under Colonial Rule: A South Indian Case*, Cambridge University Press, Cambridge, 1981.

47 The *panan* of the Sangam age also compares his patron to a god or few gods. This does not mean that the *panan* makes Sangam kingship either sacred or divine.

48 *Le Bourgeois Gentil Homme*, Act I, Scene ii.

49 The bard–king relationship of the Sangam days where support was extended through the institution of the temple in Chola times.

50 S. Seetha, *Tanjore as a Seat of Music*, University of Madras, Madras, 1981. Seetha gives a vivid picture of literary and musical compositional activity in the Nayaka court.

51 Velcheru Narayana Rao, David Shulman and Sanjay Subramanyan,

Symbols of Substance, Court and State in the Nayaka Period of Tamilnadu, Oxford University Press, Delhi, 1992, pp. 217–18.

52 Marx provides a good analysis of the site of creation of value in such a network. 'A singer who sings like a bird is an unproductive worker. When he is paid he is a wage-earner. But the same singer employed by someone else is a productive worker because he directly produces capital.' Karl Marx, *'Travail productif et travail improductif (Materiaux pour l' economie)'*, Ch. 2 in *Oeuvres Completes*, Edition de la Pleiade, Vol. 2, Gallimard, Paris, 1968, p. 393.

53 Sridara Venkatesa, *Sahendra Vilasam*, Thanjai Mannar Serfoji Saraswathi Mahal Library, Thanjavur, n.d., pp. 293–94.

54 *Reports of the House of Commons*, Vol. II, *Fourth Report from the Committee of Secrecy on the State of the East India Company*, 1782. Arasarathnam, *The Rice Trade in Eastern India, 1650 to 1740*, 1985, p. 540.

55 Ronald Lardinois, 'Deserted Village and Rural Depopulation in Tamilnadu, *c.*1730 to 1830', in Tim Dyson (ed.), *India's Historical Demography: Studies in Famine, Disease and Society*, Curzon Press, London, 1989, pp. 16–48.

56 Dedication to Persee, *'Tragedie mise en musique par M de Lully, Escuyer, Conscilier Secretaire du roy et Surintendant de la Musique de sa Majeste'*, in *Prodhomme Ecrits des musicieno*, p. 209, n. 19.

57 The word harmony sweeps its semantic zone with precision, number, artefact, well-being, language and world.

58 Exchange as locus of order, a means for the channelization of discord.

59 Jurgen Habermas observed, 'Bourgeois art is meant to satisfy those residual needs that are suppressed in daily social intercourse.' *Knowledge and Human Interests*, Heinemann, London, 1972.

60 Maurice A. Canney, *An Encyclopaedia of Religions*, Nag Publishers, Delhi, 1976, p. 137.

Pindaris, Soldiers and State Formation in Malwa, *c.* 1800–18

Amar Farooqui

The Pindaris (or Pendharis) were an invisible people almost throughout their history. They became visible very briefly during the first two decades of the nineteenth century, particularly in the years between the Second Anglo–Maratha War (1802–05) and Third Anglo–Maratha War (1817–18). But even for the few years that they were visible, they remained largely invisible in the sense that they revealed next to nothing about themselves. We know hardly anything in their own terms about their past, their traditions and what distinguished them as a group. To a large extent, this is so because the Pindari identity was primarily a colonial construct. British officials superimposed a uniform identity on an amorphous group.

Highly prejudiced servants of the East India Company are our main source of information about the Pindaris. This information is supplemented by references to them in the Maratha records. It was during the Second Anglo–Maratha War that colonial officials began taking notice of the Pindaris, and they lost interest in them soon after 1818. The views of Sir John Malcolm, the principal British official in Malwa after the Third Anglo–Maratha War, were the single most important influence on the colonial perception of the Pindaris. Malcolm first began scrutinizing the Pindaris when he was at the Sindia *darbar* during the first half of 1804.[1] Later, in his *Memoir of Central India*, written after the Third Anglo–Maratha War, Malcolm presented a detailed and connected narrative of the Pindaris.[2] This was to remain, and still remains, the standard account of the Pindaris. Most of what has been written about the Pindaris can ultimately be traced, apart from Malcolm's *Memoir*, to contemporary reports prepared by James Tod (1811), Richard Jenkins (1812) and George Sydenham (1814), and the voluminous correspondence reproduced in *Papers Respecting the Pindarry and Mahratta Wars.*[3]

The official colonial view of the Pindaris focuses exclusively on their plundering activities, completely missing out both on the disruption that colonial intervention caused, and the twin processes of social differentiation and state formation that tribal people in parts of western and central India were undergoing during the eighteenth and nineteenth centuries. This view is echoed in more recent writings on the subject as well. Thus B.K. Sinha, in his full-length study, *The Pindaris,* observes simplistically that

> the Pindaris had no political aspirations and the main underlying principle of their organization was to strike terror in the hearts of the people so that they might not offer any resistance or opposition and they might accomplish their sole purpose of plunder and return to their camps with rich booty.[4]

In colonial writings, the Pindaris are invariably labelled 'freebooters', a synonym for pirates.[5] This indicates where exactly the Pindaris were placed in colonial discourse. The 'freebooter' label ruled out the possibility of negotiating with them. The Marathas accorded a somewhat more respectable status to the Pindaris. They appeared as an adjunct to their main army.[6] For the Marathas the Pindaris were a self-sustaining auxiliary force. Apart from constituting a low-cost cavalry, the Pindaris had other uses. They effectively harassed and inflicted losses on the enemy with their hit-and-run tactics, plundered retreating troops, and served to generally demoralize the local support bases of the opponent by striking terror through their swift and unpredictable raids. The real *forté* of the Pindaris was their familiarity with difficult terrain, especially hills and jungle, their speed, and their low level of subsistence. By the early nineteenth century, 'Pindari' had become a generic expression in Malwa for bands of mercenaries who combined soldiering with rapid raiding expeditions.

The Pindaris made their appearance towards the end of the eighteenth century as a new factor in the politics of Malwa. They were originally one of the numerous people living on the fringes of settled society in Malwa. Their integration began when many of them found a place in the Maratha military organization. By the end of the eighteenth century, they had become a regular part of Maratha campaigns north of the Narmada.[7]

Some of the hypotheses about the origins of the Pindaris are so vague as to render meaningless any discussion of this problem. In one attempt to unravel the mystery of their origins, the term Pindari is linked to a variety of intoxicating drink to which the Pindaris are supposed to have been addicted;[8] in another attempt the name is linked to the word *pendha*, or bundle of straw, suggesting that the Pindaris were originally foragers.[9]

More relevant is the reference to the tribal core of the Pindaris in R.V. Russell's *Tribes and Castes of the Central Provinces of India.* According to Russell, the Pindaris descended from the Gonds and Bhils of central India.[10] There was certainly an older Pindari tribal stratum which had a strong connection with the Narmada valley and the Vindhyas. The *Settlement Report* for Hoshangabad, a district in which there had been a number of Pindari possessions, observed that their ancestors 'were generally Gonds, Kurkus, Bhils, etc.'.[11] Right until 1818, the main Pindari chiefs retained holdings in the Narmada valley and the Vindhyan forests, especially in the stretch between south-eastern Dewas and the Hoshangabad–Narsimhapur border.[12]

Parts of Hoshangabad (district) remained closely identified with the Pindaris (Handia, Harda, Timurni, Makrai, etc.). Besides, some of the adjoining areas of Dewas—Nemawar, Satwas, Kannod, Kantaphor, Bagli—were Pindari bases. In Narsimhapur (district), the two most important Pindari chiefs, Chitu and Karim Khan, had holdings at Barha and Paloha. Chitu had lodged his family in a village close to Satwas.[13] He had received Satwas as a grant from Daulat Rao Sindia, and had built a fort there. Four guns were reportedly placed at the fort. Satwas (Dewas district, Madhya Pradesh) lies south of the Vindhyas and commands the road to Nemawar. Nemawar (Dewas district) is located strategically on the northern bank of the Narmada, at a point where the river is fordable. Handia (Hoshangabad district, Madhya Pradesh) is situated on the opposite bank. Nemawar, which was part of Sindia's territories, had also been granted to Chitu who established a cantonment at the place.[14] South of the Narmada, Timurni, Makrai, Harda, Barha and Paloha were among the territories held by the Pindari chiefs. It is worth noting that in the Narmada valley most of their possessions were concentrated in the tract between Handia and Narsimhapur, that is, east of Nimar and west of Jabalpur.

In the rather remote and inhospitable Narsimhapur area, both Chitu and Karim Khan had accepted grants from Sindia. These appear to have had an almost symbolic significance. The two villages given to them (Barha to Chitu and Paloha to Karim Khan) could not have yielded a large revenue, nor were they strategically important. They are situated close to each other in Gadarwara *tehsil* in the western portion of Narsimhapur district, not far from the southern bank of the Narmada. The Shakkar river, a tributary of the Narmada, runs along the west of Paloha. Barha lies south of Paloha. Chitu had built a fort at Barha.[15] By itself the Narsimhapur area was of little consequence at that point of time. Until about the last quarter of the eighteenth century, it was unsettled and sparsely populated. Narsimhapur town, originally known as Gadariya Kheda ('settlement of shepherds') village, began to develop only during the 1780s.[16]

Chitu and Karim Khan did not have any particular personal attachment to the Narsimhapur area, since they themselves came from Mewat and Malwa, respectively, but they were keen to maintain a presence at this gateway to the Gond homeland.[17] This would have allowed them to procure fresh recruits for their raiding expeditions, most of which increasingly took place in northern Malwa. As a matter of fact, the Pindari leaders retained outposts in the Narsimhapur–Hoshangabad–Dewas stretch of the Narmada valley, partly in order to have a safe haven in case of an emergency but mainly to enlist followers from among the tribal communities of the central Indian forest (Gonds, Bhils, etc.). The lifestyles of these communities had undergone a metamorphosis due to various historical processes. The resulting 'social disintegration' led to the formation of tribal bands 'in the hills and woodlands', which engaged in plunder to support themselves.[18] These groups had a crucial role to play in the Pindari scheme of things, as suppliers of soldiers. Recruitment would have taken place during or immediately after the monsoon, when the Pindaris congregated on the banks of the Narmada to recoup their resources. They normally desisted from undertaking any expedition till the rains were over.[19]

The Pindaris were not a closed, homogeneous group. In the words of Sydenham, 'they now form a heterogeneous mass containing followers of almost every caste of Hindoos, and every sect of Mahomedans'. Similarly, a commission which inquired into an alleged Pindari raid on Guntur and some other parts of Andhra recorded that the raiders 'were composed of all tribes, from the . . . Bramin and Rajepoot, to the Paria'.[20]

Whatever little evidence we have on how the Pindaris interacted with each other indicates that members of Pindari bands did not share a primordial or permanent attachment to one another. The term Pindari does not suggest a membership composed of an entire ethnic or language group. Though several Pindari bands might have drawn together periodically, as for instance near the Narmada during the rainy season, there were no traditions that compelled them to gather regularly or permanently as a single unit. The major bands were in a constant state of flux, as smaller groups departed, families veered off in their own directions for various periods and captives married into the community.

The Pindaris must be placed against the backdrop of a continuous historical process of social differentiation in the extensive central and western Indian tribal belt. This process was linked to state formation, empire-building and the search for military recruits. The entire Madhya Pradesh–Rajasthan/Gujarat border and the Vindhya–Satpura region still has a substantial tribal population. Throughout the medieval period, the communities inhabiting this area underwent a phase of transition to class society. In the later medieval period, the pace of this transition was accelerated by Mughal expansion, the drive of the Dakhani sultanates and Maratha empire-building. The inhabitants of the central Indian hills and forests did not lead a completely isolated existence. They were suppliers of forest produce, so there was some exchange between them and settled agriculturists; strategically and commercially important routes passed through the area inhabited by them; and they could provide human resources to patrol the hill and jungle terrain they knew so well. While discussing the evolving ethnicities of the Bhils and Gonds, the two major tribal groups of the central Indian forests, Sumit Guha points out that the tribal-dominated lands of this region 'were no tranquil backwaters, isolated from the turbulent politics of the peninsula'. 'Nor indeed were they', he adds, 'inhabited by relic populations obstinately preserving their archaic life ways. They were in fact deeply integrated into the political economy of medieval India.'[21]

One important trend set in motion by changes taking place in this frontier region was the emergence of warriors in tribal societies, which was linked by Surajit Sinha to state formation, the articulation of new identities and rajputization.[22] The tribal belt would henceforth provide recruits for armies, while petty 'predatory chiefs' would add to the pool of those whose services could be enlisted by contractors for recruits.[23] Dirk Kolff's study of the phenomenon of recruitment of troopers by middlemen in medieval India, *Naukar, Rajput and Sepoy*, contains a useful discussion on rajputization and the transition from a tribal to a warrior culture based on differentiation and specialization. Kolff refers to a broader development, which includes the Pathans, whereby transition to a social formation marked by the presence of a professional warrior class led to dissolving former identities and taking over readymade new ones defined either as Rajput or Pathan. 'This may be a heretical thing to say,' Kolff argues,

> but I suggest that, according to the ways of the north Indian military labour market, in the pre-Mughal period, 'Afghan' as well as 'Rajput' were soldiers' identities rather than ethnic or genealogical denotations. It was merely to register membership of the war-band they had decided to join that until quite late on Indian soldiers were known by such names.[24]

One would like to suggest that whatever the term 'Pindari' might have originally meant, by the second half of the eighteenth century, it had come to denote an intermediate identity in Malwa and the middle Narmada. This was yet another option available to the new warriors for whom it defined an identity which could, given the right opportunity, become a sort of stepping stone to more reputed identities.

Kolff's work helps us to comprehend what was happening on the periphery of peasant societies in central India in the later medieval period. There was a connection between military service, state formation and newly acquired identities (Rajput, Pathan, Pindari). It was an indication of a society in a state of flux that social groups were not 'closed'; identities were not yet inflexible. Mughal, Maratha and Rajput states absorbed the soldiers provided by the tribal belt. Pindari chiefs became, in effect, contractors or sub-contractors looking after the interests of their respective groups and making no permanent commitments. Guha argues that 'Maratha incursions in northwestern Khandesh could hardly have been possible without at least the acquiescence of the local Bhils. Their support was also enlisted by the Mughal commanders.'[25] The support of this soldiery had to be constantly renegotiated. Whenever possible or necessary, they could go in for small-time plunder or extort money for ensuring the safety of vital routes passing through their settlements.

In the years preceding the Third Anglo–Maratha War, there were two outstanding Pindari leaders: Karim Khan and Chitu. Of the two, Karim Khan was politically more important, having been on the verge of creating an independent state. Tod remarked in 1811 that at one stage Karim Khan 'had attained a degree of established power, before unknown to these plundering unsettled Hordes'. He added that Karim possessed 'a pretty extensive, compact, fertile and well cultivated territory, containing several strongholds well garrisoned, and the appearance of a regular system of authority'.[26]

Karim Khan's territories were mainly located in eastern Malwa, especially on the outskirts of the Bhopal state,[27] that was almost on the brink of extinction after 1805. Bhopal, which had risen to prominence in the first quarter of the eighteenth century under Dost Muhammad Khan, was the main Pathan stronghold in Malwa.[28] Bhopal and the adjacent eastern Malwa *parganas* became the main target of the Pindaris. Karim Khan had established his principal cantonment at Berasia near Bhopal.[29] Sindia and Holkar preferred to confine the Pindaris to this area, at some distance from the core of their territory in western Malwa. For example, the tribute due to Sindia and Holkar from the frontier Rajgarh and Narsinghgarh principalities in northeast Malwa was formally divided between Karim Khan and Chitu who were left to deal with this difficult area.[30] For a long time the eastern Malwa *parganas* had been administered directly from Pune, but with the collapse of the Peshwa's authority they were encroached upon by Sindia, Holkar and numerous other contenders.

Significantly, the moment Karim Khan attempted to graduate to the status of an independent ruler, Sindia cut him down to size. Karim Khan was held captive by Daulat Rao Sindia from 1806 to 1811. The Sindia–Karim Khan relationship reveals the contradictions inherent in the political crisis that preceded the Third Anglo–Maratha War. Under the great Mahadji, the Sindia state initiated a military modernization programme in the last quarter of the eighteenth century. Benoit de Boigne was one of the main pillars of this programme. De Boigne's departure in 1796, the defection in 1803 of General Perron who succeeded de Boigne and Sindia's losses in the Second Anglo–Maratha War were major setbacks to the modernization programme.[31]

After 1805, the Pindaris were looked upon as useful and relatively inexpensive military allies. There was a marked increase in the number of Pindaris employed as soldiers by the Maratha states of Malwa. Jenkins estimated that their number doubled between 1804 and 1809, from about 13,000 to roughly 25,000.[32] At the same time, he differentiated between 'real' Pindaris of the pre-1805 period and the large number of new recruits, many of whom were discharged soldiers of Indian states which had been forced to scale down their military strength or disband their armies altogether after the Second Anglo–Maratha War.[33] In 1811, Sindia entered into a specific agreement with Karim Khan 'that no other persons but such as were real Pindaris should be entertained in the durrahs [*dharas*], and that other adventurers should be expelled'.[34] Senior officials of the East India Company were aware of the urgent need to provide alternative means of subsistence to former soldiers. Arthur Wellesley remarked in 1804, 'I think we run a great risk from the freebooter system. . . . Conceive a country in every village of which there are from twenty to thirty horsemen who have been dismissed from the service of the State and who have no means of living except by plunder.'[35]

Many of the new additions may have been part-time soldiers and part-time agriculturists from the Malwa villages. That the turn-of-the-century Pindaris were not necessarily outsiders and had strong local roots in the Malwa countryside is suggested by the ease with which they dispersed—dissolved is a more appropriate word—after an expedition, or when attacked. Their speed and swift dispersal was crucial to their overall strategy:

> all that a pursuing Party can on most occasions expect, is to come up with the cattle and a few attendants on Foot. . . . But even then many of the men unload their Ponies, mount them and escape, while others conceal themselves in any villages, Hills, or Jungles that may be at hand.[36]

Malcolm reported:

> If pursued, they made marches of extraordinary length . . . by roads almost impracticable for regular troops. If overtaken, they dispersed, and re-assembled at an appointed rendezvous; if followed to the country . . . they broke up into small parties. Their wealth, their booty, and their families were scattered over a wide region, in which

> they found protection amid the mountains, and in the fastnesses belonging to themselves and to those with whom they were either openly or secretly connected.[37]

It was noticed that after successful raiding expeditions, laden pack animals of the Pindaris were frequently unloaded at villages lying on the route of their return journey. This implies that many of those who had accompanied an expedition went home to their respective abodes along the way, as the Pindaris dispersed.[38]

We have already noted that Pindaris had been customarily employed by the Maratha armies in Malwa. After 1805, Pindari participation in the Maratha campaigns assumed a new significance. Yashwant Rao Holkar and Daulat Rao Sindia forged a sweeping alliance with the Pindaris, which was manifested in the Pindaris acquiring a limited share in political power. This provided the Pindaris an opportunity to enlarge the scope of their activities. Apart from being assigned specific territories, the prominent Pindari leaders were for the first time honoured with titles which announced their new status and served to acknowledge their political clout in post-1805 Malwa. Chitu was honoured with the pompous title of 'Nawab Kamal Khan Mustaqim Jang'; Karim Khan had the title 'Nawab Sarfaraz-ud-Daula' conferred on him by Sindia; and Dost Muhammad, another prominent Pindari chief, was given the title of 'Nawab'.[39] Chitu, Karim Khan and Dost Muhammad, all had the privilege, usually reserved for the aristocracy, of a *naubat* (kettle-drum).[40] After all, the Malwa states had to find a basis for the loyalty of the Pindari chiefs so as to ensure that the troops mobilized by them did not remain mere mercenaries. Had the Third Anglo–Maratha War not intervened, these gestures might have become devices for incorporating some of the Pindari military leaders within the structures of the Malwa states. Chitu's flag symbolically expressed loyalty for Sindia. He carried a saffron-coloured flag with a small white snake drawn in the centre. This snake was an insignia of the Sindias. The sticks carried by Chitu's *harkaras* (messengers) were also 'mounted by small snake's Heads, made of silver'.[41]

Given the very low social status of the Pindaris, they had so far been kept at a distance.[42] Now, for the first time, under Daulat Rao, Pindari leaders were deemed worthy of some social intercourse. To quote Malcolm:

> Although they commanded large bodies of men they were never allowed to sit down in the presence of the prince; and when Jeswunt Row [Yashwant Rao Holkar] . . . met Dowlet Row Sindia he reproached that prince for the encouragement he had given the Pindarry chiefs, by his personal intercourse with them, and by the high titles and grants of land which he had bestowed on men unworthy of such distinction.[43]

Incidentally, Daulat Rao was reputed to be 'profuse, open, easy of access and a great dissembler', which might have allowed him to be temperamentally less inhibited in his dealings with the Pindaris.[44]

Nevertheless, Daulat Rao was not willing to admit any Pindari claim to sharing political power in Malwa on a permanent basis. Hence his anxiety to keep Karim Khan under control without completely alienating him. The Company's Residents at the Sindia court remarked that Karim did not really suffer rigorous confinement.[45] What is more, even in captivity Karim maintained close links with sections of Sindia's army, particularly with the powerful faction led by Jaswant Rao Bhau.[46] Jaswant Rao was to provide shelter to Karim Khan and Chitu in the closing phase of the Third Anglo–Maratha War.

The nexus between Jaswant Rao Bhau and the Pindari leaders is illustrative of the extent to which military leaders of the Malwa states were dependent upon the Pindari soldiers. For instance, in 1814, he was reported to have taken 'an immense body of Pindarries under the notorious Cheetoo' into service at the rate of fifteen rupees per month for each horseman.[47] Jaswant Rao played a major role in cementing ties between the Pindaris and the Sindia army during the inter-war period. Jaswant Rao was a leading commander during the first quarter of the nineteenth century. His father, Jiva Dada, had been one of Sindia's chief military officers in the late eighteenth century. Jaswant Rao held the *pargana*s of Jawad, Jiran and Nimach (Mandsaur district, Madhya Pradesh) on the Malwa–Mewar border. These *pargana*s had been taken by Sindia from Udaipur. Jaswant Rao consolidated his position in this frontier region and used it as a base for encroaching upon the territories of states in southeastern Rajasthan, especially Mewar. The fortified town of Jawad was the capital of Jaswant Rao's fiefdom.[48] He constantly needed military support to stabilize Sindia rule in the area. The ubiquitous Zalim Singh, *de facto* ruler of Kota for over four decades, was also active in this area, and his intervention was often vital for Maratha expansion in Rajasthan. Zalim Singh was, among other things, an efficient military entrepreneur. He himself had an intimate connection with the Pindari chiefs. Zalim Singh assisted in negotiating the release of Karim Khan from Sindia's captivity. He facilitated the process by agreeing to stand surety for the huge sum (reportedly six to ten lakh rupees) demanded by Sindia as the price for Karim Khan's liberty.[49]

During the Third Anglo–Maratha War Jaswant Rao, ignoring the explicit instructions of Daulat Rao Sindia, actively aided Chitu and Karim Khan:

> In contempt of the orders publicly delivered to him on the part of Scindia, he not only furnished provisions, and every facilitation of progress, to the body of Pindaris retreating under Cheetoo, but he gave to that chief intelligence of the approach of the British troops, and saved him from being cut off.[50]

Seeing that Jaswant Rao 'could not be prevailed upon to move a man against him', British forces attacked Jawad and captured the town, forcing the Sardar to flee the place.[51] When the troops entered Jawad they discovered, much to their surprise, that Karim Khan too had been sheltered by Bhau and had left shortly before the town fell to the British.[52]

Subsequently, Jaswant Rao surrendered to the British (on 14 February 1818), and the following morning Karim Khan too gave himself up.[53] Sindia punished Jaswant Rao's defiance by temporarily disowning him. Jaswant Rao's possessions, which had been occupied by the British, were restored to Sindia after the war. However Sindia refused to reappoint Jaswant Rao. The Bhau continued to petition Daulat Rao, and it was only in 1821 that he was restored to favour. Even then, despite his appeals, he was not allowed to resume his former grant. An interesting postscript to this episode was that Jaswant Rao was given the *parganas* of Nemawar and Satwas, which had been earlier granted to Chitu.[54] Nimach, strategically located on the Madhya Pradesh–Rajasthan border, was made the headquarter of the Rajputana–Malwa charge by the British in 1822, and placed under David Ochterlony. Ochterlony was Resident there till 1825. A cantonment for British troops was located on the outskirts of Nimach.[55] Jaswant Rao never regained his former prestige. After 1818, parvenus increasingly dominated the Sindia military establishment. There were just a few notable exceptions to this trend, one of them being Jean Baptiste Filose, who, among the old guard, had frequently collaborated with Jaswant Rao in recruiting Pindaris and retained sufficient authority till the 1840s.

In view of the new and more aggressive role that the Pindaris were called upon to play after the Second Anglo–Maratha War, it is not surprising that when Lord Hastings embarked upon a fresh round of colonial expansionism he regarded the destruction of the Pindaris as a matter of great urgency. What is grandly referred to as the Third Anglo–Maratha War began as a campaign against the Pindaris. Hastings had been seeking sanction for launching a war against the Pindaris, and even though a conditional sanction was given, he was told that 'the authorities at home are unwilling to incur the risk of a general war for the uncertain purpose of extirpating altogether the Pindaris'.[56] Eventually, Hastings was able to convince his superiors that annihilation of the Pindaris was the key to establishing British supremacy over Malwa.

The anti-Pindari campaign was a major war effort. The Company assembled 1,20,000 troops for this war, 'the largest army collected up to that time for one purpose under the British flag in India'.[57] The Pindaris were caught in a synchronous movement from north and south. The northern army was commanded personally by the Governor General, while the southern army, led by Lt Gen. T. Hislop, commander-in-chief of the Deccan army, carried out the major operations against the Pindaris. The sheer military might of the Company resulted in victory. The success of the Company's unprecedented mobilization notwithstanding, this war produced no glorious battles, barring perhaps the Battle of Mehidpur against Holkar's troops (December 1817), in which, however, the British lost 800 men.[58] That was about all. As for the Pindaris, the bulk of them simply dissolved. There was not a single face-to-face engagement with the Pindaris, and though they were chased by the Company's contingents which criss-crossed the length and breadth of Malwa, few were captured. Only on one occasion were a sizeable number of Pindaris trapped, leaving at least 1,000 killed.[59]

The refusal of the Pindaris to be coaxed into battle was very much in keeping with the style of warfare they preferred. Malcolm was exasperated that 'nowhere did they present any point of attack'.[60] This provides an insight into the nature of Pindari formations. It was generally recognized that 'their chief strength lay in their being intangible'.[61] We have already seen how their formations dissolved after raiding expeditions. They were not burdened by elaborate paraphernalia since they marched without tents and baggage. They kept their provisions to a minimum. Their overall poverty was reflected in their frugality. The ordinary Pindari was 'satisfied with the coarsest cakes of wheat or Jowaree, parched peas or other grains'.[62] The fact that they had such few physical needs while on the march made it easy for Pindari formations to advance and retreat with great speed. Sydenham wrote admiringly, that they moved 'with a rapidity perhaps unequalled by the marches of any other cavalry in the world'.[63] Whereas they normally covered nearly 65 kilometres in a day, when pursued they could march at double that speed. In other words, it was possible for them to cross almost the entire length or breadth of Malwa in a week, 'over Roads and Hills impassable to Horses unaccustomed to traverse them'. This, according to Sydenham, was a modest estimate.[64]

Though Chitu seems to have been much more cautious than Karim Khan in that he did not overstep the bounds of his social origin in his relations with Sindia, yet, between the two, it was Chitu who symbolized much more forcefully the anti-British sentiment of the Maratha–Pindari coalition. This is not the place to go into the details of the complicated end-game of the 1818 war. What one would like to recall is the almost simultaneous movement of Peshwa Baji Rao II in the direction of Asirgarh, and the escape from British captivity and subsequent flight towards Asirgarh of Appa Sahib, the deposed ruler of Nagpur. Coinciding with this was the retreat of Chitu in the direction of Asirgarh. The Ahmadnagar Collector, H. Pottinger, reported in May 1818, that Baji Rao's force 'is said to consist of 7,000 men, and Ramdeen, Seeto Pindarry and Kana Beel are with him'.[65] In his final struggle Chitu aligned himself with Baji Rao, Appa Sahib, the Bhil chief Kanhya Bhil and Ram Din.

Ram Din headed the bloc at Holkar's court which had not reconciled itself to British supremacy over Indore. He was a key figure in Holkar's military mobilization, especially in the period between Yashwant Rao Holkar's death and the Third Anglo–Maratha War, that is, 1811–18. This brought him close to the Pindaris. Ram Din was a brahmana from north India. He started his career as an orderly of Yashwant Rao Holkar. Around 1810, shortly before the death of Yashwant Rao, he was placed in charge of Maheshwar. Maheshwar (west

Nimar district, Madhya Pradesh), on the northern banks of the Narmada, was a town of great importance. It had been the main residence of Ahilya Bai, and was a prominent ritual and commercial centre. In the intense struggle for power following the insanity and subsequent death of Yashwant Rao, Ram Din seems to have suffered imprisonment for some time. After his release, he was assigned a military charge. We do not have details about the nature of his military responsibilities but he was fairly successful, so that a faction of the Holkar army was loyal to him.[66] Like several other military entrepreneurs who were then active in Malwa, Ram Din combined various roles, including that of *sahukar* and revenue farmer. His business interests provided him with resources for recruiting soldiers and supporting armed contingents. On the other hand, the troops could be used for raiding expeditions from time to time, so that plunder constituted a source of primitive accumulation for Ram Din. Writing in 1818, a British official commented: 'Of all the freebooters who desolated Malwa there is not one whose ravages, in this quarter at least within the last six years, have been so merciless and unremitting as those of Ram Deen.'[67]

From Maheshwar, Ram Din moved to Indore and Ujjain. It was the shift to Ujjain that brought him in contact with the world of high finance, and ultimately it was big money that catapulted him to power. Malcolm noted that Ram Din was connected with 'some of the richest bankers of Ujjain'.[68] Ram Din's brother, Makhan Lal Joshi, who reportedly possessed considerable property and influence in Ujjain, was his business associate. Revenue farming was an integral part of their business activities. Ram Din had been the *ijaradar* of Indore, as well as of Betma and Depalpur (Indore district) for several years preceding the Third Anglo–Maratha War. His revenue farm was managed mainly by Makhan Lal.[69] Makhan Lal must have been an efficient manager, since Daulat Rao Sindia offered him the *ijara* (revenue farm) of several *parganas*, an offer strongly resisted by the Company, which had come to regard Ram Din as an outlaw after 1818–19.[70]

Ram Din, who was present at the Battle of Mehidpur, proceeded to Ujjain after the debacle suffered by the Holkar army. Here he was assured of the active support of Ujjain *sahukars*, and he decided to resist being captured by the British troops who had been pursuing the two brothers. The Ujjain residence of Makhan Lal was one of the few fortified buildings in the city. Ram Din had sufficient troops to safeguard his interests. Hislop, who commanded the Company's army at Mehidpur, wrote a long note to the Governor General informing him of the nature of Ram Din's resistance and the kind of support he enjoyed at Ujjain:

> It appears that the house of Makun Loll was one of the two or three fortified buildings, another of which was inhabited by an adopted son of Scindiah's; that these houses were filled with Mikrany [Arab] infantry, of which Ram Deen has a number in his pay; and to have taken Makun Loll involved the necessity not only of attacking the house of Scindiah's adopted son, but of sending a detachment of disciplined troops through the narrow streets of a large town, and under most unfavourable circumstances, and with the chance of Makun Loll making his escape after all.[71]

With the British troops indicating their reluctance to use force against Makhan Lal, he confidently departed for Indore, accompanied by Ram Din. Having settled their affairs at Indore, Makhan Lal returned to Ujjain, while Ram Din went southward towards Betma and Depalpur to rally his supporters. From there he moved in the direction of the Vindhyas, and eventually joined Chitu and the Peshwa.[72]

Unfortunately, the potential of this formidable Peshwa–Bhonsle–Pindari–Bhil–Indore convergence was never realized.[73] Chitu was forced to flee to the Vindhyan forests as the British troops closed in. Malcolm, who savoured the submission of several Pindari, Maratha, Rajput and Pathan leaders, was denied the satisfaction of capturing Chitu alive. Chitu was killed by a tiger in the dense Sita Ban jungle in Limanpur, not far from Satwas, where he had escaped. Malcolm sought the support of the local *thakurs* to apprehend Chitu. Bhim Singh of Bagli and Nana Zamindar of Kantaphor offered to help in this task. Chitu was tracked 'like a hunted animal, through the jungles, by the prints of his horse's hoofs'.[74] Nana found the head of Chitu, 'the rest of the body having been devoured by a tiger', and presented it before Malcolm.[75]

Lying on either side of the Vindhya range, Bagli and Kantaphor (both in Dewas district) were part of the Sindia state. The road from Kantaphor runs in a southeasterly direction to Satwas and Nemawar. This entire area is not easily accessible. Malcolm described the 'fastnesses between Baglee and Mudleysir [Mandaleshwar]' as being 'chiefly inhabited by Gonds', and added that 'the plundering class who lately occupied them had amongst their followers men of desperate fortunes from Hindustan and other quarters'. He mentioned some 'Native soldiers who had deserted from the service of the Madras army ten years ago [*c.* 1813]' being discovered in this locale.[76] Bhim Singh himself alluded to the fact that Limanpur could not be cultivated 'because it is a wild woody tract, the abode of thieves and robbers who have here and there inhabited a few hamlets'.[77] When a dispute arose in the 1840s over the sharing of Bagli revenues, reference was made to the service which Bhim Singh had rendered in cornering Chitu: 'Sir John Malcolm never forgot these services and always treated Bheem Singh with marked attention, giving him presents of horses, swords, and guns.'[78]

While the mass of Pindari soldiers simply returned home after 1818 and lay low, their leaders were left high and dry. We have seen Chitu's fate. Of the other Pindari leaders, Karim Khan, Namdar Khan and the son of Dost Muhammad submitted to the British; Rajjan was captured; Wasil Muhammad committed suicide.[79] When Pindari leaders surrendered, they did so individually. They had hardly any followers with them. After Karim Khan was forced to flee from Jawad, he was reduced to wandering in the neighbouring hills for a fortnight, possessing neither companions nor any means of subsistence. The bands which had been led by these chiefs mingled with the ordinary inhabitants of Malwa, the Vindhyan forests and the Narmada valley. Even Chitu, for all his heroic effort, was virtually alone in his last days.[80]

The tame surrender of many of the Pindari leaders and the willingness of the British authorities to pardon them leads one to suspect that the level of violence attributed to these 'freebooters' was grossly exaggerated by the Company's officials. Ultimately, the East India Company was keen to ensure that prominent Pindari military commanders did not compete for a share of the military labour market, which the British intended to monopolize. Karim Khan was deported to Gorakhpur, where he was given the large estate of the Raja of Barhiapar in Bansgaon *tehsil* for his support and that of his companions. He had a fairly large retinue of 600 persons.[81] Rajjan, who had been the nominal head of the contingent led by Chitu, was also sent to Gorakhpur, but he did not have adequate financial means. In 1823, he petitioned the British government to enhance his allowance so that he could arrange for his family, which had been separated from him at the time of the war, to come and reside with him:

> Your petitioner now receives 300 rupees per month, but requests that some increase may be made to it, that he may be enabled to send for his family, etc., from Bhopal. . . . Should the Gentlemen of the Sudder not approve of this your petitioner begs a grant of lands in the neighbourhood of Bhopal may be given him, as by cultivating the ground there, your petitioner will be able to support his large family.[82]

There was one military entrepreneur associated with the Pindaris who remained unscathed: Amir Khan. In fact, the British went out of their way to please him at the end of the Third Anglo–Maratha War. This has to be viewed in the context of the ability of Amir Khan to mobilize well-trained and highly disciplined troops. With an elite contingent, he was in a position to strike a good bargain with the Company, and he did rather well for himself once the war was over. The point is that among the Pindaris there was a small section that had the professional skills to be inducted into a modern army. Sydenham had reported that of a given Pindari column, on average, two-fifths would usually be composed of well-trained soldiers mounted on good-quality horses; another two-fifths would comprise *luteras* mounted on half-bred horses, who could however be very effective as fighters; the remaining one-fifth would be riding on *tattus* armed with nothing more than sticks. The effective strength of the formation was derived from the skilled riders, whose main weapon was a 12-feet-long spear. Besides, approximately 5 per cent of the men would be armed with matchlocks.[83] Use of the spear made the Pindaris more easily compatible with the Maratha military ethos, which, in the words of Stewart Gordon, was based on 'light cavalry (mounted on locally-bred horses), straight sword and shield and lance'.[84]

Right at the outset, Amir Khan concentrated on recruiting the better-quality Pindari fighters. Although Amir Khan is sometimes clubbed with the other Pindari chiefs, he had come to Malwa from Sambhal during the latter half of the eighteenth century in search of an opportunity for military service.[85] Sambhal was then part of the territories of the Ruhela chief Hafiz Rahmat Khan, whose borders touched those of the Sindia state. Towards the end of the century, Amir

Khan became a firm ally of Yashwant Rao Holkar.[86] As early as *c.* 1798, Amir Khan's troops were receiving a higher pay than even the Maratha soldiers in Yashwant Rao's army.[87] Assisted by his brother, Karim-uddin (who died quite young), he strove hard to make his contingent a disciplined and formidable fighting force.[88] After Yashwant Rao's death, Amir Khan, in partnership with his relative Ghafur Khan, continued to occupy an important place in the Holkar military structure. On the eve of the Battle of Mehidpur Amir Khan capitulated and negotiated a settlement with Ochterlony.[89] The fact that he had an elite force under him made all the difference. He entered into a contract by which the British promised employment on attractive terms to as many as 6,000 of his men. Amir Khan was paid Rs 5,00,000 to disband his army and hand over his guns. An additional sum of Rs 3,00,000 was advanced to him. A more substantial gain for Amir Khan was the newly created principality of Tonk, of which he was made the ruler. As for Ghafur Khan, he became the first Nawab of Jaora. In creating the state of Jaora, the British hoped to have the bonus of a religious conflict as well. Malcolm cynically admitted his intention of 'planting in the heart of the remaining possessions of Holkar a Mahomedan authority, which must prove a check upon the Hindoo adherents of this ruler'.[90] Of course, the principal objective of the deal with Amir Khan and Ghafur Khan was to pre-empt the possibility of their well-trained soldiers being recruited by anyone else.[91]

The suppression of the Pindaris wrecked a major large-scale attempt on the part of the war-bands of central India, with their nucleus composed of warriors from the tribal belt whose strength was augmented by discharged troopers and impoverished Malwa peasants, to move out of the narrow confines of their domains and intervene in the high politics of the plateau. After 1818, the vast majority of those who had been members of these bands were still available for service in private armed contingents of petty chiefs, landlords and powerful bankers. But the scale on which such contingents operated was too small to absorb all the former Pindaris. Thousands of these unemployed men with some military training became the mainstay of central Indian social banditry. In 1822, Ochterlony warned that 'the terror struck by the suppression of the Pindarry system is beginning to subside, and in some Quarters has subsided, and though the present Banditti have not yet assumed an open front, their aggressions are every day becoming more formidable and more regularly organized'.[92] The shortcircuiting of the Pindari experiment continued to be a source of dislocation, the consequences of which are imperfectly understood. The colonial construction of *thagi*, which belongs to the period following the Third Anglo–Maratha War, was a product of this very dislocation.[93]

Notes and References

1 See R. Jenkins, Resident, Nagpur, 'Memorandum relative to the Pindarries', 1812, in *Papers Respecting the Pindarry and Mahratta Wars*, National Archives of India, New Delhi (hereafter NAI), Foreign Department (hereafter FD) Misc., 124/A, p. 26.

2 John Malcolm, *A Memoir of Central India, including Malwa and Adjoining Provinces*, 2 vols, Kingsbury, Parbury and Allen, London, 1823, reprinted by Sagar Publications, New Delhi, 1970, Vol. I, Ch. X.

3 James Tod, 'Origin, Progress and Present State [of the] Pindarras', Gwalior, October 1811, NAI, FD Misc., 124; Jenkins, 'Memorandum'; G. Sydenham, Agent, Berar, 'Memorandum respecting the Pindarries towards the end of the year 1814', 15 October 1814, NAI, FD Misc., 124. Cf. Edward Thompson and G.T. Garratt, *Rise and Fulfilment of British Rule in India*, Macmillan, London, 1934, reprinted by Central Book Depot, Allahabad, 1976, Ch. IX; P.E. Roberts, *History of British India*, third edn, Oxford University Press, Oxford, 1952, pp. 282–84.

4 B.K. Sinha, *The Pindaris (1798–1818)*, Bookland, Calcutta, 1971, p. 61. Cf. also Malcolm, *Memoir*, Vol. I, pp. 428–29.

5 For example, Tod, 'Pindarras', p. 8; Malcolm, *Memoir*, Vol. I, pp. 431, 433.

6 S.N. Sen, *The Military System of the Marathas*, Orient Longman, Bombay, 1958, pp. 74 ff.

7 The supposed reference to the Pindaris in the *Tarikh-i-Firishta*, is a misreading. Sydenham, using Capt. Jonathan Scott's translation (*Firishta's History of the Dekkan*, J. & W. Eddowes/John Stockdale, Shrewsbury, 1794, Vol. II, pp. 121–22), stated that the Pindaris 'are first mentioned in Ferishta, . . . in his memoirs of Aurangzeb's operations in the Deckan, where he relates their having plundered the districts about Beejapore in conjunction with some rebellious Zemindars in the year 1689': Sydenham, 'Memorandum', p. 37. Sydenham compounded the error by making Firishta, who resided at Bijapur from 1591 till his death in 1623, a contemporary of Aurangzeb. The mistake was repeated by Malcolm (*Memoir*, Vol. I, p. 426 and n.), and was carelessly reproduced in later writings. The notion that the Pindaris were a product of the seventeenth century persisted in works such as those of G.S. Sardesai, which otherwise revealed a thorough grasp of Maratha history (G.S. Sardesai, *New History of the Marathas*, Vol. III, Phoenix Publications, Bombay, 1948, p. 477).

It should be underlined that the Pindaris were essentially a phenomenon of the last quarter of the eighteenth century, and more than a century separated the formation of this identity from Aurangzeb's Dakhan campaigns. Significantly, Bhimsen's important memoir of these campaigns, *Tarikh-i-Dilkasha*, written almost a hundred years after the *Tarikh-i-Firishta*, does not mention the Pindaris (*Tarikh-i-Dilkasha*, English translation by Jadunath Sarkar, edited by V.G. Khobrekar, Department of Archives, Government of Maharashtra, Bombay, 1972). Bhimsen was no stranger to the region which later became the main Pindari zone, since both he and his father had served in Malwa and Dakhan for a long time. Moreover, as Stewart Gordon observes, the Maratha identity and military ethos itself was still evolving during the seventeenth century ('Zones of Military Entrepreneurship in India, 1500–1700', in Stewart Gordon, *Marathas, Marauders, and State Formation in Eighteenth-Century India*, Oxford University Press, Delhi, 1994, pp. 193–94).

[8] Malcolm, *Memoir*, Vol. I, p. 433 n. According to Malcolm, Karim Khan, one of the foremost Pindari leaders, stated that 'he had never heard any other reason given for this name' except that it was derived from 'an intoxicated [*sic*] drink termed Pinda'. It is significant that Karim Khan showed little interest in advancing a plausible theory about the origin of the Pindaris. He appears to have casually mentioned this etymology during the course of his interview with Malcolm shortly after his surrender, when he must have had more pressing problems on his mind.

[9] Sinha, *Pindaris*, p. 2; Interview, Shri N.C. Zamindar, Indore, 1991 (Zamindar was scion of the *mandloi* family of Indore). Sardesai notes that 'the etymology of the Marathi word Pendha or Pendhar is doubtful. It means a body of stragglers': Sardesai, *Marathas*, Vol. III, p. 477, n. 8.

[10] R.V. Russell and Hira Lal, *The Tribes and Castes of the Central Provinces of India*, Macmillan, London, Vol. IV, 1916, reprinted by Cosmo, Delhi, 1975, p. 388. The Pindaris never became a fashionable subject for anthropological investigation, since they were not a typical ethnic group. Further, they had no distinctive or exotic practices and beliefs, which an anthropologist might have found exciting.

[11] C.A. Elliott, quoted in Charles Grant (ed.), *Gazetteer of Central Provinces of India*, second edn, Education Society Press, Nagpur, 1870, reprinted by Usha, Delhi, 1984, p. xcv, n.

[12] W. Irvine, in an article entitled 'Etymology of the Word Pindari' (*Indian Antiquary*, Vol. XXIX, May 1900), argued that the term is derived from the word *pandhar*, which broadly referred to a region that included Hoshangabad, Nemawar and Handia on the Narmada. Quoted in Sinha, *Pindaris*, pp. 3–4. While tracing the early history of the Pindaris, Sydenham emphasized their connection with the Narmada region: 'in 1794 they are said to have established themselves on the Banks of the Nerbudda, and from that period to have increased progressively in consequence and power.' Sydenham, 'Memorandum', p. 38.

[13] Jenkins, 'Memorandum', p. 30.

[14] Sydenham, 'Memorandum', p. 46. Malcolm, in his *Memoir*, wrongly mentions Nimar instead of Nemawar as one of Chitu's possessions. This was

apparently just a slip on the part of the author, since he was too well acquainted with the region to make an error of this kind. See Malcolm, *Memoir*, Vol. I, pp. 444–45.

15 Jenkins, 'Memorandum', p. 30; *Central Provinces Gazetteer*, p. 28; P.N. Shrivastav, *Madhya Pradesh Gazetteers, Narsimhapur*, Government Central Press, Bhopal, 1971, pp. 2, 54, n. 1, 2.

16 *Narsimhapur Gazetteer*, p. 2.

17 Sumit Guha notes that in the first quarter of the nineteenth century, 'the Gond territory extended as far west as Mandaleshwar on the Narmada river [district West Nimar], and eastward into Western Orissa and Chotanagpur': Sumit Guha, *Environment and Ethnicity in India, 1200–1991*, Cambridge University Press, Cambridge, 1999, p. 122.

18 Ibid., pp. 126–27.

19 Cf. James Tod, 'Journal', August–September 1813, NAI, FD Misc., 124, p. 30; Sydenham, 'Memorandum', p. 41.

20 'Report of Commission . . . to enquire into Pindary invasion of Guntur, Masulipatam, Cuddappa', 31 January 1817, FD, Misc., 124/A, p. 56. This report, from which later historical accounts have quoted extensively, needs to be treated with some caution, since it was very unusual for the Pindaris to operate so far down south. Moreover, this was an isolated case, which makes one wonder whether it was a Pindari raid at all. Nevertheless, what is pertinent is that contemporary officials did not have a homogeneous group in mind while describing the Pindaris.

21 Guha, *Environment and Ethnicity*, p. 121.

22 Cf. Surajit Sinha, 'State Formation and the Rajput Myth in Central India', reprinted in H. Kulke (ed.), *The State in India 1000–1700*, Oxford University Press, Delhi, 1995, pp. 304 ff.

23 Cf. Guha, *Environment and Ethnicity*, pp. 110–16.

24 Dirk H.A. Kolff, *Naukar, Rajput and Sepoy: The Ethnohistory of the Military Labour Market in Hindustan, 1450–1850*, Cambridge University Press, Cambridge, 1990, pp. 57–58.

25 Sumit Guha, 'Forest Polities and Agrarian Empires: The Khandesh Bhils, *c.* 1700–1850', *Indian Economic and Social History Review*, Vol. XXXIII, No. 2, 1996, p. 136.

26 Tod, 'Pindarras', p. 6.

27 Ibid.; Sydenham, 'Memorandum', pp. 49–51.

28 Cf. Stewart Gordon, 'Legitimacy and Loyalty in Some Successor States', in Gordon, *Marathas, Marauders*, pp. 65 ff.

29 Berasia (district Bhopal) was the birthplace of Karim Khan. Malcolm, *Memoir*, Vol. I, p. 449.

30 Ibid.; Captain William Henley, Agent, eastern Malwa, to J. Stewart, Resident, Gwalior, 19 February 1819, NAI, FD, Central India Agency Records (hereafter CIA), file no. 45; Sydenham, 'Memorandum', p. 51. For more details on the complicated tribute-sharing formula for northeastern Malwa, involving Sindia, Holkar, Rajgarh, Narsinghgarh, Zalim Singh and the Pindaris, see Amar Farooqui, 'Towards Dussehra 1831: The Revolt of Lallaji

Patel', *Indian Economic and Social History Review*, Vol. XXXV, No. 2, 1998, pp. 165–66.

31 Herbert Compton, *A Particular Account of the European Military Adventurers of Hindustan from 1784 to 1803*, T. Fisher Unwin, London, 1892, pp. 31, 46–48, 229.

32 Jenkins, 'Memorandum', p. 26.

33 Jenkins talks of 'accessions which the result of the Mahratta wars must have brought them [the Pindaris], from the starving bodies of horses which the peace dispersed over Malwah'. Ibid.

34 Ibid.

35 Quoted in C.E. Luard and D.N. Sheopuri, *Gwalior State Gazetteer, The Central India State Gazetteer Series*, Vol. I, Thacker, Spink and Co., Calcutta, 1908, p. 33 n.

36 Sydenham, 'Memorandum', p. 40.

37 Malcolm, *Memoir*, Vol. I, p. 431.

38 Sydenham, 'Memorandum', p. 40.

39 Tod, 'Pindarras', p. 7; Sydenham, 'Memorandum', pp. 45, 55; Malcolm, *Memoir*, p. 441 n. '*Mustaqim*' means faithful, firm.

40 Sydenham, 'Memorandum', p. 48.

41 Ibid.

42 Chitu, for instance, had originally been a slave. He was probably a Jat or Meo. Tod, 'Pindarras', p. 17; Sydenham, 'Memorandum', p. 44. The Pindari leaders never really managed to settle down and so were unable to manufacture impressive genealogies for themselves. Their humble origins are reflected in the commonplace names of a number of Pindari warriors: Chitu, Hiru, Rajjan, Gangola, Jangli, Kallu, Shukku, Nathu, Tukku, Buddan, etc.

43 Malcolm, *Memoir*, Vol. I, pp. 436–37.

44 R. Cavendish, Resident, Gwalior, to Government of India, 10 January 1834, NAI, FDP, 33/29 January 1834.

45 Tod, 'Pindarras', p. 17.

46 Cf. Lord Hastings, Governor General, 'Narrative of Military and Political Operations in Hindoostan and the Deccan', 1 March 1820, NAI, FD Misc., 124/A, p. 400.

47 Letter of Tod, dated 15 September 1814, NAI, FD Misc., 124, p. 88; also cf. Sydenham, 'Memorandum', p. 55.

48 Letter to Lalaji Ballal, Kamavisdar, Jawad–Jiran, etc., 23 June 1802, Sri Nat Nagar Shodh Samsthan, Sitamau, Gulgule daftar, Vol. VII, No. 227; Madhya Pradesh State Archives, Bhopal, Sitole daftar (1805 onwards); A. Stirling, Secretary, Government of India, to Gwalior Resident, 23 May 1820(?), NAI, FD, CIA, file no. 106; NAI, Survey of India Memoirs, route book No. 36/11; Malcolm, *Memoir*, Vol. II, pp. 497–98; W. Hamilton, *East India Gazetteer*, Vol. II, W.H. Allen, London, 1828, p. 34; *Gwalior Gazetteer*, pp. 245–46, 265, 275 and 293.

49 Bengal Government to Secret Committee, 16 August 1811, NAI, FD Misc., 124/A, p. 1; Tod, 'Pindarras', p. 12; Sydenham, 'Memorandum', p. 51;

Malcolm, *Memoir*, p. 455. It is not unlikely that Zalim Singh made a large profit out of this guarantee. He was an astute banker and was engaged in various commercial dealings, including the supply of opium. One suspects that some of the Pindari chiefs might have maintained accounts with Zalim Singh and that he was willing to stand surety for such a large sum precisely because he had access to Karim Khan's deposits. Given the fact that the Pindaris led a rather insecure existence and were constantly on the move, they had to rely on the services of bankers to look after their financial arrangements. In the absence of a regular treasury this was indispensable. We learn that Dhakun (Dakhan?) Seth was the main banker of Chitu's camp. Another banker, Mowjee Ram, was also attached to Chitu. These bankers and *sahukars* advanced money to the Pindaris for purchases of horses and food, and were repaid from the proceeds of tribute collections and raiding expeditions. Sydenham, 'Memorandum', p. 49.

50 Hastings to Court of Directors, 8 February 1818, NAI, FD Misc., 124/A, pp. 204–05.

51 Hastings, 'Narrative', 124/A, p. 400; J. Blacker, Quarter-Master-General, to Major-General W.G. Keir, 6 February 1818, NAI, FD Misc., 124/A, p. 332.

52 Hastings, 'Narrative', pp. 400–01.

53 Malcolm to F. Warden, Secretary, Bombay Government, 17 February 1818, NAI, FD Misc., 124/A, p. 238.

54 R. Close, Resident, Gwalior, to Major Henley, Agent, eastern Malwa, 4 November 1821; *Sanad* from Daulat Rao Sindia to Jaswant Rao, 2 Muharram 1222 fasli, tr. NAI, FD, CIA, file no. 102.

55 NAI, Survey of India Memoirs, 36/11; *Gwalior Gazetteer*, p. 275.

56 Canning, quoted in C.H. Philips, *The East India Company 1784–1834*, Orient Longman, Bombay, 1961, p. 215.

57 Major Ross-of-Blandensburg, *The Marquess of Hastings*, Clarendon Press, Oxford, 1893, p. 113.

58 Ibid., p. 130.

59 Major R. Clarke to Captain W. Henley, 14 January 1818, FD, Misc., 124/A, p. 303.

60 Malcolm, *Memoir*, Vol. I, p. 431.

61 Ibid.

62 Sydenham, 'Memorandum', p. 41.

63 Ibid., p. 40.

64 Ibid.

65 H. Pottinger, Collector, Ahmadnagar, to M. Elphinstone, 16 May 1818, FD Misc., 124/A, p. 285.

66 Malcolm, *Memoir*, Vol. I, p. 276 n.

67 A. MacDonald, Assistant to J. Malcolm, 'Report relative to Dewas', 1 November 1818, NAI, FD, CIA, file no. 78.

68 Malcolm, *Memoir*, Vol. I, p. 288.

69 Lt. Gen. T. Hislop to Governor-General, 2 February 1818, NAI, FD Misc., 124/A, p. 231; P.V. Agnew, on a mission to Holkar's court, to Malcolm, 18 February 1818, NAI, FD Misc., 124, pp. 346–47.

[70] Malcolm, *Memoir,* Vol. I, p. 288.

[71] Hislop to Governor General, 2 February 1818, NAI, FD Misc., 124/A, p. 231.

[72] Blacker to Keir, 6 February 1818, NAI, FD Misc., 124/A, p. 232.

[73] In his analysis of Bhil motives in collaborating with this subversive coalition, Guha states that the Bhils 'were not isolated remnant populations savagely defending themselves against inexorably encroaching civilization —rather they were determined to share in the goods that civilization could yield, and to secure this they were prepared to use their mutual solidarity, their knowledge of the hills and forests, of the paths and water-resources, their capacity for guerrilla war, as assets to be traded in the regional political arena. They could be allies of the Mughals, of Holkar, and offer refuge to the last Peshwa himself.' Guha, *Environment and Ethnicity,* p. 110.

[74] Malcolm, *Memoir,* Vol. I, p. 447.

[75] Ibid., pp. 447–48; R.N. Hamilton, Resident, Gwalior, to H.M. Elliot, Secretary, Government of India, 22 July 1850, NAI, FD, CIA, file no. 129.

[76] Malcolm, *Memoir,* Vol. I, p. 522 and n.

[77] Thakur Salim Singh and Kunwar Bhim Singh of Bagli to Major W. Henley, 1877 (Samvat), tr. NAI, FD, CIA, file no. 129.

[78] Hamilton to Elliot, 11 July 1850, NAI, FD, CIA, file no. 129.

[79] Cf. Hastings, 'Narrative', p. 396.

[80] Chitu only had five adherents with him. Besides, there was his son, Muhammad Punnah, who was deaf and of 'a weak intellect'. Malcolm gives a vivid, and surprisingly even sympathetic, account of Chitu's death. See Malcolm, *Memoir,* Vol. I, pp. 445–49.

[81] Malcolm to Government of India, 23 March 1818, NAI, FD Misc., 124/A, p. 260; *Uttar Pradesh District Gazetteers, Gorakhpur,* Government of Uttar Pradesh, Lucknow, 1985, pp. 35–36.

[82] Translation of a petition presented by Rajun Pindarra Chief, enclosed in A. Stoneham, Superintendent of Pindarra Chiefs, Gorakhpur, to Government of India, 19 June 1823, NAI, FD, CIA, file no. 76.

[83] Sydenham, 'Memorandum', p. 42.

[84] Gordon contrasts this with the Rajput/Mughal ethos 'with its heavy cavalry (mounted on expensive imported horses), bow and arrow, curved sword, ethic of dying for the leader'. Gordon, 'Zones of Military Entrepreneurship', p. 204.

[85] Malcolm, *Memoir,* Vol. I, p. 325.

[86] Ibid., p. 203.

[87] Ibid., p. 205 n.

[88] Cf. ibid., p. 212.

[89] Ross-of-Blandensburg, *Hastings,* pp. 128–29.

[90] Malcolm to Government of India, n.d., NAI, FD, CIA, file no. 94, Jaora, doc. 7.

[91] The proximity of Amir Khan to British officials stationed in Malwa and the British perception of his role in military mobilization is indicated by the disproportionately large space devoted to Amir Khan in Malcolm's *Memoir.*

While the history of the Sindias, who ruled over the biggest indigenous state of Malwa, is dismissed in just about twenty-five pages, nearly sixty-five pages are devoted to the career of Amir Khan. See Malcolm, *Memoir*, Vol. I.

92 David Ochterlony, Resident in Malwa and Rajputana, to G. Swinton, Secretary, Government of India, 30 April 1822, in N.K. Sinha and A.K. Dasgupta (eds), *Selections from Ochterlony Papers (1818–1825)*, University of Calcutta, Calcutta, 1964, p. 244.

93 For a reappraisal of the *thagi* phenomenon, see Stewart Gordon, 'Scarf and Sword: Thugs, Marauders, and State-formation in Eighteenth-Century Malwa', in Gordon, *Marathas, Marauders*, pp. 1–22.

Of Environment, Exchange and Economic Transactions

Water Resources and Forests in Southern Rajasthan

Glimpses from Inscriptions

(Seventh–Seventeenth Centuries)

Nandini Sinha Kapur

This essay, based on inscriptional records, examines the importance of water resources in agrarian expansion in southern Rajasthan between the seventh and seventeenth centuries. It also highlights the references to forests in this period. The essay assumes importance in the context of the historiography of environmental history in precolonial South Asia. Although the scope of debates on the environmental history of colonial India is considerably large,[1] studies of the environmental history of ancient and medieval India have largely focused on issues of evolution of ecological and settlement patterns, resource utilization such as water and hydraulic machineries, forestation and deforestation, and conservation of nature. These studies range from a general discussion of the environment and its influence on history and culture,[2] early Buddhist perceptions of the significance of forests, water resources and sanctuaries,[3] archaeological findings on ecology and deforestation in pre and protohistoric South Asia,[4] to Greek literature on Indian flora and fauna.[5] Since this essay focuses mainly on water resources and forests, we will briefly highlight the research of B.D. Chattopadhyaya and Ranabir Chakravarty on irrigational projects of early medieval Rajasthan and hydraulic machines of ancient India, respectively, and Aloka Parasher Sen's work on tribes and forests in the Mauryan period.

B.D. Chattopadhyaya, in his study of irrigational projects in Rajasthan, compares and contrasts the pattern of crop production and irrigation between *c.* 700 and *c.* 1300 with an earlier period, to note changes in this pattern. Admittedly, data for early historic Rajasthan are meagre. A discussion of Rairh, Bairat, Ahar and Rang Mahal reveals that agriculture depended more on rainfall, annual floods and rivers.[6] Chattopadhyaya provides a detailed discussion of the importance of tanks, wells and *araghattas* (water-wheels) in the expansion of agricultural fields in early medieval Rajasthan. Inscriptions from Rajasthan refer to wells with three different terms: *dhimada* or *dhivada*,[7] *vapi* (stepwell), and *araghatta* or *araghata* or *arahata*. Chattopadhyaya opines that the different terms may indicate operational variations in well irrigation.[8] The relative importance of *araghattas* may be inferred from the fact that they invariably bear separate names, and from the social status of the people who seem to have transferred land irrigated by an *araghatta*.[9] A discussion on the controversy regarding the use of Persian wheels in early medieval Rajasthan is also provided.[10] The relationship between artificial irrigation and change in crop production is analysed,[11] and the detailed and critical analysis of ownership of irrigational projects, particularly in western Rajasthan (where water was scarce), is illuminating.[12]

Ranabir Chakravarty is rightly of the view that the 'choice of habitat and the growth and decay of settlement are determined, to a considerable extent, by environmental factors'.[13] Chakravarty makes the important observations, in the context of ancient India, that human settlements could alter the existing landscape; the success of agriculture depended largely on irrigation facilities; and the Gupta and post-Gupta periods witnessed continuation of many characteristics of settlement patterns and hydraulic projects of the immediately preceding period, such as creation of new settlements and the maintenance of hydraulic projects by private agencies.[14] Inscriptional evidence from early medieval Bengal indicates the creation of settlements by royal land grants[15] and irrigational projects by royal authorities and private entrepreneurs. The *Rajatarangini* reveals royal interest in hydraulic projects in the early medieval period.[16] Two new types of artificial irrigation projects—*araghatta* and *vapi*—appear in early medieval Gujarat[17] and Rajasthan, respectively,[18] while individuals and cooperatives managed hydraulic projects in early medieval south India.[19] Bengal, being a region of better rainfall, had many natural sources of irrigation in the form of small streams or rivulets (*ganginika*), marshy lands (*jolaka*) and channels (*khatika*),[20] while a semi-arid Marwar, with less rainfall, witnessed tapping of hydraulic resources at considerable depth, leading to construction of deep wells (*dhiku*) and water-wheels.[21] Thus, Chakravarty's findings complement Chattopadhyaya's study, particularly on Rajasthan. Their work highlights not only the importance of water resources in the expansion of agricultural produce but also the socio-political significance of the ownership of artificial means of irrigation, particularly in arid regions. Control over water resources in arid regions seems to have been an important source of status for the royalty.

Aloka Parasher Sen focuses on the interaction between the state and the tribals of forests in the Mauryan period.[22] It is significant that the *Arthashastra* and Ashokan edicts highlight the royal perception towards forest-dwellers, and the processes through which the Mauryan state sought to control the forests and its populations. '*Atavika*' (forest) is a repeated reference in the *Arthashastra* and Ashokan edicts, which conveys its significance—economic, strategic and political. Sen observes that 'overall, the period of Ashokan rule, on the one hand, brought a greater awareness about the need to protect animal and forest wealth, at a time when their destruction was a potent reality'.[23] Sen rightly suggests that the impact of Mauryan policies on tribal habitats has been overestimated, as historians have tended to project the Mauryan state as a monolithic state.[24] It seems that the Mauryan intrusion into forests disturbed the socio-economic texture of life of the tribals. Disturbance of tribal habitats did not necessarily mean large-scale 'peasantization' of tribes, but a disruption of many of the food-gathering and hunting localities, particularly those bordering the plains. These areas came to depend on the produce of the plains, while large-scale forest resources began to be exploited by the 'metropolitan society'.[25]

The above survey offers us a macro-perspective of precolonial South Asia, including a big region like Rajasthan, highlighting the symbiotic relationship between man and his environment, natural resources and their utilization, tribals, their habitats and interactions with agrarian cultures.

In the background of these macro-studies, the case study of a micro-region like Mewar offers us a chronological survey of the natural environment, its function in an agrarian economy, its conservation and degradation, and human projects to manage the depleted natural resources.

A brief introduction to the geography of the region of Mewar highlights a differentiation in space, accounting for distinct sub-regions with their own nuclear or core areas and peripheries. The sub-regions of the Mewar hills and upper Banas plain comprise the territory popularly known as 'Mewar'. It consists of the districts of Udaipur,

Chittaurgarh and Bhilwara. The Mewar hills cover the whole of Udaipur district except its two eastern *tehsils*, Mavali and Vallabhnagar, the recently formed district of Rai Samand (carved out of Udaipur district), and the southeastern margin of Pali district. It touches the northern portions of the middle Mahi basin, which is largely occupied by the Bhil and Gerasia tribes. The agricultural activities are mainly confined to the valley of the Berach, its smaller tributaries and the area north of the Mahi river. This sub-region is situated between the Banas plain and the Abu block. The highest part of the Mewar hills is the Bhorat plateau (1,202 metres).[26] The rainfall is moderate (50–100 cm).[27] Its southeastern part is densely forested and the southwest is covered with jungle scrub and grass, closely-packed ridges and valleys ridden with boulder-strewn river beds.[28] Hence, its western and southern hills are unable to sustain agricultural activity because of the forests and inhospitable terrain. This sub-region has red and yellow soils in the northwest and ferruginous red soil in the southern parts.[29] It produces crops like maize, wheat, barley, gram and oilseeds. Agricultural activities are mainly confined to the valley of the Berach and its smaller tributaries. The sub-region is rich in mineral resources, especially copper, zinc, lead and silver (Zawar mines),[30] and a major route of communication in the early medieval period ran from Delhi–Agra to Malwa and Champaner–Dohad in Gujarat via Ahada in Mewar.[31] The other significant feature of this sub-region is the concentration of a tribal population on the Bhorat plateau and the adjoining hills. Here lies the land predominantly occupied by the Bhils. Even today, many of them practise shifting agriculture.[32] The Bhil-occupied territory of the Mewar hills is popularly known as Bhomat. Bhomat is again divided by a massive mountain range into a south-western division known as the Kotra Bhomat[33] and a part of the Merwara region that is inhabited by the tribe of Mers (Meda): Merwara is that portion of the Aravalli chain that runs between Kumbhalmer (Kumbhalgarh) and Ajmer.[34]

The upper Banas plain is the other sub-region of Mewar. This sub-region comprises the three districts of Bhilwara, Chittaurgarh and Rajsamand, and the two eastern *tehsils* of Udaipur district, Mavali and Vallabhnagar. It is an elevated plain drained by the Banas and its tributaries, the Khari Kothari, Berach, Gambhiri and Wagan.[35] The variety of soils ranges from thin to black in the western and southern parts. Extensive cultivation of maize, wheat, cotton, sugarcane and other crops is the dominant feature of agricultural activities. Cotton is predominantly grown on the pattern of the black soil belt of Bhilwara and Chittaurgarh districts. While the northern and central parts of Mewar have high cropping incidence, its western part, covering almost the whole of Udaipur district, has as low a cropping incidence as 52 per cent and below.[36] Excavations at Ahar, Bhairat valley and Rairh have yielded evidence of millet, rice, jowar, wheat and cotton cultivation.[37] B.D. Chattopadhyaya writes:

> while the location of the three sites indicates their possible sources of water supply, the evidence seems to be more specific at Rang Mahal, where in early times a high rainfall rate and annual flooding of the Ghaggar, facilitating rice cultivation, have been suggested. If these instances are taken to form any generalization regarding the early historic period, the organization of artificial irrigation in early medieval Rajasthan certainly constitutes a departure from the earlier pattern.[38]

A brief survey of the early historic sites in Mewar enables us to contrast their sources of water with those of early medieval Mewar. Nagari (11 miles to the north of the present city of Chittaurgarh), the capital town of the *janapada* of the Sibis (the first known political centre of ancient Mewar), has not yielded any specimen indicating an artificial source of irrigation.[39] Inscriptions from Nandsa-Yapa (Bhilwara district) and Chhoti-Sadri (Chittaurgarh district), highlighting the political, economic and religious importance of these two centres, do not reveal any artificial means of irrigation for these settlements.[40] It is important to note that all the above early historical sites were located on river banks.

Southern Rajasthan witnessed a process of local state formation and agrarian expansion in the early medieval period. It is significant that irrigational works, both individual and royal enterprises, figure in the records in the context of land grants and rural settlements. In the kingdom of the Kiskindha Guhilas, a number of irrigational projects were owned by notable members of the rural society. The Dungarpur plates of Babhata refer to a reservoir and a tank owned by Rongaraka and Pahaka, respectively.[41] This record also refers to a well named Kaccho[42] as one of the boundaries of the donated fields. The fact that these irrigational works contributed to agricultural production in the village of Mitrapallika is evident from the mention of specific quantities of yields from the donated fields. For instance, the field named Pahakapabhaka yielded five units of grains.[43]

Similar instances come from the district of Bhilwara. The village of Dhavagarta (modern Dhor, in Jahazpur *tehsil*) was a flourishing agricultural settlement in the seventh century. The Dabok inscription of the reign of the Mori king Dhavalappadeva (AD 641) refers to *saradya graismaka* fields (fields that can be tilled in autumn as well as in summer), indicating double-cropping.[44] This record also refers to *graismakaksetradi* (fields yielding crops in summer) and *saradyaksetradi* (fields yielding crops in autumn).[45] Different irrigational works in this village were owned by individuals and royalty. Two boundaries of donated fields are mentioned as *vahiyalinamaraghattaksetram* (field that was irrigated by an *araghatta* named *vahiyali*) and *Rajakiya-araghattakulya* (an *araghatta* owned by the royal house).[46] This record also mentions another field irrigated by an *araghatta*[47] (*tatha kakkatadaka cagrata-araghattaksetram*)[48] and a water reservoir on the south of one of the granted fields.[49] The fact that the Dabok inscription refers to a large number of fields owned by different individuals indicates sufficient agricultural production. The above irrigational projects and agricultural production undoubtedly contributed to the revenue base of the local Guhila state, and indicate a stratified rural society.

Udaipur district witnessed the opening up of new settlements in the forests in this period. The Samoli inscription of AD 646 records the opening up of an *akara* (a mine) at a place called Aranyakupagiri and the building of a temple of the goddess Aranyavasini by a migrating community from Vatanagar (Sirohi district).[50] The terms Aranyakupagiri and Aranyavasini indicate a forest and a hilly terrain. The name Aranyavasini (she who dwells in the forest) indicates that the temple was dedicated to the goddess of a local tribal population. Hence, the mine was opened up in the Bhil domain of Udaipur district. The mine can be tentatively located either in the zinc–lead–silver mines of Zawar (40 kilometres south of Udaipur), or in the copper belt around Udaipur. It is important to note that the Zawar mines came into operation in the seventh century—precisely the period of the beginning of the process of local state formation in Mewar.[51] The record points towards two successive stages in the development of the settlement called Aranyakupagiri. This small settlement in the hilly forested area of the tribals already had a well (*kupa*), or wells, as a means of artificial irrigation. This technology is likely to have been introduced by the migrating community in a semi-arid, hilly, tribal locality with a pre-agricultural settlement. Wells seem to have provided the best possible means of artificial irrigation in the boulder-strewn hills. Similar instances of opening up of settlements with *kupas* in the country of the Abhiras come from the Jodhpur area in the ninth century.[52]

Hence, wells seem to have played a significant role in sustaining and expanding agricultural yields within these settlements. Moreover, the area witnessed deforestation along with increasing agricultural production on the arrival of *mahajanas* at Aranyakupagiri. Besides the need for agricultural land, supply of raw materials from the surrounding forests to the nearest nodes in the Guhila kingdom, Nagda and Ahada, might have necessitated some degree of deforestation. Finally, Aranyakupagiri as a centre of mining and the presence of the temple of Aranyavasini meant the emergence of a workshop-cum-exchange centre at this settlement (the temple of Aranyavasini is stated to have been visited by bards from far and near, indicating occasional festivities necessitating weekly or occasional fairs).[53] Therefore, routes connecting Aranyakupagiri with Nagda and Ahada would have resulted in some amount of deforestation.

The phenomenon of deforestation possibly assumes significance in view of the emergence of new settlements in the post-ninth century. Inscriptional records list quite a few commercial, religious and politically important centres between the tenth and thirteenth centuries in Mewar. The emergence of temple centres such as Ekalingaji at Nagda (north of Udaipur) and Kankroli near the copper mines at Dariba, is likely to have caused some degree of deforestation, as clearances were needed for agricultural activities to sustain temples and *mathas*. The fact that the Ekalingaji temple emerged as a royal temple complex in the tenth century must have necessitated mobilization of additional agricultural resources. It is important to remember that the Ekalingaji temple inscription recording the construction of this temple in AD 971 does not mention any village as a land grant to the temple. Absence of grants of land would indicate intensification of agricultural activities at Nagda and in its surrounding hills, to sustain this royal temple complex. The opening up of the Dariba copper mines and the emergence of a pilgrimage centre (a temple dedicated to a goddess) at nearby Kankroli would have involved a similar process.[54]

Perhaps the most obvious indicator of the process of deforestation is the absence of reference to forest routes in the post-seventh century records.

It is significant that the term *vanamarggah* (forest routes), which figured in a land grant of the seventh century from the Guhila kingdom of Kiskindha,[55] is absent in the post-seventh century land-grant charters from Mewar, such as the Pratapgarh grant of the Guhila king Bhartribhatta in the Chhappan area, dated AD 942. The Pratapgarh inscription recording the grant of a field named Vavvulika by Bhartribhatta to God Indrajaditya in the village of Palasakupika near Dasapura (modern Mandasaur), does not mention forests or forest routes[56] as boundaries of the village. Some degree of deforestation must have been an ongoing process around the areas of Pratapgarh and Mandasaur in the tenth century. On the other hand, rural settlements dotted this landscape, as they figure in the grants made by others to the same temple complex.

It is significant that royal grants were usually situated near sources of water. They were thus assured of sustained agricultural production. The northern boundary of the field Vavvulika touched the stream Nandya. Also, the presence of wells in this village is clearly evident from its name, Palasakupika. The mention of the stream in the Pratapgarh inscription indicates its significance for the agricultural fields along its banks. This point is clearly evident from the mention of a number of fields as boundaries of the donated field, Vavvulika.[57] It is important that Palasakupika was linked to the village of Varahapalligrama by road.[58] There is a possibility that this village was also located on some part of the stream Nandya.

A separate plate of a Pratapgarh inscription dated AD 946 records the grant of a field named Chhittullaka, in which ten *mani*s of seeds could be sown and which was irrigated by one leather bucket,[59] in favour of God Indradityadeva at Ghontavarsika, by Cahamana Devaraja.[60] Madhava, a governor of the Pratiharas from Ujjain, donated a field irrigated by an *araghatta* located on the bank of a river (possibly on the northern side of Dharapadraka, identified with modern Dharavad in Mewar, near the boundary of the Pratapgarh state).[61]

*Araghatta*s and devices like leather buckets seem to have become popular means of artificial irrigation by the tenth century. It is also evident from these records that water-wheels and similar devices were suitable for fields which were located near river banks. These fields are likely to have been connected to rivers through water channels. The Pratapgarh inscriptions give us an idea of clusters of agricultural settlements with well-irrigated fields, drawing water from streams, rivers and wells.

We shall now shift our focus to northcentral Rajasthan. The Guhilas of Nagda–Ahada extended their power to the arid region of Pali, north of Mewar, in the eleventh century. As the ecology changed, so did the ownership of water resources. It is important to remind ourselves that irrigation works, reservoirs, etc., were owned more by individual entrepreneurs than by the government in Mewar (southern Rajasthan) between the seventh and tenth centuries. But the Kadmal plates of AD 1083, recording the grant of revenue by the Guhila king Vijayasimha in the village of Palli (modern Pali), give us an entirely different picture. This inscription records the donation of a fifth of the produce of the village of Palli, embracing all its receipts, to Unal-acharya, son of Acharya Sahiya, a resident of Nagahrada (Nagda) but whose son had probably migrated to Palli.[62] The donee was given full rights over the fifth part of every item of produce of the donated village to the extent of its boundaries, with the exception of the income of taxes and drainage, of which he received only half (that is, a one-tenth part), the other half going to the donor himself (the Guhila king Vijayasimha).[63] If not identical, a similar instance comes from Bolera (Marwar division), where a royal land grant was made in AD 994 to a brahmana, Shri Dirghacharya. It consisted of a piece of land with a share of only one-third of the water from a well (*Ghaghalikupa-tribhagodakena saha*).[64] That water was an important administrative concern in this area, is evident from royal initiative in the necessary work of construction and the nature of gift specifications.

The above evidences are important enough to probe into the nature of ownership of water resources. Chattopadhyaya asks, 'How was artificial irrigation socially organized? This question is particularly pertinent to western Rajasthan where water was scarce.'[65] An examination of the patrons of artificial irrigation works and the major beneficiaries of grants of facilities for artificial irrigation would focus on the social control of water resources. An inscriptional survey of early medieval Rajasthan reveals that grants of irrigational facilities emanated largely from the rulers and their officials. Sometimes, notable members of rural society also owned an *araghatta*.[66] This becomes rare in later times, although epigraphic references to *araghattas* are far more numerous in the later period. Apart from dynasties, the *panchakulas* (executive bodies mostly appointed by the king[67]) also transferred land and *araghattas* to brahmana donees and religious establishments and, in some cases, entrusted them with the supervision of cesses from *araghatta* fields.[68] The beneficiaries mostly consisted of brahmanas, temples, songstresses and musicians attached to temples in early medieval Rajasthan. On the basis of inscriptional survey, Chattopadhyaya observes: 'in early medieval Rajasthan [there is] a certain positive correlation between . . . "induced" irrigation organization and a general growth in agricultural production. . . . Irrigational efforts could and did to a certain extent generate economic and social power, albeit at microscopic political-spatial levels.'[69]

Hence, the state retained rights over water resources in the arid region of Pali. Without getting into the debate on the Asiatic mode of production, we can observe that the nature of royal grants in Pali indicates a certain amount of political control over water resources in the arid parts of Rajasthan. The point is that the Guhila state was obviously interested in diverting the resources from the newly acquired region of Palli towards Mewar. The Guhila state legitimized the exercise of its power in the Palli territory through a brahmana donee; it carefully retained governmental authority over the scarce resources of an arid region. Exercise of governmental authority over water resources in an arid region would indicate attempts towards Guhila control over the revenue from Pali.

Thirteenth-century records from Mewar refer to lakes/reservoirs in the context of donated land and temple centres. The Tamtarada family, in its record of AD 1274, refers to the Kalelaya lake in the village of Chirakupa, near which the donated land for the temples of Yogeshvara and Yogeshvari were situated.[70] Lake Kalelaya seems to have been maintained by the local elite of Chirakupa, and its water shared by them. The economic significance of this lake is clearly evident from its mention in the context of donated land. The donated land/fields were likely to have been irrigated by the lake. One of the older tanks at the Chittaurgarh fortress, Chitranga, continues to appear in a thirteenth-century record, indicating its maintenance and utility in this period. A Chittaurgarh pillar inscription of AD 1287, of the reign of the Guhila king Samarsimha, records the grant of a few *dramma* coins to the temple of Vaidyanatha, situated on the bank of the

Chitranga tank, by Vijada, son of Pachasiga.[71] The Chitranga tank seems to have been an important source of water inside the fortresss of Chittaurgarh for a very long time. The local elite and patrons of temples are likely to have maintained this tank.

*Araghatta*s continued to be an important source of artificial irrigation in the district of Udaipur in the twelfth century. Royal grants continued to be made in the vicinity of *araghatta*s. A land-grant charter of King Padmasimha of AD 1194 records the grant of land located in the vicinity of an *araghatta* named Gajana in the domain (estate) of Cahamana Rao Mokaja in the village of Kadmal, to a brahmana named Sivaguna, as a source of livelihood.[72] The fact that royal donations consisted of land situated near *araghatta*s indicates the premium attached to irrigated fields in southern Rajasthan. The piece of land apparently yielded sufficient amount of crops, as the land was meant for the donee's 'livelihood'.

The process of deforestation in the tribal belt of Merwara could have begun on a limited scale in the fifteenth century, with the construction of the royal fortress of Kumbhalgarh by Maharana Kumbha. Maharana Kumbha granted the village of Kachhar to the brahmana Godha Gohad, in AD 1453.[73] Land grants in the tribal tract of Merwara (occupied by the Medas/Mers) were essential for obvious political and economic reasons. However, the presence of villages in Merwara pre-dates Kumbha's arrival in this tribal tract, and indicates the emergence of rural centres under private entrepreneurship. Hence, the Guhila state alone might not have been responsible for deforestation but is likely to have accelerated such a process around the fortress of Kumbhalgarh by building roads and bringing land under cultivation. However, the rocky nature of Merwara might have increased the royal dependence on the existing villages, thereby initiating deforestation around those villages to mobilize additional resources for the administrative centre at Kumbhalgarh. Our sources indicate only one royal land grant in Merwara in the fifteenth century. This definitely indicates the difficulties and limitations of agricultural expansion in a hilly, forested terrain with scarce water resources.

Lakes continued to be an important means of irrigation in the Nagda–Ahada belt in the fifteenth century. The village of Thura (near Ahada), granted to Guru Gopalabhatta by Rana Raimalla, is described as consisting of lakes full of lotuses, fruit trees, rows of rice fields irrigated by water, a fine rosary of Mudgas and fields of sweet sugarcane.[74]

It is significant that an official record chooses to highlight the lakes and irrigated rice fields. This indicates the continuing importance of sources of water and irrigated fields in southern Rajasthan. We are able to locate some of the villages donated to the temple of Ekalingaji in the late fourteenth and fifteenth centuries in the tribal belt of Bhomat—the Bhil dominion in the district of Udaipur. Villages west of Nagda and Chirava, such as Panavadapur, Rama, Paner, Simvallipur and Kathadavan, can essentially be plotted on a map of Bhomat.[75] This points towards the gradual process of agricultural expansion in those areas of the forests of Bhomat which seem to have had some sources of water.

The royal initiative in harvesting water for the economic growth of Mewar can be best seen in the construction of a huge lake, the Raja-samudra, in the northern part of Udaipur district in the seventeenth century. Maharana Rajasimha had initiated the excavation of a few more lakes in the same district before the commencement of the construction of Rajasamudra. These lakes were excavated in those villages which had the requisite water table. The *Rajaprashasti Mahakavyam* refers to the excavation of a new lake, 'Janasagar', at the village of Bari. The excavation of this lake cost Rs 6,80,000.[76] The Maharana donated the villages of Devapura and Gunahanda to the priest Garibdas. On the same day, the crown prince Maharajakumar Jayasimha laid the foundations of 'Rangasar' lake in the city of Udaipur.[77]

The *Rajaprashasti* records the construction of the Rajasamudra lake as follows. Crown prince Rajasimha, on his way to Jaisalmer (during his wedding procession), decided to construct a lake on the boundaries of the villages of Dhayonda, Sanwar, Sivali, Bhigavada, Morchana, Pasund, Kheri, Chhaparkheri, Tasol, Mandavar, Bhana, Luhana, Bansol, Gudali, Kankroli and Madha.[78] Rajasimha acceded to the throne in AD 1718 and decided to launch the project of Rajasamudra in consultation with his chief priest. This project was supervised by different departments headed by various *samantas*.[79] Details of the engineering are vividly described. The flow of the Gomti river was obstructed by building a *mahasetu* (big bridge/sluice-gates) between two big hills.[80] A huge labour force was deployed to dig out water. A large number of *araghattas* were utilized for this purpose. Architects and villagers were also advised regarding the water table. Water gushed out and was carried to the villages listed above by canals.[81] The significance of these canals for irrigating fields is more than obvious. Once the water was tapped, the occasion for laying the foundation stone was fixed for the day of *Vaishakh Shukla*, 13th, Monday, 1721.[82] When the architects saw multi-coloured fish and turtles coming out from the other side of the bridge, they were able to predict the depth of the water.[83] The next to be undertaken was the project of building a bridge at the village of Kankroli (a mining centre).[84] Rains arrived in summer, filling up a part of the lake at Kankroli, leading to the strong masonry work (the bridge) spreading over eight years, five months and six days.

A palace, 'Rajamandira', was built on the banks of the reservoir at Kankroli in AD 1726.[85] A boat-launching ceremony was planned. But Rajasamudra did not have sufficient water for boats to sail.[86] Since there was no hope of another auspicious occasion in the near future for this ceremony, Ranavat Ramasimha, the chief manager of the Rajasamudra project, suggested that the lake be artificially filled with water for launching the boat.[87] Rains arrived soon on the performance of '*Varunasukta jap*', and Maharana Rajasimha sailed in the boat. [88] The architects closed the mouth of a canal on royal order.[89] Simultaneous embellishments at older lakes were a part of the overall project. A pavilion was built at the lake of Indrasar (Indrasarovar) at Ekalingaji, along with four new gates.[90] Details of the measurements of the main bridge over Rajasamudra are mentioned,[91] as well as details of other measurements.[92] Four structures/altars were built at the four corners of the bridge. The altar facing Rajamandira had an *araghatta* (Persian wheel) which carried water to the gardens of this temple.[93] Other bridges that were built are listed as follows: Nimba bridge, 432 *gaz* in length; Bhadra bridge, 144 *gaz* in length; bridges at the villages of Kankroli, 550 *gaz* in length; Asotia, 2,068 *gaz* in length; Vansol, 1,224 *gaz* in length.[94]

The three rivers of Mewar, the Gomti, Tal and Kelva, merged into Rajasamudra.[95] The bordering area, and a total of thirty reservoirs, tanks and wells, of the villages of Sivali, Bhingavada, Bhanah, Luhana, Vansol, Gudhali, Pasunda, Kheri, Chhaparkheri, Tasol, Mandavar, Kankroli and Sivali, were submerged by Rajasamudra.[96] The total length of the main bridge covering the lake measured 6,413 *gaz.*[97] The *Rajaprashasti* also mentions that, according to the divine engineer Viswakarma, the maximum length of any reservoir should be 6,000 *gaz.*[98] Hence, Ranachoda Bhatta (composer of the *Rajaprashasti Mahakavyam*) eulogized Rajasimha for having built such a long reservoir.[99] Ranachoda mentions that Maharana Udaisimha (sixteenth century) had made a similar attempt in the past but could not succeed; hence, he built Udaisagar.[100] Floods on the rivers Tal and Gomti largely added to the waters of Rajasamudra.[101] Architects from Lahore, Gujarat and Surat came to see the launching of boats on Rajasamudra.[102] Markets and camps were set up on its banks[103] dealing in grains and foodstuff.[104] Rajasimha's queen, Rani Shri Ramrasde, built a well at the embankment at Debari, costing Rs 24,000.[105] Another queen, a Rathaur princess, built a well at Rajanagar, costing Rs 30,000.[106]

The building of these wells and *araghatta*s attached to Rajasamudra undoubtedly indicates their irrigational capacity for the fields and gardens in all the villages listed above. The setting up of markets was an outcome of the increased agricultural production in the villages around Rajasamudra. We have already noted that canals from this lake carried water to the villages. Rajasimha made a donation of '*pancalangal*' (*mahadan*), consisting of five golden ploughshares and the village Bhavli.[107]

However, the environmental cost of such huge projects is evident from the mention of the submergence of fields and villages during the excavation of Rajasamudra.[108] A sense of loss and compensation is echoed when Ranachoda Bhatta justifies the flooding of villages in terms of the transformation of these submerged villages into pilgrimage centres (newly created lakes?), and says that these villages would henceforth serve not only mankind but also aquatic animals[109] and submerged trees.[110] Even forests were submerged. The description that forests where lions used to roar now abounded in the sound of water indicates the scale of devastation.[111] However, ultimately, the environmental and economic importance of Rajasamudra for a semi-arid region like Mewar was more significant than the costs involved.

This essay has highlighted the socio-economic significance of two important components of the environment, water and forest, in precolonial southern Rajasthan. This case study can perhaps be situated in the context of the historiography of the theme briefly discussed in the beginning. If the research on water and forest resources in ancient India by Ranabir Chakravarty and Aloka Parasher Sen broaden our perspective and knowledge of environmental history, B.D. Chattopadhyaya's work on early medieval Rajasthan focuses on the scope of a similar project in a semi-arid region. The long time-frame of one thousand years of the environmental history of an important sub-region of Rajasthan highlights the changes and continuity in the pattern of utilization of two resources: water and forest. If wells and *araghattas* initiated expansion of agricultural yield, streams, lakes and reservoirs continued to be important sources of water throughout the period. Royal control over water resources in arid localities like Pali points towards governmental authority over revenue in a newly-acquired territory. Individual ownership of artificial means of irrigation focuses on the social aspect of water resources. The drying up of the water table resulted in the construction of the huge lake of Rajasamudra in the seventeenth century. The description of the submergence of villages, wells and forests by Rajasamudra indicates the scale of environmental problems faced by the state and rural society in the late medieval period. But the state of Mewar seems to have managed this crisis through its entrepreneurship. State-engineered water resources helped to sustain agricultural production and bring back the grain market into the economy of southern Rajasthan.

Notes and References

1 The literature on the environmental history of colonial India is vast. The range includes Ramachandra Guha, *The Unquiet Woods: Ecological Change and Peasant Resistance in the Himalaya*, Oxford University Press, Delhi, 1989; Madhav Gadgil and Ramachandra Guha, *This Fissured Land: An Ecological History of India*, Oxford University Press, Delhi, 1992; Richard H. Grove, *Green Imperialism: Colonial Expansion, Tropical Islands, Edens and the Origins of Environmentalism, 1600–1860*, Cambridge University Press, Cambridge, 1995; Vinita Damodaran, Satpal Sangwan and Richard H. Grove (eds), *Nature and Orient: The Environmental History of South and South-east Asia*, Oxford University Press, Delhi, 1998; Mahesh Rangarajan, *Fencing the Forests: Conservation and Ecological Change in India's Central Province: 1860–1914*, Oxford University Press, Delhi, 1996; Chetan Singh, *Natural Premises: Ecology and Peasant Life in the Western Himalaya: 1800–1950*, Oxford University Press, Delhi–Calcutta–Chennai, 1998.

2 For instance, see M.K. Dhavalikar, 'Environment: Its Influence on History and Culture in Western India', *Indica*, Vol. 33, No. 2, September 1996, pp. 81–118.

3 Meena V. Talim, 'Forests, Ponds and Sanctuaries in Ancient India', *Indica*, Vol. 33, No. 1, March 1996, pp. 1–10.

4 Bridget Allchin, 'Early Man and Environment in South Asia 10000 BC–AD 500', in Damodaran, Sangwan and Grove (eds), *Nature and Orient*, pp. 29–50; George Erdosy, 'Deforestation in Pre and Proto-historic South Asia', ibid., pp. 51–69.

5 J. Donald Hughes, 'Early Ecological Knowledge of India from Alexander and Aristotle to Aelian', ibid., pp. 70–86.

[6] B.D. Chattopadhyaya, 'Irrigation in Early Medieval Rajasthan', *Journal of the Economic and Social History of the Orient*, Vol. XVI, Pts II–III, p. 301.

[7] *Epigraphia Indica*, XIII, pp. 208–20; *Indian Antiquary*, XLV, pp. 77 f.

[8] Ibid., p. 305.

[9] Ibid.

[10] Ibid., pp. 303–04, fn. 6.

[11] Ibid., pp. 308–10.

[12] Ibid., pp. 311–16.

[13] Ranabir Chakravarty, 'The Creation and Expansion of Settlements and Management of Hydraulic Resources in Ancient India', in Damodaran, Sangwan and Grove (eds), *Nature and Orient*, p. 87.

[14] Ibid.

[15] Kamalakanta Gupta, *Copper-Plates of Sylhet*, Lipika Enterprises, Sylhet, 1967, pp. 76–77; D.C. Sircar, *Epigraphic Discourses in East Pakistan*, cited in Chakravarty, 'Creation and Expansion of Settlements', p. 98.

[16] Pandeya Ramtej Shastri, *Rajatarangini: A Chronicle of the Kings of Kashmir*, Pandit Pustakalaya, Banaras, 1960.

[17] V.K. Jain, *Trade and Traders in Western India (AD 1000–1300)*, Munshiram Manoharlal, New Delhi, 1990, pp. 24–34.

[18] Chattopadhyaya, 'Irrigation in Early Medieval Rajasthan'.

[19] Chakravarty, 'Creation and Expansion of Settlements', p. 99; B.D. Chattopadhyaya, *Aspects of Rural Settlements and Rural Society in Early Medieval India*, Institute of Social Sciences, Calcutta, 1990, pp. 90–120.

[20] Chakravarty, 'Creation and Expansion of Settlements', p. 101.

[21] Ibid., Chattopadhyaya, 'Irrigation in Early Medieval Rajasthan', pp. 306–10.

[22] Aloka Parasher Sen, 'Of Tribes, Hunters and Barbarians: Forest Dwellers in the Mauryan Period', *Studies in History*, Vol. 14, No. 2, July–December 1998, pp. 173–91.

[23] Ibid., p. 189.

[24] Ibid.

[25] Ibid., p. 191.

[26] R.L. Singh, *India: A Regional Geography*, National Geographical Society of India, Varanasi–New Delhi, p. 557.

[27] Ibid.

[28] Morris Carstairs, 'The Bhils of Kotra Bhomat', *Eastern Anthropologist*, Vol. VII, Nos 3 and 4, 1953–54, pp. 169–81.

[29] V.C. Misra, *Geography of Rajasthan*, National Book Trust, New Delhi, 1967, p. 173.

[30] Ibid., pp. 110–11.

[31] Jain, 'Trade and Traders in Western India', see map on p. 111.

[32] O.H. Spate, *India, Pakistan and Ceylon*, Methuen, London, 1972, p. 627.

[33] Carstairs, 'Bhils of Kotra Bhomat', p. 169.

[34] Ibid., p. 181.

[35] *Gazetteer of Chittaurgarh*, Government of Rajasthan, Jaipur, 1977, p. 15.

[36] R.K. Dhabai, *Regional Structure of Mewar*, M.Phil. dissertation, Centre for

Studies in Regional Development, Jawaharlal Nehru University, 1975 (unpublished), see map on Link Routes.

[37] H.D. Sankalia, S.B. Deo and Z.D. Ansari, *Excavations at Ahar (Tambavati)*, Deccan College of Archaeology, Poona, 1969, pp. 217, 236, Appendix II; Vishnu-Mittre, 'Remains of Rice and Millet', pp. 229–35; K.N. Puri, *Excavations at Rairh during 1938–39 and 1931–40*, Department of Archaeology and Historical Research, Jaipur (n.d.), Nos 81, 82, 103, pp. 58–61.

[38] Chattopadhyaya, 'Irrigation in Early Medieval Rajasthan', p. 301.

[39] D.R. Bhandarkar, *The Archaeological Remains and Excavations at Nagari*, Memoirs of the Archaeological Survey of India, No. 4, Calcutta, 1927, p. 127.

[40] The Nandsa–Yupa inscription is dated AD 226, *Epigraphia Indica*, Vol. XXVII, pp. 25ff. See the Bhawarmata inscription and one more inscriptional record, both dated fifth century, *Epigraphia Indica*, Vol. XXX, pp. 120–27.

[41] D.C. Sircar, *The Guhilas of Kiskindha*, Sanskrit College, Calcutta, 1965, pp. 74–75.

[42] Ibid., p. 75, 1. Kupakaccho.

[43] *Pahakapabhakabhidhanapanchikaparimanam kshetram*, ibid., pp. 74, I.13.

[44] *Epigraphia Indica*, Vol. XX , pp. 122–25 , ll.4, 6, 10.

[45] Ibid., l.12.

[46] Ibid., p. 124, ll.7–8.

[47] In the majority of the translations of early medieval Rajasthani inscriptions, the term *araghatta* has been translated as either 'machine-well' or 'Persian wheel' (*Progress Report of Archaeological Survey of India, Western Circle, 1916–17*, p. 65). Irfan Habib, in 'Technological Changes and Society: Thirteenth and Fourteenth Centuries' (Presidential Address, Medieval India Section, 31st Session of the Indian History Congress, Varanasi, December 1969), argues that the alleged references to Persian wheels in early India relate more to the '*noria*' meant for drawing water 'near surface, or from a river', and in which 'there is no hint either of a chain carrying the pots, or of any gearing'. Habib places the introduction of Persian wheels proper in India in the thirteenth–fourteenth centuries as part of its diffusion from the Arab world. There has been an attempt at equating the *ghatiyantra* (a device for drawing water from a well) with the Persian wheel. Chattopadhyaya disputes M.C. Joshi's equation of a 'rotary motion well' (possibly a *ghatiyantra*) of Mandasor inscription 532 with a Persian wheel ('Irrigation in Early Medieval Rajasthan', pp. 303–04, fn. 6). Sculptures from early medieval Rajasthan show wheels with pots set on a well (R.C. Agrawala, 'Persian Wheel in Rajasthani Sculpture', *Man in India*, Vol. 46, 1966, pp. 87–88). Chattopadhyaya, on the basis of the above evidences, observes that to be set on a big well, the wheel carrying the pots required the mechanism of a chain, but the gearing mechanism which facilitated the use of animal power is likely to have come at a later stage ('Irrigation in Early Medieval Rajasthan', p. 304). It is interesting to note that sometimes human labour was also used in *araghatta* operation in early medieval Rajasthan. See the

Nanana plates dated the first half of the twelfth century, (*Epigraphia Indica*, Vol. XXXIII, pp. 238–46).

48 Ibid., 1.7.

49 Ibid., l.6, *dakshinatah tatokodakam.*

50 *Epigraphia Indica*, Vol. XX, pp. 99–100.

51 Paul Craddock, Freestone, Gurjar, Middleton and Willies, 'The Production of Lead , Silver, and Zinc in Early India', in A. Hauptmann, E. Prinicka and G.A. Wagner (eds), *Old World Archaeometry*, Deutsches Bergalu Museum, Bochum, 1989, p. 56.

52 Ghatiyala inscription of Kakkuka of AD 859, *Epigraphia Indica*, Vol. IX, pp. 210 ff.

53 Samoli inscription, ll.7–8.

54 Kankroli Road station inscription of AD 1299 records the donation of sixteen *drammas* by Karana and Sohada to a local temple of a goddess. This record is quoted in G.H. Ojha, *Udaipur Rajya Ka Itihas*, second edn, Rajasthani Granthagar, Jodhpur, 1999, p. 177, fn. 5.

55 Grant of King Babhata of AD 688; see Sircar, *The Guhilas of Kiskindha*, p. 175, l.14.

56 *Epigraphia Indica*, Vol. XIV, pp. 187–88.

57 Ibid., p. 187, ll.28–29.

58 Ibid., l.28–39, '*Patasakurika kshetramtaritam varahapalligramavartama*'.

59 Ibid., p. 187, l.31, '. . . *Kosavahe Chhittullakakshetram manivap ten sasanena pradattam*'.

60 Ibid.

61 Ibid., pp. 181, 186, l.26, '*Kacchakanam araghattan tu sambutum dattan*'.

62 *Epigraphia Indica*, Vol. XXXI, pp. 237–48.

63 Ibid., ll.1–38.

64 *Epigraphia Indica*, Vol. X, pp. 76–79.

65 Chattopadhyaya, 'Irrigation in Early Medieval Rajasthan', p. 311.

66 For instance, Vaidya Giyaka of a kayastha family in seventh-century Bhilwara area; see *Epigraphia Indica*, Vol. XX, pp. 122–25.

67 For the composition and functions of the Panchakulas, see A.K. Majumdar, *Chaulukyas of Gujarat*, M.S. University, Bombay, 1956, pp. 236–42.

68 *Progress Report of Archaeological Survey, Western Circle, 1910–11*, pp. 38–39; *Epigraphia Indica*, Vol. XXII, pp. 192–96.

69 Chattopadhyaya, 'Irrigation in Early Medieval Rajasthan', p. 316.

70 Chirava inscription, *Epigraphia Indica*, Vol. XXII, p. 291, vv.36–40.

71 *Vir Vinod*, Vol. I, Motilal Banarsidass, Delhi, 1986, p. 401, ll.1–3, '*Shri Chitrakute . . . Chitrangatadagamadhya Shri Vaidyanatha*'.

72 *Shodh Patrika*, V.S. 2010, Rajasthan Vidyapeeth, Udaipur, pp. 50–51, '*Savilarabhumyam Kardamval grame vrittisam jukta pradattam*'.

73 *Shodh Patrika*, Vol. VII, Rajasthan Vidyapeeth, Udaipur, pp. 65–66.

74 Ekalingaji Temple Dakshina Dwara Prashasti of AD 1488, *Vir Vinod*, Vol. I, Motilal Banarsidass, Delhi, 1986, v. 87.

75 See Nandini Sinha Kapur, *State Formation in Rajasthan: Mewar during the*

Seventh–Fifteenth Centuries, Manohar, Delhi, 2002, Chapter V: 'Sources of Legitimation of the Guhila State: The Religious Dimension'.

[76] Motilal Menaria (ed.), *Mahakavi Ranachod Bhatta Pranitam Rajaprasasti Mahakavyam*, Rajasthan Vidyapeeth, Udaipur, 1973, Ch. 8 , p. 88, vv.47–50.

[77] Ibid., p. 88, v.52.

[78] Ibid., Ch. 9, p. 91, vv.4–7.

[79] Ibid., p. 94, v.21.

[80] Ibid., p. 92, v.13

[81] Ibid., pp. 93–96, vv.16–30.

[82] Ibid., p. 96, v.96.

[83] Ibid., p. 99, v.34.

[84] Ibid., Ch. 10, p. 103, v.10.

[85] Ibid., pp. 101–02, v.3–4

[86] Ibid., p. 106, vv.22–23

[87] Ibid., p. 106, v.24.

[88] Ibid., p. 107–08, vv.26–31.

[89] Ibid., p. 108, v.32.

[90] Ibid., p. 110, vv.41–42.

[91] Ibid., Ch. 11, p. 112, vv.2–13.

[92] Ibid., pp. 112–14, vv.2–13.

[93] Ibid., p. 115, v.16.

[94] Ibid., pp. 116–21, vv.21–52.

[95] Ibid., Ch. 12, p. 124, v.9.

[96] Ibid., p. 125, vv.7–9.

[97] Ibid., p. 125, v.11.

[98] Ibid., p. 125, v.13.

[99] Ibid.

[100] Ibid., p. 127, vv.21–22.

[101] Ibid., p. 128, vv.25–28.

[102] Ibid., p. 131, v.36.

[103] Ibid., Ch. 13, p. 135, v.8.

[104] Ibid., pp. 136–37, v.13–16.

[105] Ibid., p. 140, vv.28–29.

[106] Ibid., Ch. 14, pp. 146–47, vv.11–12.

[107] Ibid., Ch. 10, p. 109, v.35.

[108] Ibid., Ch. 19 , pp. 202, vv.7–8.

[109] Ibid., v.8.

[110] Ibid., v.9.

[111] Ibid., p. 203, v.16.

Mughals and *Mahmudis*

The Incorporation of Gujarat into the Imperial Monetary System

Najaf Haider

The Mughal imperial power was organized around certain symbols and instruments of control through which the regime communicated with its people and executed its will in regions of the empire. The functionaries of the regime regarded money and its currency as one such means necessary to wield political authority and establish order in the domain of exchange. Although monetary movements have a momentum of their own and can silently cut through well-defined political divisions, it can be argued that the degree to which an imperial regime was able to create the basic framework to negotiate its power relations and economic interests in matters concerning the use and flow of money, as well as the extent to which it encountered resistance, constitute interesting themes in the history of the dynamic processes of empire-building.

The present study takes up the subject of the integration of a regional monetary economy into the framework of an imperial system, and concentrates on policies and institutions that helped to bring this about. The attempt here is to illustrate, through a case study of Gujarat, the process of interaction between imperial apparatuses, evolved with the intention of creating and running an empire, and regional political structures and market economies. The textual and numismatic material used for this study is drawn from mainstream sources, and an effort has been made to retrieve information of monetary significance from data lying dormant at the doorsteps of numismatists and historians for quite some time now.

On the eve of the Mughal conquest of Gujarat, the most prominent currency of the region was the *mahmudi*, a silver coin of 88 grains, first issued by Gujarat's Sultan Mahmud Shah (1458–1511). At least three varieties of the *mahmudi*, of different weights, fineness and exchange rates, all modelled on Mahmud's principal silver coin, circulated in various parts of Gujarat. It is important for our study to disaggregate the collective designation *mahmudi*, in order to observe how in each area of its circulation the local currency system encountered the Mughal efforts at standardization. In western (peninsular) Gujarat, the chieftains of Nawanagar and Bhuj coined their own respective *mahmudis* which circulated in the regions of upper and lower Kachh. The Nawanagar variety was also current in the city of Ahmadabad and its vicinity. The other region from where the *mahmudi* was diffused to the entire region of southern Gujarat was the chiefdom of Baglana. In between, around Baroda and Broach, a slightly heavier variety of the *mahmudi*, called *changezi*, was in circulation from the days of the Gujarat sultans. The trifurcation of the *mahmudi* signified the decentralization of political and monetary authority in the sixteenth century, and localization of fiscal and commercial networks within the sultanate of Gujarat.

Recoinage and Replacement of the Ahmadabad *Mahmudi*

Before the Mughal annexation, the trade balances of Gujarat with the markets of northern India were paid for either in *mahmudis* or in Iranian currencies of the Indian Ocean—*shahis* and *laris*—imported from Hurmuz and Basra, after converting them all into rupees at inland mints.[1] Alternatively, bills of exchange (*hundis*) were drawn upon the inland markets by the *sarrafs* of Gujarat, who also utilized the surplus cash available with their correspondents in the rupee areas to discount inland bills paid in *mahmudis*. Both methods of payment allowed Gujarat to maintain its regional currency system while conducting trade with the rest of the Mughal empire.

After the conquest of Gujarat by Akbar (AD 1572), the link between Ahmadabad, now the capital of the province, and the core areas of the Mughal empire became stronger.[2] Remittances of revenue from the province, routed through Ahmadabad, complemented the existing channel of precious metal flow to the inland towns through trade. Silver imported from the territories of Iran, Turkey and Iraq (*Wilayat, Rum wa Iraq*) was eventually brought for coining to Ahmadabad, the hinterland market for the port cities of Cambay, Diu and Ghogha.[3] Soon after 1572, the imperial mint of Ahmadabad began to coin rupees, a sizeable portion of which was remitted by merchants operating in Gujarat to the inland regions, to pay for their purchases. It gave them the opportunity to avoid the inconvenience of a double exchange, that is, exchange of imported coins first into *mahmudis* and then into rupees, while transporting money from the western coast to the inland regions. The recovery of numerous hoards comprising Ahmad-abad rupees in large quantities across the central regions of the empire points to the direction of the physical movement of specie (Table 1). Rupee circulation had become so widespread by 1583 that, after recapturing Ahmadabad for a very brief period, the Gujarat sultan needed to strike silver coins of the exact shape and weight as the rupee of Akbar rather than the reputed *mahmudi* of his ancestors.[4]

From 1575, a series of fiscal and monetary measures were undertaken by the Mughal state. The flow of cash income to the treasury was facilitated by centralizing mint production and integrating it with the fiscal structure. At the same time, the official exchange rates of Mughal currencies were streamlined by linking them all with a single money of account (*tanka i muradi*).[5] Also, to curb the influence of the money market on currency users, an immobilized numismatic date was given to all coins minted between 1582 and 1591 so that no arbitrary discount could be charged on full-weight coins simply on the basis of their age.[6]

Once the Mughal monetary policy on the introduction and circulation of its own currency in the core areas of the empire was put into place, the attention of the administration was directed towards regional currencies. In 1592, an imperial order was issued to demonetize all precious metal coins of previous emperors (*padshahan i sabiq*). The premium they enjoyed on account of seigniorage was abolished, and they were sold and purchased in the market as gold and silver bullion (*ba baha i tila wa nuqra*).[7] In the guidelines issued to the treasurer and the police chief (*kotwal*) in the 1590s, there was a clause that referred exclusively to the treatment of coins of previous rulers (*bastani maskuk*). It was ordered that they should be declared uncurrent (*na maskuk*), and should either be melted down (*ba gudazgah dahad*) or sent to the treasury at the value of uncoined bullion (*ba irj i na mas-kuk*).[8] Penalties were devised for offenders, and money-changers (*sarrafs*) were particularly targeted for their role in giving currency to regional coins as discounters of bills of exchange and buyers of foreign bullion.[9]

TABLE 1 ***Rupees of Ahmadabad: 1572–1605***

Years	*Number of coins (museum collections)*	*Number of coins (unpublished hoards)*
1572–76	53.50	56
1577–81	35.50	28
1582–86	46.00	71
1587–91	44.00	83
1592–96	181.00	291
1597–1601	145.50	262
1602–05	115.75	202
Total	621.25	993

Sources: Unpublished Collections of Coins and Medals, British Museum, London; Department des Monnaies Medailles et Antiques, Bibliotheque Nationale, Paris; Heberden Coin Room, Ashmolean Museum, Oxford; Maratha History Museum, Deccan College, Pune; Abdul Karim, *Catalogue of Coins in the Cabinet of the Chittagong University Museum*, Chittagong, 1979; V.P. Rode, *Catalogue of Coins in the Central Museum Nagpur*, Part I: *Coins of the Mughal Emperors*, Bombay, 1969; H. Nelson Wright, *Catalogue of Coins in the Indian Museum, Calcutta*, Vol. III: *Mughal Emperors of India*, Oxford, 1908; R.B. Whitehead, *Catalogue of Coins in the Panjab Museum, Lahore*, Vol. II: *Coins of the Mughal Emperors*, Oxford, 1914; C.J. Brown, *Catalogue of Coins in the Provincial Museum, Lucknow, Coins of the Mughal Emperors*, 2 vols, Oxford, 1920; R.B. Whitehead, *Catalogue of the Collection of Coins Illustrative of the History of the Rulers of Delhi up to 1858* AD *in the Delhi Museum of Archaeology*, Calcutta, 1910; Shamsuddin Ahmad, *A Supplement to Volume III of the Catalogue of Coins in the Indian Museum, Calcutta (The Mughal Emperors of India)*, Delhi, 1939; C.R. Singhal, *Supplementary Catalogue of Mughal Coins in the State Museum, Lucknow*, Lucknow, 1965; *Treasure Trove Reports*, Ms., State Museum, Lucknow.

The purpose of passing laws against the circulation of regional coins was to allow the Mughal imperial issues to take their place. The correlation between recoinage and regional expansion in rupee circulation becomes stronger if we relate our textual information to the numismatic material. Figures are assembled in Table I by serializing museum and hoard specimens at five-year intervals, to depict the order of magnitude of rupee production in Ahmadabad. The data for the entire period can be divided into two distinct segments: the pre-recoinage period (1572–91) and the period of recoinage (1591–1605).

The total for the first five years of recoinage (1592–96) shows a four-fold increase from the previous quinquennium in the case of the museum specimens, and a jump of three-and-a-half times in the case of the hoards. Although there is a modest but progressive decline in the figures of the last two quinquennia, the numbers still remain very high compared to the period before the recoinage. The data clearly indicate that the conversion of *mahmudi*s into rupees, which began only slowly after the annexation of Gujarat due to fiscal and commercial demands, reached its culmination in the recoinage of 1592–1605 following the new monetary policy.

By the end of the sixteenth century, in the *sarkar* of Ahmadabad, which housed both the capital city of the province and a mint, the rupee had become the sole medium of exchange to the total exclusion of the *mahmudi.* In European accounts of the trade of Cambay, the *sikka* rupee ('ropia sackey') is explicitly stated as the only coin acceptable in payment.[10] We also find that, from 1599 onwards, all bills of exchange drawn upon Cambay and Ahmadabad were written in rupees, and the bills drawn at Ahmadabad on any other city were paid in the same specie.[11]

The pattern of state income and expenditure also played an important role in the monetization of the rupee. On the fiscal front, a rare reference for 1601 suggests that a sum of one lakh rupees was annually fixed for the consumption of Prince Salim out of the port revenues of Cambay.[12] This would mean that a significant portion of urban revenue in the *sarkar* of Ahmadabad, of which Cambay was a part, was collected in rupees. With the use of the same specie for payments made to provincial officials and troopers as well as the amount spent from the personal expenditure of high officials, the rupee was gradually introduced into the markets of Ahmadabad and Cambay. The penetration of the rupee in the regional exchange network came full circle when merchants and manufacturers paid their dues either by obtaining rupees directly from the market or by changing *mahmudi*s and *lari*s at the mint and money-changers' shops.

The Mint as an Instrument of Imperial Expansion
The Case of Surat

In the rest of Gujarat, particularly in the cities of Surat, Broach and Baroda, the introduction of the rupee neither took place on a similar scale nor at the same time. The *mahmudi* was still the sole currency of exchange as well as the money of account in southern Gujarat in the early decades of the seventeenth century.[13] It was used not only by merchants, bankers (*sarrafs*), shopkeepers and transporters (*adhviyas*) for commercial transactions, but also by Mughal officials for receiving and making payments into and out of the provincial treasury.[14] A clear division of Surat and Ahmadabad into distinct *mahmudi* and rupee areas was acknowledged by the merchants trading between the two zones:

> Moneys current in Surrat is of silver, called a mamudo, being of value almost 12 d. sterling. Another coin there is of copper, called a pize, whereof you have commonly 34 in the mamudo, being so great as they are worth it, therefore as copper riseth or falleth you have more or less in the mamudos. . . . Other coins pass in Cambaya and Amadavad called rupies.[15]

There were two reasons for the continued circulation of *mahmudis* at Mughal Surat both in the market and the state sector. First, there was an obvious limitation, given the level of the minting technology and the size of the work force employed by the mint, to the volume of coin production in Ahmadabad, which could not possibly have supplied rupees to the entire province that was served earlier by at least five active *mahmudi* mints of the Gujarat sultans and autonomous chieftains. Second, while rupee circulation was restricted to the areas covered by the Ahmadabad mint in the north, the supply of *mahmudis* to Surat continued unabated from an independent source in the east.

Much of the supply of the Surat *mahmudi* came from the autonomous principality of Baglana, situated in the Sahyadri range between Gujarat and the Deccan, where it was struck in the twin fortress towns of Salher and Mulher (in the northwest corner of the present Nasik district). The chiefs of Baglana, the Bharjis, retained control over their territory and trade routes by acknowledging the authority of the rulers of Khandesh, Gujarat or the Mughals, as the situation demanded.[16] A contemporary description of the territory and its relationship with the Mughal state comes from one of the early European travellers to this part of India:

> This towne [Bhadwad] is the last of note in Pectopshaws [Pratap Shah] land, who is a small king or Rajaw, a Gentile, keeping on the top of inaccessible mountaines, which begin at Curka and extend

> many courses. He holdeth two faire cities, Salere, and the other Muliere, where the mamudees are coined. . . .
>
> The Acabar besieged him seven years, and in the end was forced to compound with him, giving him Narampore, Dayta, and Badur, with diverse other aldeas, for the safe conduct of his merchants alongst this plaine.[17]

It appears from Finch's description, which we have just cited, that the Mughal state allowed Pratap Shah to retain his possessions on the condition that he granted safe passage to merchant caravans through the northern cities of his principality. The towns of Dhaita and Navapur lay on the trade routes linking Surat with Agra (via Burhanpur), on the one hand, and with the Deccan kingdoms of Bijapur and Golconda, on the other. This arrangement also appears to have left intact Pratap Shah's right to levy a transit tax (*rahdari*) on the passing merchandise. Prince Khurram, the viceroy of Gujarat and the Deccan, refused to persuade Pratap Shah to exempt English merchants from paying *rahdari* since a part of this income formed the tribute paid to the Mughals.[18]

Another concession that the Baglana chief was able to obtain from Akbar's administration was the right to mint *mahmudi*s in the name of the Mughal emperor.[19] This can be surmised from a reading of the textual evidence on Baglana together with the specimens classified in various museum collections as 'Coins of the Gujarat Fabric' (Table 2). In weight and workmanship, all surviving specimens appear much closer to the *mahmudi* of the Gujarat sultans. However, where legends are concerned, they resemble the rupee of the reigning monarch: the *kalima* being inscribed on the obverse and Akbar's name and title on the reverse. The correlation between the two sets of evidence is strengthened by a series of contemporary documents, all coming from Surat, where the currency of transaction has been described as *mahmudi fizza Akbari* (silver *mahmudi* of Akbar).[20] A recent laboratory analysis of a specimen dated 992 AH suggests a degree of fineness (92.9 per cent) high enough to justify the designation 'silver *mahmudi*' used for them in the Surat documents.[21]

The striking of the Baglana *mahmudi* in Akbar's name for over a decade after his death suggests the continuation of the old policy of keeping southern Gujarat outside the imperial monetary system. Pratap Shah had remained a loyal tributary chieftain of the Mughal

TABLE 2 ***Surat Mahmudis Issued in Akbar's Name: Museum and Private Collections***

Year (Hijri)	*Year (Christian)*	*Weight (troy grains)*	*Number of specimens*
985	1577–1578	87.0	1
986	1578–1579	84.6	1
988	1580–1581	84.7	1
989	1581–1582	–	1
990	1582–1583	–	1
991	1583–1584	–	1
992	1584–1585	83.0	1
994	1587–1588	–	1
995	1588–1589	–	1
996	1587–1588	87.0	1
997	1588–1589	83.5*	2
998	1589–1590	–	1
999	1590–1591	87.2*	2
1000	1591–1592	–	1
1003	1594–1595	87.0	1
1004	1595–1596	87.0	1
1005	1596–1597	87.0*	2
1006	1597–1598	87.0	1
1007	1598–1599	87.0*	2
1008	1599–1600	87.8	1
1009	1600–1601	86.0*	2
1012	1603–1604	–	1
1014	1605–1606	–	1
1016	1607–1608	75.0	1
1019	1610–1611	84.0	1
1020	1611–1612	–	1
1025	1616–1617	86.4*	2
1026	1617–1618	83.2	1
1027	1618–1619	86.0	1
1215	1800	86.9	3
1217	1802	87.0*	4

* Maximum weight

Note: Undated and fractional issues are excluded. Specimens without any weights assigned to them come from G.P. Taylor's personal collection, and range between 78 and 87 grains.

Sources: References cited for Table 1; G.P. Taylor, 'On the Coins of "Gujarat Fabric"', *Journal of Asiatic Society of Bengal*, Vol. 73, 1904; *Numismatic Supplement*, II, pp. 235–39.

state as well as a part of its extended bureaucracy, and Jahangir's administration had not yet expressed the desire for formal annexation of his territory.[22]

A major policy decision taken in this direction, inspired as much by fiscal as by monetary considerations, was the commissioning of the Surat mint from 1620 onwards to strike rupees on a regular basis. The timing was decidedly opportune to instal an imperial mint at this port city. The currents of maritime trade in the western Indian Ocean were shifting away from the Gulf of Cambay towards the coast of Surat with the arrival of the Dutch and English East India Companies.[23] European merchants, the English in particular, had already announced their intention of carrying 'away callicoes and indicoes' and 'enriching', in return, the Mughal 'Kingdomes with silver'.[24] The Mughal administration was therefore gearing itself to facilitate the minting of much of the silver gravitating around the western coast in order to expand the rupee area at the expense of the *mahmudi*, still current in this part of Gujarat, and, at the same time, to earn extra income from seigniorage, hitherto appropriated by the chieftain of Baglana.

The establishment of the Surat mint was backed by a two-pronged monetary policy, the purpose of which appears to have been to guarantee an uninterrupted supply of silver to the Surat mint. First, an embargo was placed on the outflow of all foreign specie and bullion landing at Surat, as revealed by the transcript of a consultation held at Surat, on 9 January 1621, between the English factors:

> Furthermore, the exportation of royalls [reales of eight], through occation of a minte erected in this towne, being utterly debared us, and wee having sould 40, 000 royalls unto the Captain of the Castell, deputie in the Governor's absence, with condition to receive the greater partt in redye money and the resedue in bills of exchange for Amadavad and Agra. . . [S]eeinge noe perswation can prevaile with these officers for lycence to exporte our monyes, and that the Company both have and must ever undergoe such licke adventures by exchanges, it is generally thought fitting their bills should bee received and dispeeded. . . .[25]

Second, accompanying the prohibition on the sale of foreign specie at any place other than Surat, there was an increase in the mint price (coins paid out for a fixed quantity of fine metal) of silver. This can be inferred from two sets of information furnished by the factors themselves. One, a letter of 1638 in which the desirability of remitting money from Isfahan in the form of bills of exchange was defended on the ground that 'by special command from the king the mint of Suratt is made equal to that of Amadavad, and so the charge is encreased 7 per mille'.[26] Thus it appears that till 1638, the Surat mint was coining rupees at a lower cost than Ahmadabad, seven for each batch of 1,000 coins, and that once the incentive was withdrawn the Isfahan merchants preferred to convert their cash into rupees by buying bills upon Surat rather than delivering coins to the mint for conversion.

Two, a set of letters, written and received at Surat, which enables us to infer the lower minting fee charged at Surat as far back as 1622. The letters carried recurring complaints that the Surat rupee was circulating at a discount in Ahmadabad and elsewhere.[27] No reasons were cited for the lower market exchange rate of rupees minted at Surat, as against the same specie coined at Ahmadabad and other mints. A recent laboratory test conducted on a Surat rupee of 1035 AH (1625–26) suggests a very high degree of fineness (98.9 per cent) and rules out any possibility of a decline in its standard intrinsic value.[28] It is thus reasonable to assume that the discount on rupees was occasioned by a lower seigniorage charged on them that made up, among other things, the rate at which coins were exchanged for bullion and other currencies.

Just as the news of an increase in minting charges at Surat had the effect of diverting bullion away from the mint, a fall would have had the opposite effect—of attracting bullion from all competing mints—if the cost of transport exceeded the difference. In the case of Surat, the double-edged monetary policy of the Mughal administration appears to have been directed towards discouraging European and other merchants from sending their bullion, landing at Swally, to Ahmadabad, the only other rupee mint in the province, by making it both uneconomical and illegal.

How successful was the Mughal policy of using the mint as an instrument for expansion of the imperial currency, and what effect did it have on the *mahmudi*s of Baglana circulating at Surat? On both these counts, but more the first, the most helpful observation comes from Pelsaert, the Dutch factor, who witnessed and recorded the transition from regional to imperial currency around 1626:

> Formerly mahmudis, and not rupees, were current here; the mahmudi is smaller, and worth only 10 stivers by our reckoning. Rupees have come into circulation during the *last five or six years*; the mahmudi is still the nominal unit for sales and purchases, but the actual payment is generally made in rupees, which we take as 24 stivers. The king has now a mint in Surat, as in Ahmadabad and all other capital cities (emphasis added).[29]

Pelsaert's remarks date the commencement of the third phase in the expansion of rupee circulation in Gujarat, the first starting immediately after the annexation of the sultanate (1572–73) and the second operating between 1592 and 1605. The Surat mint quickly overshadowed the Ahmadabad mint, and from then on it became the major recipient of imported bullion and the largest producer of rupee coins in the Mughal empire.[30] By 1636, the mint was fully engaged during the high seasons and merchants began to experience delays in receiving the supply of fresh coins for the silver they delivered. Soon after, as we saw, the charges of the Surat mint were brought on a par with those of Ahmadabad.

Much like in Ahmadabad, rupee circulation in and around Surat was sustained partly by its use in the income and expenditure of the state, and partly by the system of payment involved in inter-regional trade. The city retained that portion of silver money that was remitted to Agra, Burhanpur and other inland areas of investment through bills of exchange.[31] In subsequent years, the rupee appeared as a currency at various levels of transactions involving the payment of bills of exchange, debt settlements, and the sale and purchase of commodities.[32]

The introduction of an official and standard currency in the market was bound to affect the fortunes of the local coin, although the Mughal administration was probably not fully confident of the rupee's ability to automatically replace the *mahmudi* in the circuits of exchange as well as in the account books. The *mahmudi* was not only present in the minds of the market people as a nominal unit of expressing values, *à la* Pelsaert, but also in the official treasuries.[33] The Mughal administration thus had to adopt a more direct policy towards the displacement of the *mahmudi* than simply expecting it to be swayed by the continued circulation of its own currency. It seems that a revival of Akbar's policy towards regional currencies, of disallowing their circulation through demonetization, took place in Jahangir's time, on the eve of the establishment of the Surat mint. An indication of this comes from the refusal of bankers and merchants to make payments in *mahmudis* for any bill drawn on Surat rather than 'in [the] current monye of the bazar'.[34] Another clue to official prohibition of the circulation of the Surat *mahmudi* is provided by the absence of available specimens from 1619 (Table 2), a year before the mint at Surat became operational.

On the face of it, the numismatic evidence makes it quite clear that the Baglana chief, apparently after giving an assurance to the Mughal authorities, refrained from minting any more *mahmudis* beyond this date. But it is likely that he found a way out of the situation, where he was obliged to accommodate both the Mughal prohibition and his fiscal interests, by fixing an immobilized date and legend on his coins, like his fellow rulers of Kachh and Kathiawar (on which see below), while quietly inviting bullion merchants to his mints with fresh supplies.[35] Whichever may have been the case, it appears that the Mughals were able, at least for the time being, to stem the supply of a competing currency to this part of the empire.

If the Baglana chief had any intention of reviving the operations of the Mulher mint on any significant scale, it must have been thwarted by Shahjahan's expansionist designs which ensured, through a military expedition launched in 1638, the annexation of his principality to the Mughal empire as a separate *wilayat.* The occupation by the Mughals of all the nine forts of Baglana, including Salher and Mulher, and the removal of the chief's residence to the nearby *pargana* of Sultanpur, completed the capitulation.[36]

Once fresh supplies of the local currency stopped from Baglana, it began to affect the circulation of the pre-existing stock in Surat as well by accelerating the displacement of the *mahmudi* by the rupee. The first problem that the *mahmudi* experienced was a progressive decline in its exchange value, particularly against the rupee, reflected in the discount (*batta*) imposed on it by the market in commercial transactions. The discount on *mahmudis* stayed throughout the seventeenth century, and became so common an element of market exchange that no contemporary ever bothered to comment on its rationale.[37] In a rare reference, the discount is explained on the basis of the fact that the *mahmudi* was 'none of the king's coyne, but coyned by the Rajah of Mallore [Mulher in Baglana], a place distant from hence [Surat] 70 course or myles, and are onely currant in these adjacent countries, not further than Barodera.'[38]

The manner in which the discount came to be accepted by the market is not clear to us although it may have in all likelihood begun as an official imposition, with the collection of taxes and other dues, by demonetizing the *mahmudi* and accepting it for bullion while disregarding the value added to it by seigniorage and the cost of minting.[39] Another reason for the discount may have been the depreciation (real or assumed) in the fine-metal content of the *mahmudi* due to wear and tear, at a rate higher than coins, such as the rupee or the reale, which were minted or recoined at regular intervals.

The strength of the rupee against the *mahmudi* was also linked to its wider area of circulation, which extended beyond the regional confines of Gujarat. This is demonstrated in the case of the grain trade which linked Gujarat to the markets of central and northern India. Since the traffic in this commodity was unilateral, the itinerant merchants (*banjaras*) who brought supplies of grain to Gujarat and received payment in *mahmudi*s, were required to carry back rupees as their capital for up-country investments. The remittance of rupees from the *mahmudi* areas invariably caused a spurt in the discount rates, which went up to 6 per cent during days of scarcity of foodgrains and other provisions.[40] The premium on the rupee also grew with the need of the Gujarati merchants themselves to send money for seasonal investments outside the *mahmudi* areas.[41] The rates returned to normal when fresh supplies of the rupee from mints and other sources brought about a relative fall in its demand.[42]

The Case of Kathiawar

The policy of establishing imperial mints with the objective of replacing regional currencies was also pursued by Shahjahan, directed towards the *mahmudi* of the Kathiawar peninsula (*Kachh i khurd*). In this region, the circulation of *mahmudi*s originated from the city of Nawanagar (Jamnagar), ruled by an autonomous chieftain (the Jam) who was a tributary of the Mughal administration at Gujarat.[43] This chiefdom could successfully maintain the circulation of its own brand of *mahmudi* (also known as *Jami* or *kori*) for both political and commercial reasons. Throughout the reign of Akbar, and possibly of Jahangir as well, the Jam remained in complete possession of his territory and control of its administration on payment of tribute.[44]

Akbar's decree of removing from circulation all non-Mughal coins effectively reached only Ahmadabad, and Kachh, like southern Gujarat, had been left out of its purview, possibly due to the complexities of carrying out such an exercise in regions where the Mughal administrative apparatus was yet to be implanted.

The chiefdom of Nawanagar bordered areas which, lying within immediate reach of the sea, had assumed the status of entrepots by linking oceanic commerce to the hinterland markets of northern Gujarat.[45] The pattern of Indian Ocean trade ensured regular exchange of bullion and foreign coins for Indian goods in the coastal emporia, and the economy of Nawanagar, based significantly on the transit trade, was able to tap the seasonal supplies of overseas silver and direct a part of it to its *mahmudi* mint. The Nawanagar *mahmudi* could thus carve an area of influence, stretching from Kathiawar to the borders of Ahmadabad, which remained largely independent of the political and economic compulsions of the rest of Mughal Gujarat.

The first intrusion into this privileged monetary domain was made on the heels of a full-scale military campaign launched by the Mughals against the Jam in 1641, three years after the annexation of Baglana. An official account of this expedition was kept for his patron by Shahjahan's court chronicler:

> During his [Azam Khan, the *subadar* of Gujarat] administration, the *marzban* (chief) Jam did not observe the same subservience in his deeds which is expected of the *zamindars*. The Khan swiftly set out to discipline him. When he reached a distance of seven *karohs* from Nawanagar, which is the place of residence of the above mentioned *marzban*, the Khan i Azam sent him a message that unless he [the Jam] agreed on the [payment of] tribute and the discontinuance of the Nawanagar mint, which is situated in the heart of his territory and where the coin *mahmudi* is struck, there would be no way out for him. The said *zamindar*, who had no choice other than offering his allegiance, gave [away] one hundred horses of Kachh and three lakhs *mahmudis* by way of tribute (*peshkash*) and consented to close down the mint (*dar uz zarb bar andakhtan*).[46]

The political offensive to shut down the mint and stifle the supply of the Kachh coin was accompanied by a decision to establish an imperial mint at Junagadh for the sole purpose of melting *mahmudis* (*bar gudaz mahmudi*) and recoining them into rupees.[47]

Although the *Mirat i Ahmadi* distinguishes the Junagadh mint as a product of the campaign launched in 1641, which appears to be logical, the numismatic evidence pre-dates rupee minting by at least two years (Table 3). Whatever may have been the actual date of the establishment of the mint at Junagadh, the intentions of the Mughal authorities were quite clear. They wanted to repeat the experiments conducted at Ahmadabad and Surat by banning the Nawanagar *mahmudi* and supplying the market with legal tender. However, the author of the *Mirat* was in no doubt that the experiment failed and the mint was discontinued. According to him, 'in view of convenience and cost effectiveness (*nazr bar suhulat wa kifayat*), merchants started coining their gold and silver, brought at Diu, there [Junagadh] rather than taking them to Ahmadabad'.[48]

The specimens listed in Table 3 suggest that the mint at Junagadh continued to strike rupees throughout Shahjahan's reign and hence contradict the textual evidence of its discontinuance. However, it is also true that the experiment was only partly successful and that it failed in one significant particular. While it allowed the imperial money to be coined and circulated in an area which was familiar only with the regional issue, it did so by diverting the flow of silver away from another Mughal mint (Ahmadabad) rather than at the expense

TABLE 3 ***Shahjahan's Rupees of Junagadh Mint* (museum collections)**

Year (Hijri)	*Year (Christian)*	*Number of specimens*
1049	1639–40	1
1050	1640–41	1
1052	1642–43	2
1054	1644–45	2
1055	1645–46	2
1056	1646–47	1
1059	1649–50	2
1060	1650–51	1
1062	1651–52	1
1064	1652–53	2
1066	1655–56	1
1067	1656–57	2

Sources: References cited for Table 1.

of the coin it was designed to dislodge. Thus, the circulation of the pre-existing *mahmudi* continued unabated since the rupee failed to replace it in the same manner as it did in Ahmadabad and Surat.

Conclusion

The Mughal monetary structure, as we know of it in the seventeenth century, emerged only after decades of intense administrative activity under Akbar and his successors. This meant a uniform and standardized currency system in place of the old regime of regional currencies, geared to a constant flow of silver through trade. Gujarat was a test case for the imperial policies in western India (the other region, Sind, had no precious metal currency of its own), being the most difficult province to be reduced to a homogenous political and economic unit. The collective circulation of Gujarat *mahmudis* by the local rulers, who deployed their geographical and political autonomy and their links with maritime sources of precious metals to sustain the legacy of the sultanate, posed a challenge to the Mughal design of carving an empire within the region. It was an affront to their claims to sovereignty and anathema to their fiscal interests.

In response, the Mughal administration moved systematically by combining military supremacy and commercial viability of the territories under its control with monetary management. The concentration of Akbar's administration on Ahmadabad, while exercising minimum intervention in the affairs of the rest of Gujarat, explains the success achieved in the first phase of the expansion of the imperial monetary system. The emergence of Surat as an entrepôt and its deepening links with the hinterland, at a time when international trade and the supply of silver was on the rise, allowed the Mughal authorities to take control of its monetary affairs essentially by using the mint as an instrument. With the bulk of the province now integrated, their attention turned towards the peninsula, and although the Kathiawar experiment did not fully meet the imperial expectations, the emission of rupees from Junagadh throughout the seventeenth century offered the kind of satisfaction to the Mughals that imperial regimes often derived from symbols rather than substance.

The story of the Mughal encounters with the *mahmudi* does not begin and end with the policies and institutions of the state alone. The market too, in a wider sense of the term, was an important player. While it reacted favourably to a new and good currency (the rupee), it also showed its resilience to the eviction of the *mahmudi* beyond permissible limits. The presence of the *mahmudi* in Saurashtra and, to a limited extent, southern Gujarat owed a great deal to the customary loyalty it commanded in its area of circulation, as well as to the buoyant economy of Gujarat where the rupee alone was unable to meet the constant mercantile demand for liquid capital.

Notes and References

1 Abu'l Fazl, *Ain-i Akbari,* 2 vols, edited by H. Blochmann, Bibliotheca Indica, 1872–77, Vol. 1, p. 19.

2 Shireen Moosvi, 'The Gujarat Ports and their Hinterland: The Economic Relationship', in Indu Banga (ed.), *Ports and their Hinterlands in India, 1700–1950,* New Delhi, 1992, pp. 123, 125.

3 *Ain-i Akbari,* Vol. 1, p. 486.

4 G.P. Taylor, 'On the Identity of the Gujarat Fabric and the Surat Mahmudi', *Journal of Asiatic Society of Bengal,* New Series, Vol. I, No. 10, 1902, *Numismatic Supplement,* vi, p. 413.

5 Najaf Haider, 'Precious Metal Flows and Currency Circulation in the Mughal Empire', *Journal of Economic and Social History of the Orient,* 39 (3), 1996, pp. 347–49.

6 Najaf Haider, 'Disappearance of Coin Minting in the 1580s? A Note on the *Alf* Coins', in Irfan Habib (ed.), *Akbar and His India,* Delhi, 1997, pp. 55–65.

7 Abdu'l Qadir Badauni, *Muntakhab u't Tawarikh,* 3 vols, edited by William Lees and Ahmad Ali, Bibliotheca Indica, 1864–69, Vol. 3, 1869, p. 380.

8 *A'in-i Akbari,* Vol. 1, pp. 284, 289.

9 *Muntakhab u't Tawarikh,* Vol. 3, p. 380.

10 Pieter van den Broecke, *Pieter van den Broecke in Azie,* 2 vols, edited by W.Ph. Coolhaas, s-Gravenhage, 1962–63, Vol. 2, p. 382. As early as 1615, the European factors noted that only rupees were current in Ahmadabad and Cambay, whereas *mahmudis* were in circulation at Surat. *De Opkomst Der Westerkwartieren van De Oost-Indische Compagnie (Suratte, Arabie, Perzie),* edited by H. Terpstra, s-Gravenhage, 1918, p. 206; *Letters Received by the East India Company from its Servants in the East, 1602–17,* 6 vols, edited by Charles Danvers and W. Foster, London, 1896–1902, Vol. 3, p. 11; *A Supplementary Calendar of Documents in the India Office relating to India or to the Home Affairs of the East India Company, 1600–1640,* edited by William Foster, London, 1928, p. 46.

11 Abu'l Fazl, *Akbarnama,* 3 vols., edited by Agha Ahmad Ali and Abdur Rahim, Bibliotheca Indica, 1873–87, Vol. 3, p. 762; *Supplementary Calendar,* pp. 64, 90, 112; *English Factories in India (1618–1669),* 13 vols (each volume titled by the year/s it covers), edited by William Foster, Oxford, 1906–27; *1618–21,* pp. 113, 181–82; *1622–23,* pp. 19, 147, 149.

[12] Ali Muhammad Khan, *Mirat i Ahmadi*, 2 vols and *Supplement*, edited by Syed Nawab Ali, Baroda, 1927–30, Vol. 1, p. 184.

[13] *Letters Received*, Vol. 1, p. 34. Also see Thomas Best, *The Voyage of Thomas Best to the East Indies, 1612–14*, edited by William Foster, Hakluyt Society, 1934, p. 35; *De Opkomst*, p. 205.

[14] *Supplementary Calendar*, pp. 56, 60, 84, 88, 117.

[15] *Letters Received*, Vol. 3, 1615, p. 11. Also see Peter Mundy, *The Travels of Peter Mundy in Europe and Asia 1608–1667*, 3 vols, edited by Richard Carnac Temple, Hakluyt Society, 1914, Vol. 2: *Travels in Asia 1628–34*, p. 311 ('Then there are Mahmoodes which goe only at Suratt and thereabouts, hardly at Ahmudavad').

[16] *Mirat-i Ahmadi*, Vol. 1, p. 21; *Akbarnama*, Vol. 3, pp. 29–30, 770; Shah Nawaz Khan, *Maasir al Umara*, 3 vols, edited by Abdur Rahim and Mirza Ashraf Ali, Bibliotheca Indica, 1888–91, Vol. 3, pp. 412–15.

[17] William Finch, *Early Travels in India, 1583–1619*, edited by William Foster, London, 1921, pp. 136–37.

[18] W.H. Moreland, *From Akbar to Aurangzeb: A Study in Indian Economic History*, London, 1923, p. 288.

[19] For a suggestion that *mahmudis* were minted at Baglana in Akbar's name, see J.F. Richards, 'Official Revenues and Money Flows in a Mughal Province', in John F. Richards (ed.), *The Imperial Monetary System of Mughal India*, Delhi, 1987, p. 198.

[20] Bibliotheque Nationale, Ms Blochet, Supplement Persan 482ff. 194a, 196b, 197a.

[21] Ms. report of a laboratory analysis conducted by the British Museum using energy-dispersive X-ray analysis (EDX) in a scanning electron microscope (SEM) and energy-dispersive X-ray fluorescence (XRF). Courtesy M.R. Cowell, Department of Coins and Medals, British Museum.

[22] *Tuzuk-i Jahangiri*, edited by Syud Ahmud, pp. 196, 203; Abdul Hamid Lahori, *Badshahnama*, 2 vols, 3 pts., edited by Maulvi Abdur Rahim and Kabiruddin Ahmad, Bibliotheca Indica, 1867–68, Vol. 1, pp. 316–17, 419.

[23] Haider, 'Precious Metal Flows and Currency Circulation', pp. 317–21.

[24] Thomas Roe, *The Embassy of Sir Thomas Roe to India 1615–19*, edited by William Foster, 1926; reprint, Delhi, 1990, p. 186.

[25] *English Factories, 1618–21*, p. 218.

[26] *English Factories, 1637–41*, p. 84. Earlier, the Surat factors wrote to the Company that 'the mint in Amadavad takes a greater allowance then this in Suratt by almost two percent'. *English Factories, 1634–36*, pp. 217–18. This figure is higher than the one quoted in the subsequent letter (0.7 per cent), and perhaps includes the cost of making a round trip from Surat to Ahmadabad.

[27] *English Factories, 1622–23*, pp. 87, 92–93; *1624–29*, pp. 235, 238.

[28] See note 20.

[29] Francisco Pelsaert, *Remonstrantie*, in W.H. Moreland and P. Geyl (trs), *Jahangir's India*, Cambridge, 1925, p. 42.

30 Moreland, *From Akbar to Aurangzeb*, pp. 176–78.

31 *English Factories 1618–21*, pp. 85, 146, 155; *1622–23*, pp. 68–69.

32 Ibid., *1622–23*, p. 97; *1630–33*, pp. 262–3; *1634–36*, pp. 55, 68–69.

33 *Tuzuk-i Jahangiri or Memoirs of Jahangir*, 2 vols. translated by Alexander Rogers, edited by Henry Beneridge, 1909–14; reprint, Delhi, 1989, Vol. 1, p. 267; *English Factories 1622–23*, pp. 205–06.

34 *English Factories 1622–23*, pp. 96–97.

35 For a discussion among the English merchants that Pratap Shah may be approached for a 'more quiatt transporte of . . . rialls to Mouler' to obtain timely supplies of *mahmudis* at Surat, see ibid., p. 25.

36 Lahori, *Badshahnama*, Vol. 2, pp. 105–09.

37 *Oxenden Papers*, British Library, Add. Ms. 40702, ff. 10b, 22b, 23b, 55b, 61b; *English Factories, 1630–33*, pp. 262–63; *1634–36*, pp. 68–69.

38 *English Factories, 1634–36*, pp. 224–25.

39 A similar policy was later adopted by Shahjahan with regard to the local coinage (*khani*) of Balkh and Badakhshan, the newly conquered provinces of Central Asia. The *khani* was first demonetized, and then restruck with changes in its alloy composition to bring it on a par with a quarter rupee. Lahori, *Badshahnama*, Vol. 2, pp. 562–63. But, unlike Gujarat, the measure here symbolized a compromise between imperial issues and Central Asian monetary standards of the kind witnessed in the case of the Shahrukhis of Babur and Humayun.

40 *English Factories, 1634–36*, pp. 68–69.

41 Ibid.

42 Ibid., p. 68.

43 O. Codrington, 'The Coinages of Cutch and Kathiawar', *Numismatic Chronicle*, 3rd Series, Vol. 15, 1895, pp. 80–81.

44 'During the reign of Arsh Ashyani [Akbar], zamindar Jam remained in possession of his territory as in the time of the Gujarat Sultans.' *Mirat-i Ahmadi, Supplement*, pp. 219–20.

45 There was a regular trade between Ahmadabad and Nawanagar based on mutual understanding not only between the merchants but also between the political authorities on matters such as payment of transit dues. Ibid.

46 Lahori, *Badshahnama*, Vol. 2, pp. 231–32. Also see *Mirat-i Ahmadi*, Vol. 1, p. 214; *Maasir ul Umara*, Vol. 1, pp. 178–79.

47 *Mirat-i Ahmadi*, Vol. 1, p. 214; *Supplement*, pp. 211–12.

48 *Mirat-i Ahmadi*, Vol. 1, p. 214. The author says that the mint was discontinued on the advice of the *diwan* of the *suba*, Mir Sabir, although the said person had already quit the office in 1638.

Nomadic or Semi-Nomadic

Banjaras and the Indian Economy, Sixteenth to Nineteenth Centuries

Meena Bhargava

Scholarly debates and researches have contributed substantially to an understanding of the Indian economy and society for the period from the sixteenth to the nineteenth centuries. However, in their analysis of the patterns of growth and development of the economy for the period, scholars have been largely biased towards the achievements of sedentary populations. Consequently, a significant section of the society, that is, a few tribes or castes or communities, although considerable in numbers and in socio-economic importance, have remained marginalized. One such tribal group are the Banjaras. There has been little scholarly attempt to focus on this tribe and to evaluate their role in the creation of the society and economy of the said period.

The Banjaras represent an inextricable intermeshing of tribal and non-tribal, sedentary and non-sedentary ways of life. Characteristically a wandering tribe, the Banjaras may not be rigidly classified as nomads for they were not merely pastoralists but performed a variety of functions. Several of their roles made them appear no less than sedentary settlers. They were carriers of goods, petty traders, grain dealers; in some regions, like in the Mughal *sarkar* Gorakhpur of *suba* Awadh, they even held the position of *ta'lluqdars*; and in several instances they were accused of being plunderers and marauders. Notwithstanding their multifaceted character, the Banjaras were undeniably nomadic in many ways. They were averse to recognizing boundaries and territories, and to building permanent homes. Vagabondage was their style, their custom. They believed that making a *pucca* home of cement and mortar, or staying in one place, was inauspicious. It was *adharma*. Hence their houses were *kutcha* (non-masonry), with mud walls and bamboo matting, and their roofs were thatched with grass or tiles or tin sheets.[1] The Banjara ethos was rooted in the philosophy that if the greatest of men have had to leave this world, then why should any human being 'stay and wait' in one place. This ideology influenced their lifestyle. Thus, whenever a *tanda* (a Banjara *kafila* or caravan) camped in a place, it did not even create a proper fireplace to cook but used a makeshift arrangement of three bricks as the hearth. Stability in life was opposed to the notions of the Banjara *samaj*.[2]

The Banjaras, however, were in many ways also tied to sedentary communities. It was a relationship of dependence and reciprocity.[3] It may be worthwhile to comment on the economic relevance of nomads to evaluate the significance of the Banjaras in the Indian economy. Emphasizing the indispensability of the non-sedentary to the sedentary and vice versa, Fredrik Barth has argued that a nomad and a villager within a single economic system or within the economic structure of an area should be regarded as specialized occupational groups.[4] In Central Asia, nomadic pastoralism and agriculture had developed as interdependent processes since early times. For instance, in the Neolithic period many Central Asian tribes, particularly those of the Jeitun settlement in southern Turkmenia, pursued both nomadism and cattle-grazing along with agriculture. Such characteristics in the economy of Central Asia continued to prevail till the eighteenth century, particularly amongst the nomads of Turkmenia, Kazakhstan and Kirghizia.[5] In West Asia too, the pastoral lands were surrounded either partly or completely by urban settlements, and the grazing lands used by the nomads formed enclaves partially or wholly within the sedentary zone.[6] Evidence indicates that pre-Islamic Arabia was interspersed throughout with nomads—herders of goats, sheep or camels. They were ubiquitous in Arabia. Yet, even in this region, to suggest a sharp distinction between the nomadic and the sedentary life would be misleading. There was but a small fraction among the pastoral people of Arabia who could be called fully nomadic, for there were a sizeable number of nomads who practised both pastoralism and agriculture.[7]

These instances of interdependence between nomadism and sedentary life suggest the importance of nomadic tribes (however peculiar they may have been in their characteristics) in the creation and consolidation of any economy and society. It therefore becomes imperative that even as we talk of agrarian territory,[8] we need to place equal emphasis on the territorial institutions[9] that provide an identity to agrarian space and constitute social power in agrarian territory. Nomads, herders, hunters, traders, shifting cultivators, or any such 'travelling' people, would have added up to perhaps half the total population at almost any point in most regions during the period before AD 1800. Therefore, what we call 'sedentary agriculture' was not really sedentary.[10] Tribesmen and nomads were not confined to any single territory; they were a wide phenomenon. Their movements, often termed 'rebellious' by historians, continued throughout the sixteenth to the eighteenth centuries. Bayly argues that the flourishing and expanding money economy of Asia and Norṭh Africa during this period stirred restive tribal groups, who sought wealth and fame either by serving or plundering kingdoms.[11] The Bakhtiari and Laks, engaged in rich caravan trade, consolidated themselves in Persia; the western nomadic Bedouin tribes moved into the rich, fertile lands of Fayum on the Egyptian delta; and the Kurds gained strength through their battles with the Ottoman provincial rulers in Baghdad.[12] In India, the Banjaras represented the migratory and nomadic people. A popular saying goes thus:

> The Banjaras are honest and never steal
> The Banjara*'s* mother watches the seasons [for her son's return from his periodical journeys]
> Watch for the homecoming of a servant, a thief, a thug and a Banjara
> Strip off her shell, O Banjara and put it on someone more worthy.
> [Refers to the shell bracelets worn by married women and to the reputation of the Banjaras][13]

Like nomadic tribes in other parts of the world, the Banjaras in India also served and plundered, and were involved in exchanges with sedentary settlers.

Contemporary Indian chronicles of the sixteenth century, like the *Baburnama* and *Akbarnama*, have supported the speculation that a certain percentage of the Indian population during this period depended on fighting for their livelihood, and many of them travelled most of the time to earn their means of subsistence. Migrations of entire communities from one region to another were a common feature. In this context, we may mention one of the Banjara tribes, the Lohanis, also known as tribal traders. The trade activities of the Lohanis were not confined to merely India; they also carried merchandise from

India to Kabul,[14] and bought and sold in Ghazni.[15] These trading patterns of the Lohanis continued into the early nineteenth century. Alexander Burnes has observed that the Lohani Afghans were a pastoral and migratory people who, joined by their families, visited India annually to purchase merchandise and carry it back to Kabul.[16]

The *Akbarnama* and the *Ain-i-Akbari* of Abul Fazl, for the first time, provided a comprehensive list of dominant lineages and communities in India. Emulating Abul Fazl, the East India Company, from 1806 onwards, initiated the task of preparing a detailed list of communities in India. However, it was the census operation from 1881 to 1941 that generated the most comprehensive data-set for India. The 1891 census report, based on ethnological, historical and functional considerations, classified the Banjaras as an occupational category. The census report of 1901, however, used another term—functional castes—to study the tribes and castes of India. The definition of functional castes was derived from their traditional occupation even though many of the members had abandoned the work of their ancestors. The adoption of new occupations or of changes in original occupation resulted in sub-divisions in the caste that ultimately developed into entirely distinct castes. In the 1901 census report the Banjaras were described as a functional caste.[17] The same report also prepared a general list of castes with a strength of 1,00,000 or more per locality. As many as 1,321 communities were identified. The Banjaras were classified as one of the major communities, along with several others.[18]

To compare and categorize different castes, anthropometrical[19] measurements of the castes of the North West Frontier Provinces and Awadh were undertaken by Surgeon Captain Drake-Brockman. The castes were grouped into three main divisions, namely, Aryan, Medium[20] and Dravidian. The last was further divided into hinduized and aboriginal, to indicate social status. To analyse the data on the basis of anthropometry, only males of 25 years and above with mature physical development were selected as subjects for measurement. Drake-Brockman studied their nasal and cephalic indices and the facial angle.[21] The Banjaras were identified as the representative caste of the Dravidian division. The facial angle of a Banjara was measured as being 66 on an average index.[22]

J.C. Nesfield, on the contrary, advocated that castes could be determined only on the basis of occupation. He argued that function alone was the foundation upon which the caste system of India was built.[23] Using the criterion of traditional occupation, Nesfield classified the Banjaras as carriers, along with other castes or tribes like the Ahiwasis, Baidguars, Belwars, Naiks and Rahbaris. Of the total number of carriers, which was 86,674 in the late nineteenth century, the Banjaras constituted the majority—67,097. The others numbered 9,502, 420, 6,194, 2,593 and 808, respectively.[24]

Crooke disagreed with Nesfield's methodology. He argued that only a few of the occupational groups, like the Atishbazes (firework-makers), Nalbands (farriers) and so on, adhered to the original trade or handicrafts of their castes or occupations from which they derived their names. Others, like the Banjaras, Nunias (salt-makers), Chamars (leather-workers), Ahirs (cattle-grazers), had at some time or the other cultivated, performed field labour, tended cattle or been traders. Crooke faced a genuine problem in framing a classification of castes on the basis of traditional occupations.[25] We share Crooke's dilemma and apprehension in categorizing the Banjaras exclusively as carriers, for they had several other attributes as well.

It is difficult to be comfortable with the word 'tribe'[26] when one studies the Banjara community. Some scholars have argued that the level of Banjara acculturation was so different from that of other tribes in India that the usual criteria adopted for assigning to any group the status of a tribe could not be applied to the Banjaras.[27] They were distinct for at least three reasons: (a) they did not accept the demarcation of any territory; (b) non-Banjaras were assimilated in their *samaj*; (c) even though they remained a segregated group, they contributed to the prosperity and development of sedentary groups.[28] The Banjaras, no doubt, had a long history of migration and of nomadism, but they were essentially an occupational community. Their social life and socialization were similar to that of non-tribals.[29] Another characteristic that distinguished the Banjaras was their firm and committed belief in *samuhik jeevan* (collective living). This aspect is clearly evident from the folk literature of the Banjaras. To illustrate, lines from a Marathi *lok geet* (folk song) can be quoted:

> *Aadhi Aadhi Rate Ro*
> *Tandlo Ye Lado*
> [The whole *tanda* has set out for trade; there is no one family; the *tanda* gives importance to *samuhik jeevan*.][30]

The Banjaras derived their name from the word *bajjika*, which means trade or business.[31] Some argue that their roots lie in the Sanskrit word *vanijya* or *banijya-kara* (merchant).[32] *Vanijya* in Sanskrit is *banaj* in Hindi, meaning those who are engaged in trade. Their origin is also associated with *banjar* (fallow land). In other words, those who lived on *banjar* lands were ascribed the status of Banjaras.[33] Yet another view holds that the term Banjara is linked to the word *banji*, meaning a pedlar's pack.[34] Despite the complexities of etymology, what emerges is that though traditionally a nomadic tribe, the Banjaras in effect were a trading community. They trace their descent from Lakhi Banjara, who had moved from one *van* (forest) to another with his merchandise. Crooke described the Banjaras as carriers of grain and supplies to armies in the field.[35] Risley, on the other hand, said that the term Banjara applied to a grain and cattle merchant who, along with several other members of his community, moved in different markets and especially accompanied troops to supply them with corn. He further argued that the epithet Banjara is particularly applicable to the tribes spread along the foot of the mountains from Haridwar to Gorakhpur. The Banjaras comprised various sub-divisions, many of which were stationary but some of which also practised agriculture.[36]

That the root meaning of the word and the descent of the Banjaras differed across states is evident from the interpretation of Denzil Ibbetson. He argued that the Banjaras and the Labana caste were identical. Both were called Banjaras in the eastern districts and Labanas in the Punjab.[37] Cutting across state boundaries, the Mathura Banjaras[38] of Andhra Pradesh were also known as Labanas.[39] Removing all doubts that the Banjaras were confined to a single territory or only to some parts of India, Grierson observed that the Lambanis in Karnataka were 'the well-known tribe of carriers who were found all over western and southern India'.[40] It is apparent then that the Banjaras in Karnataka were popularly known as Lambanis.

However, the enigma still remains as to who the Banjaras were and where they came from. S.R. Sharma has suggested that if a Banjara is ever questioned about his ancestors, he invariably and promptly replies—Rajputs. They believe that they were originally revenue assignees or *jagirdars*, and that their relatives ruled Delhi. To protect themselves from the Ghorid Sultans, they escaped to the jungles and lived the lives of nomads, sometimes working as transporters of goods and sometimes as petty traders. Sharma reiterates that 'for the sake of independence they became forest-dwellers'.[41] Sharma's hypothesis, however, runs into a problem in view of the claims of the three Banjara tribes of the Deccan.[42] Though they insist that they had descended from the Rajputs, they ascribe their tribe's segregation to irregular marriages contracted by their early ancestors. It is assumed that marriage by adventurous wanderers into distant lands initiated the break of these branches from the parent stock and planted them apart as distinct communities.[43] Some Banjara tribes of the North West Frontier Provinces and Awadh claim an even deeper antiquity, though they too trace their origin to the Rajputs. They support the speculation that they had provided refuge to the Pandavas after their exile from Hastinapur, and that it was they (the Banjaras) who had founded the town of Deoband in the Saharanpur district of Uttar Pradesh. In the Banjara *tola* of Gopamau (a town in Hardoi district), some Banjaras call themselves Sayyid Salari and descendants of the followers of the saint. The Banjaras of Madras (Chennai) trace their lineage to Sugriva, the monkey chieftain and an ally of Rama, king of Ayodhya.[44] Such diverse claims by Banjaras firmly establish that they were a mixed race, comprising contingents from various other tribes and castes who may have at different times joined the profession.

The Banjaras were an endogamous group of *patti*s, each of which included several exogamous units. However, since the Banjaras were basically wanderers and constantly on the move, they did not have a settled organization. Their community unit, the *tanda*, connotes a moving unit. The *tanda*s moved with pack-laden bullocks which were fed in open fields along the route. As the Banjaras shifted from region to region, one of the major hazards they faced was the loss of livestock from disease or natural calamity.[45] Even so, these problems did not weaken the Banjara conviction and tradition of being in constant transit. In fact, such was their importance to the Mughal economy that Aurangzeb declared illegal the levies imposed on the Banjaras for grazing their animals.[46] A Banjara *tanda* could have as many as 20,000 pack-oxen.[47] In case a large army had to be supplied, the Banjaras could collect up to 1,00,000 bullocks or more.[48] With firmly established belief in collectivity or *samuhik jeevan*, a *tanda* usually contained five to fifty families. The families were paid according to the number of bullocks they supplied to the *tanda*. None of them was permitted to maintain a separate identity. They were bound by kinship ties and had to move with the *tanda*, abiding by the orders of the *naik*—headman and chief of the *tanda*.[49] A Marathi saying, '*Naik Bole aur Tanda Chale*' (on the orders of the *naik*, the *tanda* moved), reinforces the power and authority of the *naik*.[50] In some *tandas*, a hut was set aside for Mitthu Bhukiya, a freebooter whom they worshipped. A white flag outside the hut was a sign that the camp worshipped Mitthu Bhukiya. He enjoyed the devotion of such Banjara *tandas* in particular that practised plunder and crime.[51]

The worship of Mitthu Bhukiya by a few *tandas* does not mean that the Banjaras were necessarily a criminal tribe. On the contrary, the sources indicate that their primary occupation was as traders and carriers and suppliers of *rasad* (food articles) to the army during the days of constant war expeditions by the sultans of Delhi and the Mughal emperors to the Deccan. They have been mentioned in these capacities in the fourteenth century during the reign of Sultan Muhammad Bin Tughlak, and then again in 1504 when Sultan Sikandar Lodi led his army to Dholpur.[52] The Banjaras were significantly important as carriers and petty traders during the Mughal regime. Ashraf, in fact, believes that the term Banjara had been more widely and clearly used since the Mughal period.[53] As suggested earlier, the Banjaras maintained a number of buffaloes to load and carry commodities; the larger the number of buffaloes he owned, the greater a Banjara was considered as a transporter and a trader. Reinforcing this argument, Ashraf observes that the Banjaras were an old trading group that possessed lakhs of buffaloes; sometimes their *kafila* had up to 40,000 buffaloes.[54] The Banjaras became so indispensable to the Mughal army as carriers and suppliers of *rasad* that on several occasions the army was compelled to delay its departure if they could not find a sufficient number of Banjaras to carry their *rasad*.

The growing importance of the Banjaras to the Mughal army can be further ascertained by an instance of 1630, when Shahjahan's army was led by Asaf Jan to the Deccan. Banjaras were hired to supply foodgrains to the imperial army stationed at Burhanpur. This adversely affected the transportation of grain by the Banjaras to Gujarat for trade from Malwa and beyond.[55] Nevertheless, in 1630, the Banjaras' role as carriers for the army prevailed. The Banjara *tandas* of Bhangi and Jhangi Naik (apparently brothers) and Bhagwan Das Naik, with 1,80,000 and 52,000 bullocks respectively, accompanied the imperial army. Hesitant to travel the long distance to the Deccan, Bhangi and Jhangi Naik expressed fears about the difficulty in obtaining grass and water for their cattle. But so vital were the services of the Banjaras to the Mughal army, that the imperial commander disregarded their problems as a mere excuse. To utilize the Banjaras as carriers and suppliers to the army as it moved into the Deccan, Asaf Jan had no hesitation in using coercion. He issued a *farman* to Bhangi and Jhangi Naik forbidding them from abandoning the Mughal army. He promised to overlook many of their illegitimate activities if they abided by the order. To exemplify the value and indispensability of the Banjaras to the Mughal army, it may be worthwhile to reproduce an excerpt from the *farman* (engraved on copper with gold):

> *Ranjan ka Pani, Chhapar ki Ghas, Din ke Teen Khun Mu'af*
> *Aur jahan Asaf Jan ke Ghore, Wahan Bhangi Jhangi ke Bael*
> [If you can find no water elsewhere, you may take it from the pots of my followers; grass you may take from the roofs of their huts; and if you commit three murders in a day they would be pardoned, provided that wherever Asaf Jan's cavalry moves, Bhangi Jhangi's bullocks would also be there.]

The *farman*, apparently, raised the morale of the Banjaras. It was seen as a symbol of honour; the descendants of Bhangi and Jhangi preserved the *farman* as a relic. The rulers of Hyderabad continued the practice of recognizing the contributions of the family of Bhangi and Jhangi. Emulating the custom, the Nizam of Hyderabad subsequently decorated them with *khilats* (robes of honour).[56]

The tradition of the Banjaras as carriers and suppliers of provisions to the army was carried forward during the regime of the East India Company with even greater rigour. Notwithstanding the fact that their employers had changed, the Banjaras, in their customary way, accompanied the Company's army and supplied them with grains during the war with Tipu Sultan.[57] Impressed by the attainments of this 'useful class', Lord Cornwallis instructed 'unprecedented liberality and justice' towards them. Army officials confessed that the army was virtually helpless without these 'necessary attendants'. The Company classified the Banjaras as an 'indispensable necessity'. However, the Company faced a problem in that very few Banjaras resided in the Company's territory. Pragmatism and expediency entailed inducing the Banjaras to settle there. Thus, understanding the customary traditions of the Banjaras became a major priority and preoccupation of the Company. Basing itself on indigenous knowledge, the Company awakened to Banjara practices: that they led a wandering life and carried most of their families with them; that despite this, they remained attached to a particular government or establishment and its subjects. The Banjaras were also known for their great strength and formidable unity. If an Indian ruler alienated them, the Banjaras expressed no hesitation in changing their loyalty from one army to another. Such was their usefulness that even when they deserted an Indian ruler or chieftain, the latter, instead of punishing them, attempted to hold them back for fear of losing the support of the entire Banjara clan.[58]

Realizing the utility of the Banjaras to its army, the Company decided to attract a large number of them to settle in its territory. To motivate the Banjaras to betray their local masters in favour of the Company, Lord Cornwallis initiated a process of rewarding them for their services to the Company's army during the Anglo–Mysore War of 1798–99. For instance, Lachchi Ram, the *naik* or head Banjara who attended to the Company's army at Seringapatam, was granted a tract in Baramahal on easy terms both as reward for his past services and as security for his future. The Company hoped that such encouragement would inspire the Banjaras to settle down in its territory. As a further incentive, the Company made a lucrative offer of trade, a passion of the Banjaras. They were assured that in times of peace they could carry copper and salt from the Company's districts and return from the Nizam's territory loaded with cotton. Moreover, as inhabitants of the Company's territory, they could also trade with allies of the Company.[59]

While the Company pursued the Banjaras, its war with Tipu Sultan continued. Emphasizing the status of the Banjaras as a 'useful and formidable body', the Company made specific arrangements with them for supplying the army with grain and provisions and working as carriers for the army. Lachchi Ram and Nagapa Chetti, two head Banjaras, were sanctioned the contract, since they had supplied the Company's army on the earlier occasion of its war with Mysore. These Banjara *naiks* in turn offered to procure the services of other castes under three denominations. First, the Labanas or the caste that commonly traded in salt, could be employed as carriers for the army or for moving grains from one garrison to another, and could be paid in cash or kind. The second category comprised musclemen who could be hired as monthly servants or whenever their services were required. They had to be paid in cash. The last group were the indispensable

Banjaras, perhaps the only caste that the Company sought to foster. The Banjaras volunteered to be grain-dealers, that is, to supply grains to districts that were affected by scarcity and to carry the surplus from regions which abounded in grain. The Company had obviously succeeded in rejuvenating the Banjaras. Proposals from them to serve the Company's army were widely forthcoming. As the Anglo–Mysore War thickened in severity, a Banjara called Muniapa offered to furnish a few gun bullocks to the Company's army.[60]

Proud at the fulfilment of its objectives, the Company became even more confident of achieving its ambition, that is, to procure the services of the Banjaras on its own terms. To collect the Banjaras speedily and engage them on the lowest possible terms, the Company encouraged competition in the business of supply. The Banjaras principally inhabited the interior parts of India and carried supplies to the coast. There was a constant demand for their services also by the armies of Indian rulers. But it was the Company's regime that was able to make optimum use of the Banjaras.[61] Ostensibly, the Company reformulated and recreated the norms and customs that governed the Banjaras and succeeded in enthusing the tribe.

The Banjara tradition of carrying and supplying continued into the eighteenth century, although it was reinvented in several ways. Along with this, another Banjara activity, i.e. trade, also continued to dominate the Indian economy in the eighteenth–nineteenth centuries or at least till the railways were firmly established. The Banjaras, since the Mughal period, had virtually monopolized the trade on land, particularly in commodities like foodgrains, sugar, butter and salt. Stipulating the importance of Banjara trade, Tavernier divided the Banjaras into four castes, each carrying on distinct trade in corn, rice, pulse and salt.[62] Irfan Habib, however, has discarded Tavernier's classification as 'fanciful'. He argues that it was volition that guided Banjara trade although on a few occasions they carried goods for others as well. They supplied commodities to the regions that needed them and brought back the surpluses with them.[63] The trade undertaken annually by the Banjaras was considerable in volume. This may have been owing to the low costs of Banjara transport as compared to other methods of land transport. However, since the costs incurred by the Banjaras are not stated anywhere, it can only be conjectured that the Banjara trade and transport on land were the cheapest.[64]

K.M. Ashraf has observed that Banjara trade was not limited

to the confines of Hindustan but spread to neighbouring countries like Central Asia, Afghanistan, Persia, Multan, Quetta and Khyber as well.[65] Further pointing to the significance of Banjaras as traders, some scholars have argued that the Banjaras were a group that segregated from the Rajputs and Kshatriyas, who had been engaged in trade since ancient times.[66]

To consolidate our observations about the Banjaras in the eighteenth and nineteenth centuries, a few individual examples from *sarkar* Gorakhpur of *suba* Awadh may be given, even as we study them in broader terms in other centres of the same *suba* and in the Deccan. Traders and merchants of this region formed a significant segment of the Indian economy and part of a homogenous business culture.[67] Certain castes and their families and kin groups had dominated mercantile activity for generations. Caste distinctions often overlapped the specialization and professionalism of these groups. The most dominant mercantile communities in Awadh included Khatris, Aggarwals, Brahmans, Rajputs, Kayasthas, Banias or Baqqals and Muslims.[68] Besides these, the Banjaras contributed substantially to trade in Awadh in the eighteenth century. A large number of them carried valuable items of trade between Bihar and Awadh in the 1730s. So prosperous was their trade that there were instances of the zamindars of the region plundering them. For example, in 1715, the zamindar of *pargana* Rajpur in Moradabad reportedly plundered Banjara merchandise worth Rs 4,00,000.[69] The Banjaras, a mercantile community in Gorakhpur, exemplified 'peddling trade' organized on a massive scale. Known as 'pack-bullock traders' or 'roving grain traders', some of the Banjaras also came from peasant families.[70] By the end of the eighteenth century, a Banjara *kafila* comprised several peasants who had temporarily opted to become carriers and merchants either because of a poor season or because a passing army had raised prices in some districts.[71]

Generally referred to as small traders, the Banjaras were classified as carriers of a variety of merchandise, particularly grain. However, though they were frequently hired by other merchants to carry commodities to distant or local markets, they were not merely carriers or transporters. The Banjaras were merchants in themselves who bought grain at cheap rates and sold it at profitable prices.[72] Invariably, zamindars sold their grain to Banjaras and other itinerant dealers who took it to distant markets. The income derived from this transaction was sufficient for the zamindars to pay revenue and be utilized later in the year for buying back grain from another group of Banjaras and itinerant dealers at higher prices.[73]

In most parts of north India, the Banjaras carried a large proportion of grain and salt from area to area.[74] They imported almost the entire salt of Gorakhpur from western India. They moved in caravans through the territories of the Nawab Wazir with as many as 10,000 to 40,000 oxen and bullocks, which they owned. Some quantity of salt was also imported from the dominion of the Nawab Wazir and the territory beyond Allahabad. The quantity of salt imported was probably much more considerable than has been stated here, especially as some of it was smuggled into Saran, where sea salt alone could be legally imported.[75]

The policy of the East India Company in the nineteenth century regulating salt trade and the supply of salt affected the Banjara trade. At cession, the Company introduced its monopoly of salt in the ceded provinces. Export and import of salt by private individuals were prohibited under the penalty of confiscation.[76] This meant that only agents of the Company could now undertake salt trade. Salt could be manufactured and sold only in such markets and towns of the ceded provinces that were approved by the Company. The Company also devised a system of duties to control the export and import of salt in the ceded provinces.[77] To further discourage salt trade by individuals other than the Company's agents, the Company insisted that Banjaras or any salt merchant, before crossing the frontier, would have to pay in advance the whole or at least three-fourths of the amount of the contract for transportation to distant markets.[78]

The grievances of the Banjaras and other salt and cotton merchants were further aggravated when magistrates seized their carts for military purposes.[79] The turmoil in the salt trade and its effect on the Banjaras continued throughout the nineteenth century. Another development of this time—the depression and famines of 1833–34 and 1837–38—further added to their adversities. The crisis reached its peak in 1837 when a large number of heads of cattle belonging to the Banjaras of Bayana returned unladen from the northern markets of Farrukhabad and Shahjahanpur. Usually these Banjara traders exchanged Rajasthan salt for Rohilkhand grain, but in 1837 the prices were so high that there was no hope of any gains in the western markets. Therefore, no exchanges were made.[80]

Known in north India as grain-dealers and for their trade in salt, the Banjaras represented somewhat different characteristics in Deccan. They were recognized as an established feature of the Deccan cotton trade, not only of the textile industry but also of the general exchange economy of northern Coromandel and the Deccan. It is believed that they owned the cotton they brought from the Deccan and when they sold this cotton, they purchased salt from the coastal salt pans for their return trip to the Deccan. In the early nineteenth century, 5,000 candies, or above 2,500,000 lbs, of raw cotton were sold at Hinghaun Ghat, an important Deccan market for Banjara trade. The carrying capacity of a bullock was between 240 to 260 lbs. This meant that approximately 10,000–15,000 bullocks were required to supply the total quantity, a number well within the capacity of a Banjara *tanda*. Dutch records indicate that the prices of cotton rose steadily during the period in which the demand for textiles was growing. The Banjaras, however, could profit only marginally from the growing value of the goods they carried.[81]

Economic depression and famine apart, the colonial policy of regulating trade and the strict monopoly over it, and the disproportionately high transit dues, affected the Banjaras. The free trade of the Banjaras, influenced by market forces, was drastically curtailed. With the development of the railways, which provided speedy transport to commodities, Banjara trade worsened even further.[82]

Predominant in trading activity in almost all parts of India, the Banjaras were often accused of combining trade with plundering and looting. This earned them the titles of 'mercantile robbers' and 'vagrant tribes' who moved in large hordes with men, women, children and cattle under the pretext of trading.[83] Describing the ravages of villages by the Banjaras in the Mughal *suba* of Punjab, Muzaffar Alam has argued that the sources of the period (early eighteenth century) provide no apparent reason for the resistance of Banjaras towards the Mughals. He conjectures that it could have been a reaction to the unlawful cesses extracted from the Banjaras or the inflated rates of *ijara* that resulted in an exorbitant rise in the prices of foodgrains.[84] The rebellion and resistance of the Banjaras saw no respite even as the rule passed on to the East India Company. The Banjaras were found guilty of murdering travellers, killing or wounding their opponents, ransacking the houses of peasants, and even ravishing their wives and daughters or kidnapping their children.[85] The *sazawals* or peons of the Company, deputed to restrain or discipline the Banjaras, were beaten and wounded, and deprived of their arms and belongings.[86] Notwithstanding their violent activities, since the Company considered the Banjaras to be 'useful people' who carried and distributed supplies to the army, it adopted a mild disposition towards the depredations of the Banjaras. Although the police was posted amongst the Banjaras to maintain vigilance, the Company was cautious not to alienate the 'useful tribe'. It passed a discreet order, that though the Banjaras occasionally murdered travellers, only those among them should be apprehended who were implicated in a specific crime.[87] As a further concession, the Company instructed that the best way to restrain Banjara violence was to appropriate their labour. Only in expedient circumstances were the Banjaras to be dismissed from service.[88]

The Company's liberal but apparently pragmatic approach towards the Banjaras is evident from an incident of 1799. Banjaras from a *tanda* had murdered two *raiyat*s residing in the Company's territory, and wounded another two who were not likely to survive. Their households and personal property were also plundered and devastated. The Banjaras of the *tanda* were seized to be punished for their violence, but not without an assurance that if they surrendered the murderers the others would be released without any precondition.[89]

The anarchic and devastating activities of the Banjaras made them a peculiar phenomenon in the economy of Gorakhpur in the eighteenth century. Calling themselves Banjara *ta'lluqdar*s, they assumed enormous and disturbing powers during the reign of Nawab Shuja u'd Daulah, and carved out a powerful political horizon for themselves in the eastern part of Awadh (including Gorakhpur).[90] Stealthy and armed, the Banjara *ta'lluqdar*s of Gorakhpur accumulated power to the extent of becoming a political threat, plundering all areas they found defenceless and unguarded. Claiming these plundered areas as their *ta'lluqa*s, they usurped titles like *chakledar, nazim, naib, amil* and *ta'lluqdar*. They became such a menace and a scourge to the region that the rajas of the affected *pargana*s or those in the vicinity of the strongholds of the Banjaras were compelled to build *qilacha*s or *garhi*s (mud forts) to protect themselves against the Banjara invasions. In the division of the *kotwali* of Gorakhpur, at least twenty to thirty *garhi*s were built by the rajas 'to keep off the incursions of the vagrant tribe'. With similar intentions, the rajas of Dhuliyabandar erected *garhi*s. Amongst these, a *garhi* of significance was the one at Muskaroya, about 2 miles from Mahadeva, the centre of the Banjara tribe.

This *garhi* was resorted to whenever the 'predatory merchants' plundered the *pargana*s of Bansi, Satasi and Padrauna. That these *pargana*s were the worst affected is evident from the twenty *garhi*s that were built in Padrauna itself to defend the rajas against Banjara attacks.[91]

Raja Sarabjeet Singh of *pargana* Bansi, who successfully ousted them from his dominion, ultimately chastised the Banjaras in Gorakhpur a few years before cession. In a bid to sustain his ancestral domain, the raja of Majhauli abandoned Sidhua Jobna to the Banjaras and created the two estates of Padrauna and Tamkuhi for them, with the intention of building a buffer state and securing Majhauli against not only Banjara incursions but also the vexatious tolls of the *amil*s. The new *ta'lluqdar*s, with the support of the neighbouring *pargana*s, consolidated their political power and sheltered their *ta'lluqa*s and those in the proximity from harassment by the *amils* who exacted illegal and disproportionately high cesses. Having acquired the status of *ta'lluqdar*s, they could now successfully defy the heavy duties—*rahdari* and *tanhadari*—imposed on them by the rajas and the zamindars, which, the Banjaras claimed, had always been the main source of dispute and disturbance. With no such burdens and allegedly well established in power, they were considerably quiet after cession.[92]

The Banjaras lost their indispensability as carriers and suppliers by the end of the mid-nineteenth century. With changes in and growth of the Indian economy, the Banjaras were subordinated as traders by merchant groups. Also, with rapidly expanding and diversified agriculture, they could no longer find open fields to rear their cattle. Their services became even more redundant with the widening railway network, which provided speedy transport to all kinds of commodities. The Banjaras, who had once represented a conventional form of traditional exchange, were increasingly marginalized as a people by the end of the nineteenth century. However, this did not mean that the Banjaras disappeared from Indian society. They dispersed into different regions. Acclimatizing and accommodating themselves to the changed circumstances, they chose diverse occupations ranging from cattle trade to cultivation to petty trade in clothes, artificial jewellery and cosmetics.

Identified as a major community in the 1901 census, the Banjaras are no longer a nomadic community in the true sense of the term. Certain traditions have, of course, continued. And, although they are now settled in different states in India,[93] they have not completely abandoned their Banjara habit of wandering and moving from one region to another to sell merchandise.

Notes and References

[1] S.G. Deogaonkar and S.S. Deogaonkar, *The Banjara, Castes and Tribes of India*, Series 3, Concept Publishing Company, New Delhi, 1992, p. 25.

[2] Moti Raj Rathor, *Banjara Lok Sahitya Mein Samaj Sanskriti*, Saraswati Prakashan, Kanpur, 1988, p. 66.

[3] See Chetan Singh, 'Conformity and Conflict: Tribes and the 'Agrarian System' of Mughal India', *Indian Economic and Social History Review*, Vol. XXX, No. 3, July–September 1988, pp. 319–40.

[4] For details, see Fredrik Barth, 'Nomadism in the Mountain and Plateau Areas of South-West Asia', in *Arid Zone Research*, No. XVII, *Problems of the Arid Zone*, Proceedings of the Paris Symposium, UNESCO, 1962, p. 345.

[5] Devendra Kaushik, *Central Asia in Modern Times: A History from the Early Nineteenth Century*, Progress Publishers, Moscow, 1970, pp. 15–30. Also see Meena Bhargava, 'Agricultural Technology and Patterns of Exchange: A Study of Central Asia and its Interaction with India, Tenth to the Eighteenth Centuries', in A. Rahman (ed.), *India's Interaction with China, Central and West Asia, History of Science, Philosophy and Culture in Indian Civilization*, Vol. III, Part 2, Oxford University Press, New Delhi, 2002, pp. 392–408; A. Vambery, *Sketches of Central Asia*, W.H. Allen, London, 1868, and *Travels in Central Asia*, Cambridge Scholars Press Ltd, London, 1864.

[6] See M.B. Rowton, 'Autonomy and Nomadism in Western Asia', *Orientalia*, Vol. 42, 1975; cf. Chetan Singh, 'Conformity and Conflict', p. 332.

[7] Fred McGraw Donner, *The Early Islamic Conquests*, Princeton University Press, New Jersey, 1981, p. 16.

[8] David Ludden defines agrarian territory as that 'part of agrarian space that can be effectively bounded, physically and culturally, and marked as a spatial domain for organized social power and activity'. David Ludden, *An Agrarian History of South Asia*, The New Cambridge History of India, IV.4, Cambridge University Press, Cambridge, 1999, p. 41.

[9] They comprise caste groups, lineages, clans, tribal groups, village communities, states, war, etc. Ibid., p. 43.

[10] Ibid., p. 67.

[11] C.A. Bayly, *Imperial Meridian: The British Empire and the World, 1780–1830*, Longman, London and New York, 1989, pp. 17–18.

[12] Ibid., pp. 37–38.

[13] H.H. Risley, *The People of India*, second edn, edited by W. Crooke, Oriental Books Reprint Corporation, Delhi, 1969, p. 318.

[14] Zahiruddin Muhammad Babur, *Baburnama*, edited and translated by A.S. Beveridge, Luzac & Co., London, 1921, p. 235.

[15] Abul Fazl, *Akbarnama*, edited and translated by H. Beveridge, Bibliotheca Indica: A Collection of Oriental Works, published by Asiatic Society of Bengal, Calcutta, 1921, Vol. 3, p. 1165.

[16] See Alexander Burnes, *Cabool*, Murray, London, 1842, pp. 77–79.

[17] *Census Report of India*, 1901, pp. 521–29.

[18] The other communities included Banias, Lingayats, Mals/Malas, Marathas, Brahmans, Rajputs, Khatris, Kayasthas, Bairagis, etc. *Census Report*, 1901, p. 271.

[19] Anthropometry may be defined as the science which seeks to ascertain and classify the chief types of mankind by measuring certain physical characters such as stature and the proportions of the head, features and limbs. By analysing their points of agreement and difference, it works back to the probable origin of various race-stocks. Like ethnography and ethnology, anthropometry forms part of the studies grouped together under the head of anthropology. See W. Crooke, *The Tribes and Castes of the North Western India*, Vol. I, Cosmo Publications, Delhi, 1974, p. xxvii.

[20] The Medium group contained a large number of castes which formed an intermediate type and were not capable of being classified strictly under either of the two main groups. Ibid.

[21] Drake-Brockman believed that the facial angle more or less provided the degree of prognathism and this, taken together with the nasal index, gave the best test possible. The nasal index, according to him, was the best determinant for racial distinction. Then, all the castes have cephalic indices, which show the formation of the head. Crooke, ibid., pp. xxviii–xxxii.

[22] Ibid., pp. xxvii–xxxii.

[23] To classify castes on the basis of occupation, Nesfield divided the entire population into eleven groups. He demarcated a group as 'casteless tribes', comprising the Dravidian tribes of the central Indian plateau and a collection of vagrants and gypsy-like people such as Nats, Kaṇjars, Doms and Musahars. See J.C. Nesfield, *Brief View of the Caste System of the North Western Provinces and Oudh.* Cf. Crooke, *Tribes and Castes*, pp. cxxxix–cxlii.

[24] Nesfield, *Brief View of the Caste System*; cf. Crooke, *Tribes and Castes.*

[25] Crooke, ibid., p. cxliv.

[26] There is no consensus on a definite and comprehensive explanation of what constitutes a tribe. The 1911 census report defined tribe as 'distinguished from a caste on a political rather than economic or social basis. The members of a tribe supposedly believed in a common origin, shared in a community of interests and felt the need for mutual defence, speaking the same language, which was often peculiar to the tribe.' See *Census Report of India*, 1911, p. 367. Andre Beteille makes a comparison between tribe and caste and emphasizes the 'relative isolation of tribes as compared with castes'. He argues that 'a tribe is a world within itself having few external social ties'. See Andre Beteille, *Six Essays in Comparative Sociology*, Oxford University Press, New Delhi, 1979, pp. 40–47.

[27] Deogaonkar and Deogâonkar, *The Banjara*, p. 8.

[28] Shri Ram Sharma, *Banjara Samaj*, Dakshin Prakashan, Hyderabad, 1983, p. 2.

[29] Deogaonkar and Deogaonkar, *The Banjara*, p. 9.

[30] Rathor, *Banjara Lok Sahitya Mein Samaj Sanskriti*, p. 51.

[31] K.S. Singh, *India's Communities: People of India*, National Series, Vol. IV, Anthropological Survey of India, Oxford University Press, New Delhi, 1998, p. 268.

[32] Crooke, *Tribes and Castes*, p. 149.

[33] Nanjudayya Iyer and K. Ananthakrishna, *The Mysore Castes and Tribes*, Vol. I, Mysore, 1928, p. 136, cited in Deogaonker and Deogaonker, *The Banjara*, p. 11.

[34] K.S. Singh, *India's Communities*, p. 269.

[35] Crooke, *Tribes and Castes*, p. 149.

[36] H.H. Risley, *The Tribes and Castes of Bengal*, Vol. I, Firma Mukhopadhyay, Calcutta, 1981, p. 59.

[37] Denzil Ibbetson, *The Punjab Castes*, Punjab Languages Department, Patiala, reprint, 1970, p. 145.

[38] The Mathura Banjaras claim that they were a wandering band (*tanda*) who migrated with their pack-bullocks to Vishakhapatnam from Mathura. Hence their name. See N.N. Vyas, 'The Banjara: The Mercantile Nomads of Rajasthan', *Tribe*, Vol. 3, No. 2, p. 277.

[39] Ibid.

[40] Ibid., p. 275.

[41] Sharma, *Banjara Samaj*, p. 68.

[42] Mathuriya or those from Mathura, Lavana or carriers of salt (*lavana* in Sanskrit means salt) and Charan (in Sanskrit it means wanderer or pilgrim). See Cumberlage, *Berar Gazetteer*, p. 195. Cf. Crooke, *Tribes and Castes*, p. 150. For the Charan tribe in particular, see R.V. Russell and Hiralal, *Tribes and Castes and the Central Provinces of India*, Vol. II, Cosmo Publications, Delhi, 1975, pp. 165–67.

[43] Cumberlage, *Berar Gazetteer*, p. 195.

[44] Crooke, *Tribes and Castes*, p. 157.

[45] Asiya Siddiqi, 'Introduction', in Asiya Siddiqi (ed.), *Trade and Finance in Colonial India, 1750–1860*, Themes in Indian History, Oxford University Press, New Delhi, 1995, p. 43.

[46] Irfan Habib, *The Agrarian System of Mughal India, 1556–1707*, second revised edn, Oxford University Press, New Delhi, 1999, p. 69n.

[47] Jean-Baptiste Tavernier, *Travels in India, 1640–1667*, translated by V. Ball, second edn, revised by W. Crooke, Oxford University Press, London, 1925, p. 14.

[48] Habib, *Agrarian System*, p. 69.

[49] Rathor, *Banjara Lok Sahitya Mein Samaj Sanskriti*, pp. 52, 60. Also see K.S. Singh, *Indian Communities*, p. 269.

[50] Rathor, *Banjara Lok Sahitya Mein Samaj Sanskriti*, p. 52.

[51] Crooke, *Tribes and Castes*, p. 155.

[52] Russell and Hiralal, *Tribes and Castes*, p. 170. Also see William Irvine, *Army of the Indian Mughals*, reprint, Eurasian Publishing House, Delhi, 1962.

[53] K.M. Ashraf, *Life and Conditions of the People of Hindustan*, Indus Publications, Karachi, reprint, 1978, p. 11.

[54] Ibid.

55 Habib, *Agrarian System*, p. 116. Also see Crooke, *Tribes and Castes*, p. 151.

56 Crooke, *Tribes and Castes.*

57 Extract of Fort St George, Military and Political Consultation, 9 October 1798, Boards Collections, 1798–1800, Vol. 59, F/4/59, 1313, India Office Library (IOL), London.

58 Extract of Fort St George, Military and Political Consultation, 30 October 1798, Boards Collections, ibid.

59 Ibid.

60 Extract of Fort St George, Military and Political Consultation, 4 December 1798, Boards Collections, ibid.

61 Ibid. Also, Extract of Fort St. George, Military and Political Consultation, 10 December 1798, Boards Collections, ibid.

62 Tavernier, *Travels in India*, pp. 33–34.

63 Habib, *Agrarian System*, p. 69n.

64 Ibid., pp. 70, 70n, 71, 71n.

65 Ashraf, *Life and Conditions of the People of Hindustan*, p. 11.

66 Bali Ram Patel, *Gaur Banjare Lokacha Itihas*, Deshmukh and Co., Amravati, 1939, p. 54.

67 Meena Bhargava, *State, Society and Ecology: Gorakhpur in Transition, 1750–1830*, Manohar, New Delhi, 1999, p. 231. Compare C.A. Bayly, *Rulers, Townsmen and Bazaars: North Indian Society in the Age of British Expansion, 1770–1870*, Cambridge University Press, Cambridge, 1983, p. 31.

68 Bhargava, *State, Society and Ecology*, p. 231.

69 Muzaffar Alam, *The Crisis of Empire in Mughal North India: Awadh and the Punjab, 1707–1748*, Oxford University Press, Cambridge, New Delhi, 1986, p. 247.

70 Buchanan Hamilton, 'An Account of the Northern Part of the District of Gorakhpur', Mss Eur D 91–3 (IOL), BK I, p. 172. Also see Bhargava, *State, Society and Ecology*, p. 237.

71 Compare Bayly, *Rulers, Townsmen and Bazaars*, p. 52.

72 Bhargava, *State, Society and Ecology*, p. 237. Also see Habib, *Agrarian System*, pp. 69–71; Tapan Raychaudhuri, 'Inland Trade', in Tapan Raychaudhuri and Irfan Habib (eds), *The Cambridge Economic History of India*, Vol. I, Orient Longman, New Delhi, 1984, p. 342.

73 Francis Buchanan, *An Account of the Districts of Bihar and Patna, 1811–12*, Bihar and Orissa Research Society, Patna, 1937, Table 7. Also see Bayly, *Rulers, Townsmen and Bazaars*, pp. 55–56.

74 Russell and Hiralal, *Tribes and Castes*, pp. 11, 162–72; also Irvine, *Army of the Indian Mughals*, p. 242.

75 Buchanan Hamilton, 'An Account', BK V, p. 64.

76 Translation of a Proclamation by the Lt Governor, Bisulpur, 10 November 1802, in G.N. Saletore (ed.), *Henry Wellesley's Correspondence, 1801–1803*, Selections from English Records No. 2, Government Central Record Office, Uttar Pradesh, Allahabad, 1955, pp. 84–85.

77 To the Court of Directors for the Affairs of the United Company of Merchants of England trading to the East Indies, 31 December 1804, Home

Dept Miscl. (Public) (Commercial)—Ceded Provinces (General Letters) from Bengal to Court of Directors, 1803–05, Vol. 210, National Archives of India, Delhi.

78 E.W. Blunt, Collector of Government Customs to Thomas Fortesque, Secretary to the Board of Commissioners, Farrukhabad, 7 October 1809, North West Provinces—Judicial Series, Saharanpur, Vol. 23, Regional State Archives, Allahabad.

79 E.H. Colebrooke and J. Dean to J. Lumsden, Vice President in Council, Fort William, 11 October 1809, North West Provinces—Judicial Series, Saharanpur, Vol. 23, Regional State Archives, Allahabad.

80 See Bayly, *Rulers, Townsmen and Bazaars*, p. 293.

81 Joseph J. Brenning, 'Textile Producers and Production in late Seventeenth Century Coromandel', in Sanjay Subrahmanyam (ed.), *Merchants, Markets and the State in Early Modern India*, Oxford University Press, New Delhi, 1990, pp. 69–71.

82 Compare Siddiqi, 'Introduction', p. 43.

83 Buchanan Hamilton, 'An Account', BK I, p. 161. Also Bhargava, *State, Society and Ecology*, p. 141.

84 Alam, *The Crisis of Empire*, pp. 25n, 162–63.

85 Translation of an *arzee* from the Tahsildar of Tripattur, 21 May 1799, Boards Collections, 1799–1800, Vol. 59 (IOL). Compare Radhika Singha, *A Despotism of Law: Crime and Justice in Early Colonial India*, Oxford University Press, New Delhi, 1998, p. 127.

86 Translation of an *arzee* from the Tahsildar of Kunattur, 16 May 1799, Boards Collections, 1799–1800, Vol. 59 (IOL).

87 Singha, *Despotism of Law*, p. 222.

88 Extract of a letter to Colonel Read, 29 May 1799, Boards Collections, 1799–1800, Vol. 59 (IOL).

89 To Captain J.G. Graham, Collector Ceded District from L. Mesuriir, Lt Commanding Panagre, 19 May 1799, Boards Collections, ibid.

90 Bhargava, *State, Society and Ecology*, p. 141. Compare S.Z.H. Jafri, 'Origin and Growth of Ta'alluqdari Tenures in Awadh', *Proceedings of the Indian History Congress*, 45th session, Annamalai, 1984, pp. 414, 417n.

91 H.R. Nevill, *District Gazetteers of the United Provinces of Agra and Oudh—Gorakhpur*, Vol. 31, Allahabad, 1909, p. 184; also Buchanan Hamilton, 'An Account', BK I, pp. 161, 172, 326; Bhargava, *State, Society and Ecology*, pp. 141–42.

92 Nevill, *District Gazetteers*, p. 185; also Buchanan Hamilton, 'An Account', BK I, pp. 161, 326; Bhargava, *State, Society and Ecology*, p. 142.

93 The Banjaras at present are mostly settled in the states of Madhya Pradesh, Gujarat, Rajasthan, Uttar Pradesh, Maharashtra, Haryana, Himachal Pradesh, Punjab, Orissa and the union territories of Delhi and Chandigarh. In some states, the Banjaras are notified under the scheduled caste and scheduled tribe categories. For more details, see K.S. Singh, *India's Communities*, pp. 268–72.

English Trading Methods in the Seventeenth Century and the Rajapur Experiment

Vijaya Ramaswamy

Perhaps the greatest handicap of the East India Company in India was the nature of the Company itself—its organizational problems, the state of its finances, its private traders. The Company had, on average, between ten to twelve factories in south India alone, and the enormous task of organizing the East India trade rested with them. First and foremost, communication gaps existed at virtually every level—between the Board of Directors in England and the Company's agents and residents in India; between superior factories and subordinate factories; between the agents and the factors; between the Company and the chief merchants and other intermediaries; and finally, between the intermediaries and the primary producers. Policy decisions were difficult to frame and almost impossible to coordinate.

Secondly, the position of the Company itself was not impregnable but subject to political changes, as can be seen from the royal charter granted to William Courteen's association by Charles I, or the charter of Charles II which broke the monopoly of the East India Company and permitted the operation of rival companies in the Indies. Thirdly, the functioning of the East India Company was not only limited by the political shifts in England but was constantly hampered by turbulent political changes and wars in India. In the north Deccan region this was especially true of the Mughal–Maratha wars or the Bijapur–Maratha conflicts which caused mass desertion of villages, pushed up the prices of cotton and saltpetre, and made the procurement of cloth and other goods virtually impossible.

It is against this background that the Rajapur experiment is to be viewed. In the course of the seventeenth–eighteenth centuries, while the Company muddled through its problems, certain bold innovations were attempted by some of its agents and servants. One such experiment was the attempt at Kasimbazar to set up a Company *karkhana* bringing together weavers, dyers and bleachers, in a bid to eliminate intermediaries. For about two to three years, that is, roughly the official span of that agent, the Company records were replete with a plethora of optimistic details regarding new schemes by the agent, his heated exchanges with his superiors which were also reflected in the dispatches to and from England, and usually the bowing down to the inevitable on the part of the 'innovative agent'. With a new successor, the factory would get back once more to the established grooves of official Company practice with all the internal tensions being sugar-coated by external conformity. Rajapur in the north Deccan was one such factory in the seventeenth century, and the name of its innovative agent was Henry Revington.

This essay will study the Rajapur experiment in the context of the English trading methods in the seventeenth century and the historical specificity of Rajapur. The experiment will be analysed within the context of the Company's trade, particularly in textiles, from three angles: (i) the established pattern of Company policy in India with its accompanying problems; (ii) the historical specificity of the Rajapur factory; and (iii) Agent Henry Revington's experiments and their ultimate failure, resulting in the abandoning of the factory in 1679.

Situating the English Presence in Seventeenth-Century Commerce

The directors of the East India Company were faced with the task of framing policy decisions in a situation where time and distance between the markets and the areas of production sometimes tended to reduce all normal measures of commercial risk to meaningless calculation. There was a perpetual disequilibrium between the Company policy and its implementation in India, between the demand and supply of goods. The factory system and the creation of fortified settlements were devised as a solution to the problem of long-distance operation in production centres,[1] but the system failed to solve all the problems because of the varied nature of the markets and the slowness of the process in fulfilling these demands. In the Malay archipelago, where Indian cloth was bartered for spices, the demand was usually for coarse, striped cloth like *tapechindes*, *pattas* and *sallalos*.[2] The coarse blue *salamporees* was mainly supplied to West African slaves and came to be called 'slave cloth'.[3] The European market was much more fluid. For example, in Europe the market for textiles changed every year with changing fashions.[4] A dispatch from England, dated 22 April 1681, states:

> Note this for a constant and general rule . . . that you change the fashion and flower as much as you can every year, for English ladies, and they say, the French and other Europeans will give twice as much for a new thing not seen in Europe though worse, than they will give, for a better . . . of the same fashion worn the former year.

However, the problem at the procurement end was that six months elapsed between the sending of the Company's order to Surat or Fort St George or, as in the present case, Rajapur, and the receiving of the orders. Given the highly fluctuating nature of the market, when invoiced goods were ultimately dispatched they would register a sharp loss at the auctions.

The second major problem arose from having to deal with intermediaries. The weaving centres were too many and too far-flung for the Company to maintain administrative personnel in all these regions. The problem was equally present in the case of all the commodities, including saltpetre, that formed a part of the Company trade. It was only rarely that factories could be established at the production centres themselves. Hence, by and large, the Company could operate only through intermediaries.

Intermediaries became crucial to the English East India Company's commercial set-up for several reasons. First, the English, at least in the early part of the seventeenth century, had much less liquid capital at their disposal than the Dutch. Availability of ready money facilitated the Dutch in dealing directly with the weavers since they could mobilize resources faster and buy things cheaper at the source. In fact, a *farman* of the king of Golconda given in 1605 orders that all weavers employed by the Dutch, with Dutch money in their hands, should not be interfered with in their work.[5]

Given the fact that the English, unlike the Dutch, seldom had any liquid capital at their disposal, they could only operate by borrowing heavily from local merchants who advanced money to producers of indigo, pepper and other spices, and to weavers of cotton cloth. They were indebted to many of their own chief merchants, like Uttamamoda, Kasi Viranna, Timmanna and even Mir Jumla, the Deccani potentate. Of Uttamamoda, the chief merchant at Pulicat, the English factor wrote: 'Last year he gave us credit for a 1000 rials till the arrival of our ships and now promises still greater service.'[6] In dealing with weavers the Company had to also adopt a system of advances, because at a time of keen European competition, a primary characteristic of the seventeenth century, committing the intermediaries ensured that they would not sell cloth to the Dutch or the Danes for higher profit.[7]

The practical problems arising out of dealing directly with weavers rendered the use of intermediaries necessary. The Company's reasons are best laid forth in the Pulicat factor's explanation of 1622:

> the merchants . . . have to be responsible for the money advanced through them to the weavers and painters which oftentimes pay them with a farewell. If we had to deal with them direct at the year's end, when we expected to be invested of our goods, we should find undoubtedly come short of our quantity, besides undergo a hazard of their running away where there was no hope for us to find them out or recover their monies.[8]

The underwriting of responsibility by merchants solved the problem of bad debts, which was a major source of concern for the Company. Of course, it was also the duty of the middlemen to ensure quality control. The weavers were supplied with musters through merchants, and the merchants ensured that they worked 'to the perfection of a pattern', a telling phrase that occurs in a dispatch from the Board of Directors dated 1697.

Thus developed a system of intermediaries which was highly complex and not a simple one of Company–merchant–weaver. There were chief merchants for each region assisted by smaller merchants. Below them were the *dubash* or *egyb*, brokers or interpreters, and the head broker in turn had a number of assistants. The commission of the head broker, as given in the diaries of Streynsham Master, was 1 per cent on coarse cloth and 1.5 per cent on fine cloth.[9] The *dubash* was sometimes referred to as 'Braminy' in the records because, being the only literate class, the brahmanas became the go-betweens. The brahmana thus logically became a '*dvi-bashi*', literally, 'one who could speak in two languages'. Company records refer to 'Braminy' like Vira Ragavayya in the 1670s or Chandrasekharayya in the 1680s, in the context of the settlement of new factories at Cuddalore and Porto Novo. Another intermediary who received a cut from various transactions of the Company was the *vakil* or *mulla*, whose job it was, presumably, to point out the implications of any Company policy in respect of native laws and customs.

The most glaring disadvantage of having such a vast chain of intermediaries between the Company and the producers was the cuts taken by them and the consequent reduction in the Company's profits. Besides, too many middlemen also tended to make the whole system less efficient. Too great a time-gap existed between the director's orders, the receipt of these communications at Surat and Fort St George, and the contracting of weavers by the merchant-middlemen through brokers, by which time the nature of the demand might have changed. It would by then be too late to change the cloth on the loom.

By virtue of their unique position, the long chain of intermediaries became extremely powerful in the commercial scenario of the seventeenth century. Also, the presence of a multitiered system of intermediaries increased the hiatus between the British agents at the Indian end and the policy-makers operating 'beyond the black waters'. The middlemen were well aware of their indispensability to the Company. This led the chief merchants to usurp powers and abuse their position. Malaya Chetti was one of the most powerful chief merchants of the seventeenth century. Referred to as the king's agent in one of the Company dispatches, he is said to have collaborated with the Dutch to damage English trade.[10] It was said of the brahmana intermediaries Venkata and Kannappa that they held the offices of *dubash*, governor of the Black Town, and chief *taliyar* or watchman. When Baker was the agent, Rev. William Issacs reported to the Company in England that the agent had no knowledge and no say since everything was being done by Beri Timmanna.[11] He also stated that the entire available rice was captured by him so that the weavers were compelled to increase the price of cloth. Winter, the next agent at Fort St George, wrote that Timmanna could not be dispensed with because the other merchants and weavers functioned only at his bidding.

The domination of the chief merchant meant not merely domination by one man but in fact domination by his family and succeeding generations. Elihu Yale, the agent in the 1690s, made a lengthy comment on this tendency. Timmappa, son of Pedda Venkatadry, claimed the rights of intermediary not only for himself but also for Mooda Verona, adopted son of Kasi Viranna and Durgappa, son of Chinna Venkatadry, 'who', says Yale, 'according to their rules are to succeed one another in the chief merchantship and their children after them'.[12] In the factories of the English East India Company, the system of chief merchants continued right till 1680. Streynsham Master formed the first joint stock of merchants in 1680 but, as seen by Elihu Yale's statement, even joint stocks continued to be dominated by the chief merchants and their families. In this context, the Rajapur experiment has special relevance because one of its major efforts was the elimination of intermediaries.

The line of communication between policy-makers in England and policy-implementing agents in India was rendered more complex as a result of the political pulls and pressures at both ends.

Contextualizing Rajapur

Rajapur is a small town in Ratnagiri district on the Konkan coast. It lies between Dabhol in the north, and Goa and Karwar in the south. In the seventeenth century it was at the centre of a political hotbed, with the Portuguese in Goa, the Dutch at Vengurla and the indigenous powers—the Adil Shahis of Bijapur, the Marathas and the Mughals—constantly at war. The chief merit of the place lay in the fact that Rajapur itself was comparatively insignificant and tranquil, so that, while other trading ports (Masulipatnam, for example) were hit by the wars raging around them, Rajapur could exploit the situation to corner all the trade. The inland markets of the region were Raibagh, Hubli, Belgaon and Athani.

Commercially, pepper of the variety called long pepper was the most important product of Rajapur.[13] Cardamom was also produced, mainly in the Vengurla region.[14] The eastern portion of the Deccan plateau consisted of black cotton soil. Rajapur had a flourishing industry in cotton textiles, especially *baftas*, *moorees* and silk cloth. The Company trade in these textiles was mainly directed towards Mokha and Persia, that is, towards the Red Sea trade. Some inferior indigo was produced at Dabhol, as well as seed lac and borax at Rajapur. However, although the indigo from the Rajapur region was used locally for dyeing and was even exempted by the English, it could not match that of Malwa or Sarkhej.[15] Unrefined saltpetre was also produced and exported from Rajapur.[16]

Interestingly, Rajapur was first established as a centre for trade not by the East India Company but by their arch-rivals and interlopers, the Courteens, in l636. In December 1635, Charles I granted a charter to Courteen and his associates, licensing them to trade from the coast of Africa to the Far East, on the ground that the East India Company had neglected the interests of the nation and abused the privileges that had been conferred upon it.[17] The royal charter to the Courteens was renewed in 1637. Although the English East India Company did have a tiny factory at Rajapur, it was the Courteens who put both Rajapur and Karwar on the trading map of Asia and Europe. The history of Rajapur in the next decade was one of commercial domination by the Courteens, who, despite the protests of the incumbent Company, were received with equal favour by the native sovereigns and granted the same trade privileges.

The Courteens undercut their English compatriots in Mokha, Persia and the Gombroons. Their ships—*William and Talbot* under Edward Hall and later *Loyalty* under Durston—flooded the Bijapur region with broadcloth, lead and vermilion, and loaded cinnamon, cardamom and pepper in large quantities for the West Asian market. The first Courteen expedition in 1636 under Weddell had a capital of 120,000 pounds. They met the king of Bijapur and secured the right to trade throughout his dominions as well as to establish themselves at Rajapur.[18] The Courteens soon bought up the Company broker at Rajapur, called Vittala Komati Chetti. The beleaguered East India Company simultaneously had to face fierce opposition from the Bijapur government.

Rajapur, it seemed, was no longer a viable proposition for the Company. The Courteens glutted the local markets at Rajapur and Karwar with their broadcloth and lead, the only products which seemed to have any demand in these regions. They also took away the profitable business of carrying freight goods to Persia, the Gombroons and other places. The Company's letter dated 7 September 1645 raised a storm of protest over the 'hijacking' of the goods of the 'Moors' and 'Banias' (by which nomenclatures they referred to Muslim and Hindu merchants) bound for the Gombroons. President Fremlin at Surat wrote: 'You are positively and absolutely forbidden . . . to come to any port or place in the Indies where our honourable employees have trade and residencies. Such was, is, and will be, Rajapur.'[19] Claims and counter-claims by the English East India Company and the Courteens find mention in the record books of that time as the 'Courteenians and the Cockenians', since Pitt and Company, it was said, represented not England as a whole (as they claimed) but merely William Cockayne, the then Governor of the Company.

Portuguese and Dutch rivalry compounded by the Courteens' menace resulted in virtually shutting down commercial operations by 1645–46. The British, under duress, abandoned Rajapur in 1650.

Revington, the 'Innovative Agent', and the Rajapur Experiment

During the period of open trade, the increasing demand in England for pepper, saltpetre and other items, and the obstacles placed by the Dutch in the way of obtaining pepper from Bantam or Achin, led to the reopening of the Rajapur factory in 1658. Henry Revington became the man in charge.

Revington's character is revealed by his motto: 'Idleness is a disease.' He combined unbounded energy with a certain visionary adventurism. In his dreams of the future he saw Rajapur as the centre of a vast trade in saltpetre, pepper, calico and cotton yarn, replacing Surat as the headquarters of the East India Company in the west. It would be made the site of a mint providing coinage for use all along the west. As his dreams unfolded, Rajapur would replace Surat as the headquarters of the Presidency initially due to the Maratha–Mughal–Bijapur wars, but eventually as the permanent headquarters of the English East India Company. Rajapur, under the inspired guidance of Revington, would become the greatest mart in India, and England, the greatest trading nation.

A primary aim of Revington's experiment at Rajapur was the elimination of intermediaries through the framing of a new purchase policy. He pushed inland and set up his headquarters at Raibagh (in Kolhapur district) because Goa, Vengurla and Rajapur lay triangular to it and all goods could be gathered at this point. In purchasing cotton yarn, indigo, saltpetre and pepper, he proposed to deal directly with the primary producers. In a letter to the Surat Presidency dated 4 October 1659, he gave strong justification for moving from Kolhapur into Hotni, Lakshmishvar and Hubli: 'You complain of our going to Hotni because it is a charge unto the Company. We answer we go nowhere but it is to the Company's profit . . . and go where *our business lies and not trust to Baniyas*'[20] (the word '*baniya*' is used here as a pejorative term for merchants). In November, Revington wrote triumphantly to the Board of Directors that he had purchased saltpetre at Gadag, calicoes at Lakshmishvar and Mudhol, and pepper at Hubli, at far lower prices than they had hitherto paid through intermediaries.

Revington assiduously cultivated the friendship of Rustam Zaman, the governor of Rajapur, and obtained a grant of privileges from him including a supply of 200 tons of saltpetre at 'a much lower rate and hoped to bring it down to the very cheap rate of three-and-a-half rupees per maund'.[21] He observed that the best and cheapest pepper was to be had in the region around Hubli–Lakshmisvar, Kadra, Hotni, Raibagh and Asby—and if only the Company directors would provide them with ready money they could eliminate the brokers, paying cash directly to the primary producers. Equally important was his shrewd observation that so long as the Company was forced to purchase pepper from the independent kingdoms, they would continue to exercise their monopoly and hold up the price. The only means of getting even cheaper pepper would be to militarily and politically take over Karwar.

The agent's interest extended to the weavers. Noting that the value of the excellent Kolhapur cotton yarn was reduced because it was twisted the wrong way, he persuaded the spinners to adopt the right-hand twist. Since the Rajapur weavers at this time produced only the Guinea cloth demanded by the Dutch, Revington suggested bringing in Masulipatnam weavers to teach them the technique of weaving long-cloth.[22]

Finally, Revington sought and obtained a sizeable customs remission on goods purchased by the Company. He first secured the Company's permission to ship pepper from Karwar itself, without bringing it up to Rajapur; this formed the basis of an English settlement here. Next, he secured the privilege from Rustam Zaman that Company goods would not have to pay any customs duties at Karwar but could make the payment at Rajapur, after reducing one-quarter of the total payment.[23]

In a letter of 19 November 1659, addressed to the Board of Directors, the agent triumphantly asserted that Rajapur had been able to provide during that season 900 tons of goods, consisting of pepper, saltpetre, calicoes, gum lac, cotton yarn and coffee. In his characteristically pompous style, which roused the ire of the Surat Presidency, he wrote in a letter of 10 December 1659: 'Our present business is at this present not so much about your present business as your future. . . . Therefore we come to speak of things that may be, and not what is already done.'[24]

In the context of the innovations that Revington attempted at

Rajapur, one recurrent problem was the lack of ready money. Liquid capital could make possible cheaper purchases of pepper, cloth and saltpetre, and also eliminate intermediaries. Therefore, Revington's blueprint for the future involved the setting up of a mint at Rajapur. As he picturesquely put it, 'Intention [to trade] without a stock of money is like an adjective without a substantive, which cannot stand.'[25]

The time-worn methods of vending English broadcloth or participating in the country's trade had failed. The English met with very limited success in their attempts to sell broadcloth, scarletts, rashes, aroras and other types of woollens, as also lead, copper, tin, coral, vermilion, madder, etc., at Rajapur, or, for that matter, anywhere else on the Coromandel coast. Company goods remained unsold and most of the broadcloth was given out as *peshkash* or presents to earn the goodwill of merchants and local officials.[26] While the failure of woollens in the Indian market was inevitable, given the climate of the region, the English failure to push other products like coral, vermilion and quicksilver was due to the situation of glut caused by the Dutch East India Company.

In the absence of the possibility of raising any money from off-loading woollens and other goods which had no takers in the Indian market, the agent came up with what he thought was the best alternative—the establishment of a mint at Rajapur. Revington believed that the Rajapur mint could coin silver equal in weight and firmness to the Mughal rupee, and facilitate trade at Surat. He pointed out to the Company, the following advantages.

1. By having a *taksal* (that is, a mint), the coins may be minted by the Company's servants themselves paying only mintage charges, and thus eliminate the gain of the Surat *shroff* who was the local money-changer.

2. The Company could save the 2 per cent custom imposed on imported treasure at Surat by minting the coins at Rajapur itself, besides which their silver could be used to mint more coins here than in England because of the difference in the requirement of the intrinsic value.

3. In times of war, for example, the war of succession raging in the north, the Company with its coins could not only supply other merchants at a premium but carry on its own trade unaffected by political vicissitudes.

4. Finally, using a typical bullionist argument, Revington pleaded that the Mughal rulers and the Surat governors would have greater respect for 10,000 pounds in cash than 100,000 pounds in goods.

The Presidency at Surat was not persuaded by these attractive arguments. Their dampening reply to Revington was: 'You forget what you aught to do and run into new projects which are rotten before they are ripe and so will be your *taksal* agreement with Rustam Zaman.'[27] Revington in his turn mocked at the absurdity of sending him silver for use in a country with a gold standard, 'which will neither buy anything nor sell here to anybody but the shroff who sends it to Surat again and so will pay a price accordingly'.[28] Thus, nothing came of Revington's scheme to establish a silver mint at Rajapur, but it foreshadowed the establishment, thirteen years later, of a mint at Bombay and eventually a mint in the Deccan, following the Mughal take-over of Bijapur and Golconda.

The final goal of the Rajapur experiment, as set forth by Revington in his 'Letters of 1659' to the Company in England and the Presidency at Surat, related to the manipulation of indigenous power politics and the establishment of English political ascendancy, leading eventually to a commercial take-over. In his letter of 10 December, he stated his impression that Portugal was a waning power in the area and so the English should step in to prevent an impending Dutch–Bijapur alliance (a powerful possibility in his imagination) and instead encourage Bijapur's alliance with the Portuguese, so that when Portugal eventually left Goa (something that he visualized in the immediate future but eventually happened only in 1960!), the English would be invited to fill the vacancy as the best friend and ally of Bijapur. Playing a role in the internal politics, Revington encouraged Rustam Zaman in his attempted overthrow of Ali Adil Shah of Bijapur. This was to be accomplished by allying with Shivaji and giving him control over the fort of Danda Rajapur. The letter colourfully describes Shivaji's encounter with Afzal Khan and the death of the Bijapur commander. Linked to these proposals, he sought permission to build a fort at Rajapur, thus enabling it to become the English headquarters in times of Mughal–Maratha conflict.

The Surat Presidency regarded Revington's schemes as harebrained and a blatant transgression of their authority. In a letter to Rajapur dated 24 October 1659, they asked whether Revington and his associates 'ever knew a petty factory whose conceited chief is allowed but 50 pounds per annum as salary, dare protest against a President and a Council?'[29] Issuing orders for Revington's dismissal, they wrote in a letter of 3 February 1660: 'Revington fools himself by his conceit into crime after crime.'[30]

As things turned out, Shivaji proved to be more cunning than Revington. After capturing Panhala he sacked the Rajapur factory in 1660–61. In panic, Revington changed sides and offered English aid to Sidi Johar, the Bijapur commander. The success of the Bijapur forces against Shivaji was shortlived. In September 1660, Revington fled for his life to Vishalgarh. Meanwhile, Shivaji imprisoned many of the English factors and their brokers.

The Surat Presidency was throughout very critical of Revington and the Rajapur agent's role in the matter of Danda Rajapuri. In a letter to him, dated 24 October 1659, they wrote: 'We charge you to act nothing [*sic*] without advising us so that through your vain imaginations of doing something without power you hinder not the endeavours of those that are commanded by their masters to use theirs.'

Business was at a standstill and the English debts at Rajapur were mounting. Pleading for some money, Revington wrote that the broker Bhaoji Shivpat, on hearing about the dishonouring of English bills of exchange at Surat, had immediately informed Rustam Zaman and his deputy Abdul Kareem of their insolvency. The agent bitterly complained that the broker had summoned all the merchants and *vakils* of Rajapur, and drawn up a consolidated account of English debts to them. Revington concluded: 'We are now reduced to that extremity that none will lend us one piece of money and that if it were not for our broker Valiji Chaunji, we might starve.'[31]

The Surat Presidency, on the other hand, expressed its doubts about whether it was at all necessary to have a factory at Rajapur. Writing directly to the Company on 10 January 1660, they claimed that pepper and cardamom were not grown at Rajapur but came from Karwar and Cannanore; that saltpetre could be obtained more cheaply from Agra or Sind; that the calicoes of Rajapur were ill-wrought and not to be compared with those of Navsari near Surat; and finally, that the vending of English goods at Rajapur was deeply disappointing. According to Andrews and his advisors at Surat, the strongest argument against the continuation of the factory at Rajapur was the intolerable pretensions and personality of Revington himself.

The final phase of the Rajapur experiment began with the decision of the Surat Presidency being conveyed to the Board of Directors in England. The Rajapur factory was to be closed down and it was advised that Agent Revington should be charged with insubordination. Their warning to the Board was dramatically phrased. If Revington was not charge-sheeted and punished, the result would be 'every particular factory a faction'. What is interesting is that throughout this drama, Revington's associates stood by him staunchly.

Andrews, the head of the Surat Presidency, proved to be prophetic on one point. In l661, Shivaji wreaked vengeance on the English factory for aiding Bijapur. Englishmen were massacred and Revington was imprisoned. Undaunted, Revington wrote from his prison in June l661, that the Company must on no account pay the ransom of 1,00,000 pagodas demanded by Shivaji for his release. He further suggested that the Company must hold out the threat of offering open passage to Aurangzeb for facilitating his attack on the Deccan if the factors were not unconditionally released. Revington had the boldness to propose that Shivaji be bullied into giving a port town to the English East India Company for setting up a new factory and establishing a mint! Although the letter shows Revington as a man unmatched for sheer audacity and courage, he was actually suffering from a fatal attack of dropsy which led to his death shortly after. Strangely enough, by then all hostility between the Surat head Andrews and Revington seems to have come to an end; Andrews had written to England on 17 October l761 praising Revington and praying for his recovery. Revington however died soon after.

The death of the innovative agent Revington marked the end of the Rajapur experiment, and the end of his rosy vision of Rajapur as the greatest English settlement on the west coast. Rajapur passed into Shivaji's hands who now had a personal stake in reviving trade in the region and, with this view, released Taylor and all the other English factors at Rajapur in 1663. The Maratha governor at Rajapur, Raoji Pundit, appealed to the English to reopen their factory at Rajapur. But Rajapur had faded into history.

The Rajapur experiment was by no means an exercise in futility, and the future course of English trading policy to some extent vindicated the steps taken by Revington. His concern with the domination of chief merchants was reflected in the creation of joint stock companies in 1680. A silver mint, so strongly favoured by Revington, was established in the next decade; and his scheme for a commercial take-over through political manipulations, although it proved faulty in the case of Bijapur, was adopted time and again by the English in their dealings with the Indian principalities.

This paper was originally presented at the international seminar, *Beyond the Black Waters*, held at Berkeley, California, in 1989. This essay is dedicated to my memories of Professor Partha Sarathi Gupta as mentor and friend.

Notes and References

1 The establishment of a factory was geared to the demands of the specific types of goods required and the locality where they would be available. In the context of the textile industry, the calicoes of Surat, the printed chintz and bettelles of Masulipatnam and the painted calicoes of San Thome (Mylapur), Pulicat and Saidapet (in Chennapatnam or Chennai) were the reasons for the establishment of factories in these regions. In the Consultation of 1677, the agent and Council take credit for the fact that their factory at Madapollam was 'so well seated' since 'it lyes among the weavers'. *The Diary and Consulation Books of Fort St George, 1672–1756*, Madras, 1910–41.

2 The traveller Peter Floris (1611–15) emphasized the particularity of the eastern markets—'But a great oversight hath been committed in the bespeaking of the pattas, dragons, sallalos, etc., for they have, all of them, a little narrower white edge and the upright (that is, proper) Malay cloth must be without it. . . . I had never believed it, that so small a fault could cause so great an abatement in prices.' *The Voyage of Peter Floris*, edited by W.H. Moreland, Hakluyt Society, London, 1934, p. 71.

3 This trade began around 1630 and the term for Indian calico, 'guinea', in fact comes from the Guinea coast of equatorial Africa where most of the slaves were purchased.

4 The consumption pattern in England was a changing one, from a demand for calico for curtains and coverlets to a demand for calico as a utility item of clothing and bettelles as fashion ware. The late seventeenth century was the age of a 'calico craze' in England. The changing nature of demand can be seen in the *Dispatches from England—1670 to 1758*, Madras, 1911–32.

5 The *farman* has been quoted in Joseph Brennig, *The Textile Trade of the Seventeenth Century, Northern Coromandel*, University Microfilms, Ann Arbor, Michigan, p. 25.

6 *English Factories in India*, edited by William Foster, 23 vols, Oxford, 1906–27, Vol. II, p. 154.

7 *Diary and Consultation Books of Fort St George*, 28 September 1675, p. 74: Kasi Viranna's statement that if at least half of the payment was not made

to the weavers in advance, the Dutch would run away with the whole bargain.

8 *English Factories in India,* Vol. I, 24 September 1652, p. 104, Thomas Mills and John Milward at Pulicat to the Masulipatnam factors.

9 *The Diaries of Streynsham Master* (AD 1675–80), edited by Richard Temple, 2 vols, Hakluyt Society, London, 1911, Vol. II, p. 165.

10 The share of Malaya Chetti in the financial investments of the Dutch is very revealing. In 1632, the Company invested 32,000 pagodas in textiles out of which Malaya Chetti lent 23,000 pagodas—Koloniel Archief, 5 August 1632, folio 246–47, cited in Joseph Brennig, *The Textile Trade of the Seventeenth Century, Northern Coromandel,* p. 56.

11 Original Correspondence, (O.C.) 2856 A, dated 1661.

12 *Diary and Consultation Books of Fort St George,* 5 November, 1658, p. 122.

13 Tavernier, *Travels in India (1640–60),* edited by V. Ball and W. Crooke, 2 vols, original edition, Hakluyt Society, London, 1925, reprint, first Indian edition, Munshiram Manoharlal, Delhi, 1977, Vol. II, p. 11; J.H. Linschoten (*c.* 1583), *Itinerario,* 2 vols, Hakluyt Society, London, 1984, Vol. I, p. 73, etc. In 1637, Bornford, the representative of the English Company at this place, was assured by the Adil Shahi officer at Rajapur that it was capable of exporting annually 3,000 candies (approximately 700 tons) of pepper.

14 Linschoten, *Itinerario,* Vol. II, as well as Tavernier, *Travels,* Vol. I, have several references to cardamom being traded through the Rajapur factory.

15 See, for instance, references to lac in *English Factories in India,* Vol. X, specifically letter dated 19 November 1659. Thevenot also refers to the production of lac in Rajapur: *Travels of Thevenot and Carreri,* edited by Surendranath Sen, New Delhi, 1949, p. 101.

16 *English Factories in India,* Vol. VIII, pp. 79, 186; Vol. X, p. 379, etc.

17 The nature of the charter granted to Courteens is discussed in Holden Furber, *Rival Empires of Trade in the Orient,* Oxford University Press, Delhi, 1976, p. 69ff.

18 *English Factories in India,* Vol. VI. English Company's letter to the Directors from President Fremlin and Council at Swally Marine, dated 9 December 1639 and 27 January 1640, complaining of the stiff competition posed by the Courteens at Rajapur, threatening their very existence.

19 *English Factories in India,* Vol. VI, President Fremlin and Council at Surat to Edward Hall and John Smart, dated 3 February 1640, p. 236.

20 Original correspondence, 18 October 1659.

21 *English Factories in India,* Vol. X, 19 November 1659, p. 241.

22 *English Factories in India,* correspondence between Revington and the Board of Directors, 19 November 1659, p. 241.

23 Ibid., letter to Hubli, 31 October 1659 and to Surat on 19 November 1659.

24 Ibid., p. 240.

25 Ibid., Revington from Kolhapur to the Company at Surat in his letter dated 12 October 1660.

26 *Diary and Consultation Books of Fort St George,* 14 September 1676. See

references to broadcloth given as *peshkash* to Madanna, Akkanna, Poddala Lingappa, etc.

27 *English Factories in India*, letter from Company to their Agent at Rajapur dated 24 October 1659, p. 243.

28 G/31/1 (519 T) Company Book of Letters, letter from Revington in Raybag to Surat dated 30 October 1659.

29 *English Factories in India*, letter from President Andrews to Randolph Taylor, second in command at Rajapur, dated 24 October 1659.

30 Ibid., letter from Andrew to Taylor dated 3 February 1660, p. 360.

31 For Revington's relationship with Shivaji and its impact on Rajapur, see *English Records on Shivaji*, edited by Paranjpe and Kale, 2 vols, Shivaji-charitra Karyalaya, Poona, 193l.

Social Change and Resistance

The Household, the Community and Women

Perspectives from the Early Grhyasutras, *c.* 800–500 BC

Jaya Sinha Tyagi

The notion of the *griha* in the Grhyasutras[1] included the physical structure of the house and the members of the household, and encompassed the idea that specific activities were conducted within the house. Mere co-residence did not qualify one to be a member of the *griha*; the members, who included the *grihapati*, his wife and their children, had to be connected to each other through ritual ties. In some instances, the elder son and his wife also stayed in the *griha*.[2] Within the *griha*, various activities related to production, consumption, distribution and transmission of resources and traditions were carried out, along with activities related to reproduction and forging of social linkages. The last was one of the important tasks of the *griha*.

The rites that are mentioned in the Grhyasutras can be divided into two categories—those that were confined to the household and were carried out in the presence of the members of the household, and those which took place in the presence of the surrounding community.[3] It is significant that by the time these texts were compiled, an attempt was made by the brahmanical order to not only control the complexities and hierarchies *within* the *griha* but also to manipulate the manner in which it would relate to the community *outside*. The Grhyasutras, while providing for several interactive levels through which the household could communicate with other social groups, were careful in identifying brahmanas as the ones who could control these channels of communication. The growing role of the brahmana on occasions like the *upanayana*, marriage, birth and death rites was related to the attempt to extend brahmanical control over events where the community interacted. In order to understand how the interaction was carried out, we have to first identify that social grouping which is attempted in the Grhyasutras, and the level at which the household made connections with these groups. We need to identify the areas of interaction between the household and social groups such as the village, *varna*, the *kula*, and what part women may have played in initiating or changing the nature of these interactions. But before that, it is necessary to understand the significance of rituals in establishing linkages between the household and the rest of the community.

Role of Rituals in Establishing Social Linkages

Rituals served as a mechanism through which 'communication' at different levels could be achieved.[4] In the Grhyasutras, the 'public' display of rituals was to make open declarations of changing circumstances. Marriage, birth and death rites kept the household in a state of constant flux, influencing the *griha*'s producing and consuming capacity, and causing related changes in the surrounding community.[5] Thus, the marriage of a son or daughter, the birth of a child, or even the death of a member of the household, were 'formally' announced through the performance of rites. The relations between different levels in the societal structure were so entwined that rites like marriage, involving more than one *griha*, more than one *kula* and more than one *grama*, would cause ripples in the community, besides changing the situation in the participating *griha*, *kula* and *grama*.

The other reason for the 'formalization' of relationships in public view was to display conformity with traditions in order to gain social acceptance. The need to conform is constantly reiterated in the Grhyasutras. However, conformity with traditions did not mean that there was total uniformity in the manner in which rites were conducted. The Grhyasutras hint at the underlying tensions and competitiveness that marked the performance of rituals, where each household would play the game of one-upmanship, 'cloaking conflicts', for gaining or underlining one's status, whether it was in showing adherence to traditions or in giving *dakshina* to the brahmana. The brahmanical texts ensured that in the ensuing struggle, it was the brahmana who would act as the intermediary between different participants of the ritual and the community that would stand to gain the most.

There are many instances where the Grhyasutras refer to interaction with the community, especially in marriage rites. The couple stayed with a brahmana of repute on the night of the marriage in the *Gobhila Grhyasutra* II.3.1; according to the *Gobhila Grhyasutra*

II.4.6, brahmana women 'of good character, whose husbands and sons are living', escorted the new bride into her new home once she arrived there. It also seems as if subsequent ceremonies were performed under their aegis.[6] Similarly, rituals at birth ensured that the birth of a new member aspiring towards inclusion in the community was announced. Death rites also showed participation of the community where support to the bereaved family was offered.

In fact, if one is to identify the two main events in the texts, it would be marriage and death. The preoccupation of the Grhyasutra authors with both these events is not unrelated. Marriage established the householder, gave him a certain status and allowed the birth of progeny. It would be this progeny who would look after the interests of the 'fathers' (*pitr*) after their death. Thus, both marriage and death were events that took place in the household but which involved the community. Community participation and issues of reciprocality were most evident in these two rites. Community participation allowed for a public declaration of intentions and actions, so that if there was any lapse in reciprocity or any wavering in promises the community could play a role in allowing the dues to be paid. These dues need not necessarily be material dues, but could be social, religious or ritual. In that sense, both death and marriage were occasions when the whole family could meet their kin and the village community.

The Grhyasutras refer to the fact that the householder, *grihapati*,[7] lived an active life with ample opportunities for social interaction. The *Apastamba Grhyasutra* II.4.1 refers to friends of the groom who were sent as 'wooers', supposed to be versed in the *mantras*. In contrast, there is hardly any reference to the friends that a bride may have had; in fact, a woman who had too many friends was to be avoided as a potential wife, according to the *Apastamba Grhyasutra* I. 3.11. The *Apastamba Grhyasutra* VIII. 23.6 refers to the protagonist's anxiety with regard to losing out on friendship. The text states that if he wished that 'somebody should not be estranged from him', he should pour his urine into the horn of a living animal and sprinkle it three times from right to left around the sleeping person while chanting verses.

The offering of *madhuparka*[8] to select guests in hospitality rites shows that social interaction in the Grhyasutras seemed to hinge on the expectations of certain sections of society. *Acharyas*, *brahmacharin*, relatives and travellers, in particular, depended on the hospitality of the householder for their sustenance.[9] The 'anxiety of hospitality'[10] seems to reveal an underlying current, the need to ensure harmony between the guest and the host. The delineation of boundaries and the codification of rules are towards this purpose. Yet, the question of the 'disguised' guest, one with a hidden identity that could cloak divinity, seems to show an anxiety to ensure hospitality rather than to only delineate its boundaries. The wife of the householder was included whenever hospitality was offered. The *Sankhayana Grhyasutra* II.16.3. states that if the wife, *bharya,* was present and the householder's fires were burning, then hospitality had to be extended to a guest if he came from a different village.[11] Although the wife was actively involved in assisting her husband, it is doubtful whether she could offer *madhuparka* on her own—it seems not, as there is no reference to her taking over the husband's duties in this case. Moreover, hospitality was based on reciprocity. While one can envisage a situation where the householder had occasion to receive hospitality from others, it is doubtful that women were given the same hospitality when they visited other households. Women did attend social occasions such as marriages and *upanayana*s and thus may have been guests from time to time, but they do not seem to qualify for the *argha*[12] reception of the Grhyasutras. The list of those who were *arghya* was exclusively male, and there is no reference to a visiting mother-in-law or any other woman relative. The brahmanical preoccupation with males is evident in the Grhyasutras from the manner in which special male guests—the *raja,* the *snataka* (one who has taken the bath after studentship), the *ritvij* (the learned brahmana), the *svasur* (the father-in-law) and the *mitra* (the friend) were venerated.

Griha rituals played an important role in forging linkages between the members of the *griha* and the rest of the community. It will now be relevant to see how the *griha* was projected as the centre of existence, situated within the community, and the manner in which the community itself was layered.

Social Grouping in the Grhyasutras: The *Varna* System

A study of the Grhyasutras shows that while the institution of *varna* did stratify the society, it was not the only form of differentiation, nor were *varna* divisions as watertight as is thought. There were several ways in which social stratification was achieved in the Grhyasutra texts, with separate 'categories' interspersed within the framework of the *varna* system and at other times shown to be separate from it. Thus, the *varna* mechanism coexisted with other forms of social differentiation. While there was an attempt to 'classify' all elements on the basis of *varna* in brahmanical literature, there were also situations where this was not possible. Women belonged to a 'contentious' category and were included in the *varna* mechanism, '*varna*ized' in some contexts while being separate from *varna* in other contexts.

The *Gobhila Grhyasutra* I.7.5 on the *darshapaurnamasa* sacrifice refers to the preparation of grain for sacrifice. The grain was washed three times for the gods, twice for men and once for the *pitr*. This goes to show that in the hierarchy of the social order, it was the gods who were pre-eminent, followed by men and not the *pitr*, as one would assume. The reference to 'men' is to brahmanas, as they were the ones most likely to be the recipients of any offerings in a ritual. The fact that brahmanas were regarded as superior even to the *pitr* is significant, as the *pitr* were regarded as having power over forces in a manner which could prove to be beneficiary to the householder. Thus, brahmanas were regarded as second only to the gods in terms of power.

The position of women in the social hierarchy varied according to situations. In matters relating to marriage, women were placed just below the males of their *varna* and above males of the succeeding *varna*. However, there were other instances of 'clubbing' women together when all the women were placed below all categories of men of the first three *varna*s. This was when learning or education was being imparted; no woman of any *varna* was supposed to learn the Vedas. In this situation, women were hierarchically placed below the brahmana, kshatriya and vaishya, and at par with shudra men.

The *Ashvalayana Grhyasutra* and the *Sankhayana Grhyasutra* do not classify types of marriage based on *varna*, unlike the *upanayana* rites where the *varna* of the *brahmacharin* determines the kind of learning he is exposed to. The *Paraskara Grhyasutra* I.4.8–11 refers to the fact that, depending on the *varna* of the male, marriage with a woman of each of the *varna*s was allowed. Thus the brahmana was allowed four wives, one from each of the *varna*s, the kshatriya three wives, the vaishya two, and the shudra one. The text goes on to quote some teachers that marriage with a shudra woman was to be conducted without *mantra*s. The exclusivity with which the *mantras* are used seems to show that the notion that the Vedas were not for all and sundry had crystallized by this time. The hierarchy of the castes with respect to marital and conjugal rights shows the manner in which the position of women was perceived, and how the marital rights of women of different castes were inversely proportional to the men of their castes. Shudra marriages were conducted without the vedic *mantras*. Moreover, the brahmanical order seems to have defined gender hierarchy in the society very clearly—men could have more than one marriage and could marry below their caste, while the same was taboo for women. Women of lower castes could marry higher-caste husbands but it was hardly for them to make a choice. It was more so that men had a wider range of possibilities for sexual exploitation of women through the *varna* mechanism, and the higher the caste of the men, the more diverse was their choice. On the other hand, for women it was the reverse—brahmana women were meant exclusively for brahmana men, while kshatriya women could marry brahmanas and kshatriyas; vaishya women were for brahmanas, kshatriyas and vaishyas, while shudra women were for brahmanas, kshatriyas, vaishyas and shudras. This shows that the *varna* hierarchy was used for reinforcing patriarchal hierarchies.

The *Ashvalayana Grhyasutra* III.8.11–15 refers to the fact that during the *godana* rite, the brahmana shaved the head, the kshatriya the two arms, the vaishya the belly, and all women their secret parts. This shows that while men were categorized according to the *varna*, women were in some cases identified with their *varna*, '*varna*ized' (as in marriage), and in other cases stripped of their *varna*, 'de-*varna*ized'. Marriage practices reinforced the patriarchal and *varna*-based division of society. It was only for marriage purposes that the *varna* of a woman was recognized, so that privileges (in this case, access to women) could be divided on the basis of *varna*. There is no reference to what happened when a woman of a lower *varna* married a man of a higher *varna*. Did this mean that a kshatriya/vaishya woman became a brahmana if she was married to a brahmana man? The fact that this debate is not addressed in the Grhyasutras shows that *varna* did not matter for women except where marriage was concerned, and stringent taboos against their marrying a person from a lower *varna* were laid only so that no man of a lower *varna* could have claims equal to a man from a higher *varna*. The sexual control of women was one way in which *varna* hierarchies were underlined, and brahmanas reiterated their superiority by having access to women of the other three *varna*s, without letting women do the same. Women had no *varna* of their own, they were born into a *varna* category and identified with the *varna* of their father, which would determine who had access to them and whom they eventually married. The reference to old 'brahmana' women with 'living husbands and sons' does not show that these women had a brahmana identity; rather, they were married to brahmana men and derived their status from that.

Brahmanas were placed on top of the social hierarchy,[13] yet the other two *varnas* were referred to frequently. Although one does get the impression that brahmanas were favoured, references to the other *varnas* seem to underline the fact that the social order could be envisaged only when *all* the three *varnas* were taken account of. Brahmanas, kshatriyas and vaishyas could exist only in relation to each other. Moreover, except for vedic learning and access to *dakshina* and the privilege of marrying women from other *varnas*, *varna* was not related to material well-being, which depended on access to resources and expertise, for which all three *varnas* had to compete equally. All three *varnas* were included in the rituals of the household. The fact that the three *varnas* were made to undertake similar rites like the *upanayana* shows that they were expected to have some uniformity with regard to setting up the household and performing rites. The references in the *upanayana* serve to enforce the fact that the brahmana was expected to undergo it earlier than the other two castes.[14] The texts attempted to highlight the differences between the *varnas* based on their attire, but this was not necessarily uniform for all the vedic *shakhas*, as the attire for brahmanas in one text is mentioned as the attire for kshatriyas in another.

The ideology of *varna* did not spring up overnight, but developed over a period of time. The superior status of the brahmanas was not projected from the beginning of brahmanical thought, but was assumed over time. Brian K. Smith's work shows that early texts on the origins of the *varna* scheme do not mention the social hierarchy in their taxonomies, and only later could the brahmanas claim a 'natural and sacred' status.[15] There was a definite increase in the power and status of the brahmanas within the Sutra literature as compared to the earlier brahmanical literature, the Vedas and the Brahmanas. This gradual attempt by the texts to further the brahmanical cause seems to have paralleled the growing ability of the brahmanas to usurp knowledge and project themselves as the chosen ones because of their understanding of the Veda and its rituals. However, the position accorded to brahmanas in the early Grhyasutra literature was less significant than in the later Grhyasutra and Dharmasutra literature. The fact that the position, power and status accorded to brahmanas were prone to ups and downs, and were not totally unchallenged or infallible, is discernible in the literature that we have chosen to review. In fact, the obsession with highlighting the superiority of brahmanas must have been because there was need for it in the face of competition. That there was a belief amongst the community about the efficacy of rituals is clear from the patronage given to brahmanas and the extension of the scope of brahmanas to rituals of the household. On the other hand, there was also anxiety on the part of the brahmanas to project themselves as the legitimate recipients of *dakshina*, which shows that brahmanas had to wage a constant struggle for their survival.

The early Grhyasutras that have been chosen for this work show that they were compiled at a stage when the position of the brahmana was projected to be superior in the texts but was not necessarily upheld in society, where the kshatriya and the vaishya were significant too. Although the other *varna*s could not do much to displace the brahmanas from their pre-eminent position in the ideological context, in reality they may have been powerful.[16] Moreover, as we see in the early Grhyasutras, all the three *varna*s were given a prominent role to play. When the 'separate fires were set up' the rich vaishya's house was projected as the source of the fire in the *Sankhayana Grhyasutra* I.1.8. The reason why the fire was procured from the rich vaishya's house was because it symbolized growing wealth; this shows that wealth and power did not always adhere to *varna* pretensions of the texts.

The brahmanical doctrine served to fill in the spatial gaps in the social order by formulating an ideology attempting at optimum pervasiveness. Interestingly, those *grhya* rites in which brahmanas insinuated themselves into the household rites were the ones where links between different households were being established. These were rites like marriage, the *upanayana* and death rites, where supervision by the brahmana was essential. Within the household a householder could carry out the rites himself, but in rites involving more than one household, the brahmana stood as an intermediary who would supervise the rites and control linkages between the different social categories. The development of the social order where the brahmana controlled the overlapping spaces in which social linkages between households existed, was parallel to the development of the ideology of power where the state tried to control the overlying spaces between different social levels through legitimate force.

There were other ways in which social differentiation was recorded; these were mainly for men. In matters such as vedic learning, brahmanas held a supreme position. Similarly, though kshatriyas were projected to be supreme in matters of the state and the protection it offered to subjects, the support of the vaishya was essential. As the texts deal primarily with vedic learning and interpretation of vedic thoughts, it seems as if brahmanas held a supreme position. The *Baudhayana Grhyasutra* I.VI.9 refers to different categories based on the extent of their learning. These included the brahmana, *shrotiya, anuchana, rishikalpa, bhruna, rishi* and *deva*, in a hierarchical manner. What is clear from the texts is that men held a supreme position in matters related to vedic learning and rituals, and this did have a social impact on women as it changed the manner in which their future role would be projected. While brahmana men were meant to undergo training in vedic texts, males of the other *varna*s also underwent training for their respective socio-political roles. Women were kept apart from any formal training, and hence their marginalization from socio-political and economic activities was complete.

The position that an *acharya* held in the Grhyasutras shows the manner in which the brahmana who provided vedic learning was seen to be the most important person in a householder's life. He was one of the 'special' persons who deserved an *argha* reception. The others who deserved an *argha* reception were the *ritvij*, a brahmana associated with rituals, and a *snataka*—*Ashvalayana Grhyasutra* I.24.1–4, *Sankhayana Grhyasutra* II.15.1, *Paraskara Grhyasutra* I.3.1, *Gobhila Grhyasutra* IV.10.23–26, *Apastamba Grhyasutra* I.3.9. The first person whom the new bride offered oblations to when she entered the house, was the *guru*. The *Gobhila Grhyasutra* II.3.13 refers to the fact that the bride broke her silence after marriage by taking the name of the *guru*, addressing him by his *gotra* name. When a *guru* died, an expiatory ceremony was performed on the new moon day, according to the *Ashvalayana Grhyasutra* IV.6.1. The ceremony was conducted before sunrise, and the fire together with the ashes and its receptacle was carried towards the south. The fact that the *guru* was the most important person in the hierarchy of the social order is clear, as the longest period of mourning was reserved for him. This fact seems to show that the Grhyasutras were written for students studying the

Vedas in a particular tradition; to such an audience, the *acharya* would naturally be the most significant person to be commemorated.

Brahmana households were projected as the ideal that other *grihas* had to live up to. The *Gobhila Grhyasutra* II.3.1 refers to the fact that a newly married couple stayed in the house of a brahmana located in the northeasterly direction. This shows that there were some expectations of the society *vis-à-vis* other sections and particularly the brahmanas who were being supported by the giving of *dakshina*. There is also reference to the difference in status between one who had set up the *shrauta* fires and one who had not, but the Grhyasutras are at pains to show that this difference was a nominal one. The *Sankhayana Grhyasutra* I.15.9 says that if the chariot breaks down when a couple is undertaking a journey after marriage, the *kanya* should be taken to the house of one who kept the sacred fires, *ahitagni*. This shows that keeping the sacred fires was some sort of a status symbol, a symbol for moral values and dependability.

The Grhyasutras do not refer to the manner in which members of the different *varnas* would conduct themselves. This was left for the later Dharmasutras. The texts are manuals for brahmana *shakhas* and hence we glean the most information on the brahmana *varna*. However, brahmanas served as role models for other *varnas* and in this way the ideology of the Grhyasutras was disseminated amongst other *varnas*. There are incidental references to other *varnas*. The reference to the barber in rites like the *chaula* and *godanakarma* in the *Gobhila Grhyasutra* II.9.10 shows that the barber was expected to carry out a significant function and actually was equated to 'Savitri'. Lowest in the social order were the servants. The Grhyasutras do not refer to shudras as servants, so the shudra *varna* may have been a larger category from which some of the servants were drawn. The *Ashvalayana Grhyasutra* IV.2.18–19 refers to the manner in which an aged servant could lift the widow from the pyre of her husband. This shows that in many instances the servant was like a family member who could be entrusted with such a task.

The *Apastamba Grhyasutra* VIII.23.7 refers to the manner in which servants (*dasa*) and labourers (*karmakarah*) who may run away should be controlled by putting hurdles in their path. The *Paraskara Grhyasutra* III.7.1–4 too refers to the manner in which a householder was expected to ensure that a servant does not run away. The entire manner in which servants were kept in check shows the social hierarchies. When the servant slept, the protagonist was encouraged to discharge his urine in the horn of a living animal and walk thrice around the servant, turning his left side to him and sprinkling it around him. The verse that accompanied the rite is particularly heart-rending—'From the mountain, from the mother, from your sister, from your Fathers and Brothers, from your friends I sever you.' The psyche of the protagonist is revealed by the above words. He wished to cut off the servant (*utula*) from all his kin. The master would like his servant to be animal-like in his passivity, removed from his kin and brethren, and serve the master unflinchingly. The reference to mount-ains shows that the servants may have come from peripheral areas around settlements. The use of urine, waste fluid from the master, ensured some sort of a hold on the servant. The anxiety with regard to a runaway servant is clearly indicated as the text claims that even after this if he ran away, a sacrifice was performed in a fire that was estab-lished (not in the domestic fire) and oblations of *kusha* blades were made. It was hoped that the servant would stumble and get tied with Indra's fetters. The fact that no vedic rites are mentioned and a separate fire was established is easily explained. The servant was not expected to come in contact with the sacred vedic hymns, or be associated with the sacred domestic fire. The *Paraskara Grhyasutra* II.11.4 refers to the *chandala*, seeing of whom was prohibited. This shows that the notion of segregation according to caste was in existence by the time the *Paraskara Grhyasutra* was being compiled.

Social Relations

Social relations were maintained not only with those who were alive but also with the dead ancestors. The relations that the Grhyasutras seem to be most concerned with are those with ancestors —the *pitr*. A strict socio-ethical code was enforced to ensure that rites for the appeasement of ancestors were performed in accordance with customary traditions. The texts seem to imply that the ancestors, by virtue of their death, had certain powers that had to be channellized to help the living ones. Brahmanical thought projected ancestors as being able to bestow back to the living ones in manifold, what was offered to them. Thus, food and related items of necessity were constantly offered to the *pitr*, to ensure returns in the life of the householder. The offer-ings were usually made to three generations of *pitr*, according to the *Paraskara Grhyasutra* III.10.48–55.

The fact that *shraddha* rites were conducted not only after the death of a person but also when one wanted something or gained something, shows the regard that the Grhyasutra authors had for the *pitr*. The *pitr* had to be involved in the fortunes of the family. Moreover, the texts extended the aura of the father figure, the patriarch, even after death; he was venerated in death like a deity. The only problem with this arrangement was that there had to be successors who would perform the relevant duties for the fathers. This explains the dependence on sons and the need to ensure their loyalty to the family name. Oblations to the fathers were to be made during seasonal rites, during rites of marriage and birth, and during other household rites like the *Vishvedevas*.

Social hierarchy was enforced by the texts at the cost of severe repercussions. This can be seen from the reference to the fact that the *Sankhayana Grhyasutra* II.16.4, while discussing the manner in which guests were welcomed, says that the *agnihotra*, bulls, children and personas of noble families 'burn up those who neglect them'. However, the Grhyasutras recognize the fact that these hierarchies varied according to situations. The *Ashvalayana Grhyasutra* I.24.1–4 refers to guests who should be offered the *madhuparka*. These include, in a hierarchical order of importance, the *snataka*, the *raja*, the *acharya*, the *svasur* (father-in-law), *pitrivya* (paternal relatives, male only?), *matulana* (maternal relatives, male only?). The *Paraskara Grhyasutra* I.3.1–3 also refers to six persons who deserve the *argha* reception, but the list is slightly different and the order in which their names are given also varies. The *acharya*, an officiating priest (*ritvij*), the father-in-law, the king (*rāja*), a friend (*priya*) and a *snataka* were given the reception once a year, but the officiating priest was given the reception whenever a *yagya* was performed (*Paraskara Grhyasutra* I.3.1–3). The term used for the father-in-law is *vaivaha* in the *Sankhayana Grhyasutra* II.15.6 and the *Paraskara Grhyasutra* I.3.1. This could mean all relatives through marriage, but as it is doubtful that the *argha* was offered to all and sundry it was probably confined to close relatives from marriage, like the father-in-law. Narayana in his commentary feels that it is the latter and refers to *vivahyah svasurah*.[17] The *Gobhila Grhyasutra* IV.10.23–26 refers to the fact that there are six persons to whom the *argha* reception is to be offered—the *acharya*, a *ritvij*, a *snataka*, a *raja*, the *vivahyah*, *priya* who came as guests. They should be offered an *argha* reception once a year, but repeatedly in the case of a sacrifice and a wedding. The *Apastamba Grhyasutra* has one of the briefest lists of those who were '*arghya*'—the *acharya*, a *ritvij*, his father-in-law—for a *raja*, as often as they visit his house if at least a year has elapsed. For a renowned teacher this was performed only once. The *Apastamba Grhyasutra* I.3.9 refers to the occasions for killing a cow—on the arrival of a guest, for the *pitr* and upon marriage.

The references show the extent to which relatives were venerated. The privileged ones were the learned brahmana, and then the king and the *acharya*. Next came the father-in-law. The other guests to be so honoured were members of the father's and mother's families. The fact that members of the father's family were treated as honoured guests shows that the extended family system where the father's relatives all lived together or close to each other was not that common, and that the village comprised a community of households not necessarily related to each other. The Grhyasutras refer to the relatives of the bride, the father, mother and brother who were involved in marriage rites, in the *Sankhayana Grhyasutra* I.14.15. The *Gobhila Grhyasutra* II.5.5 refers to the fact that uterine ('real' brothers and sisters) relations, *sayodaryo*, of the bride carried out the rite of the *lavanhoma*. That maternal relatives held a status on a par with paternal relatives in some texts shows that marriage-initiated ties and bonds were sought to be maintained by the future generations. Thus the son extended hospitality to the mother's relatives too. Yet, in texts like the *Paraskara Grhyasutra*, maternal relatives are conspicuous by their absence in the list of guests to whom the *argha* was extended; this shows that there was some conflict in the acceptance of these relatives as worthy of the *argha*.

There were various terms used to denote the members of the household. In the Grhyasutras at least, household members are always mentioned in relation to the householder. *Amatya* (*Ashvalayana Grhyasutra* II.1.7, IV.2.9, IV.6.8, IV.6.10) was used to denote 'his people'. They comprised the elderly, *sthavira*, and the young, *kumara* (*Sankhayana Grhyasutra* III.4.2), also referred to as *baljyestha grihya* (*Paraskara Grhyasutra* II.9.13). The eldest son, *jyestham putra*, had a special place (*Sankhayana Grhyasutra* III.4.9). The *jardasa* (*Ashvalayana Grhyasutra* IV.2.18) was the aged servant who could accompany the body of his master. There were other members of the family who may or may not have lived with the householder, but were mentioned during death rites. The *devar* guided the wife away from the pyre of her husband (*Ashvalayana Grhyasutra* IV.2.18).

Male relatives always had precedence over female relatives. *Bali* oblations to appease the 'beings' were to be made by any of the following—the son, brother, wife or student—when the householder was away. This order of persons shows that the preference was for male relatives—ideally the son, then the brother. It was only if they were not able to perform the functions that the wife or the student did the needful. The fact that only these relatives are mentioned shows the extent to which the concept of the household extended in the Grhyasutra times. The only close relatives who could take over the functions of the householder in his absence were his son, brother, wife and then the student. The household in this way seems to have been a small one comprising the householder, his wife, his children (unmarried?) and his siblings (unmarried?). From the references it seems as if the family envisaged was strictly of close blood relations.

The *Paraskara Grhyasutra* III.10.3 refers to those related by blood or marriage who took part in the death rites, the *sanyuktam* and the *maithunam*. The *Paraskara Grhyasutra* III.10.16 also refers to all relations, *sarvegyati*, to the seventh or tenth degree, who participated in death rites. It goes on to say that if they stayed in the same village, *samangramvasa*, then all were to attend as far as they could trace their relationship. The *Paraskara Grhyasutra* III.10.46 refers to the fact that water libations upon death were offered 'optionally' for the officiating priest, the father-in-law, a friend, distant relations, maternal uncle, sister's son and married women. This shows that once daughters were married the libations were optional, as the family she was married into would mourn for her.

The rites performed upon death show that there were two types of relationships—ones of the same *pinda* (*sapinda*), and ones not of the same *pinda*. The Grhyasutras seem to show that relationships that were formed as a result of performance of *grihya* rites like the *upanayana* and marriage were the non-*pinda* relationships. These placed the chief *gurus* at the top, then those of the *sapinda*, then a *guru* who was not *sapinda* and then unmarried women relations. Next in the hierarchy, according to the *Paraskara Grhyasutra* III.10.35–36, were the *acharya*, a relation who was not *sapinda* and married women relations. The *Paraskara Grhyasutra* refers to the fact that the impurity after the death of a relative lasted for one or two fortnights for the teacher, or the maternal grandfather or grandmother, or unmarried women. The *Paraskara Grhyasutra* III.10.13, 16–17 further states that the water libations to be carried out are by 'anyone who is related by blood or marriage'. The text goes on to state that all relations, to the seventh or tenth degree, descended into the water, and if they dwelt in the same village, as far as they could trace their relationship.

There are other terms like *kautamb* (large household?) that show the existence of an extended family in some instances, according to the *Ashvalayana Grhyasutra* II.6.10. From amongst the immediate members of the *griha*, the *jyayan*, the eldest son, had a special position in the *Sankhayana Grhyasutra*. There were verses that claimed that as the person would live in the other world, the son would live in this world—*Ashvalayana Grhyasutra* IV.4.1–4. This was the crux of the brahmanical need for developing the father–son bond. The anxiety to ensure a proper life after death in the other world was expressed in a manner in which responsibility for the father was squarely placed on the shoulders of the son. The weight of the responsibility and filial expectations was balanced with the promise of similar dividends in the son's life. The fact that the son was the chosen one who would bear the responsibility for the task tells a lot about the brahmanical perceptions of the social structure. Women could not even be thought of as having the capability or the resources to carry out this responsibility. That the son wins out as compared to other male relatives seems to show how kinship ties of the early vedic times had given way to closer-knit household structures. Notions of wealth and property had changed too. From the common pool of resources available to kinship groups in the early vedic times, settled life and agriculture along with dispersion of kinship groups to larger areas in the later times allowed for accruing of personal wealth and property. If this was to be handed down to the sons, then who could be better for looking after the interests of the fathers after death than the beneficiaries of their worldly possessions?

The fact that the son was an important player in death rites comes out clearly. The use of Rigvedic hymns in death rites shows that the rites existed from very early times; yet, the thorough discussion on the rites shows that the Grhyasutras presented the rites in a form that pretended to conform to vedic ideals but actually highlighted certain changes. One of the changes was that the responsibility for the dead became that of the household and, more specifically, the householder. Whereas earlier it was the responsibility of the kinship group to perform death rites and look after the dead, now, although they participated, the financial and ritual responsibility was of the immediate family or, more specifically, the younger brother or son. The wife, brother and son were the three relations who were mentioned in the death rites. That there were others who had a position of prominence in the life of a householder, for example, the friends who assembled, *sahridasamvetan* (*Apastamba Grhyasutra* II. 4.1), shows that there were other relationships that were fostered in the Grhyasutras, besides immediate relatives.

The *Kula* and the Role of Women

The identity of a person was further recognized on the basis of the *kula* that he belonged to. Although there are many references to the fact that 'kinship ties' were 'dissolving', the evidence from the Grhyasutras shows that the *kula* never broke down completely. The *Sankhayana Grhyasutra* II.16.7 states that the *kulavriddha*, the elders of the *kula*, should not be neglected. The *kula* coexisted with other ties based on bonds of matrimony and patrilineality, the *varna* identity, friendship, occupational proximity, as well as bonds forged because of 'common learning' experiences, for example, in the *acharya*'s *griha*. The *Apastamba Grhyasutra* VI.16.7 states that rituals were performed 'according to the family custom', *kuladharma*. *Kuladharma* is referred to again in the *Ashvalayana Grhyasutra* VII.20.19, and this shows that it was an accepted tradition to follow the customs of the *kula*. The *Gobhila Grhyasutra* I.1.12 refers to the fact that if the householder died, the 'chief', *paramisthikarnam*, should set up the sacred fires. This refers to the chief of the family. Besides the *kula*, there were other groupings that were adhered to. The *Sankhayana Grhyasutra* I.6.4 states that the relatives of the groom should take their *gotra* names when they go to fix the marriage of the bride. This was probably to avoid any intra-*gotra* marriage.

The exact nature of the kinship network is difficult to determine as the strength of the kinship bonds depended on different factors. J. Goody, in another context, has shown how kinship networks vary according to the class and he states that the 'highest classes usually have the most elaborated kin network'.[18] Similarly, rules pertaining to *gotra* exogamy and caste endogamy were probably most relevant in the brahmana *varna*. The fact was that the other *varna*s emulated the brahmana *varna* but were not able to keep up with the complexities that the brahmanas wove into the social framework. This enabled the brahmana to be an elite *varna* in terms of status even if this was not matched by economic power.

The presence of the *kula* was most visible in rites related to marriage and death. It is clear that besides members of the *kula*, persons of the village community also participated in these functions. References in the Grhyasutra texts to the fact that the rites should be performed according to the *gramadharma* indicate that the *grama* could have comprised *kula* members. However, although it may have been a common feature that the *griha* was situated within a *grama* comprising the *kula* of the householder, it may not have been a universal rule. The most common situation was where the *grama* comprised a heterogeneous community of people of different *kula*s living together. Social interaction between the *kula* and the *grama* overlapped during occasions of marriage and death. On such occasions, interactive relationships between the *griha*, the *kula* and the *grama* were forged at different levels, that is, between the *griha* and the *kula*, between the *griha* and the *grama*, as also between the *kula* and the *grama*. Every occasion of marriage and death (and other rites) was one that had the potential of opening up different levels of social interaction. In the death rites, there is a clear reference to the fact that the *kula* and *grama* participated along with the immediate family.

The *Gobhila Grhyasutra* I.4.24–25 refers to the possibility of food being cooked at different places for one family (*kula*), and in such a case the sacrificial food for offering *bali* had to come from the householder's house. This shows that there were occasions when a large extended family was envisaged and cooking was done at various places. Whether this was done on special occasions like marriages or ordinarily for extended families living together, is not clear. The fact that it is referred to shows that the possibility occurred but it was not a very common one. In such situations, the *grihapati*'s kitchen was the 'central' one from where ritual food was offered. The *Gobhila Grhyasutra* I.8.6 refers to the fact that family traditions had to be adhered to while considering the manner in which the *avadana*s, cut-off portions of the sacrificial offering placed in the ritual fire for burnt offerings, had to be obtained from the *havis*. The reference to family traditions shows that the rites referred to in the Grhyasutra had a history of being performed so that there were fixed family traditions that had to be followed. There is not much difference between the offering of four *avadanas* or five; all it shows is that they underlined the different identities of the families. For instance, the family of the Bhrigus referred to in the texts offered five portions instead of the usual three.

The relations who were close to the protagonist of the Grhyasutras were 'uterine' relations. However, it seems as if hierarchically they were placed below the *pitr* and the relations acquired through marriage. This may be one of the reasons for the decline of the *kula*, as postulated by many scholars of this period.[19] The *Apastamba Grhyasutra* VII.20.18 mentions uterine relations who were given the *sthalipak*, the cooked-food offering intended for the *kshetrapati*. This seems to show that the *kshetrapati* was the deity of their land and indicates some kind of ownership over the land; that is why only 'uterine relations' had the right to eat those oblations so that others could not claim what belonged to the relations. The text reiterates the point that as an alternative, the custom of the family, *kuladharma*, could be followed. This indicates that at times customs favouring 'uterine' relations may have gone against the *kuladharma*. The term 'uterine' relations would mean real brothers and sisters, while the *kula* would probably imply an 'extended' relationship transcending several generations, for example, grand-uncles, uncles and cousins. The evidence from the Grhyasutras implies that both types of interaction coexisted. Bonding between 'uterine' relations may have upstaged *kula* linkages in some instances, although *kula* linkages were still there and could be depended on as an alternative.

Amongst the bonds that wore down were the ones that related men through marriage and bonds between cousins.[20] There must have been situations where the power accrued by one family member was not permanent and could be usurped; hence the control was always in a state of flux. Rituals did harbour conflicts; we see that in many instances the rituals performed had blatant references to the fact that they were at the cost of others. For example, in the child-bearing ritual the *yajamana* says, 'giving a girl child to others, let me have a boy child.' This shows that in the ideology of the texts it was recognized that there was only a limited amount of resources that could go around, especially in terms of cattlehead. Sons and *anna* were probably forms of wealth that could be accumulated but that depended on the fertility of the wife and the land, and hence the preoccupation with progeny and wife in the Grhyasutras as compared to other relations.

The household must have housed and led to the development

of many inter-relationships within and outside it. These had to be maintained in a particular manner; that is why we find that the Grhyasutras refer to certain specific relationships that needed to be maintained and nurtured, while others like the *sapatna* and the *bhratravya* were ignored.[21] Roy refers to the fact that as the household relations were transformed and therefore needed to be defined, so did the kinship ties between men and women. In such a scenario, 'kinswomen other than the wife were accorded marginal importance and while intergenerational ties amongst men were recognized, intragenerational ties were thrust into the background'. In a situation where the texts are primarily focused on men, the statements that they make pertain mostly to male situations and need not always apply to women (although they did in many cases). However, it is erroneous to think that, because the Grhyasutras do not mention them, bonds between kinswomen did not exist. In fact, all the evidence seems to indicate that strong bonds existed between women—bonds that allowed the development of traditions which were so ingrained that the brahmanical order was not only forced to take cognizance of the traditions but also incorporate them in the literature. This entailed an outright patriarchal brahmanical encroachment into spaces that had hitherto been reserved for 'women' only. The fact that 'old brahmana women' were seen as repositories of information for the manner in which rites were to be performed seems to indicate this. Also, although one can agree with Roy that inter-generational ties were being encouraged at the cost of intra-generational ties within the *kula* members, one can see that this was true primarily for *men and it was through women that inter-kula ties were established, maintained and sustained.* The fact that the father-in-law was one of the venerated few who deserved an *argha* reception shows that these inter-*kula* ties had a long-lasting impact on the social position of both the *kula*s that were involved in a marriage. The role of the brother in the rite of *lajahoma* seems to show that the bonding between the *kula*s would transcend generations.

There were some separate channels of communication that existed among women. These are not recorded in the brahmanical texts but can be detected. Moreover, these channels were not totally separate from the male channels and the two interspersed at many levels. The other point that has to be clarified is that although women (wives, daughters and sisters) may have been the point of commonality between two *kula*s, the Grhyasutras never lose sight of the fact that interaction between the *kulas* was through the males. Thus, the father-in-law would interact with the son-in-law, and the husband with the wife's brother. The fact that the texts seem to highlight only the relationships between the males of two *kulas* is another example of the male-centredness of the texts, as some bonds must have been maintained through the women who connected these *kulas* too, but this is totally ignored.

One cannot come to a conclusion about the role of other kinswomen and compare it to the role of the wife, as the Grhyasutras do not attempt to define family structure or relationships. They focus on rituals of the household. The fact that other women of the *kula*, except the wife, had little role in such rites is clear. Yet, all the rites relating to marriage and reproduction seem to indicate that they were performed in the presence and under the guidance of several women, along with the male householder and the brahmana. In fact, one can say that it was the inter-relationships between the women of different *kulas* during these rites that created situations of social interaction. Men of the different *kulas* do not seem to have actively participated in these rites and the only males present could have been the householder and the brahmana. Women relatives figure in most of the rites—in the *upanayana* the first alms were taken from the mother or other women who would be favourably disposed towards the *brahmacharin*;[22] in the marriage ceremony several women dressed up the bride; women sang and danced in the *simantonnayana*. These and numerous other instances of interaction among women within and outside the *kula* can be discerned, which shows that the *kula* continued to exist in terms of social relationships. The reason why *kula* relationships seem to suffer a setback in brahmanical literature is probably because the *kula* ceased to play an important role in managing the resources of its members or a political role in decision-making. Many of these tasks were taken over by units like the *griha* at a lower level and the state at a higher level. However, socially, the *kula* continued to provide support to its members and members of the *kula* gathered together when rituals were being performed.

Any study of the role of women in establishing linkages cannot but take notice of the recent focus on women's role in family and societal units through 'reaching out' and 'bonding'. Gender studies are moving in a direction where there does not seem to be a need to prove that women can also do what men can, but recognize that women can evolve in different ways. The focus is on the significance of what women *actually do* and the impact it has on society even though it has been largely ignored by the patriarchal texts.[23] We have already shown that the shared 'learning' experience that males of different *varnas* underwent created special bonds between them; this bonding included male children as they were drawn into learning at a young age. However, although bonding between women was not formalized nor had ritual sanction, this does not mean that it did not exist.[24]

There are numerous references to the women of the family in the rites performed the death of a person. The *Paraskara Grhyasutra* III.10.35–36 refers to the fact that the impurity resulting from death lasted for one or two fortnights for the teacher, or the maternal grandfather or grandmother, or unmarried women. This list does not seem to be exhaustive, as there are many relations like the paternal grandparents and the father's brothers and uncles who are left out. It seems as if the list refers to those relationships that were forged through *grihya* rituals like *upanayana* and marriage, and had little to do with birth. The Grhyasutras seem to have been incorporating new categories of relations upon whose death the household was expected to be in mourning, and therefore one has a relatively smaller list that seems to focus on relationships made through women of the family (except for the *acharya*). The growing significance of the *acharya* only served to signify the growing importance of gaining knowledge.

For married women, 'others' were expected to do the rites, 'others' meaning the family into which they were married. The fact that special mention is made of this indicates that there was an attempt to clearly show the rights that the in-laws' family had over the woman, over and above her own family. This list clearly shows the hierarchy of the relatives of the Grhyasutra protagonist. That married women relatives come way down in the hierarchy is not surprising, but the fact that unmarried women relatives are high up, is. This seems to point to the fact that unmarried women relatives had some role to play in the household. These relatives do not seem to be only young, pre-puberty girls, because the term used for them is *strishu*, which signifies an adult woman. This shows that there were instances when women of the family remained unmarried and although their status in life is not recorded (the status of unmarried men is not mentioned either in the Grhyasutras), their status after death seems to be venerable.

Kinship relations through the father may have been dominant; however, some other relationships forged through marriage were also venerated. The father-in-law, maternal uncle and sister's son were all relationships that were forged through women. The first was through the wife, the second through the mother and the third through the sister.

There is reference to the fact that once the cremation rites after a death in the family were over, back in the house, the rites included young women of the household. The arrangement around the fire included bull's dung and bull's hide, fresh butter, a stone and as many blades of *kusha* grass as there were young women (*yuvati*) in the house. This seems to be a curious requirement, and in the light of the earlier statement on the mourning period for unmarried women, it seems to show that married young women also had a special status in the house. But the fact that they are mentioned only in the sections on death rites needs to be explored. The reason why young women were included in a rite to ward off the negative energy emanating from death in the household was because they were seen as particularly vulnerable. If death came to their husbands, there would be a drastic change in their circumstances. By involving them in such a rite, the texts imply that the women could thwart the negative energy. This also placed an onerous responsibility on the women as they could be held responsible for the occurrence of a death; women were associated with negative and evil power. It is worth noting that while the women are mentioned, their husbands are not referred to.

The rite was fairly elaborate. Since the young ones needed to be protected from negative forces, it was required to have as many blades of grass as there were women. The young women in the household would salve their eyes with butter with the aid of *darbha-grass* blades held between the thumb and the fourth finger, and then throw away the blades looking the other way. The performer of the ceremony looked at them while they salved themselves and recited the verse 'These women, not widows, having noble husbands' (*Rigveda* X.18.7), according to the *Ashvalayana Grhyasutra* IV.6.11, 12. The lives and fortunes of these women and their husbands were interlinked and the rite seems to establish this. The fact is that women were hardly given a place in rituals unless there was an absolute necessity for it. The presence of young women hints at the vulnerability that these women faced in society if they were widows. The very term used for them—

'not widows'—shows that this was seen as a sign of their good fortune, which was sought to be tapped and directed towards the releasing of positive energies at the crucial time of vulnerability that gripped the family when one of its members died.

We have seen how rituals worked towards forging bonds in the social fabric. However, rituals were not only meant for establishing linkages but, in many cases, they may have served to 'cloak the fundamental conflicts',[25] 'to create the impression that conflicts never existed in the first place by permitting society to maintain its sense of well-being'.[26] In the *upanayana* rites for males, the brahmanical ideology came in direct conflict with the mother's natural role as nurturer, and was sought to be 'resolved' by abrogating the mother's responsibility towards the young boy by handing him over to the *acharya*. Similarly, marriage rites concealed the tensions with regard to the changes the new bride would bring, as also the change in status of the groom. The bridegroom's family was arrayed against the bride's family, the community against the family, the bride against the groom. The natural hostility between the separate parties was sought to be resolved through rituals, but this was not always possible. The bridegroom's family may have stayed away from the rites of marriage with the bridegroom as the only representative, and even if they were present, it must have been as mere spectators. The community was invited to participate in the rituals but more as a custodian of the tradition, and the family must have rallied around the couple, protecting them from the harsh public gaze. The reference to the fact that the groom had to explain why the bride sobbed on the journey to her new home, 'for living relatives', shows that there was some accountability towards the community. That there was antagonism too, between the husband and the wife, can be seen from terms such as *patighni*—killer of husband, *prajaghni*—killer of progeny, used for the bride. These were cloaked in the mantle of subservience and silence that the bride was supposed to wear. Conflicts were sought to be suppressed under the weight of expectations *vis-à-vis* the new bride.

In child-bearing and childbirth rituals of the *griha* there was anxiety related to the paternity of the child. There was conflict regarding the prospective gender of the child; the fact that the birth of a girl was wished on 'some other' shows the intensely competitive nature of social relations and the desperation for a son. The father's role was constantly pitted against the mother's, at least in the sub-text. The father was granted an intensely ritual role as against the mother's role, which was a physiological necessity, and therefore could be marginalized.

Rituals are the means by which conformity with social laws and the desire to be one with the community are expressed, but they also have a competitive streak in them, the desire to project one-upmanship. Conflicts within rituals were often subverted through the drama of 'gift-giving'. While gifts establish contacts, and ameliorate relations, they are also misused and taken advantage of. Moreover, they are not harmless statements of intent, as is made out. As J. van Baal[27] goes on to point out, gifts invoke irrationality and recognition of competition and the power of the adversaries. Moreover, one has to analyse the psycho-social aspect of the performance of ritual, especially before a community audience—the feeling of anxiety, euphoria, satisfaction, generated for the protagonist, was pitted against friendship, support or competition and envy amongst the audience.

We have seen how rituals provided a forum in which social interaction could be monitored and controlled according to traditional norms. The giving of gifts further reinforced the bonds. When talking of bonding, one does not mean that bonding made different parties equal. Although the term 'bonding' seems to imply that the relationships forged were balanced ones, this was not so. In fact, the 'bonds' formed as a result of common ritual experiences reinforced imbalances and inequalities that were the cornerstone of the brahmanical ideology. Thus, one who conducted a *yagya* was projected as being superior and there would be a feeling of indebtedness towards one whose gifts had been accepted. This would create a condition of competition where each would attempt to outdo the other in gaining a 'superior' status, however transitory, by performing *yagya*s. The food or gifts received in ceremonies like marriages could be reciprocated when the recipients had to perform the same ceremonies in their household. Thus a series of gift-giving ties were established between individual *griha*s and the community comprising different *griha*s.[28] Initial gifting was always to establish contact, to gain acceptance with the recipient and to introduce oneself while making a statement of intent. It was only when the initial contact had been made and accepted that that relationship progressed to the stage of expectations of reciprocity. Relationships deviated and developed accordingly, but whatever the status of the related parties, for that moment it sought to bring them in proximity to each other. If a man made an offering to God, it seems as if he claimed to *have something to offer*, even though with the deities it may have been a statement of giving back part of what one had got. Thus, living in the social milieu required establishing and initiating contact with others. Contact was established with deities through *dakshina* offering, the brahmana through ritual and the community through the performance of social rituals.

Notes and References

1 The Grhyasutras are part of the Kalpa texts. Ideally, a complete Kalpa tradition would have a Shrautasutra, a Grhyasutra and a Dharmasutra. There are very few, like the *Ashvalayana*, *Apastamba* and *Baudhayana*, that have all the three texts. The Shrautasutras deal with 'solemn' rites that were conducted by a person who had established the three fires, while the *grhya* rites required only one fire. The Grhyasutras referred to in this section are the early Grhyasutras, namely, the *Ashvalayana Grhyasutra*, the *Sankhayana Grhyasutra*, the *Baudhayana Grhyasutra*, the *Gobhila Grhyasutra*, the *Paraskara Grhyasutra*, the *Kathaka Grhyasutra*, the *Manava Grhyasutra* and the *Apastamba Grhyasutra*. Though Ram Gopal seems to differ with P.V. Kane on the chronology of these texts, they can be placed between 800 and 500 BC. The chronology of Michael Witzel for the Shrautasutras also seems to place the early Grhyasutras between these dates. See P.V. Kane, *History of the Dharmasastras*, BORI, Pune, 1968; Ram Gopal, *India of the Vedic Kalpasutras*, Motilal Banarsidass, Delhi, 1983; Michael Witzel, *Inside the Text: Beyond the Text*, Harvard Oriental Series, Cambridge, 1997.

2 A man could set up 'separate fires' on any of these occasions—after studentship, after marriage or after the division of the father's property. Although 'setting up of fires' may not have always meant setting up a separate household, it did imply a separate identity, apart from the father's *grihagni*, the household fire, and would have eventually led to a separate household.

3 The former were rites like the seasonal rites performed for the proper functioning of the household or like those for the annual beginning of studies. The latter were rites performed in a public arena, involving the *griha* and the community—rites like marriage, *upanayana* or birth and death rites. Seasonal rites include rites performed on the full moon of *Shravana*, *Ashvayuja*, *Margashirsha*, and other months.

4 Scholars like J. van Baal stress the 'social' aspect of sacrificing rather than the religious aspect. Wilk and Rathje have shown that other social groups such as lineages, task groups, corporations, neighbourhoods and villages often have functions that complement, replace or even compete with the household. J. van Baal, 'Offering, Sacrifice and Gift', *Numen*, xxiii, Fasc. 3., 1976, pp. 161–78; Wilk and Rathje, *Household Archaeology*, Berkeley, 1982, p. 621.

[5] Bruce Lincoln, in another context, has drawn out the relationship that exists between rituals and society. Bruce Lincoln, *Emerging from the Chrysalis: Women's Rites of Initiation*, New York, 1981, reprint, 1992. He describes society as 'a tense and volatile amalgam' of various sub-groups, members of which hold different status from one another and have differential access to wealth, power and prestige. Rituals allowed differential access to and control over thought and speech (ibid., p. 117).

[6] The marriage ritual in the Grhyasutras symbolizes the 'brahmanization of marriage', according to Kumkum Roy, where, because of the codification the rite is 'transformed into a public event which is regulated' and is therefore conducted in the outer hall, the *brahihshala* (*SGS* 1.5.2), which was accessible from within and outside the house. Kumkum Roy, 'Marriage as Communication: An Exploration of Norms and Narratives in Early India', *Studies in History*, Vol. X, No. 2, 1994, p. 184.

[7] The *grihapati* of this period is not to be confused with the landed proprietors, the *gahapati*, in later Buddhist literature of the first century BC and first century AD. The *grihapati* of the Grhyasutras was the head of the household. See Suvira Jaiswal, 'The Changing Concept of the "*Grihapati*"', in D.N. Jha (ed.), *Society and Ideology in India*, Munshiram Manoharlal, Delhi, 1996, pp. 29–37.

[8] *Madhuparka* was a concoction made of dairy products and honey, that was offered to special guests.

[9] See Stephanie Jamison, *Sacrificer's Wife: Sacrificed Wife*, Oxford University Press, New York, 1996. She refers to the significant role that the wife plays in the maintenance of 'hospitality and exchange relations', as she calls them. Although she focuses on the *shrauta* rituals, they throw light on how the Sutra authors viewed women as conduits through which relations were to be maintained. In the Soma rite the manner in which King Soma was welcomed and received lays down the pattern for the receiving of other guests (ibid., p. 115).

[10] Jamison (ibid., p. 153) refers to 'anxieties' related to hospitality, for example, in the Sudarshana story the wife acts as a mediator for the husband in a risky and unpleasant situation, and he receives the benefits of her actions.

[11] Jamison (ibid., p. 173) refers to the myth of Manu's cups with which she shows how the wife is identified as a victim and the dangers that are inherent in the extension of hospitality to gods as guests whereby the wife is symbolically a sexual offering to the gods. The risk in hospitality is inherent, as Jamison states; once one opens the house to the gods anything can happen.

[12] *Argha* reception was accorded to special guests, those who were *arghya*. It included offering of water for washing, *madhuparka*, an *asana* or seat, and a cow which the guest could get killed or let free.

[13] Brian K. Smith, *Classifying the Universe: The Ancient Indian Varna System and the Origins of Caste*, Oxford University Press, New York, 1994. He refers to '*varna*' as 'colour', in the sense of 'characteristic' or 'attribute'. He uses

the term as a 'category' or 'class', and discusses the ways in which social hierarchy was integrated into and ratified and legitimated by a categorical system with universal scope and persuasive power (ibid., p. 3).

14 The time-period for brahmanas was eight to sixteen years, for kshatriyas eleven to twenty-two years, and for vaishyas eleven to twenty-four years, according to the *Sankhayana Grhyasutra* II.1.1–8. The *mekhla* was of *munja* grass for the brahmana, of bow-string for the kshatriya and of wool for the vaishya. There were different verses recommended for the castes: the brahmana recited the *Gayatri*, the *kshatriya* the *Trishtubh*, the vaishya the *Jagati* meter. However, the mention of the attire of the *brahmacharin* in the different texts varied.

15 In order to understand the references to *varna* in the Grhyasutras, it is necessary to understand the brahmanical ideology behind the growth of the institution. Brian K. Smith relates the evolution of the *varna* system to the brahmanical attempt to 'classify' everything into neat compartments based on thought, reason and logic. Smith shows that the earlier 'reductionist' stand taken by Dumezil and Gonda in trying to understand the reason why the society was divided into 'three' orders is misleading. He argues that tripartition derives from an actual or idealized social situation in which three, and later four, classes of society were primary. This division was secondarily represented in other realms too, besides the social realm, and 'brahmanical priests and kshatriya warriors displaced their superior status onto the natural, supernatural, religious and ritual worlds, and did so surreptitiously'. Smith claims that the *varna* system was the 'root metaphor' or 'master narrative' of vedic thought. They were 'super categories' that cut across boundaries of species or discrete classes, and ordered all realms of the visible and invisible cosmos. Through the *varna*, the cosmos could be tied together—up, down and sideways. The construct attempted to be as comprehensive as possible, including within the classification system not only human beings but all living and non-living things they came in contact with.

16 As Brian Smith shows, in such a philosophy 'where every strand within the social fabric of thought was thus reinforced by every other strand', it was difficult for those whose interests were not best served to think their way out of it (ibid., p. 7).

17 Oldenberg, *The Sacred Books of the East,* Vol. XXIX, Motilal Banarsidass, Delhi, 1964, p. 87.

18 J. Goody, *World Revolution and Family Patterns,* The Free Press, New York, 1963, p. 8.

19 Kumkum Roy refers to how the later vedic rituals seem to be 'obsessed' with negating the strength of two categories of kinsmen, the *bhratravya* and the *sapatna.* The former term may have meant a father's brother's son, yet it became 'virtually synonymous with enmity'. Roy traces this to the fight for property amongst brothers that assumed importance with the beginning of settled life, and it could also be because of possible conflicts

amongst brothers-in-law in an exogamous system. Kumkum Roy, 'Changing Kinship Relations in Later Vedic Society', *Indian Historical Review*, Vol. XVIII, Nos 1–2, July 1991 and January 1992, pp.1–17.

[20] One can agree with Kumkum Roy that certain *kula* ties were being peripheralized by closer and tighter bonds between direct descendants and between actual brothers and sisters.

[21] Roy ('Changing Kinship Relations', p. 7) refers to this when she states that: 'The theme of destroying the *bhratrvya* or the *sapatna* was not taken up in the brahmanized versions of the rites of passage as incorporated in the later Grhyasutras. This may indicate that the attempt to enforce the understanding of this relationship was so successful that further reiteration was unnecessary in a changing socio-economic context.' However, she also admits that there may have been resistance to such a conceptualization of kinship relations but that 'in no case was there an acceptance of an egalitarian, reciprocal relationship within the ritual context, although such a possibility was not openly repudiated or condemned.'

[22] The *Gobhila Grhyasutra* II.10.43 refers to the fact that the first alms begged by the *brahmachari* were from his mother and two of her women friends, *suhrdau*, or from as many neighbours as there were.

[23] Arvind Sharma refers to the manner in which male warriors were made to bond together at the cost of bonds with wives and children. Arvind Sharma (ed.), *Religion and Women*, New York, 1994, p. 11.

[24] Bonding amongst the women, according to William Divale, was already there due to the types of residences and lineages. Thus the conclusion is that the 'paternal dyad is weak; the maternal dyad is the main force'. George R. Mead's reference to the structural power of the woman in the position of wife and mother, which makes her the *de facto* leader of the family group where the husband is only the *de jure* head, shows the power of the maternal bond. According to the study, men associated relatively infrequently or at a reduced level of interaction with other members of the group, and were on the fringe of effective ties that bound the group. Cited in Arvind Sharma, *Religion and Woman*, 1994.

[25] Scholars like Heesterman have shown how conflicts were an inherent part of rituals: Heesterman, *The Broken World of Sacrifice: An Essay in Indian Religion*, University of Chicago Press, Chicago, 1993, p. 42. Sacrifice was from beginning to end a contest. Being a game, it was characterized by tension and uncertainty, and, given the maximal stakes, tension and uncertainty reached a maximal and all-but-unbearable pitch. The parties in it could not merely be antithetical. Sacrifice had to be antagonistic. The element of contest permeated the whole proceedings.

[26] Max Gluckman, cited in Bruce Lincoln, *Emerging from the Chrysalis*, p. 93.

[27] J. van Baal, 'Offering, Sacrifice and Gift', p. 170. Baal refers to the differences between high-intensity and low-intensity offerings, wherein the first is fraught with competition and dangers, and the second is the 'ideal form of relations with the supernatural', where anxiety is absent. It would seem as if

the *griha* rites strive towards being 'low-intensity' rites, especially when compared to the high-intensity rites of the *shrauta* texts—they may be low-key but it is doubtful whether they were totally devoid of competitiveness and anxiety.

28 To that extent J. van Baal is right that an offering is nothing but an attempt to establish communications. He argues that the dialectics of the human condition, the combination of being a part and yet a subject, make communication an urgent necessity. J. van Baal, 'Offering, Sacrifice and Gift', p. 167.

Symbols of Resistance

Non-Brahmanical *Sants* as Religious Heroes in Late Medieval India

Rameshwar Prasad Bahuguna

Recent trends in western writings on the *sant* movement in medieval India have focused primarily on the lives, texts and socio-religious ideas of the great *sants* of the fifteenth–sixteenth centuries, such as Kabir, Namdev, Raidas and Dadu.[1] In marked contrast, the perceptions of later *sants* and the nature of the *sant*-based religious culture of the seventeenth century have largely remained unexplored. The dominant assumption underlying most of the studies is that while the early phase dominated by the major *sants* was iconoclastic and nonconformist, the *sants* of the later period were lesser beings who could not sustain the radical tempo of the early phase and became increasingly susceptible to vaishnavite and brahmanical influences. In most of the scholarly works, it is commonplace to treat the early phase of the *sant* movement as the 'most creative' and to look upon the period of the seventeenth and eighteenth centuries as one of decline, sectarianization and 'hinduization'. In fact, the concept of 'hinduization' and its variants, such as 'brahmanization', 'vaishnavization' and sanskritization', have proved influential in various discussions of the later *sant* movement and the process of non-brahmanical *panth* formation.[2]

This essay seeks to question the validity of the commonly held assumption that the *sant* movement in its later stages withered away into the dismal channels of 'sanskritization' and 'hinduization'. We are concerned here with exploring the elements of continuity and change in the later *sant* movement. While it may not be difficult to identify the elements of ideological unity between the early *sants* and those belonging to the later phase, what is at stake here is the nature of a new and vibrant, though apparently ambivalent, religious culture rooted in the popularity and shared memory of the great *sants* of the formative period, yet freely drawing on a wide range of puranic cultural forms and practices for its articulation. The growing posthumous popularity of Kabir and other great *sants* of the fifteenth–sixteenth centuries among the later *sants* and subordinate social groups informed and shaped much of the seventeenth-century *santic* religious culture. This popularity created a following cutting across caste, regional and linguistic boundaries among lower-caste groups. The ordinary people tried to comprehend and then transform existing social relations based on the caste hierarchy and brahmanical dominance through the imagined lives of the great *sants*. By fashioning their own images of Kabir and the other major *sants*, they hoped to alter, albeit symbolically, the terms of their subordination. Great feats of religious and political subversion were attributed to the early *sants*. We have therefore suggested that, far from succumbing to sanskritization and hinduization, the *sants* and *sant*-based religious culture of later medieval north India continued to contest and resist the authority of the brahmanas and other religious elites. However, much-exalted *santic* ideals such as uncompromising monotheism and rejection of image worship were of little help to the hagiographers and ordinary followers, who possessed a strong carnivalesque desire to see the hostile brahmanas trounced at their own games. It was the celebration of the imagined triumphs of the great *sants* over powerful rulers, brahmanas and other religious authorities which became the staple source of the *sant*-oriented religious culture of later medieval north India. The *sant* hagiographers of the seventeenth century made use of vaishnavite myths and symbols, but such usage often formed part of a cultural strategy aimed at ridiculing the religious authorities and representing them as villains who had, along with contemporary rulers, tormented the *sants* and caused them much suffering.

This essay is therefore concerned with the retrieval of the history of the later *sant* movement from the historiographical marginalization to which it has been consigned by scholarly preoccupation with the formative phase of the *sant* movement, and by a misplaced emphasis on its subsequent take-over by 'hinduizing' vaishnavites. The existing scholarly wisdom that the *sant* movement was fragmented from the very beginning, with divisive *panth*s emerging during the lifetimes of the great *sants* themselves,[3] has also contributed to the erasure from *sant* history of the *sant*-based religious culture of the later medieval period. We have argued that the growth of institutionalized, inward-looking sects (*panths*), such as the Kabirpanth, was not the immediate outcome of the early *sant* movement. There existed a long period of transition (during the late sixteenth and seventeenth centuries) between the early phase of the *sant* movement and the emergence of *sant*-based sectarian *panths* during the eighteenth century. It was this period of transition that was characterized by a non-sectarian and unstructured but subversive and transgressive *sant*-based religious culture. The great *sants* were not regarded as objects of religious cults during this transitional period, but as charismatic religious heroes who challenged the established religious authorities of their time.

Early *Sants*: An Overview

The fifteenth and sixteenth centuries were the formative period of the radical religious movement associated with *sants*. The *sants* of this period were non-brahmanas, and mostly belonged to the lower and lowest castes of the society. Kabir was a weaver (*julaha*) by caste and most likely flourished during the fifteenth century. He was undoubtedly the most prominent *sant* of the early phase but was preceded by Namdev (*c.* 1300) and his contemporary, Trilochan.[4] Namdev was a calico printer by caste and Trilochan a trader. Various traditions inform us that Sen (a barber or *nai*), Pipa (a *rajput*), Dhanna (a *jat* peasant), Sadhna (a butcher or *kasai*) and Raidas[5] (a leather worker belonging to the *chamar* caste) were contemporaries of Kabir. Both Kabir and Raidas lived in Banaras (Kashi)—a citadel of brahmanical orthodoxy and ritual, a city where brahmana ideologues assiduously legitimized the inequalities of the brahmanical socio-religious order and where these inequities were observed most rigorously. The relationship of Guru Nanak (1469–1539) with the *sant* movement is a matter of debate, and the tendency to call him a *sant* or to view him as an integral part of the *sant* movement has been questioned.[6] But in so far as his religious ideas and his rejection of the caste hierarchy and contemporary religious elites created an ideological affinity between him and the *sants*, it may be pointed out that he was a major religious figure of the non-brahmanical, non-islamic religious effervescence during its formative years. There is, however, no controversy regarding the association of Dadu (1544–1603), a cotton-carder (*naddaf* or *dhuniya*) by caste, with the *sant* movement, as he was clearly influenced by Kabir for whom he had great reverence.

Contemporaries among the *sants* were aware of each other's

teachings and those of their predecessors. As we shall see later, various traditions of later medieval India linked Kabir and the other great *sants* in one way or another. Such traditions clearly indicate ideological affinity among the early *sants*. Ordinary people viewed them as part of the same religious movement throughout the later and late medieval periods. The ideological unity of the early *sant* movement is also evident from their independence from, and rejection of, the dominant and elitist religions of the time—brahmanism and orthodox Islam. The early *sants* criticized, ridiculed and rejected the social order based on brahmanical dominance and caste hierarchy. Being uncompromising monotheists, Kabir and the other great *sants* also rejected puranic modes of worship, including idol worship, and the concept of incarnation. They clearly distanced themselves from vaishnavas of various hues. However, rejection of puranic lore and vaishnavism did not imply wholesale rejection of existing cultural forms, myths and symbols. The *sants* adopted and reinterpreted many existing traditions. They composed their utterances in the same common language. The use of a common language is striking, considering that they belonged to different regions of northern India. The language used by them was a kind of *lingua franca* which the masses belonging to different regions could easily understand. The early *sants* led their lives as householders and rejected asceticism. Far from isolating themselves from society, they led a family life and pursued their hereditary occupations.

Later *Sants*: A Brief Sketch[7]

From the names of the historical *sants* mentioned in texts such as *Sarvangi* by Gopaldas,[8] Jan Gopal's *Dadu Janma Lila*,[9] the *Bhaktamals* composed by Jagga, Chain and Raghodas,[10] and other sources, we can easily conclude that a large number of *sants* flourished in the seventeenth century. Very little is known about most of them, but some of the more prominent seventeenth and eighteenth-century *sants* may be mentioned here briefly. Laldas (d. 1648) was the leading *sant* of the Mewat region. He belonged to the lowly placed Meo community and earned his livelihood by selling pieces of wood. According to a legendary account of his life, he was persecuted and imprisoned by the local Mughal *faujdar* for not making any distinction between Hindus and Muslims.[11] Pran Nath (1617–1693) lived in Bundelkhand. He was known for his extreme religious eclecticism, and it is said that the Bundela chief Chhatrasal was his disciple. Malukdas (1573–1671) was probably a trader by caste and belonged to the Lucknow–Allahabad region. Dhani Dharmadas was a *baniya* by caste and belonged to Bandhogarh in modern Madhya Pradesh. He began his religious career as a vaishnava but later became a follower of Kabir. Very little authentic information is available on his floruit, and his followers (the Kabirpanthis of the Chattisgarhi branch) claim that he was a direct disciple of Kabir. Most scholars, however, give him a later floruit. It is quite possible that he founded the Kabirpanth some time towards the end of the seventeenth century.

Some of the prominent *sant*s of the early part of the seventeenth century were Dadu's disciples. However, it must be made clear that although the Dadupanth did exist in the seventeenth century, it bore greater resemblance to a loose fraternity of non-brahmanical *sant*s than to a sect. Some of Dadu's leading disciples, such as Jan Gopal (the author of *Dadu Janma Lila*), Rajjab and Sundardas, valorized the great *sant*s of the early phase. During the seventeenth century there were many *sant*s who had joined the Dadupanth but were not sectarian followers of Dadu as such. Udadas, Jogidas and Virbhan have been linked to the 'Sadh' community of *sant*s. A modern scholar, Parashuram Chaturvedi, sees a link between the Sadhs and the Satnamis of Narnaul.[12] The identity of the person who 'founded' the Satnami community in the Narnaul and Mewat regions in the middle of the seventeenth century is not clear, but he claimed to belong to the tradition of Kabir.[13]

Yari Sahib belonged to the Delhi region and was probably a contemporary of Pran Nath. He was a sufi saint who later became associated with the Bawripanth of *sants* by becoming a disciple of Beeru Sahib. Among the eighteenth-century *sant*s, mention must be made of Dharanidas and Dariya Sahib, two influential *sant*s of Bihar. Dariya Sahib was a tailor by caste and had a large number of followers. Jagjivandas (1669–1760) was another prominent *sant* of the eighteenth century. He was the founder of the eighteenth-century Satnami sect in Uttar Pradesh. Charandas and Garibdas were two famous *sant*s of the eighteenth century in the Delhi and Haryana regions. Charandas (1702–1781) was a *dhusar baniya* by caste and interpreted the basic *sant* teachings in the eighteenth-century context. Garibdas was probably a junior contemporary of Charandas and was a *jat* peasant. He was deeply influenced by Kabir's ideas. Kabir and other *sant*s of the early phase find recurring mention in his utterances. Paltu Sahib was an important eighteenth-century *sant* who lived in Ayodhya at a time when the pilgrimage centre was becoming a stronghold of conservative Ramaite vaishanavas. Paltu Sahib's utterances clearly express his ideological debt to Kabir. He came into conflict with the powerful and orthodox vaishnavas of the city due to his condemnation of idol worship and caste exclusiveness. Since there were many similarities between his spiritual teachings and mode of utterance and those of Kabir, he has been called 'the second Kabir'. He came to be called 'Paltu' (changed or inverted) because, like Kabir, he used the popular *ultabamsi* language[14] (what Lind Hess calls 'upside-down language'[15]).

Great *Sants* as Historical Celebrities: Kabir on Top

While it may be true that the *sants* of the seventeenth and eighteenth centuries were 'obscure' figures in comparison with Kabir, Raidas and other major *sants* of the earlier period, they preached religious and social ideas that were not very different from those advocated by their predecessors. Rejection of brahmanical authority and caste hierarchy, strict monotheism, and lack of faith in image worship and incarnation continued to characterize the later *sant* movement right up to the time of Tulsi Sahib in the first half of the nineteenth century. Most of the later *sants* belonged to non-brahmanical social groups and, like the early *sants*, they represented the authentic voice of the most articulate and enlightened sections of the lower-caste population.

Within the framework of continuity, the *sant* movement underwent some important changes. The later *sants* regarded Kabir and other great *sants* as their role models. The memory and increasing popularity of the earlier *sants* came to play a major role in the later *sant* movement. Rarely do we come across a *sant* of the seventeenth or eighteenth century who does not make reverential mention of Kabir and other great *sants* of the earlier period. The later *sants* constantly sought legitimacy by invoking the memory of the earlier *sants*. During most of the seventeenth century the *sant* movement was marked by widespread valorization of the great *sant* collective, with Kabir occupying pride of place. Singing the verses of these *sants* became an integral part of the *santic* culture of the period. Travelling singers with excellent memories preserved the utterances of the pioneering *sant* figures, and orally transmitted them from one generation to another and one region to the other. As a result of the interaction between the itinerant musicians, their listeners and the regional dialects, many changes occurred in the original compositions; hence we have different variants of the utterances of the great *sants* in different regional traditions.[16]

The consciousness that Kabir and other *sants* of the fifteenth–sixteenth centuries formed an ideologically cohesive group had begun to grow right from the beginning of the *sant* movement. Kabir's younger contemporaries celebrated his greatness and showed reverence to each other in their *vanis*.[17] In the Sikh tradition, Kabir, Raidas, Namdev, Dhanna and others came to be known as *bhagats* and their *vanis* were incorporated in the *Adi Granth* compiled by the fifth Sikh guru, Arjan, in 1604. The *vani* of Guru Arjan himself contains a deep sense of respect and admiration for Namdev, Kabir, Raidas and Sen.[18] Sixty-one verses of Namdev, thirty-nine *sabads* of Raidas and a far larger number of Kabir's verses are included in the *Adi Granth*.[19] Guru Arjan's inclusion of the utterances of these and other lower-caste *bhagats* was an indication of his ideological agreement with them.[20] Before Guru Arjan compiled the *Adi Granth*, the third Sikh guru, Amar Das, added the *vanis* of the early *sants* to his collection of the compositions of his predecessors and those of his own.[21] The fourth guru, Ram Das, praises the *sants* and mentions that they all attained a high status despite their low social origins.[22] Apart from the *Adi Granth*, two other anthological traditions, the *Panchvani*[23] and the non-sectarian Fatehpur manuscript tradition,[24] include the compositions of Namdev, Kabir and Raidas in large numbers. In vaishnavite hagiography—from Anantdas and Nabhadas at the beginning of the seventeenth century to Priyadas at the beginning of the eighteenth century—Kabir, Raidas, Sen and others have been grouped together and treated as disciples of Ramanand.[25]

Representation of the collective identity of Kabir and his fellow *sants* was an integral part of the later *sant* movement and the *sant*-based religious culture of the seventeenth century. What is however clearly noticeable is the wide and unparalleled popularity of Kabir, and the central significance of his eulogization in this movement and culture. The later *sant* movement revolved around the memory of Kabir and his great deeds of defiance against the established religious elites and ruling classes of his time. That Kabir had acquired fame among various sections of society, especially among the lower castes, during his own lifetime, becomes clear from certain contemporary references to him. His junior contemporary Raidas takes pride in pointing out that, despite his low social origin, Kabir had become 'renowned throughout the three worlds'.[26] Dhanna also expresses similar sentiments about Kabir's greatness.[27] We come across numerous references to him in the vaishnavite, *santic* and Persian literature of the late sixteenth–early seventeenth century. Most of the later and late medieval *sants* (right up to the time of Tulsi Sahib and Ghisa in the nineteenth century) traced their ideological ancestry to Kabir and were influenced by his ideas or imagined deeds. The collective memory of Kabir simply overwhelmed the cultural and religious life of non-brahmanical sections of medieval Indian society in many ways. In the following discussion, we shall restrict ourselves to those references which relate to Kabir alone, to show his towering status among the *sants*.

That Kabir had acquired fame in his own lifetime is clear from the comment of Abdul Haqq who, in 1590–91, wrote in his work on Muslim saints that his grandfather (who died around 1523 and who might have been Kabir's contemporary) had told his father that Kabir was neither a Hindu nor a Muslim but a monotheist (*muwahhid*). This testimony also informs us that by the time of the death of Abdul Haqq's grandfather, Kabir's verses had become popular among the people.[28] By the end of the sixteenth century, Kabir's popularity was an established fact. Abul Fazl informs us that 'many authentic traditions are related regarding his sayings and doings to this day. He was revered by both Hindus and Muhammadans for his catholicity of doctrine and the illumination of his mind, and when he died, the brahmanas wished to burn his body and the Muhammadans to bury it.'[29] Elsewhere, Abul Fazl writes that Kabir believed in the unity of God and many verses in the Hindi language composed by him were still in circulation.[30] From Abul Fazl's account it can be easily concluded that Kabir had attained a high degree of posthumous popularity by the end of the sixteenth century, and that he was identified neither with the Hindus nor with the Muslims. It was around the end of the sixteenth century that Anantadas wrote his *Parachais* on Kabir, Raidas, etc., which implies that by this time non-sectarian vaishnavas had come to look upon Kabir and the other great *sants* of his time as vaishnava devotees. In the course of the seventeenth century, Kabir's popularity grew further. Nabhadas, who wrote his famous *Bhaktamal* around 1600, celebrated the memory of Kabir in a verse which became the basis for the future glorification of Kabir in much of the vaishnavite hagiography:

> Kabir refused to acknowledge caste distinction or to recognize the authority of the six Hindu schools of philosophy nor did he set any store by the four states of life (*ashramas*) prescribed for brahmanas. He held that religion (*dharma*) without devotion (*bhakti*) was no religion at all (*adharma*) and that asceticism, fasting and alms-giving had no value if not accompanied by adoration (*bhajan*). By means of *ramainis*, *sabdis* and *sakhis*, he imparted religious instruction of Hindus and Turks alike. He showed no partiality to either but gave teaching beneficial to all. With determination he spoke and never tried to please the world. Kabir refused to acknowledge caste distinction and the six systems of philosophy.[31]

Jan Gopal, a first-generation disciple of Dadu and the famous author of *Dadu Janma Lila*, frequently refers to Kabir's greatness and his influence on Dadu. He informs us that Dadu continuously sang Kabir's verses and became his equal in 'word and deed'.[32] The popularity of Kabir in the seventeenth century, particularly among *sants*, is clear from references to him in the *sant vanis*. Laldas, the seventeenth-century *sant* from Mewat, frequently quoted Kabir's sayings and respectfully mentioned him.[33] The tendency to mix Kabir's utterances with one's own also became a prominent feature during this period.[34] Dharmadas, who probably founded the Chhatisgarhi branch of Kabirpanth, claimed to have been converted to the *sant* ideology by Kabir himself at Mathura.[35] The link between the Satnamis of Narnaul, who revolted against the Mughal empire in 1672, and Kabir's ideology has also been noted.[36] Shaikh Muhammad, a sufi saint of the Maratha country became so popular that he came to be regarded as an incarnation of Kabir.[37] Eighteenth-century *sants* such as Dariya Sahib, Paltu Sahib, Garibdas and Charandas also came under the ideological influence of Kabir.

As Kabir's popularity increased, many different images came to be associated with him. Modern scholars like Charlotte Vaudeville and Linda Hess have spoken of different Kabirs—the vaishnavized Kabir of the 'western' tradition and the harsh, critical Kabir of the 'eastern' tradition.[38] Among the later medieval sufis, it seems that Kabir's image varied from that of a *malamati* sufi (reprehensible, unorthodox sufi) to a sufi belonging to the Firdausiya order.[39] The mid-seventeenth-century work *Dabistan-i-Mazahib* mentions Kabir as a *vairagi* and gives a detailed account of the *sant* in the section dealing with vaishnavas.[40]

Santic Perceptions of History and Authority

Remembrance of Kabir and other major *sants* of the preceding centuries was part of a broader strategy evolved by the later *sants* to invoke the past for purposes of the present. Celebration of this immediate history and then stretching it backwards so as to include in its scope oppressed heroes of the puranic–mythological past, provided a cutting edge to the contestatory character of the later *sant* movement. While there are some instances of references to, and even glorification of, victimized puranic figures such as Prahlad, Dhruv, Ambarish and Harishchandra in the *vanis* of Kabir, Raidas and other great *sants* of the early period,[41] the later *sants* repeatedly hark back to the memory of persecuted mythical and historical figures, to deny the brahmanas and the growing vaishnavite movement sole monopoly over the use of history. While Kabir and his fellow-*sants* had only persecuted mythological figures to look up to as past crusaders against brahmanical injustices, the later *sants* could claim to be the proud inheritors of a great historical tradition of resistance represented by great religious heroes—ranging from Prahlad to Kabir, Raidas and Dadu. The *sant* movement had acquired a history of its own by the later medieval period. The tendency among the later *sants* to draw more readily on puranic myths and other existing cultural forms should be viewed in the context of their contest with vaishnavas and brahmanas over the use of shared symbols. Puranic myths were a source of legitimation not only for brahmanas and vaishnavas but also for the *sants*. While the brahmanas traced back the lineages of contemporary rulers to the puranic solar and lunar dynasties, and the vaishnavas sang the glory of various incarnations of Vishnu as described in the Puranas, the later *sants* traced their own history to oppressed heroes of the puranic past. The *santic* perception of history clearly distinguished between the oppressors and the oppressed. From the *vanis* of Rajjab, Dariya Sahib (of Bihar), Paltu Sahib and other *sants*, it becomes clear that Hiranyakashipu, Kansa, Bhrigu, Durvasa, Vishwamitra, Ravana and Duryodhan were regarded as villains. The following verse of Dariya Sahib may be cited here:

O holy men, the Lord is the strength of the humble one,
But those who are filled with great pride in the world,
They are crushed under His powerful command.

Having a golden palace,
Ravana was highly conceited,
He was filled with egotism and pride.
Ravana came in collision with Ram,
And Ravana's pride brought his destruction.

Hiranayakashipu also became proud,
And thought himself to be a great warrior.
He was caught and his stomach was torn apart.
Such is the fate of those
Who are highly conceited in the world.

Kansa was a manifest form of the negative powers,
He quarrelled with Krishna,
Krishna pounced like a hawk on him,
And the foolish one was knocked down and killed.

Duryodhan made a great display of his power,
And amassed an enormous army.
But Krishna in league with the Pandavas,
Used his powers in such a way
That Duryodhan was reduced to dust.

Men who are born to die at last
Display their pride in vain.
They will come to realize, says Dariya,
When Yama twists and ties their hands behind their backs.[42]

While the brahmanical perception of *Kaliyuga* was transitory, to the *sant*s it represented a continuous and unending conflict between the forces of evil and those who were true devotees of God. Far from glorifying gods and rulers, whether mythical or historical, the *santic* perception of history depicted them as helpless victims of *kaal* (time).[43] The following verse of Dariya Sahib clearly portrays the helpless subordination of mighty kings to the dictation of *kaal*:

Many kingdoms of those mighty armed kings have fallen,
Who challenged the strengths of others.

They moved on elephants in processions
    resounding with trumpets.
And their fast horses ran with speed of the wind.
Their beautiful queens peeped through the holes
    of the latticed balcony;
They waited for their beloved
    to have a glimpse of his face.
These mighty ones remained entangled
    in the trammels of the world.
Without Nam, the whole world remains in delusion.[44]

If we draw a comparison between the vaishnavite perception of history and that of the *sants*, it becomes evident that the former was concerned mainly with the incarnations of Vishnu. Puranic figures such as Prahlad are glorified by the vaishnavite hagiographers as well, but they are not represented as victims of the combined oppression of brahmanas and rulers.

In the *santic* perception of history, past and present are joined together through a process of 'condensation' of time. The heroic deeds of Prahlad, Dhruv, Harishchandra and Ambarish on the one hand, and those of historical figures such as Mansur al-Hallaj, Baba Farid, Kabir, Raidas and Dadu on the other, are described in such a way that chronology becomes unimportant.[45] The descriptions of historical villains follow a similar pattern. The lineages of heroes and villains of the *sants* were continuous and unbroken. There is also a constant updating of the *sant* history. As time passed, the list of heroes became longer and included the *sant* figures of later medieval India. By the late medieval period, even Sarmad, a sufi saint executed by Aurangzeb, had been included in the list of persecuted *sants*.[46] References to Prahlad's greatness and suffering can be found in the poetry of *sants* ranging from Kabir to Tulsi Sahib of Hathras. Many *Prahlad charitas* came to be composed both by *sants* and by vaishnavas in the later medieval period. The composition of one of them has been attributed to Raidas.[47] The *santic* image of Prahlad as described in this *Prahlad charita* is different from the vaishnavite perception in which he is depicted as a devotee of Vishnu. In the *santic* version—as mentioned in the medieval *sant* poetry and in this text—the following aspects have been particularly stressed. (a) Prahlad constantly remembered the name of Ram, for which he was persecuted by his father, King Hiranyakashipu.

Prahlad's initiation into the name of God (*Ram nam*) is highlighted. (b) Complaints by the brahmana teachers to the king that Prahlad was indulging in remembrance of *Ram nam* rather than learning demonology. The teachers, Shund and Amark, were Shukracharya's sons.

The perception of authority as expressed in *santic* poetry and hagiography was political in many ways. The people considered rulers and religious elites to be an integral part of the same order. Opposition to brahmanas and qazis in *sant* writings and in hagiographic narratives was political opposition, because these religious elites mostly served as ideologues of the contemporary ruling classes. In this sense, opposition to brahmanas and qazis implies non-acceptance of brahmanical legitimation of the existing socio-political system. It is interesting that some of the peasant revolts against the Mughal state, such as the Satnami uprising of 1672, were anti-brahmanical in character. The popular *sant* legends and miracle stories of the later medieval period clearly indicate that the subordinate groups perceived rulers, brahmanas and qazis as constituting a single oppressive system of rule. They were aware that brahmanas and qazis sought to enforce social control and religious norms with the help of the rulers. They understood the state not in abstract or institutional terms but as an oppressive alliance of rulers, brahmanas and qazis. The consciousness that rulers considered religious conformism necessary for political stability is present in the legendary representations of the lives of the *sant*s. These episodes also testify to the popular fear that religious transgression or subversion might bring quick retribution from the authorities.

To the people, the atrocities perpetrated by the authorities on *sant*s such as Prahlad, Mansur al-Hallaj, Kabir, Dadu and Sarmad were a reminder of the oppressive power of the rulers and intolerance of the brahmanas and qazis. What the brahmanas considered as noble virtues were regarded as the worst social evils by the *sant*s. The *sant*s in their *vani*s persistently condemned plunder, greed and licentiousness. Both the donors and recipients of *daan* (gift) were condemned. *Daan* itself found no sanction in *sant* ideology. No amount of *daan*—not even *daan* of the whole earth—could bring salvation to the donor if he was not devoted to the name of Ram. Brahmanical greed for *daan* was ridiculed. Brahmanas were criticized for legitimizing acts of violence and plunder. The *sants* clearly drew a distinction between the *desh* of brahmanas and rulers and the *desh* of the *sant*s. The brahmanical land is characterized by Vedas, Nigamas, caste-based discriminations, religious sects, Mughals, Pathans, Sayyids and Shaikhs, old age, death, pain and doubts.[48] The land of the *sant*s, on the other hand, contains none of these evils. It is Begampur (without any sorrow). No taxes (*khiraj*) are imposed on the people here. There is no fear, no crime and scarcity. God is the eternal emperor of this kingdom and *sant*s are his courtiers. This *santic* notion of the state is articulated by Raidas in the following verses:

1. Begampur is the name of that place,
   without suffering or distress.
   Without anxiety, taxes or property,
   without fear of failure or fear of loss.
   Refrain I have found a good home in my own land.
   O my brother, there is everlasting well-being there.

2. Its everlasting sovereignty is firm and stable,
   there none is third or second, all are one.
   Flourishing and ever famous,
   the wealthy dwell in that town.

3. They wander around wherever they please,
   they stroll through palaces unchallenged.
   Says Ravidas, the liberated Chamar,
   whoever is my fellow citizen, is my friend.[49]

Another *santic* political perception comes from Paltu, one of the prominent *sant*s of the eighteenth century. He says that the *sant* has sovereign power over both the material and spiritual worlds. Kings are represented as courtiers of the *sant*:

> The Saint reigns supreme over the worlds temporal and spiritual.
> Reigning over the temporal and spiritual worlds,
> he keeps both contented
> Not only are his worldly needs fulfilled, he also enjoys the Divine Melody within.
> Kings and monarchs stand in court with folded hands.
> His word serves as law, and his command is readily obeyed.
> With the forces of Understanding, he demolishes the ramparts of Falsehood.
> Without his asking, treasures of both the worlds are his.
> He asks for nothing except the wealth of Contentment.

Such is the sovereign power of the Saint, O Paltu, that the Lord
Himself stands at his command.
The Saint reigns supreme over the worlds temporal and spiritual.[50]

The existing socio-political order was represented as an evil by the *sant*s and a political choice was clearly made. The brahmanas regarded the Vedas and other scriptures as sacred and held that the rulers must uphold the values enshrined in them. On the other hand, to the *sant*s they were just *pothi*s and weapons of brahmanical domination.

Rejection of the concept of incarnation by the *sant*s was not just a matter of theological choice. It had political overtones. Since the existing rulers were legitimized as incarnations of gods by the brahmanas, acceptance of the incarnation theory would have amounted to accepting the divine status of these rulers. It was a compromise that the *sant*s were determined not to make. The kings were, after all, ordinary mortals. While Kabir and his contemporary *sant*s considered ancient mythical *sant*s superior to gods and kings, their followers went on extending the list of *sant*-heroes, who were then placed on an even higher pedestal.

Sant Legends and Symbolic Forms of Resistance

What we have discussed so far is the ways in which the later *sant*s responded to the popularity of the early *sant*s and came to look upon themselves as the legitimate ideological successors of the latter. However, a distinction must be made here between the *sant* followers (that is, the later *sant*s) and ordinary valorizers. While we do come across fleeting hagiographic references to the lives of Kabir and other great figures in the utterances of the later *sant*s, their focus was primarily on reaffirming the validity of the socio-religious perceptions of their predecessors. Among the ordinary people, on the other hand, the appeal of the great *sant*s was rooted in the events and happenings, mostly imagined, in the lives of the latter. As the popularity of great *sant*s like Kabir and Raidas increased during the late sixteenth and seventeenth centuries, many legends about them developed from below. Liberal-minded and deeply sympathetic vaishnavite hagiographers took the lead in narrating these tales and added a vaishnavite flavour to their accounts; yet, the subaltern character of most of these stories, especially those dealing with confrontations between the defiant *sants* and religious–political authorities, cannot be mistaken. Those who narrated and listened to these stories seemed to revel in their desire to ridicule, criticize and ultimately overturn the socio-religious hierarchy. Most of the legends represented Kabir and other major *sants* as defiant religious heroes who suffered at the hands of religious authorities, officials and rulers for their acts of religious transgression and subversion. The *sants*, endowed with supernatural powers, ultimately overcame the opposition of their adversaries who accepted their greatness and sometimes even became their followers. We may, however, suggest that these stories underline the claims of subordinate social groups to use sacred objects, myths and symbols that were regarded as a brahmanical monopoly.

These stories clearly indicate that the ordinary people remembered the great *sant* preachers as anti-brahmanical religious heroes rather than as propagators of uncompromising monotheism. It is at the level of the social and religious aspirations of the common people, among whom the *sants* preached and who interpreted the *santic* messages in their own creative ways, that we have to look for some of the most important characteristics of the *sant*-inspired religious culture during the later medieval period. At this level, what shaped the consciousness of the people was not so much the monotheism–polytheism dichotomy, as the inspirational lives of the great *sants* who were remembered as performers of great deeds against religious authorities and rulers. While the later *sants* paid greater attention to the ideological aspects of *santic* teachings such as espousal of monotheism and rejection of idolatry (the 'higher' aspects of *sant* teaching), the ordinary followers went more by the anti-brahmanical and anti-hierarchical spirit of these teachings.

The relationship between the great *sants* and the ordinary people who preserved their memory and came to attribute supernatural feats of anti-brahmanical defiance to them, should be viewed in dialectical terms. If the memory of lower-caste, anti-brahmanical figures like Kabir, Raidas and Dadu influenced and inspired the common people, the latter, on their part, refashioned the image of the *sant*-heroes in such ways as to articulate their own brand of cultural and religious opposition to the religious and political elites. The refashioning of the lives of the great *sants*—as is evident from the hagiographic narratives of various episodes in lives of their—gave birth to a thriving *sant*-inspired religious culture among subordinate social groups. The emergence of this religious culture, which viewed *sant*s more as performers of great deeds which led to their conquest over rulers and brahmanas than as iconoclastic monotheists, constituted another important change in the *sant* movement during the later medieval period. While the early *sant*s, and to a great extent their successors, rejected polytheism and preached and propagated the 'higher' monotheistic religion, their ordinary followers understood the messages in the light of their lived experiences, and gave them new meaning to counter the brahmanical hegemony.

Hagiographic accounts of the lives of the *sant*s, like *sant* poetry, have important implications for understanding the nature of power and dominance at various levels, and also the ways in which this dominance was culturally contested. The apparently didactic poetry of the *sant*s and the stories of the lives of the *sant*s are suffused with various conflicts and counter-hegemonic designs. Roger Chartier has argued, in a different context: 'Politics lurks in unexpected places, and genres that seem totally detached from the political scene are in reality profoundly marked by political aims and political upheavals.'[51] Politics is not just about the state and open revolts against it. Since the brahmanas' legitimation of state power and their own authority assumed religious forms, more often than not, resistance to the state and brahmanical authority also assumed religious forms. D.D. Kosambi had long ago suggested that in Indian history class conflict manifested in 'religious disguise'.[52] In another context, he made the significant point that cults do not clash themselves and it is the 'people who observe the cult that find it impossible to come to terms'.[53] W.C. Smith, in his famous study of lower-class revolts in the Mughal empire, commented that in the context of medieval India, 'Religion was life, and life was religion.'[54] Various forms of dissent, resistance and political perceptions were expressed in religious terms. Irfan Habib has also suggested a link between the *sant* ideology and some of the religiously organized peasant revolts of the late seventeenth century.[55] Symbolic and ideological forms of lower-class/caste resistance, such as the narratives of their heroes, projection of their enemies as villains and fools, ridiculing those who exercise political and religious authority, and praising those who perform acts of religious subversion and transgression, constitute part of the counter-hegemonic culture of subordinate social groups. These forms may also include visions of millennial and utopian ideologies, and may negate the existing pattern of exploitation and subordination by overturning social and political hierarchies.

Religious and cultural forms of resistance were part of the everyday life of the common people, and such forms were appropriate to a position of subordination. They suggested subversion and inversion rather than open confrontation. Hagiographic accounts of the lives of Kabir, Raidas and Dadu attribute forms of behaviour to a *sant* which in actual fact constituted an integral part of the socio-religious life of the common people. Miracles attributed to the *sant*s were in fact the common people's way of overcoming their own social predicaments. Opposition to brahmanism—as reflected in *santic* poetry and hagiography—had political implications because the brahmanical elite rationalized in religious terms the domination of the ruling classes. Rejection of brahmanical ideology by those who believed in the stories about the lives of the great *sant*-heroes of the past implied rejection of the ideological basis of the existing state as well.

Some of the elements of this counter-hegemonic hagiographic culture need special mention here.

(i) While the religious necessity of pilgrimage was rejected by the *sant*s, there are several references in the *sant* hagiography where the *sant*s are shown meeting each other and confronting their brahmana adversaries at existing pilgrimage centres. Most of Kabir's legendary confrontations with brahmanas take place in already existing pilgrimage centres such as Banaras (Kashi).[56] While in actual life Kabir is believed to have rejected the idea that death in Kashi led to salvation[57] and, therefore, chosen to die at Magahar, which was considered an unholy place, most of the legendary accounts of Kabir and other *sant*s depict them as subverting the authority of brahmanas in existing pilgrimage centres.[58] Pilgrimage centres were the nerve-centres of orthodox brahmanism but the ordinary people also visited them on various occasions in large numbers. The dominant trend in hagiography was to contest the claims of brahmanical authority and priesthood in their own bastions.

As is evident from the episode in which Kabir miraculously pours water on the burning feet of the *panda* (priest) of the famous Jagannath temple of Puri, popular memory linked him to this famous temple.[59] The fashioning of the link between Kabir and the Jagannath temple became such an integral part of the popular imagination that, by the end of the sixteenth century, the tradition that his tomb was situated in this temple town had taken root in the collective memory.[60] The *panda* of Jagannath is shown telling the messenger sent by the king of Kashi that Kabir was a regular visitor to the temple. There are similar episodes about *sant*s like Namdev, who is always shown as a devotee of Lord Vitthal at Pandharpur.[61]

(ii) There was a tendency among the lower castes to appropriate existing sacred symbols and objects, though they were denied the right to use them. The legendary account of brahmanical opposition to Raidas over the latter's use of sacred objects such as the *salagram, tulsi*, sandalwood and flowers, clearly[62] reflects the wish of the ordinary people to deprive the brahmanas of their monopoly over the use of sacred symbols. The legends constantly remind us that brahmanas always resorted to seeking the intervention of state authorities to control the transgressive and subversive religious culture of the lower castes. Ritual inversion rather than 'hinduization' was the important characteristic of lower-caste religiosity.

(iii) Although the word '*sant*' was used both by vaishnavas and non-brahmanical *sant*s, it had different social meanings. Different perceptions of *sant*-hood indicate conflicting socio-religious interests. A person who was regarded as a *sant* or *sadh* by the lower and the lowest castes may have appeared to be an impostor to the brahmanas.

The lower-caste and non-brahmanical perception of *sant*-hood represented the *sant*s as spiritual warriors (*sant*s who suffered at the hands of religious authorities, officials and rulers, and yet ultimately emerged triumphant due to their superior spiritual and moral values). A kind of anti-brahmanical charisma came to be associated with the *sant* figures of the past. They came to be looked upon as persons of religious exaltation and glorification. *Sant*s are ultimately established as conquerors of rulers and brahmanas. The episode relating to Sikandar Lodi's persecution of Kabir may be cited here to bring the lower-caste perception of a *sant*-hero into clear focus. This episode is first mentioned in great detail in Anantadas's *Kabir Parachai*, but it is clear that the story was quite popular by the end of the sixteenth century as it came to be mentioned in other traditions as well, and became the basis for the narratives of other *sants*' lives as well. A summary of the story is given below.

Kabir's anti-brahmanical acts of religious transgression and his subversion of the religious position of the brahmanas and qazis of

Kashi outraged the antagonistic religious elites, who went to Sultan Sikandar Lodi. Wishing the sultan a long life and calling him their 'father', they requested him to punish Kabir for his subversive activities and for denigrating them. Sultan Sikandar Lodi arrested Kabir and put him on trial for his unorthodox views. When Kabir refused to recant his teachings, Sikandar Lodi ordered that Kabir be bound hand-and-foot and trampled to death by an enraged elephant. The enraged elephant, however, trembled in fear before the *sant.* Infuriated by this, the sultan himself mounted the howdah and goaded the elephant forward to where the *sant* lay. The elephant still refused to advance; peering down at the *sant*, the sultan saw that Kabir had turned himself into a lion. Sikandar Lodi dismounted from the elephant and prostrated himself before the great ascetic. A king holds the power of life and death over his subjects, but he finds himself powerless in dealing with a *sant* who holds the power over his life and death. While brahmanas and qazis are depicted as wishing the sultan a long life and addressing him as 'father' and 'mother', the legend shows Kabir refusing to offer obeisance (*salaam*) to him. When the qazi orders Kabir to offer *salaam* to the king, the *sant*'s reply is that he would offer obeisance only to God.[63]

Jan Gopal's *Dadu Janma Lila*—the earliest legendary account of Dadu's life, written a few years after his death—gives a similar description of the *sant*'s encounter with the qazi and *faujdar* of Sambhar.[64] The work also contains a legendary account of the acceptance of Dadu's spiritual greatness by Emperor Akbar, his courtiers and various chiefs of Rajasthan. Dadu, as a *sant,* is shown to be superior to all of them. When he is persuaded to visit Fatehpur Sikri and enlighten Akbar on spiritual matters, he establishes complete spiritual dominance over the emperor, his courtiers and brahmana ideologues. A brahmana advisor of Akbar named Tulsi (different from Tulsidas, the author of *Ramcharitamanas*) says 'Hail to the King', but Dadu ignores his greeting and instead says 'Hail to God'. He makes it clear that he would bow only before God and none else. He also refuses to accept the theory that the emperor is an incarnation of God.[65] Jan Gopal writes that in his discussions with Akbar, which lasted for forty days, Dadu 'spoke with the firmness of Prahlad and with the wisdom of Kabir'.[66]

Needless to say, the entire account is legendary and there is no documentary evidence to show that Dadu ever visited Fatehpur

Sikri or met Akbar. This fact, however, does not detract from the value of this account as this and other hagiographic accounts of the lives of the *sants* reveal the non-brahmanical perception of the qualities of a *sant*. Hagiographers often use the phrase 'victory, victory' whenever brahmanas and rulers are made to bite the dust and surrender before a *sant*. Clearly, in symbolic terms at least, the *sant*-hero becomes the new authority figure. What is significant about such a perception of *sant*-hood is that it reveals the political expectations of the ordinary people who, by imputing certain qualities to the *sants*, imagined the overturning of existing hierarchies. The harsh reality that the relations of domination and subordination remained intact did not prevent lower-caste groups from offering cultural and symbolic resistance to dominant groups. Marc Bloch, the famous French historian, noted long ago in his study of 'royal touch', that the tendency to believe something which never happened in reality or was contradicted by experience is an essential feature of the so-called 'primitive' mentality.[67]

Unstructured Solidarity and Fluidity

Sustained by the socio-religious ideas of the later *sants* and stories of the lives of the great *sant*-heroes of the past, the *sant*-based religious culture flourished during the period of transition between the early phase of the *sant* movement and its ultimate transformation into fragmented, well-organized *panths* (sects) in the course of the eighteenth century. There is not much evidence to suggest the existence of sectarian *panthic* orders based on the ritualized worship of a particular *sant* during most of the sixteenth and seventeenth centuries. Some modern scholars and sectarian followers of Kabir believe that the Kabirpanth was founded by Kabir himself.[68] However, the history of the Kabirpanth cannot be traced to a date before the end of the seventeenth century. The term 'Kabirpanth' or 'Kabirpanthi' is not found in pre-eighteenth-century sources. The author of *Dabistan-i-Mazahib*, written in the mid-seventeenth century, gives a detailed account of Kabir and attributes a large following to him, yet he does not refer to the existence of the Kabirpanth. Most of the manuscripts of the *Bijak*, the main scripture of the Kabirpanthis, belong to the post-eighteenth-century period.[69]

The term 'Dadupanth' was used by some of the seventeenth-century followers of Dadu. The author of *Dabistan-i-Mazahib* also gives a brief sketch of what he calls 'Dadu panthians'.[70] This sketch, however, deals with the teachings of Dadu rather than with a *panth*. For the most part of the seventeenth century, Dadupanth existed in the form of a loose association of non-brahmanical *sant*s who used it as a platform for religious propaganda. It was open to the followers of various *sant*s and there is little evidence to suggest that the followers of Dadu subordinated the spiritual authority of other great *sant*s to that of Dadu. From the testimony of Jan Gopal, the earliest biographer of Dadu in the seventeenth century, it is evident that Dadu's followers accorded a high position to Kabir. Dadu was himself represented as an incarnation of Kabir and as constantly singing Kabir's verses.[71] The seventeenth century saw many generations of Dadu's followers but they were scattered in various parts of Rajasthan. They sang the verses of Dadu along with those of other leading *sant*s such as Kabir. They were not organized under a single hierarchical organization. According to Daniel Gold, the Dadupanth emerged as a distinct sect only at the end of the seventeenth century.[72]

The *sant*-based religious culture of the seventeenth century contained strong elements of fluidity and was marked by unstructured solidarity among its adherents. It lacked an institutionalized character and formal organization, but still managed to transcend regional, linguistic and caste boundaries among non-brahmanical social groups. The fluid nature of the culture also created a taste among its adherents for subverting existing Hindu–Muslim and *nirguna–saguna* binary divisions. They drew on multiple cultural and religious sources for garnering support among the ordinary people. Ramanand was regarded as a *saguna bhakta* but most of the seventeenth-century hagiographic accounts look upon him as the spiritual guide of Kabir and other monolithistic *sant*s. In fact, in the seventeenth-century hagiography, Ramanand is a 'shadowy figure' who has no fixed religious identity. *Kabir–Raidas Samvad*, a hagiographic text whose composition is traditionally attributed to another *sant*, Sen, makes it clear that Raidas started his religious career as a *saguna* devotee and was later converted to the *nirguna* ideology as a result of a long religious discussion with Kabir.[73] Many anthological traditions of the seventeenth century bring together the verses of *saguna* and *nirguna sant*s. The Dadupanthi hagiographers give as much respect to the *saguna devotees* as to the *nirguna sant*s. The author of *Dabistan-i-Mazahib* placed Kabir in the category of Vairagis. A modern scholar on Kabir has found the testimony of the *Dabistan* 'confusing' and 'absurd'.[74] But this apparently confusing image of Kabir in the *Dabistan* was a result of the unstructuredness and fluidity of the seventeenth-century non-brahmanical religious culture. The *Dabistan* contains numerous cases of the blurring and overlapping of religious identities. According to its author, the Vairagi community was open to Hindus, Muslims and 'others':

> Whoever among the Hindus, Muselmans, or others, wishes, is received into their religion; none are rejected, but, on the contrary, all are invited. It is said that some Muselmans also worship Vichnu, because in *Bismilla*, they confound *Bisen* with Bishen (or Vichnu), and most of them agree about the purity and infinity of Vichnu's being.[75]

Elsewhere in the work he informs us that the Vairagis considered their way 'opposite to that of the Vedas and the Koran' and that they 'have nothing to do either with Muselmans or Hindus'.[76] It is evident that the Vairagis in the seventeenth century were an amorphous religious community which accommodated religious figures belonging to different traditions and religions. Many unorthodox and nonconformist tendencies remained hidden under the Vairagi fold. In the context of the subversive non-brahmanical religious culture of the seventeenth century, it is not surprising that a *sant* like Kabir, who had rejected both brahmanism and orthodox Islam, came to be regarded as a Vairagi. Dadupanthis and Satnamis were other examples of such broad-based non-sectarian fraternities. The non-brahmanical Satnami religious community incurred the hostility of the Mughal state officials for various reasons, one of them being the reluctance of its members to differentiate between Hindus and Muslims.[77] The Dadupanth was the leading unorganized association of *sant*s in the seventeenth century. The nature of the seventeenth-century non-brahmanical fraternities was such that people constantly moved into and out of them.

Conclusion

We have argued that uncritical acceptance among scholars of the conventional two-fold chronological–theological division of the medieval *sant* movement—a monotheistic early phase and a vaishnavized/sectarianized later phase—has led to historical marginalization of the later *sant* movement and *sant*-inspired religious culture of later medieval north India. A misplaced focus on the vaishnavization of the later *sant* movement has led many scholars to ignore the changing dimensions and resultant transformation of the *sant* movement. By delineating the process of continuity and change in the *sant* movement, we have tried to show that the later *sant* movement, far from being 'hinduized' or 'sanskritized', was immensely counter-hegemonic. It was sustained not only by the ideological relationship of the later *sants* with the great *sant*-heroes of the past but, more importantly, also by the shared remembrance of Kabir and his contemporaries as charismatic challengers of the established socio-political order.

The transitional period between the early phase of the movement and the emergence of well-demarcated, closed and hierarchical *panths* in the eighteenth century, characterized the emergence of a *sant*-based religious culture among the non-brahmanical segments of society. Collective memory of early *sants* as crusaders against brahmanical dominance; propagation of the utterances and, more importantly, the real or imagined deeds of the great *sants* through various modes of transmission; emergence of unorganized non-brahmanical solidarity around shared memories of the *sants*; articulation of a counter-hegemonic agenda and alternative political perceptions through the composite narratives of the lives of the *sants*; and, finally, fostering an image of the *sants* as anti-authority and subversive figures, to prepare the ideological basis for possible future acts of resistance to religious and political authorities, were some of the important constituents of the transitional phase of the *sant* movement in the seventeenth century.

Notes and References

[1] For a substantial collection of essays on medieval Indian *sants* by western scholars, see Karine Schomer and W.H. McLeod (eds), *The Sants: Studies in a Devotional Tradition of India*, Motilal Banarsidass, Delhi, 1987. Other major works published in recent decades include Charlotte Vaudeville, *Kabir*, Oxford, 1974, later published in revised form under a new title, *A Weaver Named Kabir*, Oxford University Press, Delhi, 1993; *The Bijak of Kabir*, translated by Linda Hess and Sukhdev Singh, essays and notes by Linda Hess, Motilal Banarsidass, Delhi, 1986; Winand M. Callewaert (ed. and tr.), *The Hindi Biography of Dadu Dayal* (a critical edition and English translation of Jan Gopal's *Dadu Janma Lila Parchi*), Motilal Banarsidass, Delhi, 1988; Winand M. Callaewart and O.P. de Beeck Bart (eds), *Nirgun Bhakti Sagar: Devotional Hindi Literature*, 2 vols, Manohar, Delhi, 1991; Winand M. Callaewart (ed.), The *Sarvangi of Gopaldas: A 17th Century*

Anthology of Bhakti Literature, Manohar, Delhi, 1993; Winand M. Callaewart and Peter G. Friedlander, *The Life and Works of Raidas*, Manohar, Delhi, 1992; Daniel Gold, *The Lord as Guru: Hindi Sants in the North Indian Tradition*, Oxford University Press, Delhi, 1987, and 'The Dadu-Panth: A Religious Order in the Rajasthan Context', in Karine Schomer *et al.* (eds), *The Idea of Rajasthan: Explorations in Regional Identity*, Vol. II, Manohar, Delhi, 1994, pp. 242–64; David N. Lorenzen (ed. and tr.), *Kabir Legends and Anantadas's Parachai*, State University of New York Press, Albany, 1991; David N. Lorenzen (ed.), *Bhakti Religion in North India: Community Identity and Political Action*, Manohar, Delhi, 1996; R.S. McGregor (ed.), *Devotional Literature in South Asia: Current Research, 1985–88*, Cambridge University Press, Cambridge, 1992; Alan W. Entwistle and Francoise Mallison (eds), *Studies in South Asian Devotional Literature: Research Papers 1988–91*, Manohar, Delhi, 1994.

2 Thus some of the contributors to Schomer and McLeod (eds), *The Sants*, have found the 'hinduization' thesis and its corollaries particularly useful in understanding the emergence of certain religious, ideological and social trends in the *sant* fraternities and *sant*-based sects. Winand M. Callewaert, in his essay in the volume ('Dadu and Dadu-Panth: The Sources', pp. 181–89), notices a tendency towards 'brahmanization' in the early hagiography of Dadu, resulting from the attempts of the hagiographers to hide his low-caste background and depict him as a brahman by birth (p. 189). Use of 'pseudo-Sanskrit' by some of the early disciples of Dadu in their compositions is, according to Callewert, an indication of the beginning of 'brahmanization' of the early Dadupanth ('The Sarvangi of the Dadupanthi Gopaldas', in Entwhistle and Mallison (eds), *Studies in South Asian Devotional Literature*, pp. 451–52).

David N. Lorenzen, in his study of the Kabirpanth, has observed that despite the existence of a strong sense of social and religious dissent in the *panth* against the hierarchical caste ideology, it has undergone 'sanskritization' and 'hinduization' ('The Kabir-panth and Social Protest', in Schomer and McLeod (eds), *The Sants*, pp. 284–96 *passim*). Regarding the nature of the legends about Kabir's life, Lorenzen points out in the same contribution (p. 288), that their general tendency 'is to make Kabir more Hindu and less Muslim. . . . However mythologized all these legends may be, they do clearly illustrate the rapid hinduization of Kabir tradition'.

In a more recent work on Kabir legends, Lorenzen has revised his position to some extent. While reaffirming his earlier view that these legends constitute an attempt to legitimize Kabir in terms of M.N. Srinivas's concept of sanskritization, he now acknowledges that this concept overlooks 'the presence in the legends of elements of both a more egalitarian ideology and reactionary anti-Muslim communalism': see Lorenzen (ed. and tr.), *Kabir Legends and Anantadas's Parchai*, p. 26. However, it seems that he has not entirely disowned the sanskritization thesis, as is clear from the following observation made by him on the hagiographical works produced by the Dharmadasi branch (also known as Chhatisgarhi branch) of Kabirpanth: 'In so far as this literature mimics *saguni* Puranas, it can be regarded as a product of sanskritization, the emulation of higher caste culture. On the other hand, Dharmadasi hagiography also aims to replace and finally subvert the *saguni* Puranas': David N. Lorenzen, 'Introduction: The Historical Vicissitudes of Bhakti Religion', in Lorenzen (ed.), *Bhakti Religion in North India,* p. 18.

Lorenzen does not, therefore, make a complete departure from his earlier thesis of the increasing tendency towards sanskritization and hinduization in the hagiography of Kabir, though his recent attempts to see this hagiography in a new perspective and decipher in it elements of socio-religious subversion and collective representations, deserve appreciation. We may also mention here that pre-nineteenth-century Kabir legends do not contain elements of 'anti-Muslim communalism'. Such legends as do betray an anti-Muslim bias are either nineteenth-century additions or the product of more recent appropriations of Kabir by the forces of Hindu communalism and communalization of certain Kabirpanthi establishments.

Taking a similar view of Kabir's 'legendary life', another eminent Kabirologist, Charlotte Vaudeville, sees a 'definite Hindu stamp' and vaishnava influence on the Kabir legends. She also emphasizes the growth of a 'strongly anti-Muslim flavour' in the vaishnavite hagiographic account of Kabir from the seventeenth century onwards, though she grudgingly acknowledges that 'a faint glimpse of the Muslim ideal of the *shahid,* the martyr of the monotheistic faith, may be perceived now and then, especially in the episode in which the saint refuses to prostrate himself before a king who is a mere man'. See *A Weaver Named Kabir,* pp. 64–65.

Another western scholar on the medieval *sant* movement, Daniel Gold, is conscious of the fact that great early *sants* like Kabir questioned the Hindu and Islamic traditions, and the later *sants* of the seventeenth and eighteenth centuries continued the radical legacy of their predecessors. Yet, he makes the observation that the later *sants* had to make ideological and religious compromises as they had to work in 'a more Hinduized milieu' (*The Lord as Guru,* pp. 3–6). According to Gold, the later *sants* 'flourished in a predominantly Hindu world where the popular religion was becoming increasingly oriented toward vaishnavite deities'. He uses expressions such as 'ordinary Hindus', 'hinduized milieu', 'general Hindu environment', 'hinduized heritage', etc., while referring to the religious climate in later and late medieval northern India. The existence of variety in the *sant*-based *panths* is attributed by him to 'the richness of the Hindu ritual life on which they draw'. Continuing in a similar vein, Gold refers to the process of the adaptation of 'Hindu forms' of worship by the later and late medieval *sant panths* and their 'increasing hinduization' (pp. 93–99). Elsewhere ('The Dadu Panth: A Religious Order in Rajasthan Context', in Schomer *et al.* (eds), *The Idea of Rajasthan,* Vol. II, p. 247), he observes that many of the *sant*-based sects underwent with their establishment 'familiar processes of routinization and sanskritization—so much so that several have been finally reabsorbed into conventional Hinduism, leaving only the memory of a past local *sant*. This early assimilation of *sant panths* into conventional Hinduism is indicative of the ambiguous role *sants* have played in the complex interaction between India's Great Tradition and the regional Little Traditions.'

The underlying assumption which informs this interpretation is that the *sants* and the *panths* were always an integral part of the Hindu religion and existed within it as 'regional Little Traditions'. During its initial radical phase, the *sant* movement broke away from the paternal religion but very soon returned to it through a process of routinization and sanskritization (or 'reabsorption' and 'assimilation'). While brahmanism is seen as constituting the 'Great Tradition', the *sant* movement and the widespread religious culture emanating from it, which created a strong awareness of broader though unstructured solidarity among large sections of the low-caste population of northern India during the sixteenth and seventeenth centuries, is reduced to one among myriad different and divisive 'regional Little Traditions'.

3 See, for instance, Karine Schomer's Introduction, in Schomer and McLeod (eds), *The Sants*, p. 4.

4 In the medieval Maharashtrian Bhakti tradition, Namdev is more famous as a leading figure of the Varkari movement which was vaishnavite in its character. The Varkaris were devotees of Lord Vitthala (a form of Vishnu) at Pandharpur. However, we must not stretch the regional variations in the image of Namdev too far, and instead comprehend them in ideological terms, for even in northern India he, along with other low-caste *sants* such as Kabir, Raidas, etc., has entered the vaishnavite hagiography of Nabhadas and Priyadas as a vaishnavite devotee. On the other hand, in the Sikh tradition, they are called '*bhagats*' and in the *sant* hagiography, each one of them enjoys the status of a *sant*. For a northern Indian vaishnavite portrayal of Namdev, see Nabhadas, *Bhaktamal, mool chhappaya* 43, p. 332, where the author describes him as a devotee of 'Bithal' (Lord Vitthala); and Priyadas, *Bhaktirasabodini, kavittas* 127–143, pp. 324–43. (All the references to Nabhadas's *Bhaktamal* and Priyadas's *Bhaktirasabodhini* in the paper are from Sitaramsharan Bhagwan Prasad Roopkala (ed.), *Goswami Shri Nabhaji Krit Shri Bhaktamal*, with the commentary called the *Bhaktirasabodhini Tika* by Priyadas, seventh reprint, Tej Kumar Book Depot, Lucknow, 1993.)

For Trilochan being a contemporary of Namdev, see Priyadas, ibid., *kavitta* 1980, pp. 382–83, who says that both Namdev and Trilochan were disciples of Jnandev. Also see Charlotte Vaudeville, 'The Shaiva–Vaishnava Synthesis in Maharashtrian Santism', in Schomer and McLeod (eds), *The Sants*, p. 216.

5 Raidas is known as Ravidas in the Sikh tradition.

6 W.H. McLeod (*Guru Nanak and the Sikh Religion*, Clarendon, 1968, reprint, Oxford University Press, Delhi, 1996, pp. 149–58 *passim*) emphasized that while Guru Nanak's religious thought was more consistent than

that of Kabir, the *sant* tradition or *nirguna sampradaya* provided the basis for the former's religious teachings. McLeod's reaffirmation of such a position in his subsequent writings (*The Evolution of the Sikh Community*, second edition, Oxford University Press, Delhi, 1996, p. 5, and 'The Development of the Sikh Panth', in Schomer and McLeod (eds), *The Sants*, pp. 229–49), has made him the target of criticism by 'the critics of critical scholarship'. For an excellent and fuller discussion of the issues involved in the debate between 'critical scholarship' (represented by scholars such as W.H. McLeod and Harjot Oberoi) and 'critics of critical scholarship' (meaning orthodox Sikh historians) on various aspects of the Sikh religion, see J.S. Grewal, *Contesting Interpretations of the Sikh Tradition*, Manohar, Delhi, 1998.

7 For the *vanis* and brief sketches of the lives of later *sants*, see the *Sant-Bani Pustak Mala* series published by Belvedere Press, Allahabad, in the beginning of the last century. The series includes a dozen volumes, each volume containing a brief account of the life of a particular *sant* followed by a collection of her utterances (*vanis*). Many reprints have appeared at subsequent dates. The pioneering studies of P.D. Barthwal (*The Nirguna School of Hindi Poetry*, first edition, 1936, reprint, Heritage Publishers, Delhi, 1978) and Parashuram Chaturvedi (*Uttari Bharti ki Sant Parampara*, first edition, Leader Press, Allahabad, 1952, third edition, Allahabad, 1972) drew upon the information provided on the later *sants* by the *Sant-Bani Pustak Mala* series. See also *Sant Mahatmaon ka Jiwan-Charitra Sangrah*, Belvedere Press, Allahabad, 1975; K.N. Upadhaya, *Dariya Sahib: Saint of Bihar*, Radhasoami Satsang Beas, 1987; Issac A. Ezekiel, *Saint Paltu: His Life and Teachings*, Radhasoami Satsang Beas, 1979; J.R. Puri and V.K. Sethi, *Tulsi Sahib: Saint of Hathras*, Radhasoami Satsang Beas, 1981. Unless otherwise mentioned, our account of the lives of later *sants* is based on these works.

8 See Callewaert (ed.), *The Sarvangi of Gopaldas*, pp. 19–29.

9 Jan Gopal, *Shri Dadu Janma Lila Parachi*, critical edition and English translation by Winand M. Callewaert under the title, *The Hindi Biography of Dadu Dayal*, Motilal Banarsidass, Delhi, 1988.

10 Agarchand Nahata (ed.), *Raghavadaskrit Bhaktamal*, with a commentary by Chaturdas, *granthank* 78, Rajasthan Oriental Research Institute, Jodhpur, 1965. The volume includes the texts of the *Bhaktamals* written by Jagga and Chain also.

11 P.W. Powlett, *Gazetteer of Ulwur*, London, 1978, pp. 52–59. Most of the subsequent accounts of Laldas, including Parashuram Chaturvedi's, are clearly based on the information provided by Powlett's *Gazetteer*.

12 Chaturvedi, *Uttari Bharat ki Sant Parampara*, p. 607.

13 Irfan Habib, 'Forms of Class Struggle in Mughal India', in *Essays in Indian History: Towards a Marxist Perception*, Tulika, Delhi, 1995, p. 244.

14 Gold, *The Lord as Guru*, p. 63.

15 Hess, *The Bijak of Kabir*, pp. 135–61.

16 See Winand M. Callewaert, 'Singing Repertoires in Western India', in R.S. McGregor (ed.), *Devotional Literature in South Asia: Current Research*,

1985–88, pp. 29–35; and 'Introduction', in his *Sarvangi of Gopaldas*, pp. 5–6.

[17] For the utterances of Raidas containing respectful mention of Kabir and other *sants*, see the critical edition of Raidas's *vani* in Callewaert and Friedlander, *The Life and Works of Raidas*, *pada* 109, pp. 166–67 and *pada* 111, pp. 167–68. For similar utterances of Dhanna, see the English translation of his *vani* in Vaudeville, *A Weaver Named Kabir*, p. 354.

[18] See Callewaert and Friedlander, *The Life and Works of Raidas*, p. 11.

[19] McLeod, *Guru Nanak and the Sikh Religion*, p. 154, n. 2 and 3.

[20] McLeod, *The Evolution of the Sikh Community*, p. 86.

[21] Ibid., p. 50.

[22] Callewaert and Friedlander, *The Life and Works of Raidas*, p. 11.

[23] For the *Panchavani* collections of *padas* of Kabir, Raidas, Namdev, Haridas along with those of Dadu, see Callewaert and de Beeck (eds), *Nirgun Bhakti Sagar*. See also Callewaert (ed.), *The Sarvangi of Gopaldas*. The *Sarvangis* of Rajjab and Gopaldas are compilations of the *vanis* of a large number of *sants* but in both of them the *vanis* of Dadu, Kabir, Namdev and Raidas figure prominently.

[24] For the Fatehpur manuscript tradition, see Callewaert and Friedlander, *The Life and Works of Raidas*, pp. 37–38.

[25] While reference to the early low-caste *sants* as the disciples of Ramanand are too numerous in Anantadas's and Priyadas's narratives to be mentioned here, in *Nabhadas's Bhaktamal*, see *chhappays* 36, p. 282, for reference to Kabir, Pipa, Raidas, Dhanna and Sen as disciples of Ramanand.

[26] Callewaert and Friedlander, 'The Vani of Raidas', in *The Life and Works of Raidas*, *pada* 111, pp. 167–68.

[27] See Dhanna's *vani* in Vaudeville, *A Weaver Named Kabir*, p. 354.

[28] For this reference, see M. Athar Ali, 'Encounter and Efflorescence: Genesis of the Medieval Civilization', *Social Scientist*, 200–01, 1990, p. 25.

[29] *Ain-i Akbari*, Vol. II, edited by H.B. Lochmann, English translation by H.S. Jarret and revised by J.N. Sarkar, reprint, Low Price Publications, Delhi, 1994, p. 141.

[30] Ibid., p. 182.

[31] Nabhadas, *Bhaktamal*, *mool chhappaya* 60, p. 479. English translation of the verse is from Vaudeville, *A Weaver Named Kabir*, p. 43.

[32] See Callewaert (ed. and tr.), *The Hindi Biography of Dadu Dayal*, 2:4.

[33] See Powlett, *Gazetteer of Ulwar*, p. 60.

[34] Ibid.

[35] *Dhani Dharmdas ki Shabdavali*, editorial introduction, Belvedere Press, Allahabad, 1980, p. 2.

[36] Habib, 'Forms of Class Struggle in Mughal India', p. 244.

[37] A.R. Kulkarni, 'Social Relations in the Maratha Country', in *Medieval Maharashtra*, Books and Books, Delhi, 1996, pp. 118–19.

[38] Vaudeville, *A Weaver Named Kabir*, pp. 109–30; Linda Hess, 'Three Kabir Collections: A Comparative Study', in Schomer and McLeod (eds), *The*

Sants, pp. 111–41; and Linda Hess's essays in Introduction to the *Bijak of Kabir*, Delhi, 1986, pp. 6–7.

39 The famous seventeenth-century sufi of Awadh, Abdur Rehman Chish'ti, in his *Mirat-ul-Asrar*, calls Kabir 'Shaikh Kabir'. His perception of Kabir is largely that of a religious figure who began and ended his career as a sufi and who during an intermediary stage of his spiritual development came under the influence of Ramanand '*vairagi*'. Under the influence of Ramanand, Kabir practised many ascetic exercises. 'The conception of oneness of God (*Tawhid*) became dominant in his mind and his discerning eyes made him very hard toward all externalists towards whom he showed no conciliatory attitude.' The externalists accused him of infidelity. The author then informs us that Kabir was a follower of the 'disorderly sect of Malamatiya' (reprehensible) sufis. But towards the end, he was initiated into the sufi order of Firdausiyas. For this reference, see Quamaruddin, 'Kabir as depicted in the Persian Sufistic and Historical Works', *Islam and Modern Age*, Vol. III, No. 1, 1972, pp. 57–75. I am grateful to Dr S.Z.H. Jafri for bringing this reference to my notice.

40 *Dabistan-i-Mazahib*, English translation by Anthony Tryoer and David Shea as *School of Religions* in 3 volumes, London, 1843. The sections dealing with 'the religious systems of the Hindus' have been reproduced as *Hinduism during the Mughal Period of the Seventeenth Century*, Khuda Bakhsh Oriental Public Library, Patna, 1993, pp. 186–91 (all references here are from the Patna reprint of the *Dabistan*).

41 For sympathetic attitude of Kabir towards Prahlad and some other puranic devotees, see Hess (tr.), *The Bijak of Kabir*, verse 12, p. 47 and verse 92, p. 72. References to puranic devotees and, in particular, to persecuted figures like Prahlad are numerous in the *vani* of Ravidas; see Callewaert and Friedlander, *The Life and Works of Raidas, pada* 84, pp. 152–53, *pada* 88, p. 156 and *pada* 97, p. 161, for such references. *Pada* 91, pp. 157–59 is a long verse (*Prahlad Charita*) about Prahlad's travails and his ultimate triumph over his tormentors. It is, however, not certain whether this verse was actually composed by Raidas or is a later interpolation. In any case, the verse clearly reveals the desire of medieval *sants* to identify with Prahlad's cause.

42 Upadhyaya, *Dariya Sahib: Saint of Bihar*, pp. 154–55.

43 Narayandas (ed.), *Shri Rajjab Vani*, Prakashanalya, Ajmer, 1967, '*Kal Ka Ang*', 84:3, p. 523.

44 Upadhyaya, *Dariya Sahib*, p. 154.

45 References to the mixed glorification of assorted persecuted figures mentioned in the Puranas and historical figures such as Kabir recur in the *sant* poetry from Rajjab in the seventeenth century to Tulsi Sahib in the nineteenth. As an illustration, we may refer here to some references in *Rajjab Vani*, 'Bhajan Pratap Ka Ang', verse 18, p. 172; 'Sanyam Kasauti Ka Ang', verses 38–40, p. 685, verse 3, p. 1353.

46 See the verse of Tulsi Sahib of Hathras in Puri and Sethi, *Tulsi Sahib: Saint of Hathras*, p. 96.

[47] For the printed version of this *Prahlad Charit*, see B.P. Sharma, *Sant Ravidas Vani* (Hindi), Surya Prakashan, Delhi, 1978; see also Callewaert and Friedlander, *The Life and Works of Raidas, pada* 91, pp. 157–59.

[48] Verse attributed to Kabir in Chandrika Prasad Jijnashu, *Sant Pravar Raidas Sahab*, Bahujan Kalyan Prakashan, Lucknow, fifth edition, 1984, pp. 147–48.

[49] The *vani* of Raidas in Callewaert and Friedlander, *The Life and Works of Raridas, pada* no. 36, p. 126.

[50] *Paltu Sahib ki Bani*, Belvedere Press, Allahabad, Pt I, *Kundali* 138. English translation of the verse is from Ezekiel, *Saint Paltu*, pp. 286–87.

[51] Roger Chartier, 'Introduction', in Roger Chartier (ed.), *The Culture of Print: Power and the Use of Print in Early Modern Europe*, Polity Press, Cambridge, 1989, p. 13.

[52] D.D. Kosambi, *In Introduction to the Study of Indian History*, Popular Prakashan, Bombay, 1956, revised edition, 1975, p. 373.

[53] D.D. Kosambi, *Myth and Reality*, Popular Prakashan, Bombay, 1962, p. 2.

[54] W.C. Smith, 'Lower Class Uprisings in the Mughal Empire', reprinted in Muzaffar Alam and Sanjay Subrahmanyam (eds), *The Mughal State 1526–1750*, Oxford University Press, Delhi, 1998 (originally published in *Islamic Culture*, Vol. XX, 1946, pp. 21–40), p. 325.

[55] See Irfan Habib, *The Agrarian System of Mughal India*, 1556–1707, second rev. edn (first published in 1963), Oxford University Press, Delhi, 1991, pp. 395–96. See also his 'Forms of Class Struggle in Mughal India', p. 244.

[56] See, for instance, the meeting of Kabir, Raidas and Sen as depicted in *Raidas Parachai*, translated and edited by Sukhdev Singh, Vishwavidyalaya Prakashan, Varanasi, 1993, Rest 9 and 10, pp. 76–78; see also *Kabir–Raidas Gosthi*, which is believed to have been compiled by their fellow-*sant*, Sen the barber (included in Sukhdev Singh, ed., *Raidas Parachai*).

For hagiographic narratives of the various confrontations between Kabir and the brahmanas of Kashi, see Anantdas's *Kabir Parachai*, section 3, section 5 and sections 7, 8 and 9.

For almost similar versions of this account, see Priyadas, *Bhaktirasabodhini, kavittas* 272–79, pp. 484–89. Similar stories may be found about other *sant*s such as Raidas and Namdev. In the *sant* hagiography, for references to Kabir's encounters with the brahmanas of Kashi and Sikandar Lodi, see Chaturdas's commentary on Raghodas's *Bhaktamal*, verses 108–12, pp. 53–54.

[57] In medieval times, Magahar near Gorakhpur was looked down upon as a wretched place where death would lead to rebirth as a donkey. Magahar was inhabited by low-caste *julaha*s and was regarded as unclean and barren. Kabir lived for most of his life in Kashi and, therefore, his decision to go to Magahar to die should be seen as an attempt to strike at the root of a long-held brahmanical belief. For Kabir's position, see his verse in Hess, *The Bijak of Kabir, sabad* 103, pp. 75–76.

[58] See footnote 56 above.

[59] See *Kabir Parachai*, section five; *Bhaktirasabodhini*, *kavitta* 275, p. 486.

[60] See Abul Fazl, *Ain-i Akbari*, Vol. II, p. 141. See also *Dabistan-i-Mazahib*, p. 191.

[61] See Nabhadas, *Bhaktamal*, *chhappya* 43, p. 322; Priyadas, *Bhatkirasabodhini*, *kavittas* 127–43, pp. 324--42.

[62] See Anantadas, *Raidas Parachai*, Rest 5. See Priyadas, *Bhaktirasabodhini*, *kavitta* 266–67, pp. 478–79, for a similar description of brahmanical opposition to lower castes for their use of sacred symbols and religious practices. For the legends regarding Namdev's visit to the temple of Lord Vitthala at Pandharpur, see *Bhaktirasabodhini*, *kavittas* 136–137, pp. 334–36; see also the *Bhaktamal of Raghodas*, *Namdevji Kau Mul*, *pada* 199, p. 86; Chaturdas's commentary verse 224, p. 88; *Brahmadas's Bhagatmal*, second section, verse 10, pp. 23–24.

[63] For different detailed versions of the story, see Anantadas, *Kabir Parachai*, sections 6–9; Priyadas, *Bhaktirasabodhini*, *kavittas* 277–279; Raghodas, *Bhaktamal*, *pada* 127, p. 54; Chaturdas, *Tika*, *padas* 111–12, p. 54; and Brahmadas, *Bhagatmal*, second section, *pada* 8, p. 22.

[64] Jan Gopal, *Dadu Janma Lila*, chapter 3, pp. 1–17. The account can also be found in later hagiographies such as Raghodas's *Bhaktamal*.

[65] *Dadu Janma Lila*, chapters 5 and 6.

[66] Ibid., chapter 7: 1.

[67] Marc Bloch, *The Royal Touch*, English translation, Routledge & Kegan Paul, London, 1973 (originally published in French in 1924).

[68] See, for instance, the official Kabirpanthi biography of Kabir written by Gangasharan Shastri, *Kabir Jivan Charitra* (Hindi), Varanasi, 1976.

[69] Hess, Preface to the English translation of the *Bijak of Kabir*.

[70] *Dabistan-i-Mazahib*, p. 233.

[71] Callewaert (ed.), *The Hindu Biography of Dadu Dayal*, 1:17, 2:4.

[72] Gold, 'The Dadu-Panth: A Religious Order in its Rajasthan Context', p. 249.

[73] For the printed text of *Kabir–Raidas Samvad*, see Sukhdev Singh (ed.), *Raidas Parachai*, pp. 41–54.

[74] Vaudeville, *A Weaver Named Kabir*, pp. 49–50.

[75] *Dabistan-i-Mazahib*, p. 185. The term 'Vichnu' has been used by the author for Vishnu, whom the vaishnavites (including vairagis) regard as the highest deity.

[76] Ibid., p. 193.

[77] Ishwardas Nagar, *Futuhat-i-Alamgiri*, translated by Tasneem Ahmad, Pragati Publications, Delhi, 1978, p. 94.

The Bhils in Colonial Mewar

Hari Sen

This is a discussion of the changing cultural and political location of the Bhils in nineteenth-century Mewar, and an attempt to explore some of the transformations that occurred under colonialism. The Indian state of Mewar, with an area of 12,691 square miles (approximately 32,870 square kilometres)[1] and a population of over 1.7 million in 1891,[2] was in the extreme south of the modern state of Rajasthan. In the nineteenth century, most of the Bhils in Mewar lived in the hilly southern part of the state, south of the city of Udaipur which was the seat of the maharana's *darbar* or court and bordering on the neighbouring states of Idar, Dungarpur, Banswara and Pratapgarh, and in the Aravalli hills in the southwestern part of Mewar along the border with the state of Sirohi. The region had two kinds of territories. One was ruled by the allegedly primordial lineages of the Bhumia *thikanedar*s (holders of revenue grants), and was thus referred to as Bhumat in Mewar. The other was made up of those areas where the maharana of Mewar's administration collected the revenue and were a part of the Mewar *khalsa*. This second category of territories was known as the Magra; literally, the hills.[3] The entire region—Bhumat and Magra together—was an area about 70 miles north to south and about 100 miles east to west. This southwestern part of Mewar was rocky, hilly and densely forested, and in the southern part of this area, locally known as 'Chappan', the Aravalli range was broken into numerous low hills with narrow valleys between them. In the early nineteenth century, the British concern for the security of the trade routes that passed through the area, and for 'law and order' in general, took them to these hills, which they named 'Hilly Tracts Mewar'. Predictably, they brought with them new histories for the Bhils. One might even say, 'When Tod[4] comes, can history be far behind?'

The maharanas of Mewar had a much older and interestingly equivocal relationship with the Bhils. In the legends of Bappa Rawal, the founder of Mewar in the eighth century, and of Rana Pratap, the sixteenth-century hero of the battles against the Mughals, the Bhils were represented as friends, allies and even saviours of the Sisodia Rajput rulers of Mewar, but there is another note in the histories of the Bhil–Sisodia relationship which tells us that the rulers of Mewar conceived of the Bhils as a volatile presence that had to be circumscribed. The ambiguity in the relationship between the Bhils and the maharanas was evident in the custom that when a new maharana succeeded to the throne, the *raj tilak* was done with blood taken from the thumb or toe of a Bhil from a particular family in Oghna in southwest Mewar, 'in recognition of services rendered to Bapa Rawal in the eighth century'.[5] While the 1908 edition of the *Rajputana Gazetteer* noted that this practice was 'said to have been discontinued after Rana Hamir Singh's (d. 1364) reign',[6] Tod, who published his *Annals and Antiquities of Rajasthan* in the years 1829–32, wrote:

> It is pleasing to trace, through a series of ages, the knowledge of a custom still 'honoured in the observance'. The descendants of Baleo of Oguna and the Oondree Bhil still claim the privilege of performing the *teeka* on the inauguration of the descendants of Bappa . . . (the Oghna chief) is a Bhoomia Bhil of mixed blood, from the Solanki Rajpoot, on the old stock of pure (*oojla*) Bhils, the autochtones (if such there be of any country) of Mewar. Besides making the *teeka* of blood from an incision in the thumb, the Oguna chief takes the prince by the arm and seats him on the throne, while the Oondree Bhil holds the salver of spices and sacred grains of rice used in making the *teeka*.[7]

But Tod's use of the present tense could be no more than a romantic indulgence. Shyamaldas, in his otherwise detailed account of the accession of ten maharanas between 1751 and 1874, makes no reference to the custom,[8] and there is no mention of it in accounts of the accession of the last two maharanas. However, a Presbyterian missionary who worked in Mewar wrote in the 1920s that the custom was still alive.[9] Whether this tradition was alive in the twentieth century or dead by the fourteenth, it was certainly a part of the popular constitution of the monarchy in Mewar. K.D. Erskine, writing in the Mewar section of the 1908 edition of the *Rajputana Gazetteer*, argued that

> the Rajputs considered this to be a sign of Bhil allegiance, but it seems to have been rather a relic of Bhil power. The Bhils persistently tried to keep this practice alive, despite the belief that the man whose blood was used would die within a year. But the Rajputs were anxious to end this custom as they shrank, they said, from the contact with impure Bhil blood. But perhaps the real reason for their anxiety was that the ceremony acknowledged the need for investiture by an older and conquered people who could still upset the Rajput control.[10]

Perhaps, as caste identities hardened in the course of the nineteenth century and the British became the guarantors of the regime, the context for power based on inter-community unions disappeared. It is possible that this happened even earlier, when Mughal resources replaced local alliances as the basis of political authority.

When the Rajputs first settled in the area, they frequently intermarried with the Bhils and there were instances when children of marriages between Rajput men and Bhil women were recognized as Rajputs. Similarly, there were cases of Bhil men, particularly clan and territorial chiefs, marrying non-Bhil women. These inter-community marriages led to the division of the Bhil clans into separate endogamous groups with exogamous *septs* within them; the *ujale* (pure) clans which were descended from those Bhils who only married other Bhils, and the *mele* (impure) clans descended from the offspring of inter-community marriages. The dark-skinned *ujale* or pure clans were prohibited from eating anything white in colour (sheep or goat), but it was they, and not the relatively fair-skinned *mele* clans, who had commensal relations with the Rajputs.[11] In a reversal of the popular (north Indian) Hindu classification, the Bhils and the Rajputs considered the dark-complexioned Bhils to be *ujale* or pure, and the fair-complexioned clans claiming descent from Rajputs to be *mele* or impure. It would be interesting to speculate on how this came about. Groups like the Rajputs, who lived by the purity of their carefully constructed genealogies, could hardly accept claims to a privileged status based on avowed miscegenation, but how and when did the Bhils come to esteem the darkness of their skins? Did they have a conception of purity of descent? When did it develop? Was it an assertion of somatic pride? Or did they, in intellectual and social collaboration with brahmanical theories of hierarchy and the writings of James Tod, begin to believe in purity of blood by the nineteenth century? We have very little evidence to support any of these possibilities, but the last two seem to be the most plausible in the context of the Bhils' beleaguered position in recent times. However, it must also be remembered that social relations continually contested the normative realm; in reality, most Rajputs in the nineteenth century avoided any social proximity with Bhils.

As affinal relations among the Rajputs became more rigidly ideological, intermarriages between Bhils and Rajputs seem to have become rare and their occurrence in the past was probably suppressed. By the nineteenth century, while the Bhils in general sank to the position of outcastes in Hindu society, most of the Bhumia chiefs in the Bhil areas reiterated claims to a Rajput status,[12] without any real success as far as marriages with Rajput families were concerned.

T.B. Naik's summary of the Sanskrit narratives makes it clear that the 'twice-born' had traditionally assigned a particularly low position to the Bhils.

> In ancient Sanskrit and later Apabhramsa literature there are references to Bhils. But in most cases the word Bhil and some similar terms used by ancient writers includes almost any forest people and one has therefore to be on one's guard while generalizing about the Bhils from these references. . . . The 'Nishadas' are first referred to in the later Samhitas and Puranas. The word seems to denote not a particular tribe, but was a general one for the non-Aryan tribes who were not under Aryan control, as the shudras were. . . . In Yaska's 'Nirukta' the 'Nishadas' have been distinguished from the four varnas. . . . According to B.C. Law (*Ancient Indian Tribes*, Vol. II, p. 61), the word 'Nishada' as used in the *Vajsaneyi Samhita* is explained by the commentator Mahindra to mean Bhil or Bhilla. . . . Manu, the famous legist, explains the origins of the Nishadas as the offspring of a Brahmin father and a Shudra mother. The social duty enjoined on the Nishadas was to kill and provide fish for consumption by the people.
>
> The Pauranic account of the Bhils traces their descent from the thigh of Vena, son of Anga, a descendant of Manu Swayambhu. Vena was childless and the sage therefore rubbed his thigh and produced 'a man like a charred log with a flat face and extremely short'. He was told to sit down (*ni shad*) and was so known as

> Nishada,[13] 'from whom sprang the Nishadas dwelling in the Vindhya mountains, distinguished by their wicked deeds' . . . (a different) version of the Vena episode specifically mentions the Bhils. Vena was tainted by sin and so the rishis went to him; but he signalled them to depart by a wave of his hand. At this, one of them, Angira, cursed him. Due to this curse, the offending hand was turned into a churning stick, from which sprang Nishada. When the rishis began to churn with the left hand, three more men came out, Mushahantara, Kolla and Villa, the first ancestors of the Mushahars, Kols and Bhils.[14]

We do not know the extent to which these brahmanical accounts informed the interaction between the Bhils and those who were socially and politically privileged in their society, but they certainly reinforced the social and cultural representation of the Bhils as profane.

Another—though not altogether different—construction of the relationship between the Bhils and the caste hierarchy is implicit in the stories that the Bhils tell about their origins. Two of these stories are recorded by C.S. Venkatachar in the Census of India, 1931.

> One relates that a dhobi (launderer) who used to wash his clothes in a river was one day warned by a fish of the approach of a great deluge. The fish informed him that as he had always fed those of his species he had come to give him the warning and to urge him to prepare a large box which would enable him to escape. The dhobi prepared the box and got into it with his sister and a cock. After the deluge Rama sent out his messenger to inquire into the state of affairs. The messenger heard the crowing of the cock and so discovered the box. Rama then had the box brought before him and asked the man who he was and how he had escaped. The dhobi told his tale. Rama then made him face in turn north, east and west and swear that the woman with him was his sister. The dhobi remained firm in asserting that she was his sister. Rama then turned him towards the south, upon which the dhobi contradicted his statement and said she was his wife. Rama then asked him who told him how to escape and on hearing at once had the fish's tongue cut and since then that kind of fish has been tongueless. Rama then told the dhobi to set about repopulating the world. The dhobi married his sister by whom he had seven sons and seven daughters. Rama presented the first-born son with a horse but the recipient of this gift, being unable to ride, left

the horse on the plain and went into the forest to cut wood. He and his descendants became the foresters and started the Bhil tribe.

Another tale relates how on the creation of the Bhils, five men went to see Mahadev. Parvati, seeing them approaching, said to her spouse, 'Here come five of my brothers to ask *dahej* (bride-price) of you consequent to my marriage with you.' Mahadev gave them a feast and then explained that except for his bull Nandi and his *kamandalu*, he had nothing to give. They therefore went home. In order to give them something, however, Mahadev placed a silver stool in their way, but they were incapable of seeing this. Parvati, noticing how they had missed the gift, sent for them and told them what had happened, pointing out that as they were not able to see the stool, there was little hope of their prospering, but she would do what she could, and so informed them that they must be very careful of the Nandi whose hump was full of wealth untold. On reaching home one of the five suggested slaying the Nandi and obtaining the wealth; the others demurred, but he prevailed. No wealth was found in the hump and the five were dismayed. Parvati now appeared and told them that they should have yoked the bull to the plough and thus gained wealth from the mother-earth, but as they were so foolish as to slay the sacred animal, she would never look on their faces again, and left in high displeasure. For thus killing the sacred animal the Bhil has ever lived a miserable existence and been of no caste.[15]

Despite the odd flourish of Old Testament prose, Venkatachar's rendering of these myths is elided and dull in comparison to the Bhils' own telling of the stories, particularly the second one. This is probably so because Venkatachar's purpose is ethnographic, while the Bhils invest the stories with much greater significance. For them the stories seem to constitute a prophetic tradition which was repeatedly substantiated and constantly renewed. Their telling of them is much more evocative, full of detail and of contemporary references.[16] But the stories themselves—in any telling—are powerful and tragic.

The stories also help us to understand the Bhils' construction of their present. In discussing the myths of the Trobriand islanders in his *Myth in Primitive Psychology*, Bronislaw Malinowski wrote that the myths conveyed

much more to the native than is contained in the mere story . . . that the real meaning, in fact the full account, is contained in the

> traditional foundations of social organization; and that this the native learns, not by listening to the fragmentary mythical stories, but by living within the social texture of his tribe. In other words, it is the context of social life . . . which brings home to him the full account and the full meaning of his myths of origin.[17]

Malinowski was 'doubtful how far we can carry out historical reconstruction from the myth', but he asserted that the myth was 'to a native neither a fictitious story, nor an account of a dead past; it is a statement of a bigger reality still partially alive. It is alive in that its precedent, its law, its moral still rule the social life of the natives.'[18] Like the Melanesians, and many other pre-industrial societies, the Bhils also believed in maintaining an unchanging society and culture even though this was certainly only a paragon by the colonial period; but, as Malinowski wrote, 'it is clear that myth functions especially where there is a sociological strain, such as in matters of great difference of rank and power, matters of precedence and subordination, and unquestionably where profound historical changes have taken place.'[19]

The nineteenth and early twentieth centuries were indeed a period of significant historical changes, and these may have prompted the Bhils to seek cognitive sustenance in their myths. Perhaps these stories were dreams fostered by all that was not possible in society; perhaps they were allegories. But there can be little doubt that the stories helped the Bhils to address their contemporary condition.

This is not to argue that Bhil society, culture and politics were rigidly assembled by a reified past, but that one of the reasons they told these tales was to make their present more accessible to themselves. This is perhaps particularly and unusually so in the case of the Bhils because they selfconsciously historicized their myths and so determined our reading of them as oral history. For the Bhils, history was not any written record but stories about people and events passed down from generation to generation. Often, there were a number of different stories about a person or an event in the same narrative. These stories were not arranged—or told—in a chronological sequence but according to the intensity of experience in the story and its significance.

Like in so many myths of origin among the tribes of India, Shiv/Mahadev makes an appearance, with the familiar affinal links with the tribe. There is also an association with Mahadev's characteristic renunciation of accumulating material wealth,[20] reinforced in the second story by the Bhils' own inability to 'see' material wealth even when it is miraculously put before them. But there is also the tragic self-image of a people who lost cultural and social opportunities, which accepts the caste hierarchy as socially superior. There is the birth of the tribe in a period of disorder (flood, incest) from lowly progenitors (dhobi) who intervene in liminal periods and take on the danger of pollution. Most of all, there is the inability to accept a gift from God (the horse, the bullock), which excluded them from the system of reciprocity, and from the coveted status of either those who (had the horse and so) wielded power or those who cultivated the land (with the bullock). There is an irony in this because the Bhils of Mewar were in fact good agriculturists in the nineteenth and early twentieth centuries,[21] and they were always skilled auxiliaries in the Rajputs' struggles against the Mughals and the Marathas. Perhaps these were metaphors for the loss of control over the material and cultural conditions of their own lives. There is also a claim to an 'adivasi' status: that they re-populated the world after the flood. 'On the one hand, a myth always refers to events alleged to have taken place long ago. But what gives a myth an operational value is that the specific pattern described is timeless; it explains the present and the past as well as the future',[22] wrote Claude Levi-Strauss. In that sense, the stories are sequences of events in the past and also ones full of meaning in the present. These stories seem to tell us that the Bhils believed that the differences between them and others in Mewar had originated in a cultural disability, which had then given rise to their political, social and material incapacities.

In the nineteenth and early twentieth centuries, Indians and Europeans strengthened these distinctions, and the Bhils' self-deprecation, with their own representations of the Bhils. In the 1870s, an Indian student in an examination for a university degree described the tribe thus: 'The Bhil is a very black man, but more hairy [*sic*]. He carries in his hand a long spear, with which he runs you [*sic*] when he meets you, and afterwards throws your body into the [*sic*] ditch. By this you may know the Bhil.'[23] George Carstairs, a missionary otherwise sympathetic to the Bhils, wrote: 'As a working definition this is not to be despised.'[24] The nineteenth-century Mewari historian Shyamaldas called them 'wild forest-people, like animals'.[25] James Tod, in his *Annals and Antiquities of Rajasthan*, called them 'children of nature'.[26] The *Rajputana Gazetteer* (Mewar), 1908, declared that 'The Bhils, as a whole, have always been lawless and independent, fond of fighting, shy, excitable and restless . . . (and) truthful';[27] the archetypal 'noble savages'. These potent fictions had become hegemonic facts in colonial Mewar.

Carstairs, the missionary, wrote in 1926:

> To the Hindu the Bhil is an outcaste and a barbarian. If he leaves his own hilly country, and seeks the softer life of village or town, he is treated almost as a serf. In his own land he is feared if not respected, for the Bhils are born robbers, and do not hesitate to use violence.
>
> . . . For centuries—indeed for millenniums—the Bhil has been looked down upon by the proud Aryan conqueror . . . he has long been accustomed to being regarded by the Rajputs as an outcaste and a menial, and the sense of subjection has had its effect upon his character. Those especially who live on the fringe of the Bhil country and in close contact with the Hindus develop the slave-mentality and quickly degenerate. . . . The Hindu has given him little cause to love him. He is often compelled to do forced labour. He has to pay his tribute in grass and firewood. No attempt is made to develop his country. No hospital or school is opened; no irrigation work carried out to improve his agriculture; no roads are made. He is made use of when he can be useful, and that is all. In revenge, he takes what he can lay his hands on without scruple, and is a very skilful thief.[28]

Another missionary, the widely respected Rev. Dr James Shepherd of the Presbyterian Church, constructed the distinctions between the Bhils and other Mewaris in another way, and saw an opportunity in the difference. Shepherd, who worked in Mewar between 1877 and 1920, describing his first visit to the Magra in 1877, wrote:

> By this visit we intended to make the acquaintance of some of the Bheels, of whom we had heard so much, and who, although an aboriginal race, untramelled by caste prejudices, are extremely friendly and loyal to the British. . . . A tribal meeting was arranged (at Kherwara by the British C.O. of the Mewar Bhil Corps) and some prayers said. . . . We were . . . impressed with the hopeful field for mission work presented to us by these Bheels, an impression which is now taking practical effect in the operations carried on round our recently opened station of Udaipur.[29]

Shepherd believed that the Bhils were essentially human, but that the 'child-like' Bhil could be 'civilized' by conversion to Christianity; that the Bhil would have to be effaced to save the man. Shepherd's sympathy for the Bhils as human beings and his Christian commitment to saving their souls, together led him to reinforce the archetypal image of the Bhils. He wrote: 'At his (the Bhil's) best he is frank, affable and kind; at his worst he is treacherous, drunken and dishonest, and a notorious cattle-lifter.'[30] Other than the last detail, the same could have been said of anyone, but of course Shepherd did not say it of anyone in Mewar but a Bhil. He too was complicit in producing and propagating these prejudices.

The Bhils of Mewar lived in *pals* or groups of widely dispersed huts which covered large areas. The *pals* were villages in a social sense, and were not always spatially nucleated. 'The huts are built on separate hillocks at some distance from each other—apparently to prevent anyone from surprising them. The jungle on the larger hills in the vicinity is allowed to grow to provide cover in case of attack.'[31] The Bhils were, by and large, successful subsistence agriculturists, but by the middle of the nineteenth century, they had lost control of the more fertile irrigated lands in the plains around the hills to Rajputs and peasant colonists—a process that reverberated in their myths. In the second half of the nineteenth century, they cultivated only about 25 to 33 per cent of the lands in their villages because most of the land they controlled was 'of a rocky and sterile nature'.[32] In the monsoon, the Bhils planted their staple crop maize, and also flax, sesame, rice, turmeric, ginger and some lentils. In the winter, they cultivated wheat, barley, gram and sugarcane.[33]

In the early twentieth century, the Bhils were divided into a number of 'clans' based on patrilineal descent. Mewar had approximately sixteen such clans, while the neighbouring states of Dungarpur and Pratapgarh had twenty-six and thirty-seven, respectively. The majority of the *pals* were inhabited by a single clan, and the *pal* and clan were both considered to be exogamous units. Each village (or clan) had a *gameti* or head.[34]

A census of the population was conducted in Mewar for the first time in 1881. 'Because a disturbance of the peace was feared if enumeration was forced on the Bhils, it was decided to count the houses and allow an average of four persons per house. . . . By this, Bhils in Mewar numbered 51,076.'[35] In the 1891 census, the same procedure was used again for the Bhils, and their estimated number increased by an incredible 163 per cent, to 1,34,429.[36] This was clearly an incorrect estimate of their numbers.[37] It was in the census of 1901 that 'for the first time, the Bhils of Mewar were included',[38] in the sense that they were enumerated. Out of a total population of 10,18,805 in Mewar, the Bhils numbered 1,18,138,[39] or approximately 11.6 per cent of the total population.

The late eighteenth and early nineteenth centuries were very difficult years for Mewar, and particularly so for the Bhils. The whole region had been ravaged by the Maratha and Pindari armies[40] who were especially brutal to the Bhils, burning their villages and abducting their women. The distress and dislocation was compounded by scarcity and famine,[41] and, as the old state system crumbled under the pressure of Maratha looting, there was a brutal rise in the state's levies and their rapacious collection. The 1818 treaty with the British rescued the ruling lineage from the Marathas, but for the Bhils it marked the beginning of a labyrinthine, demanding and often violent negotiation with a new regime.

In the first few years after 1818, one of the priorities of the Anglo–Sisodia[42] regime was to encourage trade and increase the resources of the state. In the early days of the new regime, the British decided to secure the Udaipur–Ahmedabad road (the Udaipur–Kherwara section of this road went through the Bhumat and the Magra) and thus aid the resuscitation of commerce in Mewar. To fulfil this objective, Col. James Tod, the first British resident in Mewar, tried to resume 'all taxes levied by the Bhils on their neighbours and to which they considered themselves entitled by prescriptive right'.[43] The state had often tried to prevent the levying of these taxes in the past 'whenever it was strong enough to do so, but had never tried to abolish them openly as Tod did'.[44] The Bhils resisted these efforts in what became their first collective encounter with colonialism. The two taxes involved in this confrontation were *bolai*, which the Bhils levied on travellers and merchandise, for whose secure passage the Bhils then took responsibility, and *rakhwali* (called blackmail by the British in the first few years of their presence in Mewar),[45] which was paid by travellers and villages to neighbouring Bhil communities for duties performed as watchmen (*chaukidari*). But in times of scarcity the Bhils probably did plunder passing merchants and neighbouring villages, and around the turn of the eighteenth century they might have emulated the Marathas and collected ransoms for themselves.

The Bhumia *thikanedars* in the area were also interested

parties. Those who had Bhil *pals* along the road in their grants, took a *biswa* (literally, one-twentieth, but often more than that) of the *bolai* collected. They also joined the resistance, and often organized it.[46] In October 1822, the Rao of Jawas—the largest of the Bhumat estates—was in 'a state of turbulent and rebellious independence'.[47] He argued that the maharana's regime had no right to abolish *bolai*, because he was a Bhumia and so did not hold his revenues by a *sanad* (grant or patent) from the maharana but by a prior prescriptive right.[48] The disputes between the new colonial regime and the Bhumat chiefs, often supported by their Bhil subjects, continued throughout the early decades of British control in Mewar. The British conducted military operations against the Bhumias and the Bhils in 1824, 1826 and 1827. Sometimes, as in the case of Jawas, even when the chief of the estate agreed to surrender the rights to *bolai* and *rakhwali* under British military pressure, the Bhils defied the terms of the agreement and continued to collect both.[49] The Bhils of the *khalsa pals* in the Magra and Bhumat estates tried to assert their rights to the collection of *bolai* and *rakhwali*, but it was usually difficult to do so when the *darbar* and the British took the same side over the issue. However by the mid-1850s, the British had changed their position, and were keen to let the Bhils—particularly those in the *khalsa pals*—retain the *bolai* levies, because they believed that if the Bhils had a reasonable income from *bolai* and *rakhwali* they would have a stake in keeping the roads secure and usable. In 1855–56, the *darbar* took away the *bolai* dues collected by the *pals* of Paduna and Beeluk, and so the Bhils refused to protect travellers and both sides declined to repair the road; the *darbar* held that it was the responsibility of the *pals*, and the Bhils insisted that they would repair and protect the road only if they retained the *bolai* levies.[50]

The *bolai* and *rakhwali* tolls were systematic and organized. In 1869, the journey from Udaipur to Kherwara involved making fourteen separate regularly fixed payments to the Mewar *darbar* and the various *pals* and estates along the road, with the rates varying according to the number of persons or the quantity of goods making the journey. The charges for the journey from Udaipur to Kherwara amounted to Rs 2–12–0 (all figures are in Udaipuri rupees, as rupees–anna–pice) per cart of travellers, Re 0–15–4 per pack bullock, Re 0–14–7 per horse, Re 1–8–10 per camel, Re 0–9–4 per man, and Rs 3–8–10 per four-bull grain cart. If the travellers stopped for the night at one of the villages along the route, they paid 2 pice per person and 1 anna per cart as *rakhwali* (*chaukidari*).[51]

In the late nineteenth century came a new railway line, and with it, gratifying central control of the *bolai* levies on opium for the colonial bureaucracy. In the early 1880s, the *bolai* and *rakhwali* levies were reorganized because of the cities of Bhilwara and Chittaur in Mewar being connected by rail to Nasirabad (near Ajmer) in the north and Nimach (in the modern district of Mandsaur in Madhya Pradesh) in the south on the Rajputana–Malwa railway system, and the consequent rearrangement of the opium trade in Mewar.

Poppy was an important winter crop in Mewar, and in the southeastern part of the state, bordering on Malwa, it was as common as wheat or barley, in the second half of the nineteenth century. Some estimates put the acreage under poppy to be about 50,000 acres in the state during that period.[52] From 1869 onwards, the opium produced in Mewar was brought to Udaipur, weighed and then sent to Bombay via Kherwara and Ahmedabad. Between 1870 and 1882, an average of 6,392 chests of opium went from Udaipur to Ahmedabad every year on this route, through the Bhumat and the Magra.[53] The Bhil *pal*s along the Udaipur–Kherwara road earned about Rs 8,000—and sometimes up to Rs 10,000—per annum in *bolai* and *rakhwali* from this traffic, and from the sale of grass, wood, etc., when the opium caravans halted overnight.[54]

With the inauguration of the Rajputana–Malwa line, the opium merchants in Mewar offered to pay an extra amount of Rs 10 per chest of opium as duty, if the *darbar* shifted its central opium-weighing depot from Udaipur to Chittaur. The merchants of Bhilwara, north of Chittaur on the same railway line, offered to pay an extra duty of Rs 15 per chest if the opium scales were shifted to Bhilwara. The opium traders were eager to profit from the cheaper, faster and safer transport provided by the railway, and the *darbar* wanted the greatly enhanced income from the higher duty. Eventually, Maharana Sajjan Singh decided to move the scales to Chittaur, because it was the old capital of Mewar.[55] Following this, the bulk of the opium grown in Mewar was transported by road to Chittaur, and then onwards to Bombay by train. This meant that the Bhil *pal*s along the old opium route on the Udaipur–Kherwara road lost a significant income, because most of the opium traffic now went west to the railhead in Chittaur without going through the Bhumat or the Magra. The little that remained on the old road from Udaipur to Kherwara was exempted from paying *bolai*.[56]

Afraid that the loss of about Rs 8,500 per annum could lead to discontent in the area, the *darbar* decided to use a part of the income from the increased opium duties to establish a series of posts staffed by salaried Bhil road-guards along the road. The *darbar* hoped that this would make the road safer, and also indirectly compensate the Bhil *pals* for the loss of opium levies.[57] The *darbar* also decided to establish primary schools in two *pals* in the area, and to spend Rs 1,500 every year on their maintenance. An additional sum of Rs 3,000 was to be spent annually on the construction of tanks, wells, etc., to encourage cultivation and employ the Bhils. The expenditure on the road-guards was to be Rs 2,400 per annum.[58] These sums added up to less than what the *pals* received directly from *bolai*, and the amount that each *pal* received for the road-guards was much less than what they got as escort fees. For example, the Bara *pal* received Rs 275 for the Rs 750 lost,[59] Tidi Rs 400 for the Rs 1,125 lost, Paduna Rs 200 for the Rs 562.5 lost, Pipli Rs 140 for the Rs 375 lost, and so on.[60] These were considerable losses, and they must have contributed to the distress and dislocation in these *pals* in the early 1880s.

The British officers in Calcutta would have preferred it if the Mewar *darbar* had abolished *bolai* on all traffic on the Udaipur–Kherwara road, and they asked it to consider such total abolition but the *darbar* rejected the proposal. The *darbar* argued that abolition of *bolai* on all traffic on the Udaipur–Kherwara road could not be considered unless it was part of total abolition of *bolai* all over the state, and that such an action 'or even declaration of intention would be certain to arouse the Bhil tribes, who attach an imaginary importance to this right of levying *bolai* wholly at variance with, and totally disproportionate to the actual material benefits they reap therefrom.'[61]

In reporting the *darbar*'s reluctance to abolish *bolai* completely, the resident acknowledged the significance of *bolai* for the Bhils' sense of autonomous territorial authority, and agreed with the *darbar* that the new arrangement would encourage the *pals* to guarantee the safety of the Udaipur–Kherwara road. In a complete reversal of the British position over the preceding half-century, which characterized *bolai* and *rakhwali* as 'blackmail', 'highway robbery' and an impediment to trade, in 1882 the resident wrote:

> the nature and light incidence of the tax is such that it is cheerfully paid by the wayfarers principally using the route, from whom no complaints on this subject have ever been received. The principal income to the Bhils on the Kherwara road under this head of *bolai* is derived from the pilgrims to the Hindu [*sic*] shrine at Rikhabnath (Rikhabdeo), who readily pay the small amount demanded from them for safe conduct, more especially as, in the case of loss, the Bhil *pal*s acknowledge the responsibility with regard to compensating the sufferers and arresting the offenders. . . . The *bolai* tax is not one that can in any way be considered as pressing heavily upon or discouraging trade. It is thoroughly understood by and acceptable to all the travellers through the Bhil districts, and it could not be discontinued without imposing on the *darbar* the unwelcome duty of making arrangements for the safety of all the routes through the Hilly Tracts—a measure that could not, I think, and save at a great expenditure, be made so efficient and satisfactory, as that at present existing, under which by a trifling payment the traveller procures the safe conduct from *pal* to *pal* of himself and his property.[62]

The Calcutta government accepted the resident's advice, and as far as the British government was concerned, there the matter rested; but the Bhil *pal*s on the Udaipur–Kherwara road lost a sizeable part of their annual income, and the *darbar* and the opium merchants gained much larger ones. Also, these changes marked a victory for the process of centralizing authority in the Magra in the hands of the colonial administration; in this case, classically accompanied by the coming of the railways.

The establishment of the Mewar Bhil Corps (MBC) was another step in the same direction. The popular resistance to the new regime in the Magra and the Bhumat in the first decade after the 1818 treaty, and the maharana's inability to deal with it, convinced the British that a military force should be expressly raised to establish and exercise their control over the area. In 1838, the British decided to raise the Mewar Bhil Corps[63]

> for the peace and good order of the Hilly Tracts of Mewar consequent on the want of power in the Udaipur State to keep its turbulent Bhil population in subjection. It was also deemed necessary to protect . . . our (British Indian) subjects in Gujrat . . . from the inroads of the Bhils, as well as to prevent any disaffected Thakurs of

> those Districts finding the ready shelter in the wild and mountainous country, which they had been accustomed to do.[64]

Recruitment began in 1841, and by 1844 cantonments had been established in Kherwara to the south of Udaipur city and Kotra to the south-west of the capital. Headquartered at Kherwara, the MBC had ten companies of about 90 soldiers each. The maharana contributed Rs 50,000 annually towards the expenses of the Corps and the British met the remainder—usually an equal but often a smaller amount.[65]

The British wanted to recruit the Mewar Bhil Corps mainly from among the Bhils,[66] because one of the reasons for raising the unit was to 'give Bhils employment and keep them from their plundering propensities'.[67] The expectation was that the Bhils who enlisted 'would be a restraining influence on their friends and relatives in the villages'.[68] By the early twentieth century, the MBC had shrunk to eight companies (a total strength of 718 men), of which seven were recruited mainly from among the Bhils and the eighth was composed largely of 'Hindustanis', but the British were proud of their success in other respects. The 1908 edition of the Mewar section of the *Rajputana Gazetteer* proudly proclaimed: 'Much good has been effected by the entertainment of these hill-men. Through the influence of those in the service, and of numerous pensioners, the entire Bhil population of these parts has been leavened with the germs of civilization'.[69] To ensure the Corps' effectiveness both as an instrument of political control and as an agent of the new order, its composition and deployment were carefully engineered and regulated. This meant that even promotions in the MBC had to be considered in terms of 'caste [*sic*] proportions'.[70] In 1892, a Hindustani *havildar*'s promotion was approved because, 'although a Hindustani by caste [*sic*], (he) has no Hindustani prejudices'. His father was an MBC *havildar* before him, and he was born in Kherwara and grew up with the Bhils. He spoke their language like a native and knew all 'their habits and customs', and so his promotion would 'not cause any discontent among the Bhils of the Corps'.[71]

There is a striking resemblance between the MBC of the nineteenth century and the United Nations-sponsored 'peace-keeping forces' of a century later. The disputes over funds, the fear of popular opposition, the initial hope that competent policing would lead to peace, the carefully enforced rules of engagement, the convenient insistence that the local authorities must carry their weight, and the eventual preoccupation of the Corps with protecting itself, are all reminiscent of our own times. The significant dissimilarity with the twentieth-century United Nations troop contingents is that the MBC was locally recruited and so had to bear the additional responsibility of being the agent of 'civilization' among the Bhils. This made the British even more wary of deploying the MBC in conflicts with Bhils, particularly in those instances where they did not themselves endorse the purpose.

In 1848, the Mewar *darbar* asked for help from the MBC in operations against 'plunderers and outlaws' in the western Magra, and the political agent in Udaipur asked the commanding official (CO) of the MBC to keep two companies ready to accompany the *darbar* troops in the operation. He instructed that the MBC troops should 'under no circumstances be used for anything but dealing with the outlaws', that the European officer in-charge of the MBC contingent should not take any orders from the *darbar* officials, and that he should 'try and prevent the Raj (*darbar*'s) troops from harassing or molesting the peaceful inhabitants of the area, as any excess committed by them might be construed by the ignorant Bhils as having our countenance.'[72]

These precautions would seem adequate to us for sanitizing the involvement of the MBC in these operations, but the MBC did not participate in them because of logistical problems[73] and because the CO of the Corps felt that 'putting a European Officer under the control of Raj (*darbar*) officials might tend rather to disparage us in the eyes of the Native Chiefs and other authorities of the country, and thus eventually to aggravate the evil which it is the object of the expedition to remove.'[74]

In April 1849, a similar request from the *darbar* for the MBC's assistance against some Bhils in the Bhumat estate of Panarwa was refused, with the comment that it would be provided 'only in cases of serious disturbances, or where the general peace of the country is endangered'.[75] However, later that same year Robinson, the fastidious political agent in Mewar, agreed to send two companies of the MBC to protect Rikhabdeo while the *darbar*'s troops attacked a nearby Bhil *pal* allegedly responsible for 'harassing' travellers and pilgrims on their way to the town. But this was only after the Mewar *darbar* had satisfied Robinson's deputy that the charges against the *pal* were true, and that the *darbar*'s contingent was adequate for the operation.[76] The first condition was a reasonable one; the purpose of the second was to ensure that the MBC would not participate directly in any offensive action against the Bhils. It would only defend Rikhabdeo in case of an attack. This defensive involvement was probably permitted because Rikhabdeo was an important centre of pilgrimage for Jains from all over the subcontinent,[77] and so, providing for its security would be an emblematic success for *Pax Britannica*. In 1852, the MBC joined the *darbar*'s troops in long operations against bandits in southwest Mewar and neighbouring Sirohi, but the reluctance to assist the *darbar* against the Bhils remained.

The British were obviously trying to establish their credibility as well-wishers of the Bhils so that they could then further the cause of 'civilization' among them, but the Mewar *darbar* saw matters rather differently. They argued that since they paid approximately half the annual cost of maintaining the MBC, they had every right to ask for its deployment. The British emphatically disagreed. 'Notwithstanding repeated explanations in this matter,' wrote the CO of the MBC,

> the Rana persisted in considering that the MBC was constituted for the purpose of coercing his refractory Bhil subjects, whereas such was never the intention with which the Regiment was raised, nor indeed would it be politic to employ its members on such a delicate duty as coercing their brethren. Time after time, it has been distinctly pointed out to His Highness that he, and he alone, is responsible for peace and good order being kept in his dominions, and that he need never expect armed assistance from us in maintaining the same. Notwithstanding these explanations, the Minister constantly alludes to the sum paid by the Udaipur government for the maintenance of the Bhil Corps as constituting a right for its services to maintain the peace of Mewar.[78]

A later CO reiterated the same position and added that the Corps' 'being mixed-up with the indisciplined rabble comprising the *darbar* troops in the Hilly Tracts would, I think, detract greatly from its influence, and the estimation in which it is held by the people of the country generally.'[79] It was plain that maintaining the 'civilizing' credibility of the MBC among the Bhils was an important consideration for the British.

This attempt to 'civilize' the Bhils raised more fundamental issues also: the belief in witchcraft among the Bhils, and the right to life over the question of 'witch-swinging'—the brutal torture and murder of women alleged to be witches. At one level, the British officers of the MBC looked at the issue of witchcraft in terms of martial law, its jurisdiction and military discipline;[80] but at another level, they were forced to deal with the Bhils' belief in witchcraft and its juridical place in Mewar. In September 1849, at one of the earliest trials for the murder of an alleged witch in the area,[81] three men were sentenced to seven years in prison. At the trial, one of the accused stated that, 'on a former occasion before the introduction of British authority in these districts, the villagers had killed a witch, at which the *kamdar* (the local revenue official) had expressed his satisfaction.'[82] The British officers in Mewar were convinced that the Bhils and their beliefs belonged in the past and not the present. In fact, the culture of the Bhils helped them to gather their own imagined past. In 1851, the CO of the MBC wrote:

> A reference to the state of feeling in England some two or three hundred years ago will best describe the firm and implicit belief in the existence of witches, which now prevails not only among the Bhils themselves but also among the foreigners from Hindoostan, who may chance to have occasion to visit the country.... When the Bhils have indigestion or any other pain elsewhere in the body, they cauterize the spot and the relief thus received is ascribed to the witch who has seized upon them being afraid of fire. . . . Bhils will not marry into a family in which there is no witch to protect them from other witches, and these family witches encourage the belief in their powers because it gives them influence. . . . When Bhils fall ill, the *Bhopa* (shaman) is called in and a witch pointed out. If the ill man dies, the witch is swung by her heels with chilly-bandaged eyes as Bhils drink and dance around her. After two or three days of swinging, if she confesses to being a witch, she is killed if she has allegedly killed many people, otherwise she is branded, her hair cut off, made to swear she will not bewitch again, and turned out as an outcaste. But if she becomes faint or ill from the torture, she is let free as these ordeals are supposed to have no effect on witches.
>
> It is difficult to suppress all this. Even if we wanted to do something impolitic like sending armed men to stop it, we could hardly send people who believed in it, as the MBC Bhils do . . . in the

> present wild and barbarous state of the country we cannot hope to eradicate one of the most natural and universal of all superstitions, and which has been known to prevail in all countries till long after they have made considerable advances in civilization . . . the death of a witch, however inhumanly caused, is accounted in this part of the country as not a justifiable, but even a commendable act by the educated classes, as well as by the ignorant.[83]

In April 1853, Sempla, a Bhil *sipahi* of the MBC, was tried for the murder of his grandmother about two years earlier. The trial was held under British law in Nimach, because the MBC was considered to be a British corps. Sempla confessed to having killed his grandmother 'because she was a witch and had killed three or four people'.[84] At the trial, Sempla said that five years earlier his uncle had taken ill and had wandered about the country trying to find out who had bewitched him. Having failed in his search, he died within fifteen days. Ten months later, another uncle had died in a similar way, and eleven months after his second uncle's death, his father had died. Soon after that, he (Sempla) had fallen ill, and a buffalo and two bullocks which belonged to him had also died. 'On this . . . the villagers of Barla (Sempla's village) assembled to find out the cause of the deaths, no others having occurred in the *pal*.'[85] The *bhopa* was consulted and he declared that witchcraft was responsible for the deaths. After various ordeals, the shaman pronounced that Sempla's grandmother Homa, and another old woman Nanee, were both witches, and that unless they were 'swung' all of Sempla's family would die. Nanee was 'swung' till she was rescued by the British doctor attached to the MBC, but Homa fled to the forest to save her life. Soon after these events,

> the people of Barla and three or four other villages assembled and told him (Sempla) that if he did not kill Homa, he would be excommunicated and would not be allowed to marry. So he stoned her to death, reported it to the village and said that they could burn or bury her.[86]

Having killed the witch, Sempla then mourned the death of his grandmother by shaving his head.

In his statement at Sempla's trial, Havildar Major Bhagwan Deen of the MBC testified that among the Bhils if one did not 'swing' an acknowledged witch in the family, one was

> excommunicated and no marriage can take place in the family in which a witch exists. . . . The belief in witches is inherent in all Bhils. A *naik* of the Regiment (MBC) lately killed his aunt as a witch, and on a party being sent by the CO to seize him, he fled to the hills and has not since been heard of.[87]

Further, Bhagwan Deen stated that the night that Sempla was to leave for his trial in Nimach,

> two Bhil sepoys came into my hut and said that they had come on behalf of all the Bhils to request that the CO would hear their case before he sent Sempla off. . . . The next day several Bhils came to me and said that they wished to speak to Capt. Brooke (the CO). . . . They went with me and petitioned that as hitherto in destroying witches they had only followed the customs of the country and had never been called to account for it, they hoped that Sempla would not be punished this time for doing what many of them had done. Were he punished, all would be frightened. That now they know that the British government does not approve of it. If they wanted to 'swing' witches, they would take their discharge, but if they did it in future while in service, they were prepared to stand the consequences.[88]

The testimony of Nanjee, a *sipahi* in the MBC, supported what Sempla and Bhagwan Deen had said. Nanjee stated that neither he nor any of the other Bhils felt that Sempla had committed a crime, and that 'all considered, he had done right. Such is the law with us Bhils.'[89] He also said that they were not aware that the British government considered the killing of a witch to be punishable as murder.

Capt. J.C. Brooke, the CO of the MBC, advised the government against a charge of murder or a severe sentence because

> at the time of the perpetration of the act, the sepoys though aware of our desire to dissuade them from the abominable custom, had never been told that they would be held answerable further than by dismissal from the service for the swinging or death of women accused of sorcery, and though the prohibition of having engaged as principals in these superstitious rites was subsequently made more stringent, no specific penalty was even then affixed to the violation of the order. . . . But for this, I would have recommended the prisoner's being placed on trial for his life.[90]

Together with Bhagwan Deen and Nanjee, Brooke too was saying that Sempla could not be punished for something that he did not know to be wrong. What is interesting is that, like them, he also argued that it was not merely a question of Sempla not being aware of his culpability but that the issue was the Bhil belief in the legitimacy of 'witch-swinging'. Brooke wrote that Sempla did not kill Homa 'of his sole will and accord . . . (but) . . . according to the rites and customs usual among the Bhils in cases of witchcraft', and so it was not a case of 'wilful and malicious murder, punishable by death'. He argued that the proceedings of the court of enquiry had shown that Sempla 'had been the executioner of the will of the community'. Brooke's contention was that if Sempla was given a severe sentence, then many others in the MBC would be answerable to the same punishment, and that it would be unjust 'to visit an ignorant savage with the penalty of the law of a more civilized country for a deed committed before he had become aware of his amenability to such a law'.[91]

Brooke was also sympathetic to the cultural geography of the Bhils. He wrote:

> Those who have not lived among the Bhils are little aware of their great reluctance to quit even temporarily their native hills or to proceed more than a few miles from their homes. For two or three years after the Corps was raised (in 1841) the Bhils used almost invariably to desert on being warned for command at Neemuch, and so extremely ignorant were they that a considerable panic and desertion was traced to a faqir in the lines spreading a story that it was the intention of the Bengal Officers to put them into ships at Neemuch and sink them.

Brooke felt that while this fear of leaving their homes had been partly overcome among Bhils in the MBC, other Bhils were still unwilling to go as far as Nimach.

> If they were forced to go to Neemuch, they would leave their homes and turn outlaws. For this very reason, imprisoning Sempla at Neemuch will be tantamount to transportation to the Bhils . . . a feeling prevails that Sempla by being ordered to Neemuch was being taken away to a species of death, and it was mentioned to me that he had a wife and two children, the former of whom would abandon her home and the latter be turned into beggars. . . . The Bhils wanted

> a petition forwarded on their behalf requesting that Sempla be imprisoned in his own country on the plea that the crime . . . had been committed in utter ignorance and during the period they had been led to consider that their customs on the subject of witchcraft would not be interfered with. . . . I trust that this will be taken into account and Sempla imprisoned at Kherwara, and also seeing Sempla in irons here will have a good effect on the Bhils.[92]

Brooke's arguments were persuasive. Presiding over the courtmartial, Col. George St Patrick Lawrence, political agent in Mewar, found Sempla guilty on the basis of his confession and sentenced him to seven years of imprisonment in Kherwara, not Nimach. In forwarding the case to his brother and administrative superior Henry Lawrence, agent of the governor general in Rajputana, George Lawrence recommended mercy because 'witch-swinging' was not hitherto a cognizable offence, and because Sempla had killed his grandmother at a time when the maximum penalty for killing witches was dismissal from service. George Lawrence also wrote that another extenuating circumstance was the fact that Sempla had acted in accordance with the customs of his community and 'his sovereign the Maharana of Mewar recognizes it as legal.'[93] Acknowledging this, Henry Lawrence wrote that Sempla was a subject of Mewar, and that 'the Maharana of Udaipur himself believes in and has heretofore punished witches. Indeed, upto the accession of the present chief (Sarup Singh, 1842–61), witches, I am informed, were burnt alive at Udaipur.'[94] Within a month of the trial, Governor General Dalhousie had accepted these recommendations and remitted a part of the sentence.[95]

There is much evidence from late twentieth-century India to show that the belief in witchcraft was often alloyed with greed as men sought to deprive women of their rights within the household and outside it, but while that may have been the cause of Homa's death, there is no direct evidence to make that argument in this case. However, it is possible that with changes in the society and economy in the nineteenth century, the customary systems of support for older women, widows in particular, began to break down, and this made it possible for such older women to be denounced as witches when they made demands on the family and the village and then fortified these with spells and curses.[96] The guilt of those charged with such unfair treatment—usually men who controlled the resources of the family—might often have led to accusations of witchcraft. Large-scale disasters like famines or epidemics were seldom attributed to witchcraft. Accusations of sorcery nearly always arose from personal misfortunes and disputes within the family or the village. Also, older women might well have cultivated a reputation for witchcraft to ensure fair treatment in their families and villages.[97]

Keith Thomas, in his study of popular beliefs in sixteenth and seventeenth-century England, has argued that sometimes witchcraft worked as 'a conservative force, acting as a check upon undue individual effort'.[98] Employment in the Mewar Bhil Corps made new economic and political means available to the Bhils who enlisted. These resources may have attracted new demands within the family or the village, which were then sought to be deflected by accusations of witchcraft. A large majority of the people charged with offences related to allegations of witchcraft in nineteenth-century Mewar were employees of the British or their dependents. While this was partly because these were the only cases reported and investigated, the large number of such charges within this group might be evidence of conservative social restraint.

What is clear is that the Bhils—including those in the MBC—did not see Sempla's actions as unlawful. They said that many of them had 'swung' witches in the past; now if they 'wanted to "swing" witches, they would take their discharge, but if they did it in future while in service, they were prepared to stand the consequences.'[99]

The Bhils who spoke at Sempla's trial and those who discussed the charges outside the courtroom understood their subjection to the British, but they believed it to be a qualified one—like a limited contract. They did not necessarily share an understanding of all its stipulations with the British, but, like colonized people elsewhere, they knew they had to submit to the new regime in some crucial aspects of their public lives because of the punitive capacity of the British and their ability to bring benefit to the Bhils in the new political and economic environment. It was a contract not in the sense of a voluntary and symmetrically reciprocal agreement, but an arrangement that the Bhils confined to specific parts of their lives. They obviously believed that they could sever the bond if they wished to do something which was unacceptable to the British; that the substance of the relationship lay in keeping to the terms as they understood them and not in accepting a pervasive social and political authority. The Bhils clearly believed that the British jurisdiction did not extend beyond their working lives as soldiers in the MBC. However, Sempla's trial must have convinced them of what many of them probably feared; that they could lose their lives if they did not submit to the new laws which came with the British. Before the establishment of British control in Mewar the maharana's government, and others in power, had used their domination to attack Bhil villages as a punitive measure against banditry or some perceived recalcitrance, and many Bhils had died in those operations. It was a conflict the Bhils knew; it was a contest between the powerful and the weak. But, unlike the succession of the maharanas and the Marathas, the British confronted the Bhils with the strength and energy of a new regime with an agenda of cultural transformation. The colonial officers were using the punitive authority of law to change culture. This element of the colonial project surprised and challenged the Bhils.

In the late nineteenth century, officers of the maharana's government, who considered the Bhils to be barely human, joined the British in the campaign against 'witch-swinging'. In April 1882, some Bhils died of small-pox in Kaliawas, a village southwest of Udaipur, and their deaths were attributed to the sorcery of a woman who was alleged to be a witch. She was beaten, stoned and hung by her heels from a mahua tree till she died. 'In this the whole *pal* was involved.'[100] When the police went to investigate the case, the Bhils tried to prevent them from reaching Kaliawas by cutting down trees across the road. They also refused to surrender the alleged culprits. The resident advised strong action against the Bhils of Kaliawas, and Maharana Sajjan Singh and his *diwan*, Mehta Pannalal, agreed.[101] In December that year, a large contingent of troops, including 150 infantrymen and 75 cavalrymen of the *darbar*, and some soldiers of the *thikanedar* of Jharol (in whose *thikana* Kaliawas was), went to the village to punish the Bhils. They found the *pal* deserted, but they seized 200 heads of cattle grazing near the village and 160 maunds of grain stored in the houses, and sent a message to the Bhils of Kaliawas that they must surrender those guilty of killing the woman.

> When after two days, the allotted time, they made no move to do so, 62 mahua trees were cut down and the houses of those most implicated destroyed. . . . While the cutting of the trees has been a severe measure, many trees are left, the crop on the ground is unhurt

> by the orders of His Highness (the maharana), and the grain will probably be returned after the criminals are surrendered . . . care has been taken to see that neither is the *pal* ravaged beyond rehabilitation, nor are the Bhils driven into rebellion from sheer necessity[102]

wrote the Mewar resident. The severity of the punitive measures against Kaliawas also marked a change in the *darbar*'s relations with the Bhils. Till then 'witch-swinging' and homicide in general among the Bhils were usually punished by inflicting a fine on the guilty or on the *pal* as a whole.[103]

The action against Kaliawas was declared to be a model of the *darbar*'s penal will for the future. On 3 March 1883, Mehta Gobind Singh, the *hakim* of the Magra, Phul Chand, the *naib hakim*, and C.K.M. Walter, the resident in Mewar, met over 400 Bhils, including seventeen *gameti*s (headmen) of important *pal*s in the Magra, at Rikhabdeo.[104] At the gathering, 'the chief man amongst them (the Bhils) quite spontaneously made a short speech in which he said that one and all were deeply sorry for what had occurred . . . that the past should be forgiven and forgotten by the sarkar, and that they would be loyal, peaceful and obedient in the future.'[105] Resident Walter told them that they would be forgiven, but if they did not keep their word the *darbar* would severely punish those who defied its authority. He told them that the *darbar* and the British government were determined to stop the torture and killing of women on the plea of their being witches, and he asked the headmen present to ensure the prevention of such acts in the future. The *gameti*s discussed this with the assembled Bhils for about ten minutes and then told the resident

> that they would do all in their power to prevent the ill-treatment of women accused of being witches in the future, but that they were a stupid race,[106] and that if some fool amongst them forgot himself and misbehaved, they would at once give him up to the *darbar* for punishment.

The Resident insisted that a verbal promise was not enough, and so, after some more discussion among the Bhils, the *gameti*s decided that their assurances should be engraved on an *agat* (stone tablet) and placed in the Rikhabdeo temple, in which the Bhils revered their sacred deity 'Kalaji'. The next morning, the *agat* was duly engraved, consecrated and ceremonially embedded in the ground to the right of the temple's doors.[107] In the inscription, the Bhils of the seventeen *pals* pledged:

> both for ourselves and for all the *pals* of the Magra . . . that we shall never kill a woman on the plea of her being a witch. If we have any suspicion of a woman being a witch, we will complain to the sarkar, who will punish the woman. We will not ourselves kill witches and this determination will go down from generation to generation. If we break this pledge, may Kalaji deal with us. . . . Should any ruffian or reprobate secretly commit the crime of witch-killing, we will hand him over to the Raj for punishment. In this there will be no deviation. We have caused the embedment of this stone of our own free will and regard the inscription on it as binding on us.[108]

Resident Walter was satisfied with this turn of events, even though the Bhils had reasserted their belief in witches in the text of the engraved agreement. The Bhils had agreed to accept the Anglo–Sisodia regime's jurisdiction over the punishment of alleged witches, although they did not renounce their belief in sorcery.[109] They had also agreed to hand over to the maharana's officers anyone who killed a woman accused of being a witch, and these commitments had been reinforced by the sanctity of Rikhabdeo. The Mewar *darbar* was also publicly committed to strong action against those who killed alleged witches. Pleased, Walter gave the Bhils a feast.[110] These developments demonstrated that as far as 'witch-swinging' among Bhils was concerned, the British were anxious to assert their control over punishment, because they assumed that punishment would undermine the Bhils' belief in sorcery.

For the Mewar *darbar*, witchcraft was not the most significant site of conflict with the people of the Bhumat and the Magra in the nineteenth century. In the middle decades of that century it tried to assert its economic, political and cultural control over the Bhumat and the Magra in various ways. The Bhumia *thikanedars* and the Bhils resented this, and both sides turned to the British for help; not because of any devotion to the British but because the Company had established itself as a powerful arbitrator in disputes between the rulers and the ruled in the Indian states.

Some of these disputes concerned ceremonial observances. When Maharana Sardar Singh died in 1842, and again when Maharana Shambhu Singh died in 1874, the *darbar*'s officers tried to enforce in the Magra, the rites of mourning that were followed in the rest of Mewar, by penalizing men who did not shave their heads and faces. In 1842, the British and the *darbar* accepted the exemption of *thikanedars* and others of the Magra from this ritual, and that convention was upheld in 1874, notwithstanding the *darbar*'s attempts to the contrary.[111]

There were other contentious issues raised by the *darbar*'s fiscal rule in the Magra, besides the *bolai* and *rakhwali* levies. Officers of the maharana's government in the Magra rarely missed an opportunity to raise the revenue collected from the Bhils.[112] This was particularly so from the 1820s, when the protective strength of British arms became available to the *darbar*, in rhetoric, if not always in fact. From the 1820s, British officers repeatedly commented on the fact that 'the disturbed state of the country was caused very much by the oppressions and lawless exactions of the Maharana's officers'.[113] There were uprisings against the *darbar* in the area in the 1820s and 1830s, and in 1835 the Bhils overran or surrounded all the *darbar*'s posts in the Magra in the course of one night.[114] By the middle of the century, Bhil villages were petitioning British officers against oppression at the hands of the *darbar*'s officials. Such petitions created tension within the process of centralization, which was usually resolved by the British taking more powers into their own hands and pressurizing the *darbar* to fall into line.

In 1856, the Bhil *pals* of Peepli and Paduna petitioned the assistant political agent in Mewar against the unjust levies of the *darbar*. The Bhils of Paduna argued that before the 1840s, when the *pal* was a part of the Thakur of Persad's estate, it had been assessed for a *hal barar* (a tax on ploughs) of Rs 60 per annum. But after Paduna was resumed into the *khalsa*, the *darbar* continued to levy *hal barar* at Rs 50 per annum and also tried to collect an additional levy of *koot* (a share of the grain collected from the threshing floor). In the 1840s the *darbar* was not always successful in collecting these levies because Paduna and the neighbouring *pals* controlled the roads in the area, and the *darbar*'s troops hesitated in attacking the villages.[115] But by 1850, the Bhils had lost much of their control over the Udaipur–Kherwara road (the arterial route to Ahmedabad in Gujarat) because of British military operations to secure the road for commercial traffic, and the *darbar* used the road to mount military expeditions against the Bhil *pals* and enforce the collection of taxes. In March 1850, a large force of *darbar* troops plundered and burnt Paduna, seized all the cattle and sold them in Udaipur, and inflicted a heavy fine on the Bhils in Paduna and the neighbouring *pals*. Then, the troops marched on Beeluk *pal* (near Rikhabdeo), carried away 3,000 heads of cattle from the village and sold them in Udaipur. They also levied a fine of Rs 11,000 on Beeluk *pal*, and collected additional fines from the neighbouring villages. The leader of the expedition, who was the *diwan* of Mewar's son—and probably also the revenue farmer of the area—'returned to Paduna with about Rs 45,000 in cash besides the cattle'.[116] As a consequence of these exactions, many of the villagers emigrated to Gujarat and Paduna became a much smaller *pal*. This did not stop the local *kamdar* from forcing the Paduna Bhils to pay *tirsala* (a tax levied every third year, in addition to the revenue), besides *hal barar* and *koot*. Also, the amounts levied as *hal barar* and *koot* increased. In 1855 Paduna paid Rs 250 as *hal barar* and *koot*, and in 1856 Rs 375 was demanded on these two accounts.[117] All this clearly increased the fiscal burden on those who remained in the village.

The petition from the Bhils of Peepli told a similar story. In the 1820s they had paid Rs 52 as the annual *hal barar* and *koot* on all the lands of the village and nothing as *tirsala*. But in the 1840s, soon after the MBC was raised in 1841, 'a *fauj barar* (tax for raising and maintaining troops) was levied twice as contribution for troops under the name of *tirsala*'.[118] The villagers of Peepli argued that they could not pay the unjust levy of Rs 200 every third year, besides the usual *hal barar* and *koot*.

Capt. J.C. Brooke, CO of the MBC, wrote in 1856 that the material condition of the Bhils in the *khalsa pals* had greatly deteriorated in the few years that he had been in Mewar. The population of *pals* like Paduna and Peepli had fallen by half over the fifteen years since the MBC was raised in 1841. With this decline in population, cultivation had also fallen. In his remonstrance the *gameti* of Paduna pointed out that twelve families had left the *pal* in 1855, and Brooke wrote:

> Bhorai (a Bhil *pal*) has diminished from about 500 houses to about 150. The head *gameti* told me last year (1855) that he had sold his own child to meet the exactions of the *raj kamdar*, while Beeluk, which had from 1000 to 1200 houses, has not now more than a third of the number. . . . The present demands for *tirsala* have driven the remaining inhabitants away from Beeluk. Many will not return, for

> I have observed that each such flight causes the well-behaved men, who resent the oppression, to emigrate into either Dungarpur or the Mahi Kantha, where a fixed demand on each house is all that is taken from them. . . . The *tirsala* is a tax which was never levied on the hill Bhils, whose crops, entirely dependent on the annual rains, are too precarious to enable them to meet it. . . . In November 1855, the *gametis* of all the principal *pals* in the area came to Udaipur to meet me (the visit to Udaipur being an unprecedented occurrence), and I spoke to the Maharana about their complaints . . . (he) said that if the *tirsala* was a fresh tax on the Bhils, it should not be levied . . . enquiry proved that it was . . . but later, when it was pointed out how much would be lost by this (ending the collection of *tirsala*), the *pals* were notified that it would be collected. The Bhils then decided that rather than pay it, they would emigrate in a body after this season's crop had been gathered. Though this might not be done, some will definitely leave. . . . The levy is unjust and there is no proof to show that it was levied ever before the Bhil Corps was raised.[119]

It is interesting to see Brooke supporting the Bhil cause so enthusiastically. He must have been concerned about the migrations and the loss of revenue, and the possibility of unrest leading to an upheaval. But in all likelihood his sincere paternalism readily found a voice on the issue of *tirsala*—and its being a *fauj barar* in disguise—because of the link between its levy and the establishment of the MBC, and the obvious implication that the British were responsible for the additional taxes.

Notwithstanding any of Brooke's anxieties, the grievances listed by the Bhils make it obvious that the various officers of the Mewar government in the Magra devoted considerable attention to collecting as much money as they could during their tenure, and to retaining as much of it as possible. This was facilitated by the fact that, in most cases, the *hakim* of the Magra was also the revenue farmer of the area. In 1862, administrative work in the Magra was held up because the *hakim* was away in Udaipur for over six months, apparently settling his accounts with the *darbar*.[120] In 1863–64, Mehta Phul Chand, the *hakim* and revenue farmer of the Magra, procrastinated whenever he was asked to show his accounts; on one occasion he pleaded illness, certified by an (pliable ?) MBC doctor. When Mehta Phul Chand did go to Udaipur, work in the Magra was held up because he often did not return for six to nine months. In 1865 he was succeeded by Mehta Madho Singh, who similarly spent long periods in Udaipur lobbying for military assistance to coerce the Bhils to pay taxes.[121] In 1866, there were a number of complaints that the *hakim* and the *naib hakim* of the Magra, Raghunath Singh and Moti Singh, were levying fines indiscriminately without trying to settle the disputes which led to the fines. The British political superintendent of the Hilly Tracts, Mewar, wrote that the *hakim* 'thinks of nothing but collecting and squeezing money from the Bhils. I have found his *kamdar*s attempting to levy the revenue twice and only stopped doing so on the Bhils complaining to me about it.'[122] These British criticisms of the *darbar*'s officers are legitimate to us, but some of them must have seemed incomprehensible in a context where the *darbar* asked only that the revenue be collected without the expense of military operations, except when absolutely necessary to safeguard the revenue, and the officers had to recoup the *nazrana* (fee of investiture) they had paid for their appointments and amass fortunes to pay the next one. To the Bhils, these levies were thoroughly unjustified.

I am grateful to Professor Sumit Sarkar and Dr Radhika Chopra for their suggestions and comments on a draft of this paper. The responsibility for any errors that remain is mine alone.

Notes and References

1 K.D. Erskine, *Rajputana Gazetteers, Vol. II–A: The Mewar Residency*, Government of India Press, Ajmer, 1908, p. 5.

2 Ibid., p. 31.

3 While most of the Magra was made up of *khalsa* villages, there were some exceptions. By the early nineteenth century, some relatively small grants of revenue had been made in the Magra.

4 James Tod, author of *Annals and Antiquities of Rajasthan* (2 vols, first published in 1829 and 1832, reprinted, M.N. Publishers, Delhi, 1983), was the East India Company's first political agent in Mewar, and so charmed was he by the romantic glory of mythic Mewar and its legendary nobles, that he thought of himself as its curator.

5 Erskine, *Rajputana Gazetteers, Vol. II-A*, p. 228.

6 Ibid.

7 Tod, *Annals and Antiquities*, p. 183.

8 Shyamaldas, *Vir Vinod: Mewar ka Itihas*, Vol. II, Motilal Banarsidass, Delhi, 1986, pp. 1535–2141. Perhaps Shyamaldas deliberately chose not to mention the custom because he thought the Bhils were no more than 'wild forest people, like animals' (ibid., p. 2217, my translation).

[9] G. Carstairs, *Shepherd of Udaipur and the Land He Loved*, Hodder & Stoughton, London, 1926, p. 25.

[10] Erskine, *Rajasthan Gazetteers, Vol. II-A*, p. 228.

[11] Ibid., p. 229. Some of the Bhils claimed descent from specific Rajput clans, and prefixed Bhati, Chauhan, Gehlot, etc. (names of Rajput clans), to their names (ibid.).

[12] C.S. Venkatachar, 'An Ethnographic Account of the Bhils of Central India', in *Census of India, 1931, Vol. I, Part III B*, Government of India Press, Simla, 1935, p. 52; Erskine, *Rajasthan Gazetteers, Vol. II-A*, p. 229; T.B. Naik, *The Bhils*, Bharatiya Adimjati Seva Sangh, Delhi, 1956, p. 19.

[13] Conventional wisdom among the 'twice-born' held that they were thus named because of their distinctive (and allegedly profane) posture when sitting. Unlike the 'twice-born', they squatted in the same way to eat and to defecate (Conversations in District Udaipur, November 1981).

[14] Naik, *The Bhils*, pp. 11–12.

[15] Venkatachar, 'An Ethnographic Account' p. 52. Another version of the second story is recorded thus: 'A tradition ascribes the origin of the Bhils to Mahadev who was said to have fallen in love with a forest girl. He had numerous progeny by her. One of them was ugly and vicious and he distinguished himself finally by slaying his father's favourite bull, and for this he was expelled from the habitation of men. From this son descended the Bhils' (Naik, *The Bhils*, p. 13). Naik also writes that there is a reference in the *Mahabharata* to 'Mahadev being bewitched by the beauty of a Bhil girl, who was in fact Parvati' (ibid.). According to Naik, the *Ramayana* has a number of references to Bhils. 'Valmiki was himself a Bhil highway robber named Valia. Shabari of the *Ramayana* is known as one of Rama's greatest devotees. She was a Bhil woman' (ibid., pp. 13–14). The last point is an interesting one because the maharanas of Mewar claimed to be descended from Ram, and the privileged relationship between Ram and Shabari was often used as a metaphor for the Maharana–Bhil relationship.

[16] I was present at a telling of the second story in Kherwara, District Udaipur, Rajasthan, in November 1981. As the storyteller moved in and out of the obviously familiar basic narrative with tragic tales of contemporary injustice, the grim stillness of the small audience seemed to reinforce the fateful power of the story. After the story was told, the two conversations I had with my fellow-listeners were both discussions of the present and not of the past. Many in the audience believed that the story was portentous.

[17] B. Malinowski, 'Myth in Primitive Psychology', in *Magic, Science and Religion and Other Essays*, Souvenir Press, London, 1974, pp. 115–16.

[18] Ibid., p. 126.

[19] Ibid.

[20] 'They seemed to think it legitimate to plunder Hindu society. When arrested a Bhil would say "I am not to blame; I am Mahadeo's thief"' (Erskine, *Rajasthan Gazetters, Vol. II-A*, p. 230). It is interesting that some Bhils used the same justification—rooted in their subsistence ethic—for

similar actions in the 1980s. And yet, the Bhils also had a peasant's pride; they would almost never beg for food individually. During the early part of the famine in 1899, before hunger drove them to utter desperation, some Bhils preferred to starve or take food by force from strangers, that is, society, rather than beg for it. 'The Bhils . . . who by nature and tradition are very averse to begging, became much demoralized. At the commencement of the famine, a Bhil in his native hills, although he might have a few qualms of conscience about lying in wait on a hill pass to attack and rob some unwary traveller, considered it derogatory to his tradition to beg. Besides this, when working together, if, by chance, one Bhil had no provisions for the day when the meal time came, he would go off, and sit somewhere out of sight, for fear the others seeing him without food, should insist, as was their custom, on him taking a share of their provisions' ('Famine Report for Udaipur State', No. 829 of 1900, p. 36, Abu Collection, Central Library, University of Rajasthan, Jaipur).

21 'Generally speaking, they (the Bhils) produce very fine crops', wrote the superintendent of the Hilly Tracts Mewar, in his Report dated 30 March 1869: File No. 1 of 1837, Mewar Residency, National Archives of India (hereafter NAI).

22 C. Levi-Strauss, *Structural Anthropology*, Penguin Books, Harmondsworth, 1977, p. 209.

23 Erskine, *Rajputana Gazetteers, Vol. II-A*, p. 231.

24 Carstairs, *Shepherd of Udaipur*, p. 226.

25 Shyamaldas, *Vir Vinod*, p. 2217, my translation.

26 Tod, *Annals and Antiquities*, p. 400.

27 Erskine, *Rajputana Gazetteers, Vol. II-A*, pp. 230–31.

28 Carstairs, *Shepherd of Udaipur*, pp. 39, 233–34.

29 Quoted in ibid., pp. 80–81.

30 Ibid., p. 234.

31 Erskine, *Rajputana Gazetteers, Vol. II-A*, p. 33.

32 Report on the Hilly Tracts Mewar, dated 30 March 1869: File No. 1 of 1837, Mewar Residency, NAI.

33 Ibid.

34 Erskine, *Rajputana Gazetteers, Vol. II-A*, p. 229; Carstairs, *Shepherd of Udaipur*, p. 231. In these sections both Erskine and Carstairs seem to be using the word clan to demarcate the exogamous unit. Perhaps the word lineage would have been more appropriate.

35 *Census of India, 1881, Vol. XIX, Rajputana*, Government of India Press, Bombay, 1882, p. 6.

36 *Census of India, 1891, Vol. XXVI, Rajputana, Part I*, Government of India Press, Calcutta, 1892, p. 58.

37 Erskine, *Rajasthan Gazetteers, Vol. II-A*, p. 32.

38 *Census of India, 1901, Vol. XXV, Rajputana, Part I*, Government of India Press, Lucknow, 1902, p. i.

39 Erskine, *Rajputana Gazetteers, Vol. II-A*, pp. 32, 35.

40 Shyamaldas, *Vir Vinod*, p. 1743.

41 Erskine, *Rajputana Gazetteers*, p. 60.

42 The maharanas of Mewar belonged to the Sisodia clan of Rajputs.

43 J.C. Brookes, *History of Meywar*, Baptist Mission Press, Calcutta, 1859, p. 72.

44 Ibid.

45 Ibid.

46 Ibid.

47 Ibid., p. 73.

48 Ibid.

49 Ibid., pp. 74–81.

50 Asst Pol. Ag. Mewar to Pol. Ag. Mewar, 6 December 1856: File No. 1 of 1837, Mewar Residency, NAI.

51 The amounts levied by each *pal* and estate were fixed by category, and the highest rates for each category were collected by the Mewar *darbar* (Annexure B, Report of the Pol. Supdt., Hilly Tracts Mewar, dated 30 March 1869: File No. 1 of 1837, Mewar Residency, NAI).

52 Erskine, *Rajputana Gazetteers, Vol. II-A*, p. 44.

53 Proceedings; Mehekma Khas Udaipur to Resident Mewar, 23 April 1882; A–Political–I, 30–47, November 1882, For. Dept, NAI.

54 Ibid., and Proceedings; Resident Mewar to 1st Asst AGG, 18 July 1882; A–Political–I, 30–47, November 1882, For. Dept, NAI.

55 Proceedings; Mehekma Khas Udaipur to Resident Mewar, 23 April 1882.

56 Traffic other than opium would continue to pay *bolai.*

57 Proceedings; Resident Mewar to 1st Asst AGG, 18 July 1882, and Proceedings; Mehekma Khas Udaipur to Resident Mewar, 23 April 1882.

58 Proceedings; Resident Mewar to 1st Asst AGG, 18 July 1882.

59 The figures for losses are annual averages.

60 Mehekma Khas Udaipur to Resident Mewar, 11 July 1882; A–Political–I, 30–47, November 1882, For. Dept, NAI. This substantial reduction—of more than 60 per cent—in the direct income of the *pals* must indeed have caused hardships. The average price of maize in the decade 1881–90 was 20.1 seers per rupee (1 seer = approx. 933 grams), and that of wheat 14.8 seers per rupee (Erskine, *Rajputana Gazetteers, Vol. II-A*, p. 16). The prices of these staples give us an idea of the purchasing power lost by the Bhils.

61 Resident Mewar to 1st Asst AGG, 2 December 1882; A–Political–I, 25–27, February 1883, For. Dept, NAI.

62 Ibid.

63 Hereafter MBC.

64 Offg. Supdt, Hilly Tracts Mewar, to Pol. Ag. Mewar, 3 October 1861; 2 of 1836, Mewar and Southern Rajputana States, Pt. II, Conf., NAI.

65 Ibid.

66 Note by the For. Dept, n.d.; Int.–B, 91–92, March 1895, For. Dept, NAI.

67 Note by the For. Dept, n.d.; General B, 162–167, July 1892, For. Dept, NAI.

68 Ibid.

69 Erskine, *Rajputana Gazetteers, Vol. II-A*, p. 79.

70 Note by the For. Dept, n.d.; General B, 162–167, July 1892.

71 Ibid.

72 Pol. Ag. Mewar to Asst Pol. Ag., 22 March 1848; 18 of 1865, Mewar Residency, NAI.

73 Pol. Ag. Mewar to CO, MBC, 26 April 1848; 18 of 1865, Mewar Residency, NAI.

74 CO, MBC to Pol. Ag. Mewar, 23 April 1848; 18 of 1865, Mewar Residency, NAI.

75 Pol. Ag. Mewar to Asst Pol. Ag., 2 April 1849; 18 of 1865, Mewar Residency, NAI.

76 Pol. Ag. Mewar to Asst Pol Ag., 4 December 1849; 18 of 1865, Mewar Residency, NAI.

77 Rikhabnath or Rikhabdeo (also known as Dhulev, sometimes corrupted into Doolia by the British) was a small town about 40 miles south of Udaipur city, built around the thirteenth-century Jain temple of Rikhabnath (Rikhab Deo), the first of the Jain Tirthankars. The Hindus worshipped the black marble idol as an incarnation of Vishnu, and the Bhils venerated it as 'Kalaji'. It was probably the most sacred site for the Bhils of Mewar.

78 CO, MBC to Pol. Ag. Mewar, 9 September 1860; 18 of 1865, Mewar Residency, NAI.

79 CO, MBC to Pol. Ag. Mewar, 4 October 1865; 18 of 1865, Mewar Residency, NAI.

80 Offg. Agent to the Governor General (hereafter AGG) Rajputana to Offg. Secy, For. Dept, GOI, 20 January 1853; Cons. 121, 16 February 1853, For. and Pol. Dept, NAI.

81 The trial was held in Nimach, and the murder had been committed in Shingoli, on the British–Indian side of the Mewar border with the then Central Provinces. Nimach and Shingoli are both in the modern district of Mandsaur in Madhya Pradesh.

82 Pol. Ag. Mewar to Asst Pol. Ag. Mewar, 7 April 1851; Cons. 122, 16 February 1853, For. and Pol. Dept, NAI.

83 CO, MBC to Pol. Ag. Mewar, 7 April 1851; and CO, MBC to Pol. Ag. Mewar, 27 July 1852; Cons. 122, 16 February 1853, For. and Pol. Dept, NAI.

84 Proceedings of the Trial of Sempla Bhil, Sepoy of 10th. Co., MBC, Kherwara; Cons. 58, 13 May 1853, For. and Pol. Dept, NAI.

85 Ibid.

86 Ibid.

87 Ibid.

88 Ibid.

89 Ibid.

90 Capt. J.C. Brookes, CO, MBC to G.St.P. Lawrence, Pol. Ag. Mewar, 29 March 1853; Cons. 55, 13 May 1853, For. and Pol. Dept, NAI.

91 Ibid.

92 J.C. Brookes, C.O. M.B.C. to G.St.P. Lawrence, Pol. Ag. Mewar, 1 April 1853; Cons. 59, 13 May 1853, For. and Pol. Dept, NAI.

93 G.St.P. Lawrence, Pol. Ag. Mewar, to H.M. Lawrence, AGG Rajputana, 18 April 1853; Cons. 57, 13 May 1853, For. and Pol. Dept, NAI.

94 H.M. Lawrence, AGG Rajputana, to C. Allen, Secy., For. and Pol. Dept, GOI, 23 April 1853; Cons. 56, 13 May 1853, For. and Pol. Dept, NAI.

95 Minute by the GG dated 7 May 1853; Cons. 59A, 13 May 1853, For. and Pol. Dept, NAI.

96 The evidence that I could find showed that all the accusations of witchcraft in ninteenth-century Mewar were made against women at least a generation older than the accuser, and most of them were made by men against women in their families.

97 'These family witches encourage the belief in their (own) powers because it gives them influence', CO, MBC to Pol. Ag. Mewar, 7 April 1851; Cons. 122, 16 February 1853; For. and Pol. Dept; NAI.

98 K. Thomas, *Religion and the Decline of Magic*, Penguin Books, Harmondsworth, 1973, p. 643.

99 Proceedings of the Trial of Sempla Bhil, Sepoy of 10th. Co., MBC, Kherwara.

100 Resident Mewar to 1st Asst AGG, 13 June 1882; A-General I, 51–58, January 1883, For. Dept, NAI.

101 Ibid.

102 Resident Mewar to 1st Asst AGG, 9 December 1882; A-General I, 51–58, January 1883, For. Dept, NAI.

103 Ibid.

104 Resident Mewar to 1st Asst AGG, 5 March 1883; A–Political–I, 66–73, April 1883, For. Dept, NAI.

105 Ibid. Walter's account of the meeting is slightly different: 'The headmen on entering the shamiana, threw down their turbans at my feet and said that as their misdeeds had been pardoned by their own *darbar*, they trusted that I, as the representative of the British Government, would also forgive them.' Political Administration Report, Rajputana, 1882–83, Rajasthan State Archives, Bikaner (hereafter RSA, Bikaner), p. 80. Unlike in the account of the meeting sent by Resident Walter to the AGG, in this one it is clear that the *hakim* of the Magra had already agreed to forgive the Bhils, thus paving the way for the agreement. Here the *darbar* does have a discernible voice, distinct from that of the British officers.

106 Unfortunately, we do not know the exact words translated thus by Resident Walter.

107 Political Administration Report, Rajputana, 1882–83, p. 81.

108 Resident Mewar to 1st Asst AGG, 5 March 1883; A–Political–I, 66–73, April 1883, For. Dept, NAI. The full text of the translation of the undertaking on the *agat* (enclosed with Resident Mewar to 1st Asst AGG, 5 March 1883; A-Political-I, 66–73, April 1883, For. Dept, NAI) is as follows.

'On the occasion of the tour of Col. C.K.M. Walter, Resident Meywar, when the officer was encamped at Doolia (Rikhabdeo) on the 3 March 1883 (Phagun Bid 9 Sambat 1939) the Gametis and Bhanjgurreahs of the under-mentioned *pals* were presented before him by Mehta Gobind Singh, Hakim of the Magra: 1. Biluk 2. Baluna 3. Pipli 4. Sagtari 5. Surara 6. Sepur 7. Naniodo 8. Danhawara 9. Nathara 10. Rajol 11. Bichiwara 12. Baran 13. Paduna 14. Barapal 15. Chenaoda 16. Seron 17. Tidi. With regard to the practice of the *pal* men killing women on the plea of their being witches, the Resident directed that arrangements should be made to put a complete stop to the crime.

'We, therefore, the above-named *pal* people, both for ourselves and for all the *pals* of the Magra, do for our own advantage agree that we shall never kill a woman on the plea of her being a witch. If we have any suspicion of a woman being a witch, we will complain to the Sarkar, who will punish the woman. We will not ourselves kill witches and this determination will go down from generation to generation. If we break this pledge, may Kalaji deal with us. Let the Raj punish anyone who disregards the terms engraved on this stone. We all combined have, of our own free will, consented to the embedment of this inscriptional slab and will hold it as binding. Should any ruffian or reprobate secretly commit the crime of witch-killing, we will hand him over to the Raj for punishment. In this there will be no deviation. We have caused the embedment of this stone of our own free will and regard the inscription on it as binding on us. Done through Bhandari Jowarji Khemraj, and signed on behalf and at the request of all the Gametis assembled, by Purshottam.'

109 In fact, the inscription made it clear that the Bhils were to hand over alleged witches to the British for punishment. From the Bhil point of view, this meant that the British had assumed the responsibility for punishing witches. However, I could not find any evidence of a case in which the Bhils handed over an alleged witch to the British for punishment.

110 Resident Mewar to 1st Asst AGG, 5 March 1883; A–Political–I, 66–73, April 1883, For. Dept, NAI.

111 Asst Pol. Ag. Mewar to Pol. Ag. Mewar, 17 August 1842; Pol. Ag. Mewar to Pol. Supdt., Hilly Tracts Mewar, 29 October 1874; Pol. Supdt, Hilly Tracts Mewar to Pol. Ag. Mewar, 5 November 1874. All in File No. 18, Udaipur Residency Customs (12), RSA, Bikaner.

112 In the 1860s the *darbar* received between Rs 1 lakh and Rs 1.25 lakh annually as taxes from the Magra (Report of the Pol. Supdt., Hilly Tracts Mewar, 30 March 1869; File No. 1 of 1837, Mewar Residency, NAI).

113 Asst Pol. Ag. Mewar to Pol. Ag. Mewar, 6 December 1856; File No. 1, 1837, Mewar Residency, NAI.

114 Ibid.

115 Ibid.

116 CO, MBC to Pol. Ag. Mewar, 9 June 1851; File No. 18 of 1865, Mewar Residency, NAI. The soldiers probably took much more than the money and material that was recorded by the leader of the expedition. In 1869, the *darbar*'s *sawars* (cavalrymen) were paid Rs 16 per month, and they had to horse, clothe and arm themselves within it. The *paidals* (foot-soldiers) had to clothe and arm themselves within a monthly salary of Rs 6 (Report of the

Pol. Supdt., Hilly Tracts Mewar, 30 March 1869; File No. 1 of 1837, Mewar Residency, NAI). In comparison, in 1861 ordinary soldiers in the Mewar Bhil Corps were paid a monthly salary of Rs 5–8, besides being supplied their uniforms and arms (all these figures are in Udaipuri rupees; in the 1860s, 1 British Re = approx. 1.27 Udaipuri rupees) (Pol. Supdt., Hilly Tracts Mewar, to Pol. Ag. Mewar, 3 October 1861; File No. 2 of 1836, Part II, Confdl., Mewar and Southern Rajputana States, NAI). In May 1869, a period of scarcity made worse by epidemics of cholera and malaria, 1 British Re purchased about 14 seers of maize or 10 of wheat in the Kherwara bazar. In May 1870 the prices were lower: 1 British Re bought about 17.5 seers of maize or 14.5 seers of wheat (1 seer = approximately 933 grams) (Report of the Pol. Supdt., Hilly Tracts Mewar, to Pol. Ag. Mewar, 10 May 1870; File No. 1 of 1837, Mewar Residency, NAI).

117 Asst Pol. Ag. Mewar to Pol. Ag. Mewar, 6 December 1856; File No. 1 of 1837, Mewar Residency, NAI.

118 Ibid.

119 Ibid.

120 Pol. Supdt, Hilly Tracts Mewar to Pol. Ag. Mewar, 10 October 1862; File No. 1 of 1837, Mewar Residency, NAI.

121 Proceedings, n.d.; File No. 1 of 1837, Mewar Residency, NAI.

122 Pol. Supdt., Hilly Tracts Mewar to Pol. Ag. Mewar, 16 December 1866; File No. 1 of 1837, Mewar Residency, NAI. In contrast, the political superintendent wrote in 1869 that 'The Bhils of the Bhumia estates in the Kherwara districts have almost entirely given up their predatory habits and are much more peaceful than those of the *khalsa pals*. This is because . . . they are not subjected to the tyranny and exactions of the *raj kamdars*' (Report by the Pol. Supdt., Hilly Tracts Mewar, 30 March 1869; File No. 1 of 1837, Mewar Residency, NAI). However, a decade earlier J.C. Brookes had implied that *kamdars* in the *thikanas* were also subjected to demands from the *thikanedars*, which probably led them to the same course. He wrote: 'The chiefs' estates are managed by *kamdars* who are not paid. They supply the chief's immediate wants and are fined a small sum on occasions of marriage &c.' (Brookes, *History of Mewar*, p. 56).

Negotiating with Dharma Pinnu

Towards a Social History of Smallpox in Colonial Orissa

Biswamoy Pati

This essay explores various complexities associated with smallpox in colonial Orissa, in eastern India. Although there has been a shift towards region-based studies to unravel the specificities and diversities of South Asia, *adivasis* (indigenous, tribal peoples) continue to remain at the periphery of the existing scholarship.[1] The attempt here is to take up the comparatively ignored indigenous tribal communities of Orissa, and examine the issue of smallpox against the canvas of social history. I do not see the indigenous cultures as autonomously generating their own ideas, notions and solutions, independent of the non-tribal communities and colonialism.[2] Instead, I accept interactions among them and highlight areas of contestation as well as acceptance of the colonial power/knowledge system. What is thus woven is the worldview of the tribal communities and popular culture, in an attempt to reach out to voices that are often difficult to hear.

Perhaps more importantly, this paper projects a process that seems to have eluded social historians, namely, the highly complex phenomenon of the hinduization of tribal communities. It was through this process that the *adivasis* were sought to be 'integrated' with Hindu (caste) society, with the obvious idea of exploiting and exercising power over them. From the point of view of the *adivasis*, hinduization implied acceptance as well as rejection of various features of non-tribal Hindu society. This coexisted with a contestatory aspect *vis-à-vis* the Oriya (non-tribal) community.

I also examine specific elements of the non-tribal groups, including certain practices like inoculation, black magic and subversive cults, demonstrating the close affinities some of these features had with those of the tribal communities. I touch upon certain aspects of the

Oriya middle class and the way it located colonial interventions related to smallpox.

Geographically, the present-day province of Orissa borders West Bengal in the east, Bihar in the north, Madhya Pradesh in the west and Andhra Pradesh in the south. Orissa is a very diverse region, historically marked by economic, social and cultural variations. By the time of the Mughals, who held sway over Orissa between 1578 and 1751, it had been divided into two parts, based on geographical, ecological and economic divisions: the *moghulbandi* areas, which was under the Mughals, who collected tax in cash through their *subahdar*s or administrative heads (*subahs* = administrative units); and the western interior, which was under the princes who were taxed by the Mughals. Whereas the *moghulbandi* area comprised the coastal plain, the western tract was hilly and heavily forested.

In 1751 Orissa was taken over by the Marathas, and then by the British in 1803. Until 1947, when India became a free country, it comprised twenty-four princely states, a number of *zamindari*s (estates) and the coastal tract of Cuttack, Puri and Balasore, which was under direct colonial administration. The British colonization of Orissa saw major interventions in the nineteenth century that were primarily centred around the agrarian settlements. Thus, whereas the land settlements with the princely states and the *zamindar*s (landlords) were made on a long-term, permanent basis, the coastal tract directly under the British saw temporary settlements. Attempts to settle directly with affluent sections of the peasants or with the villages saw the emergence of the *ryotwari* (*ryot* = peasant) and *mahalwari* settlements (*mahal* = village), respectively. Whereas the former was confined to some parts of Ganjam, the latter prevailed in the Sambalpur region which had been taken over by the British in 1818 but was united with the Central Provinces till 1905, when it became a part of Orissa. The agrarian interventions led to a host of changes over the nineteenth century, including the emergence of private property rights over land, commercialization of agriculture and increasing monetization. The polarized social stratification implied a consolidation of the exploitation, power and dominance of the upper castes, like the brahmanas and the khandayats (the Orissan variant of kshatriyas), and, simultaneously, led to increasing marginalization of the *adivasi*s and the outcastes (namely, the shudras, who were considered untouchable and in this sense were outcastes). This becomes particularly relevant if we bear in mind that the western tract, for example, had/has a large tribal population.[3]

I

The colonization of Orissa inaugurated many shifts and changes which were reflected in various ways, including the manner in which the tribal communities related to disease/health and medicine, especially smallpox. Among the prominent tribal communities, one ought to refer to the Kandhas, Santals, Mundas, Gadbas, Hos, Bhuyans, Koyas, Juangas, Parajas, Sauras, Kols, Bhumijs and Bondas. The indigenous communities had (and still have) an oral tradition that offers us fascinating clues as to their vision and worldviews on health/disease and medicine. That health was considered extremely vital is reflected in the importance attached to medicine-men and women. This not only illustrates a constant battle with certain forces but also the necessity of a virtual 'specialist'.

How did the tribal population locate smallpox? Nothing specific can be cited here, though the discourses of colonial officials and bureaucrats offer mono-dimensional explanations, often associated with the world of magic, spirits and ghosts.[4] Such constructions appear to ignore the philosophy of disease and instead project the stereotypical image of irrational/unscientific indigenous people. What is rarely mentioned in these discourses is an underlying set of interconnections between the colonial military inroads made into the Kandha 'country', smallpox and the negotiations that this entailed.[5]

In fact, it was smallpox that brought out hidden tensions and complexities in *adivasi* society in the sharpest possible way. The Kandhas, for example, around the early decades of the nineteenth century, identified it as a disease caused by Joogah Pennoo, the god of smallpox. Joogah Pennoo sowed smallpox just as men sowed seeds in the earth. We are told about Kandhas deserting their villages when struck by smallpox. Those who remained made offerings of buffaloes, hogs and sheep to appease the smallpox god. The Kandhas of neighbouring hamlets attempted to prevent Joogah Pennoo from reaching their village by planting thorns in the path that led to the affected village.[6]

A part of their survival strategy made the Kandhas resort to the *meriah* (human) sacrifice. Although it is beyond the scope of this essay to examine the details associated with it, this sacrifice, among other things, sought to protect them from diseases.[7]

For the Kandhas of Subarnaghurry, smallpox spelt doom in 1860. The Kandhas, we are told, had refused to be inoculated and in November 1860 some of them, led by Jagooah Pojaree and the Kandhas of Kranjah went over to Subarnaghurry. Here they collected the Kandhas and told them that the problem of smallpox was due to the presence of Paikas in their country. The Paikas, an erstwhile martial caste which got increasingly involved in agriculture, were 'the means of getting the *sircar* (the government) and causing smallpox to prevail among them'. If the Paikas were expelled, then they would enjoy peace and comfort. On the following day, about fifty Kandhas, accompanied by Jagooah Pojaree and armed with battle-axes, bows and arrows, went to the village of Goomahgoodah and 'shouted aloud to murder all the Paikas who hid in their houses'.

Encounters with smallpox continued to plague the Kandhas in the second half of the nineteenth century. Thus, the Kandhas of Panigoodah and Guddapoor sought the help of three or four people in the 'low country' (that is, non-tribals) who, they had gathered, could prevent smallpox through inoculation. These 'adventurers' travelled various *mootahs* (administrative units) and are said to have 'inoculated' several hundred Kandhas and 'reaped an abundant harvest' (that is, made a lot of money). Several of the Kandhas were reduced to poverty, and some had to mortgage their children in order to obtain the resources to meet the demands of the 'inoculators', to get themselves and their families inoculated. This experience in fact made them appeal to Captain Mcneill to send a '*sircar*' vaccinator.[8]

The Kuttia Kandhas also invented Dharma Pinnu—the smallpox goddess—to cope with the disease. Dharma Pinnu was seen as the source of smallpox and worshipped at all agricultural festivals. Interestingly, she was identified as an Oriya (Hindu) goddess living in the lap of luxury.[9] Ceremonies were performed in her honour just before sowing in the hill clearings. The invocations at her special ceremony were made in Oriya, and the offerings were not the normal millet and rice beer but milk, *ghee*, rice and *mohwa* liquor.[10] That this reflected a part of a broader survival strategy of the indigenous people becomes clear from the fact that tribals like the Didayi too invented their own goddess Mata, a close parallel to Dharma Pinnu of the Kandhas.[11]

When smallpox became virulent, a little cart was made on

which a saffron-stained grain of rice representing every soul in the village was placed. After numerous offerings it was dragged, with the necessary ceremony, to the boundary of the village. Through this the influence of the deity bringing smallpox was sought to be transferred across the village limits. Neighbouring villages too followed this practice, moving the cart with ceremonial accompaniments. After touring a whole set of villages, the cart was abandoned in some lonely spot.[12] A similar trend has been observed in the Gujarat region by Hardiman, where the smallpox goddess was 'made' to enter a buffalo or goat and driven far away from the village. A more common practice was to entice her through offerings of food and sacrificial victims to quit the village. A large basket was filled with cooked rice and red powder. This was then taken to the border of the village, where it was buried. In some cases the basket passed from village to village till it reached the sea, where it was immersed.[13]

Another closely related method implied offering the smallpox goddess a sweet drink called *pana*, at the junction of the roads leading away from the village. Through this the goddess, it was hoped, would leave the village without striking it with the dreaded disease. This latter method seems to have been adopted to keep out goddesses of other diseases as well.[14]

Although the tribal *adivasi* society was tuned to patriarchal practices, the way smallpox polarized gender tensions is striking. A reference from the early 1870s from Gangpur (a princely state) provides evidence. When smallpox broke out in Kurumkel it was attributed to witches, and the village headman sent four 'witch-finders', who located four women. The headman sent a report to the raja who sent an official (Gajendra Babu) to enquire. He, in turn, ordered all witches to restrain from mischief and restored peace in the village. The matter seems to have attracted a lot of attention, since the raja came and camped at a nearby village.

A small amount of hair was cut from the heads of each of the four women who had been identified as witches, and burnt. This was supposed to deprive the witches of their power. Then the four women were tied to posts and after being questioned, were ritually tortured. One of the women denied that she was a witch and was beaten with a cane which split into two. Then she was beaten with the green stalk of a castor oil plant. After about half a dozen blows she confessed to being a witch and fainted on being released. Another of the women had to go through the same ordeal and both of them died—one the following day and the other a few days later. Of the other two, one admitted that she was a witch and gave the names of the spirits responsible for the outbreak of smallpox, whereas the other denied any knowledge of witch-craft. Both were released with a warning and sacrifices were made to the *bhoots* (ghosts) named by the 'witch', after which '*saltanat* peace' returned to the village. What perhaps needs to be emphasized is that the raja was fined Rs 2,000 by the colonial administration, and awarded a year's rigorous imprisonment for his complicity in the matter, though he was not sent to the common jail but detained at Ranchi in Bihar.[15] This indicates the way the colonial establishment let off its collaborator (the raja of Gangpur) with very mild punishment, although he was involved and sanctioned the torture of the women, two of whom were murdered.

The dislocations that affected the indigenous societies were reflected in some of the perceptions that we have sought to highlight. The colonial order, and the opposition to it, was not monodimensional. Thus, the Kandhas associated the '*sircar*'—in metaphorical terms, colonialism—with smallpox, and this coexisted with knocking on the doors of the colonial establishment for help after having tried out non-tribal inoculators. Thus, colonialism, which was associated with the new order, was simultaneously feared, admired, revered, appeased and coaxed through a host of complex negotiations. The awesome hold of the colonial authority on indigenous communities coexisted with a subversive element when it came to smallpox. To explain this merely in terms of the intensity of the disease would be inadequate. What we see is the fusion of a set of highly complex strands.

One should also note the attempt to 'resist' the vaccination offered by the colonial authorities and to first try out alternatives available from the plains, as in the case of the Kandhas of Subarnaghurry. Nevertheless, this 'resistance' needs to be critiqued and problematized. David Arnold, in fact, refers to favourable accounts (mostly by European doctors and surgeons) of variolation in eastern (and northern) India prior to 1800. However, with the introduction of vaccination they tended to become sceptical and 'frankly contemptuous' of this rival practice. Arnold points to the conceptualization of the disease by the Indians and the Europeans. He delineates the importance of Sitala and the fact that she was worshipped/propitiated—with smallpox being seen as a mark of her divine presence rather than a disease. He also points to the idea of a controlled and moderated form of the disease through variolation/inoculation, through live smallpox matter, to protect the individual against a subsequent attack.[16] Here one can see a meeting point between the Indian and European methods of prevention. This should make us careful about not overemphasizing the dividing line often drawn between vaccination and inoculation.

Sanjoy Bhattacharya, while focusing on the diversities associated with the process of vaccination itself, argues that in different parts of rural India it was really a form of inoculation. He refers to reports from the localities in all the Presidencies, which often complained about the fact that local vaccinators used humanized —and usually unattenuated—lymph when the preserved animal lymph transported from the district depots lost its potency. This unattenuated lymph could, and often did, have serious side-effects, which in turn increased the opposition to a practice that was considered unreliable, especially when the unattenuated or inert lymph proved unable to provide resistance to smallpox after a painful operation. Given this, he emphasizes the existence of a two-tiered system of vaccination: an urban vaccination programme that was based on current and tested technologies, and a rural vaccination scheme in which outdated and suspect technologies were often used.[17]

The point regarding the lymph losing its effectiveness is perhaps indicated by some of the sources (see Table 1).[18] The gap between the number of people vaccinated and those in whose case it was reported to be 'successful', illustrates the problems associated with defective lymph supplies and the process of vaccination outside urban centres. These points should be borne in mind while seeking to explain the opposition to vaccination.

One should also point out that these were years marked by major rebellions, when the Kandhas fought against colonialism and the new order that was being imposed on them.[19] This assumes

TABLE 1 ***Statement showing the Operation of Vaccination in the Hill Tracts of Ganjam in the Years 1882–83 and 1883–84, and 1886–87 and 1887–88***

	1882–83	*1883–84*	*1886–87*	*1887–88*
Number vaccinated	5421	12571	4941	6066
Number successful	5134	12242	4764	5822

significance if seen in the light of the fact that historians have been generally insensitive to the connection between colonial conquests of *adivasi* (tribal) tracts and disease. Consequently, the vaccination option—associated with the colonial health establishment —was not readily available, and hence, alternatives from the plains were tried before knocking on the doors of the colonial administration for a '*sircar*' vaccinator.

A similar picture emerges when it comes to the tribal approach to non-tribal people from the plains, some of whom were distinctly associated with their exploitation. This explains the anger against the Paikas, who were favoured feudal retainers settled in the hill tracts by feudal chiefs. They were also hated because they were incorporated by and associated with the colonial agency. There is an observable link established in popular cosmology between the colonialist and the non-tribal exploiter, when it came to the outbreak of smallpox. One needs to bear all these complexities in mind since many of the movements of the Kandhas in the nineteenth century were against both these exploiters—internal and external. And, given all this, one needs to be more open to questions related to the meaning of 'science' and 'progress' among *adivasis* in the colonial world.

Significantly, some of the goddesses that emerged out of the complex interaction with the process of hinduization, occupied a rather central position. Nothing illustrates this better than the emergence of the smallpox goddess. The offering of *mohwa* (liquor) and *pana* (a ritualistic drink), the special invocations to her in Oriya and abandoning her at a lonely spot outside the village limits illustrate two simultaneous processes—contesting the Oriya (Hindu) identity and an effort to accommodate her in the tribal world. Moreover, it is worth speculating if the idea of planting thorns on the paths that led to a village affected by smallpox and abandoning the small cart with the saffron-stained rice grain in a lonely spot—outside the village limits—had anything to do with an awareness of human transmissibility.[20]

The way the indigenous tribal society consolidated its patriarchal position with the outbreak of smallpox illustrates its inner tensions and contradictions. The ritual torture of alleged witches and the symbolic cutting of their hair in order to deprive them of their power suggest selective targeting of the female identity. Witchcraft seems to have enjoyed fairly wide acceptance if one bears in mind the role of the Gangpur raja. Moreover, the measures taken against him by the colonial administration for the killing of the two 'witches' reveal a level of collaboration which was based on political constraints and considerations, and undermine the normally constructed image of a scientific and progress-based west.

II

The non-tribal people responded to smallpox in various ways. The Mastan brahmanas were hereditary inoculators against smallpox and also pursued cultivation. They normally inoculated children between two and eight years of age. These people were scattered all over coastal Orissa, though they seem to have been heavily concentrated in the Salepur area of Cuttack district. Their work season spanned the beginning of November until the beginning of March. They collected the calluses from smallpox victims on the twenty-first day, covered them with cotton wool and placed them in a hollow bamboo, sealed with *sola* corks. Within three or four days, the cotton wool was moistened with water and squeezed into a small snail shell. An incision was made on the skin of the victim using a small piece of iron, shaped like a 'country' nail-parer, with a sharp edge, to which the fluid was applied.

The child with fever was kept in confinement and it was assumed that the goddess Sitala had possessed her/his body. A serious effort was made to appease the goddess through a host of rituals and offerings, which included coconuts, curd, cheese, plantain, rice and vermilion. The child was treated very gently and fed rice, *dal* (lentils) and fried plantain during this period, since Sitala was supposed to be residing in her/him.

What is striking is that this was a skilled profession practised by a section of brahmanas, which appears to imply a certain degree of transgression of the structure of caste. Nevertheless, the caste hierarchy accommodated this, with the Mastan brahmanas located as 'low' brahmanas, given the fact that they were cultivators. The hereditary outcastes, Panas, who performed the role of inoculators in the princely states, provide another example.[21] This specialized job was accepted and accommodated by the order of the caste system since it involved collection of calluses, which could have been considered to be polluting by the upper castes, and also perhaps because of the preponderant tribal population in the region. In the Sambalpur tract there were hereditary *tikadars* (inoculators) and it was compulsory for a member of a *tikadar* family to follow the same occupation.[22] There was also a gender dimension to this system of inoculation, with the inoculators in coastal Orissa charging higher fees to inoculate boys than girls,[23] indicating female devaluation.

It has been suggested that the annual *rathajatra* at Puri, during which the trinity—Jagannatha, Balabhadra and Subhadra—go out on their annual visit to the Gundicha temple, has some connection with the ritual of clearing the main temple of smallpox. The nine-day festival corresponds with the duration of the disease; the sweeping of the chariots illustrates the wiping away of the disease; and the word Gundicha itself means smallpox (*gundi* = pox).[24] One can thus clearly see the possible linkage and interaction between the Jagannatha cult and the popular tradition related to appeasing Sitala and coping with the disease.

It has been correctly argued that Sitala was both the source of smallpox and the means of getting protection from it. However, the idea that she was a 'folk deity', not a part of the original Hindu pantheon, who had gained gradual entry into and recognition by brahmanical Hinduism,[25] does not seem particularly convincing. After all, it is impossible to locate the so-called 'original Hindu pantheon'. Instead, what needs emphasis is the specificities of her presence in the world of the indigenous people and the attempt to accommodate her in a complex way, which had some association with the process of hinduization in the colonial period.

III

Smallpox vaccination was undoubtedly one of the most serious health interventions undertaken by the colonial administration in Orissa. The context in which certain tribal communities 'sought' help from the colonial administration and the '*sircar*' vaccinator has already been highlighted. What perhaps remains to be articulated is the approach to the problem of vaccination and the constraints it suffered from. The financial implications were carefully assessed by the colonial administration in the case of any such welfare scheme. Engaging three vaccinators for the Kandhas of the hill tracts of Orissa would have meant an expenditure of Rs 400 annually (Rs 10 per month as their salary plus other expenditures). The concern about expenses occupied as important a position as the perception that this would be a 'boon' for the Kandhas.[26] There were also some in the medical establishment who did not exert themselves during the outbreak of smallpox, and the illness of some of the vaccinators sometimes constrained the operations. In other instances, there was the problem of defective lymph supplies from Calcutta. Moreover, in some areas, like Singhbhoom, the chiefs demanded 25 per cent of the vaccination fees and opposed the vaccination drive since no fees were charged.[27]

The problems faced by this intervention are also visible from tracts that were published in support of the vaccination drive, printed in Oriya at the Cuttack Mission Press. One such tract laments how only the *saheb*s (westernized men) supported it, whereas the *murkha*s (uneducated) and *agyani* (ignorant) people did not like vaccination. The author argues that it was the duty of all to first convince and explain to their domestic servants about the usefulness of vaccination. Sometimes, when *tikadar*s (vaccinators) visited villages, the women hesitated to vaccinate their children, which resulted in the large-scale deaths of children.[28] The system of vaccination implied a dependence on *zamindar*s, since it was felt by the colonial authorities that if persons of influence supported vaccination the process would be smoother.[29]

The print culture also gave prominence to certain diseases like smallpox, which struck with severity. Thus, a problem in a mathematics textbook asked: 'In a place 25 per cent of the people died of smallpox and 3,600 are now alive. What was the population of that country?'[30] Through cases like these and others, the middle classes did to a certain extent legitimize the colonial interventions associated with smallpox.[31]

One can refer to some details here to illustrate the magnitude of the vaccination drive in the early twentieth century (see Table 2).[32] This increase was not uncomplicated since we are told about the unpopularity of vaccination fees 'amongst all classes but especially among the poor' in north Orissa.[33] Although not grasped by the colonial officials, these sentiments seem to have been incorporated into

TABLE 2 ***Vaccinations in the Early Twentieth Century***

Years	*No. of vaccinations*	*No. of re-vaccinations*
1906–07	165,967	43,498
1912–13	387,190	215,438
1917–18	526,410	330,938
1936–37	603, 006	—
1939–40	706,275	—

the anti-imperialist struggle, if one goes by the decline in the number of people vaccinated in 1921 and 1929, years that converged with the mass Non-Cooperation movement (1920–22) and Civil Disobedience movement (1929–34) in Orissa.[34]

However, in the princely states the vaccination programme made rapid strides[35] and its 'remarkable progress [was] under the supervision of the Political Agent'.[36] Besides marking the triumph of colonial power/knowledge as a 'saviour' (as in the case of the Kandhas discussed earlier), the 'success' of the vaccination drive was also a result of the terror and coercion that frequently accompanied it. Here one has to bear in mind that the vaccination drive coexisted with authoritarian practices and arbitrary taxes.[37]

The picture will not be complete unless we refer to the contestations as well. Vaccination was much more than the substitution of one regulatory technology by another, especially since variolation was associated with a religious act along with prevention, while vaccination was seen as a secular act that had an alien origin. The latter's association with colonial state power reinforced this difference in perception.[38] However, one has to keep in mind the complications arising from defective lymph supplies, which created the space for opposition.

The restrictions on inoculation was viewed in some quarters as an insult to Sitala.[39] The restrictions imposed by the colonial administration were violated as the inoculation process shifted from being a public affair to a private one. One sees the virtual emergence of a subversive cult which aimed to continue with the indigenous system of inoculation. *Puja*s (religious ceremonies) with drums and cornets were no longer performed openly. Secret or hidden parts of the body came to be selected, and the inoculation spot chosen changed from the forehead (viz. between the eyes) to the upper arm, knee or back of the hand. Another method of subversion was to reject government vaccinators on grounds of caste,[40] which do not appear convincing since we have already seen that Mastan brahmanas (who were cultivators and hence considered 'low' brahmanas) and Panas (outcastes) were inoculators in the coastal tract and the princely states, respectively.

Conclusion

This essay has explored the processes of and the complexities generated by the interactions between colonialism, the *adivasi*s and the non-tribal population, and the bearing they had on smallpox.

During the 1942 Quit India movement, vaccinators were 'attacked' in parts of coastal Orissa.[41] Were they seen merely as symbols of the colonial state during this powerful, anti-colonial mass struggle? In the light of the preceding discussion, these should be seen as responses to deeper problems posed by the colonial vaccination policy. Instead of posing them as binaries, the major meeting points between inoculation and vaccination, especially in the nineteenth century, should be emphasized. This situation was altered over the twentieth century, with the development of better preservation techniques.

Health issues can become part of discriminatory practices directed at women, who are located as the 'other'. The way smallpox was identified with witches and led to the torture and murder of two women indicates this, in the context of tribal society. That the non-tribal Oriya (Hindu) society located the male child as hierarchically superior is evidenced in the way higher inoculation fees were paid for boys. This perhaps illustrates how patriarchy subsumes social differences and targets women, irrespective of whether they are tribals or non-tribals.

The severity of smallpox created possibilities for transgression of the caste system. Mastan brahmanas ('low' brahmanas) and even Panas (outcastes) were accommodated as *tikadar*s (inoculators), given their specialized skills.[42] This makes it difficult to accept resistance to vaccination on grounds of caste. In fact, the problems and insecurities were related to the working of the vaccination policy, which entailed—outside the urban environment—defective lymph supplies and the problem of contracting smallpox despite the painful process of vaccination.

There is a remarkable continuity with some of these issues today. Is Dharma Pinnu really dead? On the contrary. And, even if it is assumed that she is no more, the post-colonial situation remains strikingly similar when it comes to questions centred around health and the indigenous people. After all, goddesses are invented even today. The dependence on Dharani Khunti—invented in the mid-1980s to cope with and counter meningitis—and locally available roots and potions at Maksapadar (Kalahandi)[43] supports such an assertion. These not only echo the period studied but also demonstrate how the teeming millions in present-day India are virtually out of the framework of civil society and its agendas related to health.

This is the revised version of a paper presented at the 73rd Annual Meeting of The American Association for the History of Medicine at Bethesda, 18–21 May 2000, and subsequently published in the *Canadian Bulletin of Medical History*, Vol. 19, No. 2, 2002. I would like to thank the British Academy for a visiting fellowship in 1998, which made it possible for me to collect materials from various libraries and institutions in England. Dr Sanjoy Bhattacharya, Dr Mark Harrison and Professor Michael Worboys extended every possible help at the Department of Cultural Studies, Sheffield Hallam University, to which I was attached during the tenure of this fellowship.

Notes and References

1 We can refer here to David Arnold (ed.), *Imperial Medicine and Indigenous Societies*, Oxford University Press, Delhi, 1989, and *Colonizing the Body: State Medicine and Epidemic Disease in Nineteenth Century India*, University of California Press, Berkeley, 1993; Poonam Bala, *Imperialism and Medicine in Bengal: A Socio-Historical Perspective*, Sage, Delhi, 1991; Mark Harrison, *Public Health in British India: Anglo–Indian Preventive Medicine 1859–1914*, Foundation Books, Delhi, 1994; and Biswamoy Pati and Mark Harrison (eds), *Health, Medicine and Empire: Perspectives on Colonial India*, Orient Longman, Hyderabad, 2001.

2 Arnold correctly speaks of a method that should not compartmentalize the western and the Indian systems but accept interactions (*Colonizing the Body*, p. 291). However, as we shall see, this itself simplifies things since his method does not seem to recognize complexities and pluralities in the context of the indigenous communities. The method of K.N. Panikkar ('Indigenous Medicine and Cultural Hegemony', in *Culture, Ideology, Hegemony: Intellectuals and Social Consciousness in Colonial India*, Tulika, Delhi, 1995, pp. 145–75), recognizes this dimension. Note: non-tribal = the Oriya/Hindu people, who formed a part of the caste system.

3 In fact, even today the western portion of Orissa contains a large tribal population. For example, according to the *District Statistical Handbook of Koraput, 1972–73* (Orissa Government Press, Cuttack, n.d., p. 29), tribals constitute 56.34 per cent of the population of Koraput district. For details related to Orissa's colonization, the agrarian interventions and the allied changes, see, Sanjib Rout, 'Rural Stratification in Coastal Orissa, 1866–1900', *Social Science Probings*, 3, 1, 1986, pp. 136–50; Pradipta Chaudhury, 'Peasants and British Rule in Orissa', *Social Scientist*, 19, 7, 1991, pp. 28–56; Biswamoy Pati, *Resisting Domination: Peasants, Tribals and the National Movement in Orissa, 1920–50*, Manohar, Delhi, 1993, Ch. 1; and Shakti Prasad Padhi, *Land Relations and Agrarian Development in India: A Comparative Historical Study of Regional Variations*, Centre for Development Studies, Thiruvananthapuram, 1999, especially for the variations between the coastal and the western tracts.

4 This has remarkable continuities even among present-day scholars. P.K. Nayak and Anil Mahajan (eds), *Human Encounter with Drought*, Reliance Publishing House, Delhi, 1991, p. 119, for example, refer to the villagers in

the Kalahandi region being 'totally in darkness in regard to modern concepts of health and disease.'

[5] Very few scholars seem to view things holistically—disease, colonial wars on the *adivasis* and the shifts and changes that these reinforced. One can refer to exceptions here like Sumit Guha, 'Forest Politics and Agrarian Empires: The Khandesh Bhills, *c.* 1700–1850', *Indian Economic and Social History Review*, 33, 2, 1996, pp. 345–59; and David Arnold, 'Disease, Resistance and India's Ecological Frontier, 1770–1947', in Biswamoy Pati (ed.), *Issues in Modern Indian History: For Sumit Sarkar*, Popular Prakashan, Bombay, 2000, pp. 1–22.

[6] S.C. MacPherson, *Report Upon The Khonds Of The Districts Of Ganjam and Cuttack*, Military Orphan Press, Calcutta, 1842, p. 69.

[7] European MSS D/1112, extract from Dispatch, dated 19 February 1837 . . . from Henry Ricketts, Commissioner Cuttack, to the Government of India, India Office Library, London (hereafter IOL). One might add here that the *meriah* sacrifice was also supposed to ensure good crops and prevent accidents.

[8] Home Dep. (Public Branch) Nos. 60–61 (A), 24 January 1861, National Archives of India, Delhi, (hereafter NAI). Note: *moothas* = administrative units.

[9] Dharma Pinnu should not be in any way mistaken for Laxmi—the Hindu goddess of prosperity. The difference in spelling between Pennoo (in the case of Joogah Pennoo) and Pinnu is because I have retained the way they are referred to in the sources.

[10] N.A. Watts, *The Half Clad Tribes of Eastern India*, Orient Longman, Bombay, 1970, p. 65.

[11] Uma Guha, M.K.A Siddiqui and P.R.G. Mathur, *The Didayi: A Forgotten Tribe of Orissa*, Anthropological Survey of India, Delhi, 1968, p. 186.

[12] Nrusinha Charan Behuria, *Final Report on the Major Settlement Operations in Koraput District, 1938–64*, Orissa Government Press, Cuttack, n.d., p. 30.

[13] David Hardiman, *The Coming of the Devi: Adivasi Assertion in Western India*, Oxford University Press, Delhi, 1987, pp. 25–26.

[14] Kunja Bihari Das and L.K. Mahapatra, *Folklore of Orissa*, National Book Trust, Delhi, 1979, p. 100; the reference here is to chickenpox, cholera, measles and the plague epidemic.

[15] C.L. Philips, 'Confidential History of Gangpur State' (upto 1927), Crown Representative Papers, R/2 306/121, undated, IOL, London; Indrabilas Mukherji, *Final Report on the Land Revenue Settlement of the Gangpur State 1929–1936*, Berhampur, 1938, p. 5, contains a brief reference to this incident.

[16] Arnold, *Colonizing the Body*, pp. 120, 126. Whereas inoculation, as we will see, operated with the method of callus collection and a process that required special skill, and was a caste profession in colonial Orissa, vaccination was associated with the colonial health establishment and a technological process which prepared the vaccine using animal lymph. For

a detailed analysis based on archival materials seen on the subject of smallpox and its eradication in India, we have to wait for the monograph of Dr Sanjoy Bhattacharya, arising out of a Wellcome-funded project.

17 Sanjoy Bhattacharya, 'Re-devising Jennerian Vaccines?: European Technologies, Indian Innovation and the Control of Smallpox in South Asia, 1850–1950', *Social Scientist*, 28, 306–307, 1998, pp. 27–66. Arnold, *Colonizing the Body*, p. 156, also mentions the lack of preservation techniques which meant low level of immunity for those who were vaccinated, and the problems of creating a reliable vaccinating agency. As suggested, these problems were similar to Europe's own experience.

18 Based on Ganjam District Records, Orissa State Archives, Bhubaneshwar, Accession Nos 1292G and 1953G.

19 For details, see for example, Biswamoy Pati, 'Environment and Social History: Kalahandi, 1800–1950', *Environment and History*, 5, 3, 1999, pp. 345–59.

20 The lack of any evidence, based on the sources I have seen, inhibits me from making any serious formulation here.

21 This is based on the Report of Major J.T. Calvert (undated), IMS Civil Surgeon, Cuttack, cited in L.S.S. O'Malley, *Bihar and Orissa District Gazetteers: Cuttack*, Superintendent of Government Printing, Patna, 1933, pp. 69–71. That the inoculators were either 'low' brahmanas or outcastes reveals a dependence that is particularly striking, given the hold of the brahmanical order and the caste system.

22 This is based on the Report of J. Short (1855), Assistant Surgeon, cited in L.S.S. O'Malley, *Bihar and Orissa District Gazetteers: Sambalpur*, Superintendent of Government Printing, Patna, 1932, p. 109.

23 O'Malley, *District Gazetteers, Cuttack*, p. 70; this was 2 *annas* for girls and 4 *annas* for boys.

24 F.A. Marglin, 'Smallpox in Two Systems of Knowledge', in F.A. Marglin and S.A. Marglin (eds), *Dominating Knowledge: Development, Culture and Resistance*, Clarendon Press, Oxford, 1990, pp. 135–36. *Rathajatra* is the annual festival at Puri—Orissa's famous temple town—associated with Jagannatha, Balabhadra and Subhadra.

25 Arnold, *Colonizing the Body*, pp. 121, 124.

26 Home Dept (Public Branch), Nos 60–61 (A) 24 January 1861, NAI. Arnold, *Colonizing the Body*, p. 121, while discussing the hurdles met by the vaccination policy, also mentions, among other things, the reluctance of the colonial state to shoulder the financial burden of mass vaccination.

27 Home Dept (Sanitary Branch), Nos 7–10, November 1881, and Home Dept (Medical Branch), Nos 68–71 Part (A) January 1880—'Report on Vaccination—Bengal 1878–79', NAI. Singhbhoom was a princely state.

28 John Shortt, *A Popular Treatise on Vaccination in Oriya*, Orissa Mission Press, Cuttack, 1867, p. 39.

29 Home Dept (Sanitary Branch), Nos 7–10, November 1881, NAI.

30 Radhanath Ray, *Ardhaprasnabali, Part 1*, Balasore, 1878; Vernacular Tracts, IOL, p. 19; translation mine.

[31] Thus Arnold, *Colonizing the Body*, p. 157, suggests that by the 1880s the Indian middle classes began to support the vaccination policy.

[32] Based on S.N. Tiwari, *Annual Statistical Returns and Short Notes on Vaccination in Bihar and Orissa for the Year 1918–19*, Superintendent of Government Printing, Patna, 1919, p. 3; G. Verghese, *Annual Public Health Report of the Province of Orissa for the Year 1936 and the Vaccination Report for the Year 1936–37*, Orissa Government Press, Cuttack, 1938, p. 19; G. Verghese, *Annual Public Health Report of the Province of Orissa for the Year 1939 and the Annual Vaccination Report for the Year 1939–40*, Orissa Government Press, Cuttack, 1941, p. 33.

[33] Verghese, *Annual Public Health Report*, p. 36.

[34] W.C. Ross, *Annual Sanitary Report of the Province of Bihar and Orissa for the Year 1921*, Superintendent of Government Printing, Patna, 1922, p. 3; and J.A.S. Phillips, *Annual Public Health Report of the Province of Bihar and Orissa for the Year 1928 and the Annual Vaccination Report for the Year 1928–29*, Superintendent of Government Printing, Patna, 1923, do refer to the decline in the number of people vaccinated. Needless to say, 1929–31 were years of acute economic pressures, with the colonial economy reeling under the throes of the 'Great Depression'.

[35] L.E.B. Cobden Ramsay, *Bengal Gazetteers: Feudatory States of Orissa*, Calcutta, 1910, reprint, Firma K.L.M., Calcutta, 1982, p. 70.

[36] W.C. Ross, *Annual Sanitary Report 1916*, Superintendent of Government Printing, Patna, 1917, p. 32.

[37] This was true for most of the princely states and some of the *zamindaris*.

[38] Arnold, *Colonizing the Body*, p. 120.

[39] In fact, Marglin, in 'Smallpox in Two Systems', p. 139, echoes this sentiment. Hardiman, *The Coming of the Devi*, pp. 24, 52–54, refers to the feeling among the village folk of Gujarat that government methods of restricting her progress would enrage Sitala. This got polarized with the goddess spreading the message of the 'Mahatma', getting associated with social reform and emerging as a vehicle of protest against the Parsi exploiters by 1921–22. However, this trend was not visible in Orissa.

[40] Home Dept (Medical Branch), Nos 68–71 Part (A), January 1880, NAI, Interestingly, the reference is to people asking for a brahmana vaccinator, but refusing his services after he joined.

[41] See Pati, *Resisting Domination*, p. 64, for details.

[42] Although it is outside the scope of this essay, the magnitude of the problem during a smallpox outbreak in colonial, nineteenth-century Orissa can be, perhaps, compared to AIDS in the present-day context.

[43] Biswajit Das and Biswamoy Pati, 'The Eternal Famine: Poverty, Food Scarcity and Survival in Kalahandi (Orissa)', Occasional Paper No. XC, Centre for Contemporary Studies, Delhi, 1994, pp. 47–48.

A Note on Jobbers and Jobbery

Partho Datta

I

The jobber or the *sardar* and the *sardari* mode of recruitment is one of the most fascinating and intriguing aspects of the history of early Indian industrialization. Traditionally seen as a more articulate member of the working class and its natural leader, the jobber, it is argued, played the pivotal role of bridging the gaps between workers and mill owners, on the one hand, and among workers, on the other. The jobber and the prevalence of jobbery was certainly a ubiquitous feature of Indian factories in the past (and some would argue, also in the present), and many government reports, contemporary studies and historical monographs testify to this.[1] Traditional labour histories, though wide-ranging in scope (but perhaps not in depth), from Karnik to Revri, Sen and Saha,[2] have little to say about or often gloss over the role of the jobber. Perhaps this was a function of the kind of history they were writing, which was often elitist, focusing only on well-known and well-publicized strikes. The other reason for this bias could be that the writers often used as sources, documents and books written by trade unionists themselves, who, being active participants and enthusiastic organizers of that vague collectivity called 'the worker', perhaps overlooked internal contradictions. However, recently, the jobber has attracted renewed attention. Historians are claiming that the social history of the working class will be incomplete if the role of the jobber is not evaluated. Dipesh Chakrabarty has made the jobber a point of entry into the study of working-class culture.[3] In this short note I propose to re-evaluate the existing views on jobbers and jobbery by focusing on some evidence from Bengal, specifically for the period 1918–24 which saw a spate of strikes in the greater Calcutta region just after the First World War.[4]

II

The *sardar* (literally, headman) was the chief recruiter for the mill managers and was primarily responsible for the supervision of labour inside the factory. As the *Report of the Royal Commission on Labour* (hereafter *RCL*) put it:

> one of the most remarkable [elements] . . . of Indian factory organization [the jobber] . . . usually combines in one person a formidable series of functions. He is primarily a chargeman. Promoted from the ranks after full experience of the factory, he is responsible for the supervision of labour while at work. . . . Many jobbers follow the worker even further than the factory gate.[5]

Outside the factory the *sardar*, whose social origins were similar to that of ordinary workers, often controlled access to housing, food and credit.[6] Dipesh Chakrabarty has shown that *sardars* dominated the caste *panchayats* of up-country Hindus and were important patrons of *ulemas* in the mill areas. In other words, they were leaders of the local community. Mosques named after *sardars* still existing in the jute mill areas of Bengal testify to their influence.[7] It may even have been 'an example of a pre-colonial, pre-capitalist institution being made an essential feature of the process of industrialization in a colony'.[8] Ranajit Dasgupta has also shown how jobbery was a traditional form of bondage for Indian labour, to which the colonial employers acquiesced in their quest for cheap labour supply to the local mines, tea plantations and jute mills. In stressing the point Dasgupta has exploded the myth of 'free' labour in an 'open' labour market structure.[9] *Sardari* was certainly an important institution in the early years of industry in India, when labour supply was erratic and *sardars* had to be sent to villages to recruit people. The *RCL* has observed that this led to a situation in which, 'in some areas recruiting was confined to a few villages where connections had been established, adjacent villages making no contributions'.[10] In later years, mill managers retained the system of *sardari* because it was a cheap method of maintaining supervision over and communication with workers.[11]

The *sardar* was therefore an important and influential figure both inside and outside the factory. The worker recognized this in his payment to the *sardar* of *dastoory* (variously translated as fee, 'cut' or petty bribe).[12] His position had distinct social advantages too. In some fascinating evidence of sanskritization, R.N. Gilchrist, the labour intelligence officer for Bengal in the 1920s, noted that jobbers would 'change their names from their artisan appellation to a name signifying a high caste'.[13] I want to end this section with a quotation from the evidence that the Bengal government gave to the touring *RCL*, which sums up the prevailing views on the jobber:

> The immediate employer of a worker is his sirdar. The sirdar gives him his job and it is by his will that the worker retains it. . . . The sirdars are the real masters of men. They employ them and dismiss them, and in many cases they house them and unhouse them. They may own or control the shops which supply men with food. The operative, too, pays his lump or recurring sum to the sirdar to retain his job. His life, indeed at every turn, is coloured by sirdarism.[14]

III

Let us now look at the *sardar* in the light of evidence from 1920s' Bengal. The strikes in this period coincided with the Khilafat Non-Cooperation movement which added to working-class volatility. Since these accounts are based on conventional sources like government reports and newspapers, the narrative is rather patchy.

Both the nationalists and the British authorities understood well the advantage of having community leaders and *sardar*s on their side. It is therefore not surprising that both used this leadership for policing functions. In December 1919, for instance, just after the war, the nationalists decided to boycott the peace celebrations organized by the colonial government in Calcutta city. To make it effective, the nationalists enlisted the *sardar*s of local jute mills and *maulvi*s to keep the workers away.[15] Similarly, on 24 December 1921, the day the Prince of Wales was to arrive in Calcutta, the government thought it prudent to enrol *sardar*s and foremen as civil guards in the mill areas of Twenty-four Parganas to prevent, as a government report put it, 'an excited mob from flowing into Calcutta, when the Prince . . . arrived'.[16] This proved to be a case of the authorities learning tactics from the nationalists.

Let us look at some more examples. As the Non-Cooperation movement gathered momentum, a variety of ways was used to force the colonial government's hand. Boycott became popular amongst workers, especially commercial boycott against shopkeepers who refused to close shop on *hartal* days.[17] Arbitration courts, ignoring the government machinery, were set up and panchayats sprang up in their place. This is confirmed by a confidential government report which noted that 'it was not uncommon for sirdars or foremen to set themselves up as courts and enforce their decisions by intimidation'.[18] The prevailing atmosphere of strikes and the enthusiastic participation of the working class of Calcutta city in the struggle against British rule found expression in the Bengal Labour Conference organized in 1921. This initiative may partly have been the direct result of a decision by the Congress to support the All India Trade Union Congress (1920). It is interesting that the preliminary meeting in preparation of the main conference, which was to be held on 17 April 1921, had among its participants not only prominent leaders and trade unionists like J.N. Roy, C.R. Das, N.C. Sen, S.N. Haldar, K. Chaudhury, Erfan Ali and Mohammad Daud, but also mill *sardars* and secretaries of many labour unions (who were often workers).[19] On the day of the conference, which was held in the hall of the Indian Association, worker participation was widespread. It will perhaps not be out of place to hazard a guess that part of the mobilization was done by *sardars*. Although, for the period under discussion, there is no direct evidence of *sardars* leading strikes, they must surely have been active. This is illustrated indirectly, for example, by a strike in a jute mill in Champdany, where the workers refused to work unless their *sardar* who had been arrested was released. Fearing trouble, the authorities had to release him on bail.[20]

IV

The general picture of the jobber that has emerged from the preceding section, as the natural leader of the working class, fits in well with the evidence on jobbers that can be gleaned from official documents. The jobber as a figure of power and authority is also substantiated. R.K. Newman and Dipesh Chakrabarty, modern scholars who have written most eloquently about the jobber, seem more or less to concur with this view.[21] R.N. Gilchrist, the labour intelligence officer for Bengal, has written of the 1920s that 'the recorded strikes of Bengal show only one instance of a strike caused by a demand for dismissal of a *sardar* because of exactions'.[22] Closer reading of the evidence, however, reveals a different picture. Gilchrist's is probably a good case of recording what he uncritically believed.

Let us look at the period from which we have been citing examples so far. In January 1919, the *Amrita Bazar Patrika* correspondent reported a strike by the weavers at the old Champdany Jute Mill. It was reported that the workers wanted Mia Jan, the *sardar*, dismissed, because he 'was not well disposed towards them'.[23] This was not an isolated incident. In the Wellington Jute Mills, workers on strike wanted Sardar Bhagloo dismissed. It was reported that the workers 'held a private meeting (panchayat) in which it was decided to socially boycott Bhagloo'.[24] In another instance intimidation was used to enforce the boycott, as the case of Safiat Sardar shows. Safiat Sardar had dismissed his brother-in-law and for this offence he was called before a workers' *panchayat* which ordered him to pay a sum of Rs 125 as fine, and carry the shoes of the *panchayat* members on his head. When he refused to do this, in a collective act of retribution, the workers looted his shop.[25]

Here are some more examples from the period when the Non-Cooperation movement was at its height. Workers were recruited for picketing duty and it seems they were enthusiastic volunteers. Initially, the mill managers were wary of re-employing such workers, till sympathetic strikes by workers in the mills forced their hand.[26] The nationalist movement and the resultant mobilization among workers was not just irksome for the white mill managers who had to perforce admit workers who had abandoned work for picketing duty, but was also eroding the authority of the *sardar* whose job was to keep the workers in control. Take the case of what happened in the Northbrook Jute Mills, Champdany. When 500 worker volunteers who were out on picketing duty returned to work, the mill authorities thought it prudent to admit them. This time, it was their *sardar* who was against their reinstatement. When word of this got around, *all* the workers of the mill walked out, demanding the dismissal of the *sardar*.[27]

One last example from the jute mills. The cause of the Gandhi-inspired anti-drink movement was being zealously espoused and had caught the imagination of the nationalistic Hindu *bhadralok*, whose spokesman, the *Amrita Bazar Patrika*, noted patronizingly that 'through the kind intervention of the public-spirited *moulvis* the labourers have been made to understand what moral degradation and miserable poverty they have been driven to and this at once opened their eyes and they took the solemn oath not to touch the poison again.'[28] How did this affect *sardari* authority in the mills? In Howrah,

10,000 workers of three jute mills stopped work because of a *sardar* named Dhonai. As the newspaper report put it, 'the majority of the mill hands advocated the cause of anti-drink movement', but Dhonai and his men were against it. The workers demanded his dismissal.[29]

V

What are we to make of this evidence? It now seems possible to modify the prevailing view of the jobber. And it certainly does not warrant the view of the government of Bengal that *sardars* were 'the true masters of men' or that the life of workers was 'coloured' at every turn by '*sardar*ism'.

First of all, the evidence from the strikes against *sardars* points to their shrinking and limited hold over the workers. It is also clear that the violence that was directed against the *sardar* by the workers was not indiscriminate. Certainly, the experience of participation in strikes and the nationalist upheaval threw up new possibilities of mobilization to the workers. It seems likely that in cases of working-class protest either the jobber had to restrain the workers to his own detriment or go along with them and lead the strike.[30]

Secondly, the dependence of the mill managers on the *sardar* is also exaggerated. Janet Harvey Kelman has written:

> the Calcutta sirdar has probably more influence than is usually wielded elsewhere, because in so many cases the managers and assistant managers under whom he works are European. Even if they have acquired a certain knowledge of Bengali and Hindustani, there are still four or five other languages which it would be necessary for them to know in order to talk freely with all their workers.

Continuing more generally, Kelman has written that 'it is not difficult to realize the kind of pressure that is brought to bear on the manager to increase output and to reduce expenditure. In his effort to secure these ends he is confronted with the sirdar or jobber.' Such was the hold of the *sardar* that, 'if the employer or the manager went to his mill gates, or to the coolie bazaar, and asked for workers, he would be received with laughter.'[31] This view of the jobber certainly invites scepticism. Even if the jobber was indispensable to the manager, it is a well-documented fact that overall management decisions like hours of work, pay, leave and general discipline were still the prerogative of the mill manager.

This brings us to the question as to why the *sardar* is so prominent in official reports and files. Can it be argued that *sardari* power is a construction available in the documents of the ruling class? Statements made by the Bengal government and by contemporary observers like Kelman (quoted above) should be carefully weighed against the conditions of work, where the authorities were not willing to grant even minimum facilities, like housing, pension, provident fund or sickness insurance, to the workers. In such a situation, the *sardar* became a convenient scapegoat. *Sardari* authority was increasingly depicted in official documents and files as a deterrent and obstacle to official welfare measures. By buttressing the myth of *sardari* power, the authorities could plead helplessness. Lack of interest in worker welfare and inertia were thus conveniently hidden behind the thin veneer of *sardari* authority. We have already mentioned that for mill managers and factory inspectors, the *sardar* was often the only source of information and knowledge, since they never bothered to learn the local language. There was thus an automatic magnification of the importance of the *sardar* in official reports. The possibility of the *sardar* himself boasting about his control of labour can also not be discounted.

It is now possible to see the *sardar* and *sardari* authority in a new light. While a case for *sardari* leadership in mill areas cannot be ruled out, it seems that the informal leadership that the *sardar* exercised was limited and was threatened the moment the workers decided to act themselves.

This essay was originally published in the *Proceedings of the Indian History Congress*, 52nd Session, New Delhi, 1991–92. I remember with gratitude the generous help and encouragement received from the late Professor Partha Sarathi Gupta when I was researching this essay. He was also kind enough to let me consult the calendar of files that he had prepared for his own research on labour in Bengal.

Notes and References

1 *Indian Industrial Commission*, Government of India, Calcutta, 1918; *Report of the Royal Commission on Labour (RCL)*, Government of India, Calcutta, 1931; Janet Harvey Kelman, *Labour in India, A Study of the Conditions of Indian Women in Modern Industry*, George Allen & Unwin, London, 1923; G.M. Broughton, *Labour in Indian Industries*, Oxford University Press, Bombay, 1924; Morris D. Morris, *The Emergence of an Industrial Labour Force in India*, Oxford University Press, Bombay, 1965; Chitra Joshi, 'Kanpur Textile Labour, Some Structural Features of Formative Years', *Economic and Political Weekly*, 17, Special Number, November 1981;

Eamon Murphy, *Unions in Conflict: A Comparative Study of Four South Indian Textile Centres, 1918–39,* Manohar, Delhi, 1981; C.P. Simmons, 'Recruiting and Organizing an Industrial Labour Force in Colonial India: The Case of the Coal Mining Industry *c.* 1880–1939', *Indian Economic and Social History Review,* Vol. 13, No. 4, 1976.

[2] V.B. Karnik, *Strikes in India,* Manaktalas, Bombay, 1967; C. Revri, *The Indian Trade Union Movement,* Orient Longman, Delhi, 1972; Sukomal Sen, *Working Class of India,* K.P. Bagchi, Calcutta, 1977; P. Saha, *History of the Working Class Movement in Bengal,* People's Publishing House, Delhi, 1978.

[3] Dipesh Chakrabarty, 'Conditions for the Knowledge of Working Class Conditions: Employers, Government and Jute Workers of Calcutta, 1890–1940', in Ranajit Guha (ed.), *Subaltern Studies,* Vol. II, Oxford University Press, Delhi, 1983.

[4] For details, see Partho Datta, 'Strikes in the Greater Calcutta Region, 1918–1924', *Indian Economic and Social History Review,* Vol. 30, No. 1, January–March 1993.

[5] *Report of RCL,* p. 23.

[6] Dipesh Chakrabarty, 'Communal Riots and Labour: Bengal's Jute Mill-Hands in the 1890s', *Past and Present,* No. 91, May 1981, pp. 151–52.

[7] Ibid.

[8] Ibid.

[9] Ranajit Dasgupta, 'Structure of the Labour Market in Colonial India', *Economic and Political Weekly,* Vol. 17, Special Number, November 1981.

[10] *Report of RCL,* p. 22.

[11] Kelman, *Labour in India,* p. 104.

[12] Ibid., p. 107.

[13] R.N. Gilchrist, *Payment of Wages and Profit Sharing, With a Chapter on Indian Conditions,* Government of India, Calcutta, 1924, p. 247.

[14] *RCL,* Vol. V, t 1, p. 153.

[15] Kenneth McPherson, *The Muslim Microcosm: Calcutta 1918 to 1935,* Steiner, Wiesbaden, 1974, p. 58.

[16] Government of Bengal, Pol. [Conf.], 395[1–3]/1924, West Bengal State Archives.

[17] Ibid.

[18] Ibid.

[19] *Amrita Bazar Patrika,* 16 April 1921.

[20] *Amrita Bazar Patrika,* 20 May 1920.

[21] R.K. Newman, 'Social Factors in the Recruitment of the Bombay Millhands', in *Economy and Society,* edited by R. Dewey and K.N. Chaudhuri, Oxford University Press, Delhi, 1979; and Dipesh Chakrabarty, 'Conditions for Knowledge', p. 293 and *passim.*

[22] Gilchrist, *Payment of Wages and Profit Sharing,* p. 328.

[23] *Amrita Bazar Patrika,* 13 January 1919.

[24] *Amrita Bazar Patrika,* 3 March 1921.

[25] *Amrita Bazar Patrika*, 27 March 1921.

[26] *Amrita Bazar Patrika*, 26 December 1921.

[27] *Amrita Bazar Patrika*, 3 January 1922.

[28] *Amrita Bazar Patrika*, 30 January 1921.

[29] *Amrita Bazar Patrika*, 5 April 1921.

[30] As argued by Dick Kooiman for Bombay mills in his 'Rural Labour in the Bombay Textile Industry and the Articulation of Modes of Organization', in Peter Robb (ed.), *Rural South Asia: Linkages, Change and Development*, Curzon Press, London, 1983, p. 147.

[31] Kelman, *Labour in India*, p. 104.

World War II and the Politics of Loyalty and Defiance in Bengal, 1939–42

Srimanjari

Initial Reactions to the War

In 1939, World War II presented an opportunity to many to profess their loyalty to the British. They expressed their eagerness to 'serve their king and country'. Some of the other planks on which loyalty or a pro-war stand was based were a demand for extension of recruitment and faith in the post-war plans of the British government. Contrary to this, aspects of defiance of support to the British in the war were based mainly on criticism of imperialism in India and the failure of the British government to announce favourable post-war plans for India. This essay explores, rather broadly, the different hues of loyalty and defiance at the time of the war in Bengal.

The war offered an occasion to many individuals and organizations to reject the importation of the 'non-martial' category, so often applied to Bengalis. However, in many quarters, the rejection was based not so much on the irrelevance of the concepts of martial and non-martial races. The impassioned plea for rejecting these was that the Bengalis had always been steadfast in their devotion to the call of duty and that they were loyal to the core. For instance, B.N. Ray Choudhury, a councillor and a representative of the Bengal Ex-Servicemen's Association, held the opinion that:

> If the Bengalee Regiment is revived and recognized, we may be assured of a big fresh response from the younger generation of Bengalis who are only too eager to serve their king and country . . . for the improvement of the morale of the Bengalee race a pure Bengali Regiment is a necessity.[1]

Speeches exhorting the Bengali youth 'to prove their mettle' indicate that it was not unknown that Bengalis did not figure in the list of fighting races, which included Sikhs, Rajputs, Garhwalis, Jats, Dogras, Marathas, etc.[2] However, what was more important to some, a view that perhaps percolated down from the authorities, was that the anti-war views could be dispelled by encouraging pro-war sentiments. Major D.N. Bhattacharjee, commanding officer of the Calcutta University Training Corps, was quite sure that though 'a group of people holding certain political views had a great sway over the minds of the student community in particular', students would 'respond to the call of their country and the Empire'.[3]

Pro-war proclamations by sections of the aristocracy and the titled were in a way assurances to the authorities that they had remained unaffected by political passion that was damaging to the British. It is not surprising that individuals like the nawab of Murshidabad, B.P. Singh Roy, a lawyer with extensive business interests, and Abdul Halim Ghuznavi, a landlord and merchant who was also president of the Muslim Chamber of Commerce (1939–40), threw in their lot with the British who had protected them for so long. Discrediting the era of mass politics, B.P. Singh Roy observed that 'the foundations of India's political freedom were not laid on the Indian soil—not in the *pandals* of political meetings and assemblies—but on the battlefield of France in 1914.'[4] As is obvious from this comment, the past was invoked not to condemn the colonial system but to show oneness with it. For this section of the Indian public, the nationalist movement was by and large an anathema. Abdul Halim Ghuznavi made somewhat similar observations when he objected to references to Bengalis as a non-martial race, and said: 'The Government overlooks the fact as to who defended Bengal and who fought on the side of Clive. Did the Punjabis come and fight on either side?'[5]

War and the Choice of Political Causes

The clamour for recruitment increased when expansion of the army became inevitable. New regular units were raised to procure wider provincial representation in the army. It is difficult to ascertain exactly the total number of Bengalis in the combatant and non-combatant forces, but the opening up of clerical and specialists' posts, with the expansion of the military branch of the Indian Medical Service (IMS) and the Indian Medical Department, created avenues for the educated unemployed in Bengal. From 1942, professional and specialized training to IMS doctors was imparted in Poona and at the School of Tropical Medicine in Calcutta. The Indian Electric and Mechanical Engineering Services (IEMS) was formed in May 1943 and this could have further opened avenues for engineering graduates.

There was another angle to the demand for militarization of the Bengali 'youth'. From the 1930s, both the Rashtriya Swayamsevak Sangh (RSS) and the Hindu Mahasabha penetrated new regions in India.[6] Their ideological trump-card, which was based on the logic of *Hindutva*—primarily to hinduize politics and to militarize Hindus—could now be shown boldly. While the tone was militarist and separatist in the all-India context, in Bengal, Syama Prasad Mukherjee adopted the strategy of projecting 'Bengali Hindus' as highly vulnerable people who had to be armed since their life and property were in danger. In a speech delivered at the Calcutta War Committee meeting in 1940, he said, 'today there exist genuine fears in the minds of a large section of Hindus of Bengal that the war situation may develop as to render their lives and properties specially unsafe.'[7]

There was a subtle hint here of what their propaganda would revolve around. It was going to be that the 'Hindus of Bengal' were in danger of some kind of a backlash from members of other communities, especially the Muslims. Events after the war proved how the fear psychosis encouraged during the war was exploited to further instil mistrust between the two communities. As of now, as the war drew closer and the issue of recruitment grew more contentious, Syama Prasad Mukherjee and Sir B.P. Singh Roy emerged as spokespersons of the 'Hindu *bhadralok*'. Subsequently, Governor John Herbert was warned in no uncertain terms that a civil war was in the offing if middle-class Hindu youth were not recruited.[8]

The war, it must be remembered, was an occasion for the fulfilment of different political purposes. Politics is after all based on a choice of causes. The choice of the cause that the Krishak Praja Party (KPP) espoused in the context of recruitment posed a greater threat to the manner in which the authorities wanted the war to be perceived. In 1940, Krishak Praja Party members were active among the Indian Seamen's Union, dissuading peasants and labourers from joining as *lascars*.[9] Their politics of defiance was in tune with their anti-war position. In north Sylhet, during the Krishak Conference on 28 February 1940, speeches were made to the effect that false hopes had been given to the *lascars* to induce them to join ships while the true particulars of the loss of ships had not been published. A resolution was passed at the meeting warning peasants and labourers to be cautious about accepting marine service.[10] An attempt, but of a different kind, was being made here to establish connections between rhetoric and reality.

The time was also opportune to demand a hike in wages by the Indian Seamen's Union, which enjoyed the protection of H.S. Suhrawardy, Minister of Commerce and Labour. The government, on its part, was not willing to dispense with the *lascar*s whose services were indispensable for the transportation of war materials on ships. Propaganda was thus undertaken with the help of official publications like the *Banglar Katha*, which reached the interiors of Sylhet, Noakhali and Chittagong, some of the places from where the *lascar*s were recruited. Officers of the National Welfare Units undertook similar work.[11] The authorities were of the opinion that propaganda in Bengali and by officers specially assigned for this job could be quite effective.

Scepticism about the expansion of the Indian army, however, remained intact. The secretary of state, Amery, even admonished Wavell, the commander-in-chief, against arming Indian soldiers with modern weapons.[12] The spectre of the 'mutiny' of 1857, it was believed, was a grim reminder of such 'mistakes'. In September 1943, the Home Department sent a telegram stating that three ex-soldiers had been convicted 'for conspiring to cause Mutiny'.[13] The fact that the accused were Bengalis whom the government did not want in Bengal confirmed the fear of recruitment from Bengal. It became easier for the authorities to denounce the abilities of recruits from this region towards the end of the war. For instance, it was observed that the 16th Bengali Battalion was inadequately officered, that the rank-and-file was drawn from the salaried classes and not from among cultivators, and that there was lack of enthusiasm for physical training. According to Col. Batty, chairman, GHQ Selection Board, psychological tests conducted on the soldiers showed that the 'main things lacking in Bengali character are initiative and aggressiveness'.[14] Suspicion about the *babu*s of Bengal, whether regarding their political inclinations or their supposed aversion to physical work, had persisted.

The time was also ripe for an ebb and flow of political passions. The results of the 1937 elections were such that all the three leading parties—the Congress, the Muslim League and the Krishak Praja Party—failed to secure an absolute majority. The ministry was a motley crowd of an independent Congress member (Nalini Ranjan Sarkar), caste Hindu members (B.P. Singh Roy, Sirish Chandra

Nandi), independent scheduled caste members (P. Deb Raikat, M.B. Mullick), KPP members (Fazlul Huq, Nausher Ali) and Muslim League members (B.M. Habibullah, H.S. Suhrawardy, Khwaja Nazimuddin).[15]

Organizational and factional politics and the stand of various political groups towards the war and the post-war programme caused considerable unsettlement in the province. The very nature of the coalitions was enough to provoke quibbling and charges and counter-charges. During the time of such uncertainties, the war augmented the political impasse and leadership crisis in regional politics. The role of individuals in mainstream politics cannot therefore be overlooked. And here it is necessary to mention that the war performed a dual role. It helped both in creating that extra bit of space in regional politics which helped some to temporarily acquire an edge over their 'national' counterparts, and in jeopardizing the prospects of some others.

It is interesting to note the effect the war had on the moves made by individuals and groups that either enabled them to move centrestage or forced them to bid a retreat from active politics. Fazlul Huq, the premier of Bengal, whose public image was as spokesperson of the '*projas* and *krishaks*' of Bengal, now couched his pro-war sentiments in a sectarian language. The metamorphosis was perhaps to get even with the political leadership of the Muslim League, which had constantly sidelined him. Changes were also at work in the Congress and the Hindu Mahasabha. While the Congress Working Committee banned participation in the war efforts, the Hindu Mahasabha instructed its members to join the war committees in their individual capacity. Nalini Ranjan Sarkar, who had joined the coalition government after the election of 1937, had to obey the Congress high command now. He abstained from voting on the war resolution and resigned from the cabinet. With the distancing of the All-India Congress and the Bose group, and the split in the Bengal Congress, individuals like him were marginalized.

The authorities also began to paint Subhas Chandra Bose's image in black. Government sources referred to a pact between him and the Hindu Mahasabha to field a common set of candidates for the Calcutta Corporation elections. There were allegations of a pact with the Muslim League as well.[16] However, the strategy of isolating Bose could not be carried out successfully. His rhetoric, particularly the emphatic declaration that, 'War or no war, we demand our freedom and we must have it', rejuvenated parties like the Madaripur Jugantar Party, Anushilan and the Bengal Volunteer Corps.[17]

Desperate to show that the increase in his popularity was inconsequential, some of the officials reported almost incongruously: 'His popularity and influence continue to decline except with college students, school boys and adults whose mental development had been arrested at a comparable stage.'[18] About the spread of nationalist ideas, it was felt that 'boys catch this contagion in boarding schools and so a teacher's responsibility extends to the student's extra-academic activities and parents also need to guard against the evil propensities of their sons'.[19] Warnings of this nature enabled the authorities to re-implement, with amendments, the Bengal government's (political) conduct rules.[20] Rules such as these gave the government the power to penalize government employees for the 'unlawful activities' and political inclinations of their close relatives.

Certain voices were loud and clear in their denouncement of the war. For instance, Syed Nausher Ali, a member of the KPP who had been ousted from the ministry for holding radical views on its functioning, described the war resolution as 'a big fraud on Bengal'.[21] According to Niharendu Dutta Mazumdar, a member of the Barrackpore Registered Factories, although World War II was ostensibly being fought for the defence of democracy, the basic aim behind it was extension of boundaries.[22] The Communists, whose intentions were suspect throughout the war, defied unequivocally, till 1941, the unjust measures that were implemented in the name of the war. Thus, along with supporters of the Forward Bloc, they were accused of 'inciting peasants and labourers'.[23]

Propaganda, Surveillance and a Growing Mood of Defiance

It is obvious that the officials found it difficult to come to terms with the growing mood of defiance that was apparent in many parts of eastern India. It is also not surprising that from the start of the war, the government was wary of any propaganda against it. Press censorship and proscription of leaflets and literary pieces became a routine matter. A leaflet called *Juddher Samaye Swadhinatar Jannye Juddha Koro* was proscribed because Fairweather, the commissioner of police, Calcutta, felt that it was written in an inflammatory language and sought to instigate workers and peasants against the 'rich man's war'.[24]

Since repressive policies were inadequate to deal with the

situation, attempts were made to formulate a propaganda strategy aimed particularly at the educated in the *mofussils* and in Calcutta. Through prominent newspapers like the *Amrita Bazar Patrika* and *Ananda Bazar Patrika*, people were virtually warned of what would follow if Britain lost the war. As the war drew closer to the borders of Bengal it was frequently mentioned that the 'enemy' watched them. The authorities also knew that the activities of the well-to-do and prominent citizens of Calcutta carried considerable weight with the middle class. The Calcutta War Committee that was founded to convey the government's position in the most favourable and positive manner was therefore a virtual who's who.[25] The authorities thus left no stone unturned to show how deplorable the anti-war stand was.

One of the most difficult things to do, however, was to control ideas inimical to its interests. At times censorship and proscription of literature were not resorted to, for fear that such actions would further the cause of a civil disobedience movement. This is evident from the treatment meted out to Amalendu Das Gupta's book, *Detenu*. The book was a record of the writer's experiences when he was interned in different jails. It contained conversations with the Chittagong Armoury Raid prisoners. Extracts from the book were published in Bengali journals like *Bharati* and *Mandira*, and this created quite a ripple in official circles. Apart from criticizing colonial rule, the book criticized the physical torture meted out to prisoners by Indian officials. For instance, at one stage the detenu in conversation with a sub-inspector of police says: 'when there does not arise in your mind the slightest hesitation or shrinking in oppressing the native people, and doing harm to them, such vile manliness in you appears intolerable to me. This is the reason why political officers, in spite of their being natives, are murdered now and then.'[26]

The debate that centred on the question of proscription of this book highlighted a very tricky issue, of whether the government was prepared to contradict these allegations. The public prosecutor, Rai Bahadur Prabodh Gopal Mukherjee, was of the opinion that the authorities could penalize the journals that carried the extracts of the book and the author only if they had sufficient evidence to counter the allegations. In the meantime, the demand for the release of the Chittagong Armoury Raid prisoners had increased in intensity. Ultimately, in 1940, the government decided not to take action against the book.

Proscription, it felt, would make both the writer and the book more popular.

There was definitely a change in public mood and behaviour, and the government was not going to take any chances. This was, to some extent, evident in the size of the mainstream political parties. Membership of the Congress increased from 49,040 primary members in 1936 to 464,167 primary members in 1939.[27] So-called terrorist groups like the Jugantar and Anushilan Samitis now preferred to join the mainstream political parties as the Forward Bloc, the Revolutionary Socialist Party and the Communist Party. Middle-class, educated Muslims were attracted to parliamentary politics in sizeable numbers. The calculated and cautious approach was also evident in the factional differences, for instance, within the Bengal Congress. The lukewarm response to the individual *satyagraha* campaign launched in 1941 was perhaps a casualty of such differences.

The political activists in this province realized the inefficacy of these *satyagrahas* when, at the time that they were conceived, efforts were made to confine them to members of the Congress. In reply to a question raised by Arun Chandra Guha, secretary of the Bengal Provincial Congress Committee (BPCC), whether non-Congress members could offer *satyagraha*, Gandhi had declined. He had replied that it could be offered by only those who had become 'four-*anna*' members of the organization and also fulfilled other conditions.[28] Militancy had to be kept at bay and violence had to be shunned. The organization was in no mood to encourage defiance on a large scale. What was not fathomed was that these determinants were in reality superfluous. Unlike in the United Provinces, in Bengal the movement failed to evoke a positive response. In official circles the movement came to be perceived as being 'still-born'. The district magistrate of Burdwan observed that the *satyagrahis* were 'becoming impatient with the restriction on their activities imposed by Mr Gandhi and there was every possibility of their attempting "a more active programme"'.[29]

The success of the *satyagrahas* was based on the patience and endurance of individuals. These qualities were hard to sustain in the face of severe state repression. Since the local conditions were shaped by scarcity, price rise and autocratic measures, acts of daring and aggression alone could make an impact. The success of many political parties thus depended on whether they could influence the public by launching a programme of action on these issues. There were two diametrically opposed reasons for some of these groups keeping aloof during the individual *satyagrahas*. Members of the BPCC were not enthusiastic because the movement had not actually threatened the state. On the other hand, fledgling groups like the Jugantar Party were reluctant to jeopardize their position in the BPCC 'by risking the arrest of too many important leaders'.[30]

Yet, what could not be gauged easily was that the mood was vengeful. While the *satyagrahis* remained more or less peaceful, their filial, caste and regional ties to villagers resulted in 'politicization' of sorts. In Twenty-four Parganas, for instance, when a police party arrested an agitator/*satyagrahi* for making an anti-war speech, a group of about 500 cultivators seem to have attacked the police in a bid to rescue him. But, by and large, issues concerning the people were at variance with the moderate stand adopted by the Congress at this stage. Communal disturbances in Dacca ultimately sealed the fate of such efforts.

Role of the Communists in Protests and Strikes

It was feared that the Communists would utilize the tensions between zamindars and peasants regarding rent dues, to stabilize their own position in the rural areas. Burdwan was in the forefront of such developments. Nazimuddin remarked in this context: 'Side by side with action against the Communists, Government must redress the legitimate grievances of the tenants. . . . If necessary the zamindars should be prosecuted. This will have a good effect on the tenants.'[31] The government was very apprehensive about the consequences of the tour that some of the Communist leaders, like Muzaffar Ahmad and Somnath Lahiri, had undertaken, after being externed from Calcutta. These leaders had also apparently sought cooperation from Anushilan activists like Narendra Das and Rabindra Sen Gupta.[32] However, precisely at the time of their increased participation in local affairs, their relations with the Congress soured or became tenuous. As per the instructions of the Communist Party of India (CPI) at the time of the individual *satyagraha* campaigns, only the 'less important members of the CPI' were to sign the *satyagraha* pledge and the leading members were to remain free for party work.[33] Notwithstanding such differences, even official sources were forced to acknowledge that the party was confident of weaning away the police, military and other units of the administration.

Protests and strikes against wage cuts and retrenchment of workers were the main planks on which some of the trade unions mobilized workers for their anti-war agitations. There was a general uneasiness among the working class. The disparity in the price–wage index had increased the economic vulnerability of labour. Since the 1870s, while foodgrain prices had risen by 38.5 per cent, the wages of unskilled labour had increased by only 15 per cent and of skilled labour by 25.4 per cent.[34] The majority of the workers worked under the increased strain of war production, diminished leisure-time and lessened contact with their families at a time when trade union activities were being repressed.

Jute mills were exempted by the government of Bengal from the provisions of certain sections of the Indian Factories Act, for instance, Section 34 (weekly hours), Section 35 (weekly holiday), Section 36 (daily hours), Section 37 (intervals for rest), Section 45 (further restrictions on the employment of women).[35] The workers of jute mills were paid an 'amenity allowance' linked to attendance rather than a dearness allowance. The European members of the Legislative Assembly and the ministerial authorities did not accept a non-official resolution on the war bonus demand of workers introduced in the Bengal Assembly by Dr Suresh Chandra Bannerjee, a trade union leader.[36] In fact, N.A.M. Walker, a representative of the European bloc, pointed out that the increase in earnings due to increased hours of work and overtime charges had covered the cost of living adequately.[37] H.S. Suhrawardy (Minister of Commerce and Labour and Rural Reconstruction) added most incongruously, that the prices were actually falling![38]

At this time, Mrinal Kanti Bose (president of the Bengal Provincial Trade Union Congress, henceforth BPTUC) made attempts to dispel the notion that the war had not jeopardized the standard of living of workers, when he pointed out that workers in Bengal were working for nearly 60 hours a week to meet the additional demands of the war but were given a mere 10 per cent increase in wages. As he observed, 'The relief due to the war did not however help them to return to the normal standard of life for the price of necessaries went up.'[39] By this time the Communists had begun functioning with renewed confidence. Their work among the mill workers during the noncooperation movements, particularly among the workers of the East India Railway workshop at Liluah and the jute mills in 1927 and between 1937–41, enabled them to conduct anti-war propaganda with relative ease. A plethora of pamphlets and posters, like *Natun Diner Alo, Bharat barsher samasta sona o rupa Ingrej bilate laiya gelo, Tomar Desh Paradhin* and *Juddher Samaye Swadhinatar Jannye Juddha Koro,* were written with the purpose of clinching the two issues of an anti-imperialist struggle and a communist struggle.[40]

Some of the most important Communist Party manifestos addressed the jute mill workers. One of the obvious reasons for this was that this industry was functioning in the capacity of a war industry, geared completely towards meeting the demands of the war. In 1940, a Communist Party leaflet titled *Communist Party ka Chatkal Mazdoor ke Nam Salam* mentioned that due to persistent struggle, the workers had won six *paisa* extra per rupee of their wages.[41] The argument was that since mill owners were reaping huge profits due to an increase in the price of gunny cloth and bags, they had no right to indulge in wage cuts and retrenchments. The leaflet advocated strikes against such measures.[42] Another Communist Party manifesto urged the workers to strike for a 25 per cent hike in dearness allowance. The mill owners were criticized for collecting war contributions under the pretext of providing entertainment with cinema shows. It was alleged that the workers were threatened with dismissal if they failed to comply.[43]

Both the mill owners and the government were at the receiving end of such propaganda work. Since most of the allegations were true, a majority of the workers gave the Communist activists a patient hearing. Workers in jute mills, the railways and metal industries were further informed that the government had converted the Kanchrapara Railway Workshop into an arms and ammunition factory. A diabolical image was drawn of the government to prove the excesses it committed. It was alleged that it could transfer workers in any factory and make them work according to its wishes: 'If any worker protested government would be competent to throw them into prison.'[44] To show that the government's financial position was precarious, the manifesto added: 'The government cannot cash even a five-rupee note today. They have issued a one-rupee note. They are reducing the silver in eight-anna bits.'[45] The news, particularly the last one, was alarming. The government's credibility was at stake. In fact, this was far more damaging than a call for a strike. No wonder it was alleged that propaganda of this nature was meant to instigate workers and the government was quick to proscribe these leaflets. Such measures were resorted to when the BPTUC also passed a resolution on 14 February 1941, demanding an increase in dearness allowance corresponding to the increase in prices.[46] The organization sought the workers' right to strike. All affiliated unions were asked to inform the All India Trade Union Congress (AITUC) about the pressure being exerted on workers to invest in war savings certificates.[47]

Although there was enough incentive for the workers to agitate and they did strike work on the issues mentioned above, the government left no stone unturned to divide their ranks. The work of categorizing trade unions as white flag unions (government-backed) and red flag unions (Communist or Congress-backed) had begun before the war broke out, in September 1939. The Trade Union Constitution Tribunal recognized only 27 out of the 61 unions that applied for registration.[48] Other unions were eliminated both on the basis of their political affiliation and organizational strength. The government thus built up a back-up force for some of its war-time policies in Bengal. This was evident in the pro-war labour rally organized on 5 January 1941. A majority of the unions which were backed by the government attended the rally.[49] Also, the manner in which some of the unions disaffiliated from the AITUC due to its anti-war attitude shows that the authorities were doing enough by way of repression and sowing dissension to divide the workers.

Efforts at Containing Defiance

Besides workers of the organized sector, around 1,500 scavengers struck work in March 1940 and demanded a 25 per cent increase in wages.[50] At this time, the Calcutta Corporation had granted a compensatory allowance of Re 1 a month to all employees drawing a salary of less than Rs 30 per month. The paltry amount fell far short of the rapid increase in prices. Although the scavengers rendered indispensable civic services, their demands were treated with middle-class apathy and neglect. The committee appointed to consider the matter was of the opinion that since the wives and sons of the scavengers had earning capacity, their condition compared very favourably with that of clerks from middle-class families![51] An unreasonable and biased comparison of this kind could be made due to the weak bargaining power of the scavengers. Despite the temporary inconvenience that their strike caused they were not indispensable for the 'war efforts'. And so, when they joined work after eleven days, the system of four roll-calls a day was enforced very strictly, and the workers were taken back only as new recruits.[52] Not only had their demands gone unheeded, the agitating workers were also punished for their action. Nearly nine months after the strike, in December 1940, the Calcutta Corporation relented to pay the war allowance of Re 1 a month.[53]

It was under the pretext of maintaining war production that the government came down with a heavy hand on workers' meetings and strikes. In 1942, when some of the unions responded to the call for a renewed nationalist movement, the authorities were afraid that the workers would quit work, damage machinery and bring the production process to a halt. They were desperate to divide the work force and also to demonstrate that the government was willing to protect those who produced for the war. Stafford Cripps, a Labour member of the War Cabinet, who had come to negotiate on the post-war dominion status of India, made a very pertinent observation at this time. According to him, 'If the British government could enlist the sympathy of the workers and peasants by immediate action on their behalf, the struggle in India would no longer be between India and Britain upon the nationalist basis, but between the classes in India upon an economic basis.'[54] When put into action, the Priority Classes Scheme was the result of such endeavours.

Under this scheme, the war industries and essential services could purchase large stocks of foodstuff in order to provide them to their workers at subsidized rates. The authorities were quite sure that 'the refusal of labour to be drawn into the present movement will continue as long as they are assured of adequate food supplies'.[55] The question of food could thus generate resentment among some other sections. They resented the discriminatory treatment that the state rendered, and complained that the mill-hands and factory workers received 'the largest and the most immediate attention from the authorities and employers'.[56] The scheme bore fruit when attempts at joint action by different sections during the Quit India movement were met with apathy.

Since the support of mill owners was necessary for unabated work in the mills during the war, the authorities made efforts to protect them from some of the eventualities of the war. For instance, the War Risks (factories) Ordinance of April 1942 guarded mill owners against any threat of potential loss due to war damages. In November, the ordinance was extended to include compensation to business interests for losses due to the Denial Policy.[57] Mill owners were also compensated when the military requisitioned factories. The provisions of the War Risks Ordinance were absolutely one-sided. They did not guarantee job security to the workers. When factories like the Ganges Jute Manufacturing Co., Gangabhai Jute Mills and Ludlow Jute Mills (Howrah) were requisitioned for war work, the workers found that the compensation and *khoraki* given were insufficient.[58] More difficult times awaited them in the years to come.

It is difficult to find any reference to a grant of compensation for injuries during raids. On the other hand, workers had to work double shifts to make up for the loss due to requisitioning of some mills by the military authorities.[59] Migrant labour thus preferred to risk their jobs and left for home in good numbers. This was the case throughout the year 1942. The 'bad news from Malaya and Burma' and the trying experience of watching large numbers of refugees crossing Calcutta along the Grand Trunk Road would have prompted a large section of labour to do likewise.[60] Occasions such as these were used by the mill owners to bully labour into passivity, once the air-raids were over. One of the district officials reported in early 1943 that the mill owners had adopted a policy of 'not displacing even inferior hands to make room for those who fled away during the bombing . . . and of re-employing them, when necessary, only as new hands'.[61] Although the War Injuries (Compensation Insurance) Act was introduced in November 1943, the provisions of compulsory insurance were not binding on certain agencies like the British Crown or the Federal Railway Company, unless the central government ordered likewise.[62] The majority of the port workers and railway employees could not thus be covered under the act.

Rules, acts and amendments passed both before and during the war could be extended to either commit acts of repression or to elicit sympathy and support for the war and a political climate that was not troublesome for the authorities. However, the times were very different from earlier occasions when defiance of the state was restricted to specific issues. The war and the possibility of significant political changes after the war encouraged visions of a future more realistic than any imagined or planned earlier. And one of the reasons why acts of defiance acquired greater relevance was because the government's financial and military credibility was constantly at stake during the years of the war. This was evident in the way Burma fell to the Japanese and the Japanese air-raids began in December 1941. The above discussion has thus been an attempt to show that it was futile to expect that the war would induce some kind of selective amnesia, with people willing to support the war efforts unmindful of the government's lack of war-preparedness, especially in Calcutta and Chittagong, and the high-handedness of the authorities, inflationary conditions and the stealthy approach of famine.

This essay is a brief attempt at tracing the attitudes which both posed a threat and assured the authorities while World War II was on. However, I have deliberately avoided references to the Quit India movement and the famine of 1943. These have been discussed in 'Denial, Dissent and Hunger: War-time Bengal, 1942–44', in Biswamoy Pati (ed.), *Turbulent Times: India 1940–44*, Popular Prakashan, Bombay, 1998.

Notes and References

1 *Amrita Bazar Patrika*, 4 September 1939.

2 *The Indian Year Book 1939–40, Statistical and Historical Annual of the Indian Empire, with an Explanation of the Principal Topics of the Day*, edited by Francis Low, Bennett, Coleman & Co. Ltd, Bombay, Calcutta, p. 313. That the 'fighting races' had to be of good stock with capacity for initiative, good physique and high mental calibre had earlier been confirmed by Major D.H. Cole, *Imperial Military Geography: General Characteristics of the Empire in Relation to Defence*, Sifton Praed, London, 1935, pp. 41–47. A discussion on the 'martial classes' has also been undertaken by Philip Mason, *A Matter of Honour: An Account of the Indian Arny, Its Officers and Men*, Jonathan Cape, London, 1974, pp. 350–61.

3 *Amrita Bazar Patrika*, 4 September 1939.

4 *Amrita Bazar Patrika*, 8 September 1939. Sir B.P. Singh Roy was a member of Calcutta Volunteer Rifles (1913–19), president of All India Khatriya (Rajput) Mahasabha (1939), and minister-in-charge, Local Self-Government and Revenue Department, Government of Bengal, 1937–41.

5 Ibid., 30 September 1939.

6 Tapan Basu, Pradip Dutta, Sumit Sarkar, Tanika Sarkar, Sambuddha Sen, *Khaki Shorts, Saffron Flags: A Critique of the Hindu Right*, Orient Longman, Hyderabad, 1993, p. 23.

7 *Amrita Bazar Patrika*, 21 June 1940.

8 Dr Syama Prasad Mukherjee's letter to John Herbert, Governor of Bengal, 26 July 1942, Home Poll. Miscell., National Library Annexe, Calcutta.

9 Home (Poll) Confid. 38/40, West Bengal State Archives, Calcutta (hereafter WBSA).

10 Ibid.

11 Ibid.

12 Penderel Moon (ed.), *Wavell: The Viceroy's Journal*, Oxford University

Press, Delhi, 1973, p. 3. In his book *Armies of the Raj: From the Mutiny to Independence 1858–1947*, Byron Farwell also informs us that before the revolt of 1857 there was heavy recruitment from among the high-caste brahmanas of Bengal. It was subsequently observed that the officers of the Bengal army had given too much attention to Hindu religious scruples. It was felt that the 'clever' Bengali brahmanas had been 'overly represented, unreasonably pampered'. Byron Farwell, *Armies of the Raj: From the Mutiny to Independence 1858–1947*, W.W. Norton, New York, 1989, p. 179.

[13] Home (Poll) Confid. 93/43, 1943, Jails, WBSA.

[14] Richard G. Casey, Personal Diary, 21 August 1945. The note was based on his discussion with James Buchanan and Maj. Lahiri, p. 158 (microfilm), Nehru Memorial Museum and Library (hereafter NMML).

[15] The first coalition ministry functioned from 1937 to 1941. The second ministry was formed in December 1941 and lasted till March 1943. The Progressive Coalition Party, comprising the KPP, Forward Bloc, Hindu Mahasabha and independent scheduled caste members, headed it. The Muslim League was out of power in these years. Fazlul Huq, who had been the premier in both the ministries, was forced to resign in March 1943. Under Section 93 of the Government of India Act 1935, governor's rule was imposed on 28 March 1943. On 13 April 1943, Governor Herbert allowed Nazimuddin to form a new ministry comprising only the Muslim League. This ministry lasted till 28 March 1945 and was succeeded by the ministry headed by H.S. Suhrawardy in April 1946.

[16] John Herbert, Governor of Bengal, to Linlithgow, 21 December 1940, Linlithgow Collection, p. 4 (microfilm), National Archives of India (hereafter NAI).

[17] Subhas Chandra Bose, *Crossroads (1938–40), Being the Works of Subhas Chandra Bose*, Netaji Research Bureau, Calcutta, 1962, p. 139.

[18] Home (Poll.) Confid., Fortnightly Report for first half of April 1940.

[19] Home (Poll.) Confid. 226/40, 1940, WBSA.

[20] Ibid. The Rules were initially implemented in 1932.

[21] *Bengal Legislative Assembly Proceedings*, Sixth Session, 1939, Vol. LV, No. 3, p. 217.

[22] Ibid., p. 246.

[23] Home (Poll) Confid., Fortnightly Report for the second half of December 1940. For a detailed and cogent examination and reassessment of the relationship between the colonial state and the Communist Party of India (1942–44), see Sanjoy Bhattacharya, 'An Extremely Troubled Relationship: The British Colonial State and The Communist Party of India, 1942–44', in Biswamoy Pati (ed.), *Turbulent Times*, pp. 138–66.

[24] Home (Poll) Confid. 553/39, 1939, WBSA.

[25] Some of the most prominent members of the Calcutta War Committee were: Mrinal Kanti Bose (journalist), Badridas Goenka (industrialist), Maharaja of Burdwan, B.M. Birla (industrialist), N.C. Chatterjee (Hindu Mahasabha), Fazlul Huq, Tushar Kanti Ghosh (editor, *Amrita Bazar*

Patrika and founder of *Jugantar*), A.H. Guznavi, Nawab Bahadur of Dacca, H.S. Suhrawardy (Muslim League), M.A.H. Ispahani (industrialist and Muslim League MLA), Iswardas Jalan, D.P. Khaitan (industrialists), Dr S.P. Mukherjee (Hindu Mahasabha), Nazimuddin (Muslim League), N.R. Sarkar (ex Finance Minister), B.P. Singh Roy, and Tamizuddin Khan (Minister, Public Health, Medical, Agriculture and Veterinary Dept). *Amrita Bazar Patrika*, 21 June 1940.

26 Home (Poll) Confid. W–101/40, 1940, NAI.

27 A discussion on the organizational strength of the Congress at this time figures in Bidyut Chakrabarty, *Subhas Chandra Bose and Middle Class Radicalism: A Study in Indian Nationalism 1928–1940*, Oxford University Press, Delhi, 1990.

28 *Amrita Bazar Patrika*, 1 March 1941.

29 Home (Poll) Confid. S–24/40 (41), S. No. 1–17, WBSA.

30 Home (Police) 75/10/42, 1942, NAI.

31 Ibid., W–325/40, 1940, WBSA.

32 Ibid., W–498/40, 1940, WBSA.

33 Ibid.

34 *Imperial Gazetteer of India*, Provincial Series, Bengal, Vol. I, Usha Publications, Delhi, 1984, p. 72.

35 MS 86/v/8/11/1, 1940. The Samnuggur Jute Factory Co. Ltd. Samnuggar South-Nos 1 and 2 mills, Manager's Report to the Directors, 1941, p. 66. Records of Thomas Duff & Co. Ltd. , managing agents of jute mills, Dundee University Library, Archives and Manuscripts Department, UK.

36 *Amrita Bazar Patrika*, 2 March 1940.

37 Ibid.

38 Ibid.

39 Ibid., 6 March 1940.

40 Home (Poll.) Confid. W–60/41, 1941, WBSA.

41 Home (Poll) Confid. 37/25, 1940, P.C. Joshi Archives, Jawaharlal Nehru University, Delhi.

42 Ibid., 37/99/1940.

43 Ibid.

44 Home (Poll) Confid. 37/99, 1940, P.C. Joshi Archives.

45 Ibid.

46 *Forward*, Vol. V, No. 4, 15 February 1941, p. 14.

47 Ibid.

48 Shila Sen, *Muslim Politics in Bengal 1937–47*, Impex India, New Delhi, 1976, p. 107.

49 The pro-war rally was attended, among others, by the Bengal Jute Workers' Union, Port Trust Employees Assiciation, Indian Seamens' Union, Bengal Motor Workers' Union, Calcutta Street Hawkers and Vendors' Union, Tittagarh Jute Workers' Union, Jagaddal Jute Workers' Union, Calcutta Tramways Employees Association. *Independent India*, 12 January 1941.

50 *Forward*, Vol. III, No. 10, 30 March 1940, p. 14.

51 Ibid.

52 Ibid., Vol. IV, No. 9, 14 September 1940, p. 6.

53 *Amrita Bazar Patrika*, 18 December 1940.

54 Nicholas Mansergh (ed.), *The Transfer of Power,* 2 vols, Her Majesty's Stationery Office, London, 1971, 1973. Vol. II: Cripps' note of 2 September 1942, Document 678, p. 884. Home (Poll) Confid., Fortnightly Report for second half of August 1942, WBSA.

55 Home (Poll) Confid., Fortnightly Report for second half of August 1942, WBSA. *Star of India*, 18 June 1943 (microfilm), National Library, Calcutta.

56 *Star of India*, 18 June 1943 (microfilm), National Library, Calcutta.

57 *The Statesman*, 28 November 1942.

58 Home (Poll) Confid. 159/44, 1944. WBSA.

59 MS 86/V/8/14/1, The Angus Co. Ltd. Angus Jute Works, Manager's Report for 1943, Dundee University Library, Archives and Manuscripts Dept, UK, p. 2.

60 MS 86/V/8/13/1, ibid., Manager's Report for 1942, Dundee University Library, Archives and Manuscripts Dept, UK, p. 72.

61 Home (Poll) Confid., Fortnightly Report for first half of February 1943, WBSA.

62 *Indian Information*, 1 January 1944, p. 41.

Contributors

R.P. BAHUGUNA teaches at the Department of History, Motilal Nehru College, University of Delhi. He is currently a UGC 'Career Awardee', working on non-brahminical religious communities in late medieval Rajasthan.

MEENA BHARGAVA teaches at the Department of History, Indraprastha College, University of Delhi, and is the author of *State, Society and Ecology: Gorakhpur in Transition, 1750–1830* (1999).

PARTHO DATTA teaches at the Department of History, Zakir Hussain Post Graduate College (Evening), University of Delhi. He has published papers on labour and the urban history of Calcutta.

AMAR FAROOQUI is with the Department of History, Hansraj College, University of Delhi, and is currently a Fellow at the Nehru Memorial Museum and Library, New Delhi. He is the author of *Colonial Forest Policy in Uttarakhand, 1890–1928* (1997) and *Smuggling as Subversion: Colonialism, Indian Merchants and the Politics of Opium* (1998). He has edited *Remembering Dr Gangadhar Adhikari: Life, Reminiscences, Selected Writings* (1998 and 2000).

NAJAF HAIDER teaches at the Department of History, University of Delhi, and has published papers on money, banking, prices and wages in medieval India and Iran.

NANDINI SINHA KAPUR teaches at the Department of History, PGDAV College, University of Delhi. She is the author of *State Formation in Rajasthan: Mewar during Seventh–Fifteenth Centuries* (2002).

NAYANJOT LAHIRI teaches at the Department of History, University of Delhi. She is the author of *The Archaeology of Indian Trade Routes* (1992) and *Pre-Ahom Assam* (1991), and co-author of *Copper and its Alloys in Ancient India* (1996). She has edited *The Decline and Fall of the Indus Civilization* (2000).

BISWAMOY PATI teaches at the Department of History, Sri Venkateswara College, University of Delhi. He is the author of *Resisting Domination: Peasants, Tribals and the National Movement in Orissa, 1920–1950* (1993), *Situating Social History: Orissa, 1800–1997* (2001) and *Identity, Hegemony, Resistance: Towards a Social History of Conversions in India, 1800–2000* (2003). He has edited *Turbulent Times: India, 1940–44* (1998) and *Issues in Modern Indian History: For Sumit Sarkar* (2000), and co-edited *Health, Medicine and Empire: Perspectives on Colonial India* (2001).

VIJAYA RAMASWAMY teaches at the Centre for Historical Studies, Jawaharlal Nehru University, New Delhi. She is the author of *Walking Naked: Women, Society, Spirituality in South India* (1997), *Divinity and Deviance: Women in Virasaivism* (1996) and *Textiles and Weavers in Medieval South India* (1985). She has edited *Re-searching Indian Women* (2003).

KUMKUM ROY teaches at the Centre for Historical Studies, Jawaharlal Nehru University, New Delhi. She is the author of *The Emergence of Monarchy in North India, c. 8th–4th centuries* BC, *as Reflected in the Brahmanical Tradition* (1994), and has edited *Women in Early Indian Societies* (1999).

BHAIRABI PRASAD SAHU teaches at the Department of History, University of Delhi. He is the author of *From Hunters to Breeders: Faunal Background of Early India* (1988), and has edited *Land System and Rural Society in Early India* (1997).

HARI SEN teaches at the Department of History, Ramjas College, University of Delhi. He has worked on the social history of colonial Rajasthan.

SRIMANJARI teaches at the Department of History, Miranda House, University of Delhi. Her present research is on famine and related themes in the context of the Bengal famine of 1943.

JAYA SINHA TYAGI teaches at the Department of History, Sri Venkateswara College, University of Delhi. She is currently finalizing a manuscript on gender equations and patriarchy in ancient India.

T.K. VENKATASUBRAMANIAN teaches at the Department of History, University of Delhi. He is the author of *Political Change and Agrarian Tradition in South India, 1600–1800* (1986), *Environment and Urbanization in Early Tamilakam* (1988), *Societas to Civitas: Evolution of Political Society in South India* (1993) and *Rhythm in Historical Cognition* (1993).

Index